Introduction to Programming for Researchers

James R. Derry

Introduction to Programming for Researchers

Learning Programming Fundamentals Through Dataset Processing in Bash and Python

Apress®

James R. Derry
Austin, TX, USA

ISBN-13 (pbk): 979-8-8688-1614-7   ISBN-13 (electronic): 979-8-8688-1615-4
https://doi.org/10.1007/979-8-8688-1615-4

Copyright © 2026 by James R. Derry

This work is subject to copyright. All rights are reserved by the Publisher, whether the whole or part of the material is concerned, specifically the rights of translation, reprinting, reuse of illustrations, recitation, broadcasting, reproduction on microfilms or in any other physical way, and transmission or information storage and retrieval, electronic adaptation, computer software, or by similar or dissimilar methodology now known or hereafter developed.

Trademarked names, logos, and images may appear in this book. Rather than use a trademark symbol with every occurrence of a trademarked name, logo, or image we use the names, logos, and images only in an editorial fashion and to the benefit of the trademark owner, with no intention of infringement of the trademark.

The use in this publication of trade names, trademarks, service marks, and similar terms, even if they are not identified as such, is not to be taken as an expression of opinion as to whether or not they are subject to proprietary rights.

While the advice and information in this book are believed to be true and accurate at the date of publication, neither the authors nor the editors nor the publisher can accept any legal responsibility for any errors or omissions that may be made. The publisher makes no warranty, express or implied, with respect to the material contained herein.

Managing Director, Apress Media LLC: Welmoed Spahr
Acquisitions Editor: Celestin Suresh John
Development Editor: James Markham
Coordinating Editor: Kripa Joseph

Cover designed by eStudioCalamar

Cover image designed by TyliJura on pixabay.com

Distributed to the book trade worldwide by Springer Science+Business Media New York, 1 New York Plaza, New York, NY 10004. Phone 1-800-SPRINGER, fax (201) 348-4505, e-mail orders-ny@springer-sbm.com, or visit www.springeronline.com. Apress Media, LLC is a Delaware LLC and the sole member (owner) is Springer Science + Business Media Finance Inc (SSBM Finance Inc). SSBM Finance Inc is a **Delaware** corporation.

For information on translations, please e-mail booktranslations@springernature.com; for reprint, paperback, or audio rights, please e-mail bookpermissions@springernature.com.

Apress titles may be purchased in bulk for academic, corporate, or promotional use. eBook versions and licenses are also available for most titles. For more information, reference our Print and eBook Bulk Sales web page at http://www.apress.com/bulk-sales.

Any source code or other supplementary material referenced by the author in this book is available to readers on GitHub. For more detailed information, please visit https://www.apress.com/gp/services/source-code.

If disposing of this product, please recycle the paper

To My Students,
Who Shaped the Class and Made It What It Is

Contents

About the Author xv
About the Technical Reviewers xvii
Acknowledgements xix
Introduction xxi

1 Introduction 1
   1.1   Modern Computers and Their History 1
        1.1.1   Today, Most Personal Computers Are Used Primarily As Communication Devices 1
        1.1.2   A Brief History of the Computer Age 2
   1.2   Our Modern Idea of Computers: A Theory of Computation 11

2 Digital Computation 15
   2.1   Fundamentals of Computation I: Transistors, Logic Gates, and Moore's Law 15
        2.1.1   Transistors and Moore's Law 15
        2.1.2   The Transistor Is the Fundamental Physical Unit of Computation 16
        2.1.3   Transistors Are Organized into Logic Gates 17
        2.1.4   Moore's Law 18
        2.1.5   The Transistor Budget 18
   2.2   Fundamentals of Computation II: Bits, Boolean Logic, and the Digital Age of George Boole & Claude Shannon 20
        2.2.1   George Boole 20
        2.2.2   Claude Shannon 21
   2.3   Fundamentals of Computation III: Data, Instructions, & Pointers 22
   2.4   Code and Data: Cycles of Fetch, Decode, and Execute, Over and Over 24

3 Operating Systems 27
   3.1   Operating Systems and Linux 27
        3.1.1   A Brief History of Operating Systems, with an Emphasis on UNIX 28
   3.2   The UNIX/Linux Filesystem 30
   3.3   The Memory Manager and Process Scheduler 31
   3.4   Working with Datafiles in Linux 32
   3.5   An Introduction to the Process Scheduler 33

4 Introduction to Bash 35
   4.1   The Bash Shell 35
   4.2   Changing the Bash Prompt 36

	4.3	Navigating Bash History and the LINUX Filesystem	37
	4.4	Files in LINUX	40
		4.4.1 Clobbering a File	42
		4.4.2 Changing File Permissions	43
		4.4.3 Setting the Session noclobber Flag	45
	4.5	Character Encoding and Text File Formats	45
	4.6	The UNIX Philosophy: An Introduction	48
	4.7	The Bash Interpreter	49
		4.7.1 Variables	49
		4.7.2 The Bash Environment	50
		4.7.3 The Bash Interpreter	51
		4.7.4 The Symbol Table and Variables	51
	4.8	Some Bash Tools for Working with Datafiles	52
	4.9	The General-Purpose Bash Commands *time* and *watch*	54
	4.10	The Bash Pipeline	55
	4.11	Some Advice for Writing Bash Scripts and Pipelines	57
5	**Bash: Combining Commands and Variables to Make Pipelines and Scripts to Process Data**		61
	5.1	Introduction to vim and the Bash script: How to Make an Executable Script That Runs On the Command Line & Takes Arguments	61
		5.1.1 Linting Our Executable Script	70
		5.1.2 Review	72
	5.2	tr Command: Translate or Delete Characters	72
		5.2.1 A Bash Pipeline Spellchecker	72
		5.2.2 A DOS to Linux Files Converter	81
	5.3	Extracting and Analyzing Data from Datafiles Using Bash Pipelines	82
	5.4	gawk: How Many Named Stars Are There?	88
	5.5	Getting Resultsets from Bash Queries	92
		5.5.1 Advanced Subject: Format Printing	94
	5.6	How to Make an Executable Script That Prompts Users for Input	95
	5.7	Datetime in Bash	96
	5.8	Introduction to Regular Expressions Using *grep -E*	98
	5.9	Words You Can Make on a Calculator	104
	5.10	Regular Expressions, sed, & tr: Reformatting Records In a Dataset	105
	5.11	Finding Approximate Matches with *agrep*	108
	5.12	Write Once, Run Everywhere: Embedding Our Executable Scripts in Pipelines & Invoking Them in Other Scripts	109
6	**Algorithms and Coding**		115
	6.1	An Introduction to Algorithms	115
		6.1.1 Recipes as Algorithms	118
		6.1.2 Definition of an Algorithm from *The Art of Computer Programming* . . .	118
		6.1.3 Control Flow	119
		6.1.4 Euclid GCD Algorithm	123
		6.1.5 The Little Hummer Card Trick	124
		6.1.6 The Bubblesort Algorithm	125
		6.1.7 Notes on the Mystical History of Algorithms	129
	6.2	An Introduction to Programming Style	130

		6.2.1	Richard Hamming on Programming Style, As Told by Brian Kernighan 131
7	**Floating-Point Numbers** 133		
	7.1	Floating-Point Numbers 133	
	7.2	Working with Floats: Rules of Thumb 136	
	7.3	Arbitrary Precision Math with *mpmath* 137	
	7.4	Improving the Accuracy of Floating-Point Calculations with *Herbie* 138	
8	**Introduction to Python** 141		
	8.1	Python Primer 141	
		8.1.1	Python Comes With Built-Ins: Built-In Functions, Built-In Data Types and Collections, and Built-In Modules 142
		8.1.2	Python Comes with a Built-In Error-Reporting Module Called the Traceback 143
		8.1.3	The IPython Interactive Shell I 144
		8.1.4	In Python, Everything Is an Object 147
9	**Using Python As a Calculator** 151		
	9.1	Datetime I: Duration of the COVID-19 Pandemic 151	
	9.2	Datetime II: Solving Date Problems 153	
	9.3	Heat Loss 154	
	9.4	Find the GC Content Percentage of a Nucleotide String 155	
	9.5	Stoichiometry with SymPy 157	
	9.6	Ideal Gas Law 161	
	9.7	Work Performed by Expanding Gas 163	
	9.8	Acceleration of Sun on Earth 163	
	9.9	Sound Level 164	
	9.10	SymPy on Jupyter Notebooks 165	
		9.10.1	The Jupyter Notebook 166
	9.11	Falling Bodies 168	
	9.12	Spherical Trigonometry in Navigation 171	
	9.13	Climate Data 173	
	9.14	Digital Signals 179	
	9.15	Image-Driven Data Analysis: Flood Mitigation 182	
10	**Programming** 189		
	10.1	Our First Program: Of Functions, Modules, Garbage Filters, Tests, & Docstrings 190	
		10.1.1	The Least Necessary to Write a Working Function 191
		10.1.2	The Least Necessary to Write a Useful Function 192
		10.1.3	Documenting Our Function for Coders and Users 193
		10.1.4	Saving Our Function to a Module 195
		10.1.5	Autoreloading Edited Module Content to an IPython Session 196
		10.1.6	Writing Garbage Filters: Handling Bad Input 198
		10.1.7	Automating Testing Our Code Using Unit Tests 200
		10.1.8	Linting Our Code with Pylint 203
	10.2	Introduction to Programming I: Implementing Algorithms 206	
		10.2.1	The IPython Interactive Shell II 208
		10.2.2	Back to Python and Coding 209

	10.3	Testing If Symbol in String Is Nucleotide	211
	10.4	Euclid GCD	214
	10.5	Converting Decimal Fractions into Binary	218
		10.5.1 The More You Know: Brahmagupta (598–668CE)	225
	10.6	Introduction to Programming II: Unit Testing	225
		10.6.1 Unit Tests and Our unittest_template.py File	225
	10.7	Finding the Reverse Complement of a Nucleotide String	230
		10.7.1 A Brief Introduction to the Python Dictionary	231
		10.7.2 Developing Code by Test-Driven Development (TDD)	234
	10.8	Counting Symbols in a String	238
		10.8.1 Error-Trapping	239
	10.9	IPython Magics	240
	10.10	Introduction to Programming V: Good Programming Practices	241
	10.11	Programs = Algorithms + Data Structures	243
	10.12	Interlude: Ilayda Develops Her Stoichiometry Code	244

11 Functions ... 247
- 11.1 Subroutines: The Genesis of Functions in Programming Languages ... 247
- 11.2 Functions ... 248
- 11.3 Modules ... 249
- 11.4 Documenting Your Functions, Making Them Robust with Error-Trapping and Exception Handling, and Proofing Them ... 250
- 11.5 Positional vs. Named Arguments ... 251
- 11.6 Multiple Return Values from a Python Function ... 253
- 11.7 Lambdas ... 255
- 11.8 Matters of Style When Writing Functions ... 256
- 11.9 A Calculus Primer: Numeric Integration & Differentiation Using Python ... 256
  - 11.9.1 Numerical Integration ... 257
  - 11.9.2 The More You Know ... 258
  - 11.9.3 Back to Numerical Integration ... 259
  - 11.9.4 Using Python and Numpy for Numerical Integration ... 262
  - 11.9.5 Numerical Differentiation ... 264
  - 11.9.6 Numerical Calculus with SymPy ... 266

12 Software Design ... 269
- 12.1 Writing Programs: Top-Down Design Methodology ... 270
- 12.2 Writing Programs: Converting a Top-Down Design Into A Program of Subroutines ... 271
- 12.3 Writing Your Code Base As a Set of Files ... 273
- 12.4 Writing Programs: A Practical Perspective ... 274

13 Working with Datasets ... 277
- 13.1 Accessing the Tabular Contents of Datafiles in Python Using a List of Lists (LoL) ... 277
- 13.2 Nested Collections ... 280
- 13.3 Finding the Minimum and Maximum Values in an Unsorted Collection ... 281
- 13.4 Parsers ... 282
  - 13.4.1 Revisiting fasta Parsers ... 282

	13.5	Too Big To Handle: Pre-Processing Large Datasets, Extracting Only Needed Dimensions 287
	13.6	One Record per Text File 288

14 Programming Efficiency 293
- 14.1 The Analysis of Algorithms 293
- 14.2 O(n): Finding a Value in an Unsorted Collection of Index/Value Pairs 295
- 14.3 $O(n^m)$: Nested Loops and Their Time Complexity 297
    - 14.3.1 Illustrating Executing Nested Loops with Nested Dolls 297
    - 14.3.2 The Output from Running Our Example Nested Loop 303
    - 14.3.3 Can We Do Better? Algebra to the Rescue! 303
- 14.4 $O(\ln_2 n)$: Binary Trees 304
- 14.5 Functional Equivalence and Profiling Code 308
    - 14.5.1 Dictionary As Lookup Table vs. Conditional Testing 308
- 14.6 Finding Min and Max Values in an Unsorted Collection II 309
- 14.7 Multiple Passes Through Dataset vs. Single Pass 310
    - 14.7.1 An Outline of the Problem and a Solution 310
    - 14.7.2 Extending the Solution 314

15 Other Subjects 317
- 15.1 An Introduction to Graph Theory 317
    - 15.1.1 Saving Our Python Collections by Pickling Them 322
- 15.2 Writing Python Scripts That Write Scripts 323
- 15.3 Interactive Scripts That Prompt Users for Input 327
- 15.4 The Python Half-Open Interval, Range Objects, and Slicing 328
    - 15.4.1 The Python Half-Open Interval 328
    - 15.4.2 The Range Object Revisited 329
- 15.5 Finding Intervals with Overlap 329
- 15.6 Finding Interval Overlap in Genomic Sequences 332
- 15.7 Slicing Lists and Strings 338
- 15.8 From Nucleotide String to Amino Acid Strings 339
- 15.9 Comprehension 342
    - 15.9.1 Slicing LoL, Extracting Columns with Comprehension 343
- 15.10 The Sieve of Eratosthenes 344
- 15.11 Transposing a Matrix 345
    - 15.11.1 Transposing Tabular Datasets in Python 347
- 15.12 Stacks and Queues 348
    - 15.12.1 Stacks 348
    - 15.12.2 Queues 349
    - 15.12.3 Algorithm: The Josephus Problem 350
- 15.13 Recursion 354
    - 15.13.1 A Few Recursive Functions 356

16 SciPy 359
- 16.1 matplotlib: Graphics with SciPy 360
- 16.2 NetworkX: Working with Graphs 366
- 16.3 NumPy: Foundational Library of SciPy 368
    - 16.3.1 The ndarray 368
    - 16.3.2 Linear Algebra Has Three Objects: Scalar, Vector, and Matrix 369

		16.3.3	Single-Instruction Multiple Data Registers in CPUs	370
		16.3.4	Universal Functions (ufuncs) and Vectorized Operations	370
		16.3.5	Row and Column Vectors in Memory and Data Processing	371
	16.4	Linear Algebra		372
		16.4.1	Datasets As Matrices I	372
		16.4.2	Making a Rotatable 3D Graph from Data in a Dataset	376
		16.4.3	Datasets As Matrices II: Partitioning a Matrix	379
	16.5	Pandas: Working with Labeled Datasets in Pandas		382
	16.6	Pandas: Using Masks to Query Recordsets		384
	16.7	Pandas: Getting Statistics on Datasets		385
		16.7.1	Using Seaborn	388
	16.8	Pandas: Processing Datasets Programmatically		389
	16.9	SymPy: Symbolic Python		391

17 Odds and Ends 395
- 17.1 Writing Programs: Writing, Rewriting, and Matters of Style 395
- 17.2 Python Sets 396
- 17.3 Datetime in Datasets 397
  - 17.3.1 Filling In Missing Datetime Entries 397
- 17.4 Introduction to Parallel Programming 402

18 Writing a Large Project 407
- 18.1 Putting It All Together: Solving Triangles 407
- 18.2 Design Considerations 409
- 18.3 Input and Output 410
- 18.4 Organization of the Code 410
- 18.5 Test-Driven Development (TDD) and Unit Testing 411
- 18.6 Linting Our Code 411
- 18.7 Pencil to Paper: Our Top-Down Design 412
- 18.8 Our First Unit Test 413
- 18.9 Our First Draft of solve_triangle.py 414
- 18.10 Running Our First Unit Test 415
- 18.11 Running solve_triangle Function the First Time 416
- 18.12 A Note on Structured Design 417
- 18.13 Adding Design Comments 417
- 18.14 Writing Our First Draft 420
- 18.15 Testing Our Code 422
- 18.16 The Garbage Filter: Writing Unit Tests and Coding 424
- 18.17 Finishing solve_triangle(), v1 426
- 18.18 Improving solve_triangle(), v1 426
- 18.19 TI-59 Calculator: Triangle Solution, Master Library ROM Module—A Different Approach 427
- 18.20 Losing the *rnd* Bool from the Argument List 428
- 18.21 Rethinking the Main Section of solve_triangle() 429
- 18.22 solve_triangle(), v2 431
- 18.23 What's Left to Do? 433

Suggested Reading 437
    Chapter 1 437
    Chapter 2 438
    Chapter 3 441
    Chapter 6 442
    Chapter 7 442

References 443
    Chapter 1 443
    Chapter 2 443
    Chapter 3 444
    Chapter 4 444
    Chapter 5 444
    Chapter 6 445
    Chapter 7 445
    Chapter 9 445
    Chapter 10 446
    Chapter 11 446
    Chapter 12 446
    Chapter 14 446
    Chapter 15 446
    Chapter 16 447
    Chapter 18 447

Index 449

About the Author

James R. Derry is a seasoned professional with 32 years of experience at UT-Austin, where he has served as a Senior Systems Administrator. For the past 14 years, he has also been an educator, teaching the course "Introduction to Programming for Researchers." His extensive background in both systems administration and programming education uniquely positions him to impart valuable computational skills to researchers in natural sciences and engineering, enhancing their productivity and efficiency in handling complex datasets.

About the Technical Reviewers

Karanbir Singh is an accomplished Engineering Leader with over 7 years of experience leading AI/ML engineering, distributed systems, and microservices projects across diverse industries, including fintech and automotive. Currently working as a Senior Software Engineer at Salesforce, he focuses on backend technologies as well as AI. He specializes in time series analysis, RAGs, and AI agents. His career has been marked by a commitment to building high-performing teams, driving technological innovation, and delivering impactful solutions that enhance business outcomes.

At TrueML, as an Engineering Manager, he managed a critical team to develop and deploy machine learning models in production. He successfully expanded and led engineering teams, significantly improving feature development velocity and client engagement through strategic collaboration and mentorship. His leadership directly contributed to increased revenue, client retention, and substantial cost savings through innovative internal solutions. His role involved not only steering technical projects but also shaping the company's roadmap in partnership with data science, product management, and platform teams.

Previously, at Lucid Motors and Poynt, he developed critical components and integrations that advanced product capabilities and strengthened industry partnerships. His technical expertise spans across AI/ML, cloud computing, and software architecture, and he is adept at utilizing cutting-edge technologies and methodologies to drive results.

Karanbir holds a master's degree in Computer Software Engineering from San Jose State University and has been recognized for his innovative contributions, including winning the Silicon Valley Innovation Challenge. He is passionate about mentoring and coaching emerging talent and thrives in environments where he can leverage his skills to solve complex problems and advance technological initiatives.

Krishnendu Dasgupta is a computer science engineer with nearly 14 years of experience. He is currently working on vision language models and distributed and decentralized inference, with a strong focus on healthcare and advanced computing. He is a sole proprietor and the former Head of Machine Learning at Mondosano GmbH, where he led data science initiatives in clinical trial recommendations and patient health profiling using disease and drug data.

With over a decade of experience in applied machine learning, he has held key roles at DOCONVID AI [Co-Founder], NTT DATA, PwC, and Thoucentric. His research interests span graph machine learning, medical imaging, and privacy-preserving AI solutions. He has also contributed to AI risk assessment research. He is an alumnus of the 5th Cohort of the MIT Entrepreneurship and Innovation Bootcamp (2018). He also volunteered as a Section Leader for Stanford University's Code in Place Initiative, teaching programming online for the 2024 cohort. In addition, he dedicates his time to voluntary research collaborations with research NGOs and universities.

Acknowledgements

I wish to thank Dr. Jennifer Morgan, who was the first to underwrite this class so that I could teach it; Dr. Hans Hofmann, who next underwrote the class; and to Mark McFarland, who allowed me to continue teaching it once I was reassigned from the School of Biological Sciences to the Office of Information Technology, College of Natural Sciences.

I wish to thank my colleagues for their unflagging support and suggestions to improve the Linux and Bash content, especially Eric Rostetter, Dr. Maorong Zou, and Hampton Finger.

And I wish to thank the students who provided data and suggestions on how to make the class better, which I have discovered is itself a never-ending project. Your contributions made it more interesting and engaging than it would have been otherwise.

Introduction

In 2011, I proposed to teach a class to biology grad students meant to prepare them for courses in the university catalog that have a substantial programming component. Over the next 14 years, the class has grown in audience and scope and evolved in approach. This book is a product of that class.

If you are a student working toward a career in STEM, or a scientist or engineer who missed out on programming classes, and you're looking for a book that uses a hands-on approach to teach you how to program in Python, this may be the book for you.

We start with an introduction to Linux and Bash, and in Bash, we move quickly to writing small scripts and pipelines to process datasets. Some of the Bash tools that we learn, like sed and vim, we use throughout the book.

After gaining a familiarity with Bash, we move on to learning algorithms and programming in Python. And programming in Python gives us access to a wealth of tools written and used by STEM researchers known collectively as SciPy.

The bulk of this book, like the bulk of the class, deals with writing programs that use these tools to work with and process datasets. And as we learn how to use these tools, we will also learn about and incorporate best programming practices into our work, including communicating effectively within our code to users and other programmers, testing user input to ensure it is expected input, handling bad input and exceptions, organizing code into modules and functions, and linting and unit testing our code.

Altogether, I hope to teach you how to write code that is not only correct but also robust, as easy to use as you can make it, and easy to maintain.

And by the time you finish, a whole new set of tools will be available to you to analyze datasets, automate tasks, and improve efficiency.

Introduction 1

With regard to computational might, most modern personal computers are greatly underutilized. In this brief introduction, we look at the history of the Computer Age, with a focus on their growth in power and capabilities. We finish by considering the universal Turing machine and comparing modern personal computers to the ideal UTM.

1.1 Modern Computers and Their History

> The purpose of computing is insight, not numbers.
>
> —Richard Hamming

1.1.1 Today, Most Personal Computers Are Used Primarily As Communication Devices

Most personal computers today are not used to compute. They are used to access sites on the Internet, to send and receive email, to read articles posted on news websites, to chat in real time audio-visually with family and friends all over the world, and to exchange posts on social media platforms. In other words, most personal computers today are used as communication devices.

And yet, most personal computers today, benefitting from market demand and tremendous progress in the manufacture of computer components, have capacities in mass storage, memory, and computation cycles to serve as much more than mere communication devices.

When used as computation devices to process datasets, most personal computers today can do in microseconds what researchers need months to do when working by eye and hand alone—or even when using a spreadsheet application (but not automating that work with the app's ability to run scripts).

It is the speed and ability of computers to execute repetitive tasks without error that make them ideal tools to process datasets, and this is how we will learn how to use them. In other words, we will be using our personal computers as the first computers of the Computer Age were used—as computation devices.

© James R. Derry 2026
J. R. Derry, *Introduction to Programming for Researchers*,
https://doi.org/10.1007/979-8-8688-1615-4_1

1.1.2 A Brief History of the Computer Age

Before the Computer Age, the word "computer" applied to humans, either for their mathematical abilities or their job.* The word was later applied to machines as a metaphor or analogy to describe to lay audiences the kind of work these machines performed. For years after the rise of these machines, the word "computer" still applied to clerical staff who did mathematical computations, often with slide rules and mechanical calculators.

Figure 1-1 The Harvard Observatory computers with the director of the observatory, Charles Pickering. May, **1913.** File: **Edward Charles Pickering & His Computers, 13 May 1913.** Public domain

Famous among the computer staffs of universities are the Harvard Observatory computers; and for their achievements, they deserve special mention.

The story goes that the observatory's all-male staff of computers made so many errors in cataloging and computation that Pickering fired them and put his housemaid, Williamina Fleming, in charge of hiring and managing a new staff of computers. She hired all women.

---

* Alan Turing in his doctoral thesis (1936), in which he invents the theoretical machine that would later be called a "Turing Machine," refers to such a person as a "computer."

Ex gratis, Turing's first references read: "The behaviour of the computer at any moment is determined by the symbols which he is observing, and his 'state of mind' at that moment. We may suppose that there is a bound B to the number of symbols or squares which the computer can observe at one moment. If he wishes to observe more, he must use successive observations. We will also suppose that the number of states of mind which need be taken into account is finite."

A.M. Turing. "On Computable Numbers, with an Application to the Entscheidungsproblem". *Proceedings of London Math Soc.*, 1937. pg 250, 251, 252, 253, and 254.

1.1 Modern Computers and Their History

Not only did the women prove themselves adept at the clerical tasks of computation and cataloging; but from their experience, they also developed such expertise in the subject that they went on to make significant contributions in astronomy. Indeed, they are now considered astronomers.

Most notable among them are Annie Jump Cannon and Henrietta Swan Leavitt.

Harvard Observatory was an early pioneer in the use of photography in astronomy, a marriage of technologies that allowed astronomers to capture permanent images of the observable universe for cataloging and more objective observations than could be done by a single astronomer staring into a telescope's eyepiece while scribbling notes and sketches.

As keepers and catalogers of Harvard Observatory's photographic plates, Annie Jump Cannon developed our current stellar classification scheme, while Henrietta Swan Leavitt discovered the period-luminosity relationship for Cepheid variables that astronomers still use to determine interstellar, even intergalactic, distances.

> In his essay "Mathematical Creation," Henri Poincaré wrote: "Every good mathematician ought to be a good chess player, and inversely; likewise he should be a good computer. Of course that sometimes happens; thus Gauss was at the same time a geometer of genius and a very precocious and accurate computer."[a]
>
> ---
> [a] Ghiselin, Brewster. *The Creative Process: A Symposium*. CALIFORNIA PAPERBACK EDITION, 1985. pg 23.

World War II by convention marks the start of the Computer Age, when two computation machines were built with no moving parts to do the computation—all computation was done electrically. Both were built to support the war efforts of Allied nations. The first, Colossus, was built by the British at Bletchley Park to decipher messages encoded by Lorenz cipher machines. The second, ENIAC, was built by the Americans to calculate artillery firing tables.

Before the Computer Age, computation machines used moving parts to do their computation. Alan Turing's famous Enigma-decoding bombes are a well-known example.

To decrypt Enigma messages, Alan Turing invented an electromechanical device called a "bombe," which contained a spinning cylinder, simulating the action of an Enigma rotor. In other words, moving parts were central to the bombe's ability to decipher Enigma-encoded messages.

Built by Tommy Flowers (team leader for the Mark I) and Allen Coombs (team leader for the Mark II), Colossus is the first computer whose computations required no moving parts and is considered the first computer of the Computer Age.

It was built in Bletchley Park, which also housed Turing's bombes, but it was so classified that not even Alan Turing knew of its existence.

It is believed that as many as eight Colossi were built though most were decommissioned and destroyed after the war to preserve the secret of their existence. There was a compelling reason to do this.

Although Colossus is the first all-electrical computer built and put to use, popular myth holds that ENIAC was the first machine to usher in the Computer Age. The reason for this confusion is that at the end of the war, the Americans were able to declassify ENIAC and announce its existence to the world; whereas during the Cold War, the British used Colossus and its successors to decipher Soviet communications sent between Lorenz cipher machines throughout most of the Cold War. These were Lorenz cipher machines that the Soviet Army had captured as it overran Wehrmacht strategic commands. The Soviet government, not having been told that the British had cracked the Lorenz ciphers and believing them to be uncrackable, put these machines to use in Soviet embassies throughout Eastern Europe and used them in daily radio communiqués to Moscow.

Figure 1-2 Wartime picture of one of Alan Turing's bombes. File: Wartime_picture_of_a_ Bletchley_ Park_Bombe.jpg, 1945. Public domain

For as long as the Soviets kept the Lorenz machines in service, Colossus and its descendents deciphered their encrypted messages, and their existence was kept a state secret.

ENIAC's first programmers were all women computers who at the time were working for the U.S. government. Among these programmers, Kay Antonelli, née McNulty, deserves special mention. Irish-born Antonelli, working with ENIAC's co-inventor Mauchly, first described the general usefulness of subroutines, which can be thought of as the forerunner to Python functions. She was also the first to implement subroutines on the ENIAC.

The inventors of ENIAC, John Mauchly (a physicist) and J. Presper Eckert (an electrical engineer), contributed even more to the technology of modern computers. After the success of ENIAC, they proposed a new computer, the EDVAC (Figure 1-5). This computer used binary, or ones and zeros, to store data and instructions. The greatest technical innovation in EDVAC is that the data and instructions were stored in the same memory, just as they are in computers today. This greatly lowered the cost of early computers, making them affordable to more than governments.

The polymath John von Neumann, who published the first description of shared memory used in EDVAC, in 1945 used the array data structure to implement a sorting algorithm he invented, the merge sort—the array data structure is the basis of Python collections like strings and lists, while merge sort is a recursive sorting algorithm used in production software today.

To understand why the United States figures so prominently for roughly the next 35 years in computer development, it is important to appreciate how things stood for nations after WWII that before WWII had the industries that could have competed toe-to-toe with US industries.

Figure 1-3 Colossus, Mark II. File: **Colossus. 1943**. Public domain

Figure 1-4 Electronic Numerical Integrator and Computer, or ENIAC. Pictured in the photo are two of ENIAC's first six programmers. File: **Two women operating ENIAC (full resolution).jpg** Created: 1946. Public domain

Figure 1-5 Electronic Discrete Variable Automatic Computer, or EDVAC. File: **Edvac.jpg**. Public domain

To put it euphemistically, these nations spent years trying to pound each other back into the Stone Age during the war, with the United States itself piling on while being largely spared from having to endure the same kind of beating—thanks to two great oceans.

Furthermore, the United States had become the primary war material supplier to those nations that FDR referred to as the "United Nations" in their fight against fascist states.

As a result, the United States emerged from WWII with an economy that was not only intact, but that had doubled in size over the war years. The United States was rich, and it had the resources to invest in new programs.

As the war was drawing to a close, FDR became convinced that science and technology could benefit a peaceful world as much as they had benefitted wartime belligerents; and he tasked his science advisor, Vannevar Bush, with developing a post-war plan for investing in science and technology and directing them in ways that benefitted civilians.

The results were profound and benefitted medicine, public health, and technologies whose applications had peaceful purposes. US public optimism in what scientists and engineers could achieve, the problems they could solve, was, I believe, never higher.

It was in this environment that the computer industry took root and flourished in the US economy. The United States had the resources to invest in massive technological R&D, and invest them in computers it did.

Innovations in computer hardware and software picked up pace throughout the 1950s and 1960s. These include the invention of operating systems, the replacement of vacuum tubes with transistors, the creation and widespread use of compilers, and the use of silicon as a semiconductor.

The 1950s marks the start of the Digital Revolution, when digital electronics started replacing analog electronics. By "digital," we mean information created, transmitted, and stored in two-state sequences. (Think of strings of 1s and 0s; e.g., "100110111" or "000101010.") In general, physically in our devices, these two states exist as changes in magnetic polarity or electrical voltages and may be moved between machines as changes in voltage or pulses of light. Depending on the context, we commonly represent these two states as ones and zeros, as "on" and "off," or as "true" and "false."

Today, our digital computers can bring in analog information from their environment and convert it to digital information, or they can send out digital information in analog form to affect physical environments. For example, microphones and tactile sensors take in analog information from their environment, and it is converted to digital information for storage and processing. In the other direction, speakers, LEDs, and robot motors use digital signals converted to analog ones to influence the environment. Although today we take it very much for granted, our digital computers manage well in an analog world.

The manufacture of computer components has undergone tremendous progress, thanks largely at first to military demands, and currently to market demand and the massive funding of research and development by component manufacturers. The challenge of early component manufacturers was to fit smaller and lighter avionics and guidance packages into missiles and combat aircraft, while the challenge of manufacturers today is largely to try to outdo each other in size, speed, features, and cost of components—all for our money in a global consumer market.

The result of all these efforts is that computers have gotten smaller, faster, and cheaper over time—with more features!—a trend that was first put on paper in 1965 by Intel co-founder Gordon Moore and is known as Moore's Law.

Thanks to Moore's Law, which is less a law and more an observation of trends in computer development, our laptops are many times computationally more powerful than mainframe computers were just a generation ago—computationally, we can do more, and do it faster and cheaper, than researchers could do on the most powerful computers that existed just 30 years ago.

Thanks also to Moore's Law, a transition took place away from giant, expensive, multiuser mainframes and miniframes, to personal computers. The first modern personal computers were generally expensive 8-bit hobbyist kits that users assembled and programmed without the benefit of operating systems.

These hobbyist personal computers premiered in the early to mid-1970s. Notable among them are: (1) the Altair 8800, which came out in 1974 and for which Bill Gates and Paul Allen first wrote the BASIC interpreter that would start the fortunes of Microsoft; and (2) the Apple I, designed and hand-built by Steve Wozniak in 1976, which would establish Apple Corporation.

As the first commercially successful personal computer, the Altair 8800 deserves special mention. Its CPU was the 8-bit Intel 8080. The system included slots for expansion boards. Instructions were entered using toggle switches on the front panel. The 8-bit instructions meant that for each instruction, the programmer had to set eight toggle switches to their correct positions, then flip a toggle switch to input the instruction.

Figure 1-6 The MITS Altair 8800, 1974 C.E. File: **Altair_8800_Computer.jpg**. Public domain

Tedious, but hobbyists enchanted with having a powerful and expandable computer didn't mind.

Knowing that personal computers would remain a niche market for hobbyists unless they were made easier to write applications for and use, programmers wrote and licensed operating systems for these 8-bit computers. Notable among these are CP/M, written in 1974, and Apple-DOS, written by Steve Wozniak in 1978.

The Age of Personal Computers began when IBM released the first machines meant for mass personal use in 1981. Although at the time IBM was the world's largest OS provider and CPU manufacturer, IBM did not believe that personal computers had a significant future; and so it licensed the operating system for the PC from Microsoft and used an Intel 16-bit CPU in its line of personal computers.

This failure to predict the future of PCs would cost IBM dearly.

In the meantime, Steve Jobs was pursuing his vision of future personal computers. Jobs had visited Xerox PARC in 1979, where he had gotten a demonstration of the Xerox Alto. Introduced in 1973, the Xerox Alto is the first computer whose operating system was designed to support a graphical user interface (GUI). The Alto's GUI was the now-familiar mouse-driven desktop. The design philosophy of the GUI was to make computers intuitively easy to use. Among its innovations, the Alto also had WYSIWYG* document editors and skeuomorphic icons.

After his tour of Xerox PARC, Steve Jobs is reported to have said, "I have seen the future."

Touted by some as the world's first personal computer, the Alto deserves special mention. Although touted as the world's first personal computer, it in fact required a dedicated miniframe to run it, making it prohibitively expensive for personal use. It did, however, demonstrate what was possible in future personal computers. Its many innovations, meant to make it intuitively easy to use, inspired Steve Jobs to come up with more economical versions: first, the still prohibitively expensive Lisa; then "Lisa's little brother," the affordable Macintosh.

---

* The acronym from "What You See Is What You Get," a catchphrase of comedian Flip Wilson's popular character Geraldine Jones, whom he played in drag.

1.1 Modern Computers and Their History

Figure 1-7 The Xerox Alto. File: **Xerox_Alto_mit_Rechner.jpeg**. Public domain

Figure 1-8 The Digirule 2U, an 8-bit microcomputer designed to emulate the Altair 8800 in performance, surface-mounted on a ruler

Yet another example of Moore's Law is the Digirule 2U, 2020 C.E. In power and function, the Digirule 2U is comparable to early hobbyist personal computers of the mid-1970s. It is powered by a coin-cell battery (center). To the right of the battery is the on/off switch, and beside it, the CPU.

As with the Altair 8800, instructions are entered one at a time (by pressing buttons). A programmer can also connect the Digirule via USB to a laptop or desktop, making it easier to write and debug programs.

Figure 1-9 Click or scan QR code to go to Digirule 2U site on GitHub. https://github.com/bradsprojects/Digirule2U

Figure 1-10 The instruction set and reserved registers of the 8-bit computer Digirule2U. Note that they are entered as 1s and 0s

A simple Digirule counting program rendered in assembly (mnemonics) and machine code (binary). Colors map assembly to their binary equivalents (Table 1-1).
Line 1: The program is initialized by setting the speed of execution.
Line 2: Copy the literal value of "1" into the special LEDREGISTER. The value in this register corresponds to the row of 8 DATA LEDs on the face of the 2U. A literal value of "1" lights the LED D0.
Line 3: Increment by 1 the value in the LEDREGISTER.
Line 4: Move the program counter to the instruction at ADDRESS 5—we index on zero, one byte occupies each address location, so the INCR instruction is at ADDRESS 5—and run the code again from there.
In other words, execute again:
INCR LEDREGISTER
JUMP 5. # Effectively, this instruction creates an infinite loop in which the value in LEDREGISTER is incremented by 1 each pass through the loop.

Table 1-1 A simple Digirule counting program rendered in assembly and machine code

(a) assembly

SPEED 128

COPYLR 1 LEDREGISTER

INCR LEDREGISTER

JUMP 5

(b) machine code

00000010	10000000
00000101	00000001 11111111
00011110	11111111
00101000	00000101

1.2 Our Modern Idea of Computers: A Theory of Computation

> Although our technological environment is permeated with computational devices (IoT appliances, microcontrollers, etc.), in common parlance, we tend to restrict naming machines "computers" to virtual universal Turing machines (vUTMs). A Turing machine (TM) is a machine that follows instructions to solve a problem or perform a task.
>
> A Turing machine that can follow the instructions to solve any problems or perform any tasks that any other Turing machine can do is called a universal Turing machine (UTM).
>
> Microcontrollers are programmed to perform just one task at a time. They are examples of Turing machines, or TMs. Most, like the ones in your thermostats, TV remote controls, and microwave ovens, perform just one task for as long as they're in use, which can be years, even decades.
>
> We might consider our general-purpose computers to be universal Turing machines, or UTMs, except that universal Turing machines as conceived by Alan Turing have infinite time and infinite space (memory) to solve problems or perform tasks.
>
> The UTM remains a mathematical ideal of general-purpose computers. It illustrates the limits of what computers can do.
>
> Because we don't give our computers infinite time or space to solve problems or perform tasks, we classify them as virtual universal Turing machines, or vUTMs.

In 1936, Alan Turing submitted for publication his doctoral thesis, in which he put forth the idea of hypothetical machines that later would be called "Turing machines," machines that would come to be known for their computational power.

Ironically, the focus of Turing's paper was not on the immense power of such machines, but on one of their most basic, universal limitations.

Turing, A. M. "On Computable Numbers, with an Application to the Entscheidungsproblem". *Proceedings of the London Mathematical Society, Vol.s2-42 (1)*. 1937. p.230–265.

The German mathematician David Hilbert had posed a deceptively simple question, which is whether a general algorithm can be crafted that uses math and logic alone to decide ("yes" or "no") if a statement is universally valid.

One of the great achievements of mathematics in the early 20th century was to answer this question decisively. The answer is "no."

The question had already been answered when Turing wrote his doctoral thesis. His doctoral advisor, Alonzo Church, had just proved the undecidability of what was known as "Hilbert's *Entscheidungsproblem*" using lambda calculus. But the proof by lambda calculus was not easy even for other mathematicians to follow.

Turing's approach on proving the undecidability of the *Entscheidungsproblem* was not only different from Church's, it was also easier to follow.

At the heart of Turing's approach lies a hypothetical, extremely simple machine modeled on ticker-tape machines. The machine itself starts as a metaphor for a person slavishly following an algorithm to compute a number:

> We may compare a man in the process of computing a real number to a machine which is only capable of a finite number of conditions $q_1, q_2...q_\mathbb{R}$ which will be called "m-configurations". The machine is supplied with a "tape" (the analogue of paper) running through it, and divided into sections (called "squares") each capable of bearing a "symbol".

—Alan Turing. *ibid.* p.231

Turing then goes on to describe the operations this machine can perform on the tape, which Turing later requires to be infinite in length. It can move the tape one square at a time left or right. It can read a symbol in a square. It can erase a symbol. It can write a symbol in a blank square.

It can, in fact, execute machine algorithms written for it. In *The Emperor's New MInd*, Nobel laureate Roger Penrose writes out an implementation of Euclid's GCD algorithm that runs on this machine.* Turing designed his machine so that it can execute any machine algorithm.

While Turing designed his machine to show that, for a machine that can execute any machine algorithm, there does not exist a general algorithm to decide ("yes" or "no") if every program written for it halts or not (an incarnation of the *Entscheidungsproblem* known as the "Halting Problem"), in doing so he designed a machine that also shows just how computationally powerful such a simple machine is.

Section 6 of his doctoral thesis[†] Turing titled "The universal computing machine," wherein he shows how a machine can be made to run any program that any other machine can run:

> It is possible to invent a single machine which can be used to compute any computable sequence. If this machine $\mathfrak{U}$ is supplied with a tape on the beginning of which is written the S.D. [standard description] of some computing machine $\mathfrak{M}$, then $\mathfrak{U}$ will compute the same sequence as $\mathfrak{M}$...
>
> It is not difficult to see that if $\mathfrak{M}$ can be constructed, then so can $\mathfrak{M}'$. The manner of operation of $\mathfrak{M}'$ could be made to depend on having the rules of operation (i.e., the S.D.) of $\mathfrak{M}$ written somewhere within itself (i.e. within $\mathfrak{M}'$); each step could be carried out by referring to these rules. We have only to regard the rules as being capable of being taken out and exchanged for others and we have something very akin to the universal machine.

ibid. pp. 241-2

Turing then proceeded to provide the one thing missing for what was later called a "Universal Turing Machine," or UTM. A truly astonishing feature of UTMs, though one taken for granted today, is that a UTM can emulate any Turing machine—including another UTM!

---

* Roger Penrose. *The Emperor's New Mind, With A New Preface By The Author*. Oxford University Press. 1989. p.54.

[†] *ibid.* p.241.

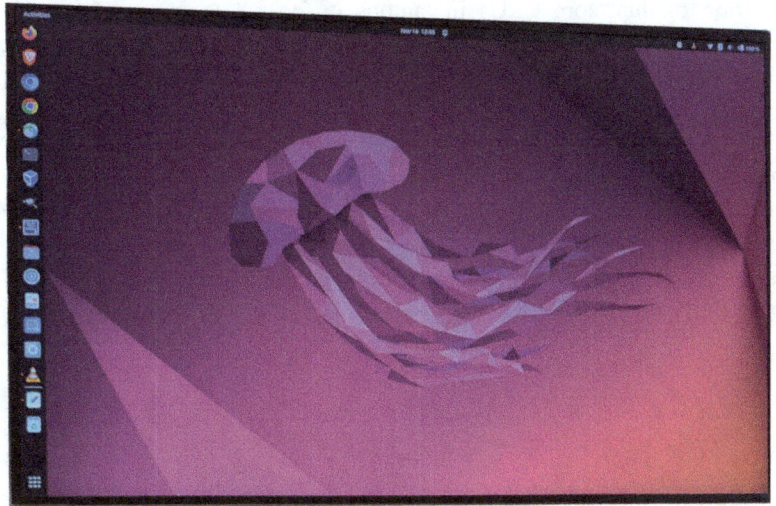

Figure 1-11 An example of a virtual universal Turing machine, or vUTM

We call implementations of universal Turing machines virtual because they lack one feature of UTMs—infinite memory.

A UTM can do any task that any Turing machine can do—even emulate another UTM! This is why we can run virtual machines on laptops. A Windows laptop, for example, can run a Linux VM, allocating the VM enough resources in memory and cores so both can run smoothly at the same time.

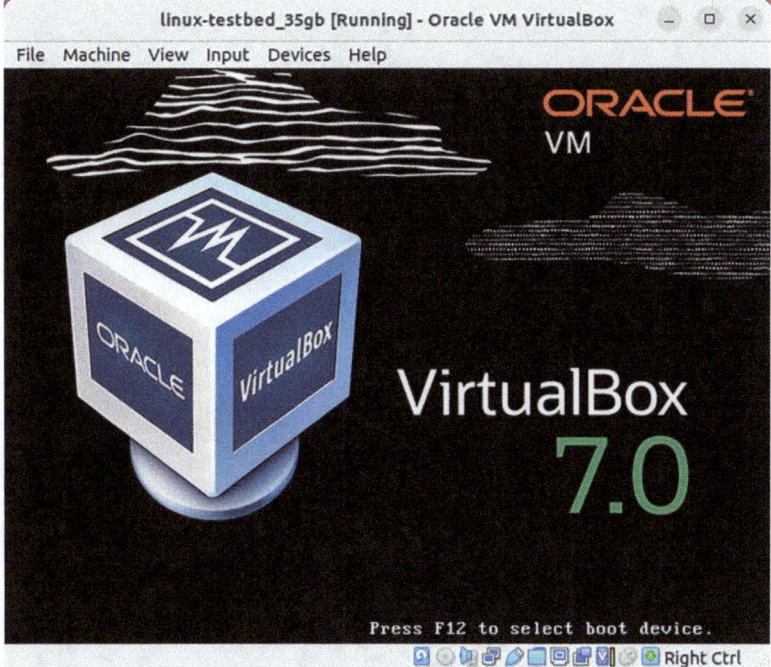

Figure 1-12 Another example of a virtual universal Turing machine: a Linux VM starting up

The introduction of dual-core CPUs in laptops in 2005 C.E. gave laptops the computational resources to run VMs, though initially, without enough RAM, relatively slow CPU speeds, and slow platter hard drive disks, even simple VMs running not-normally-stressful processes on the laptops still ran slow and could drag down the overall performance of the laptop.

Chapter Summary

Personal computers, with their multicore CPUs, many gigabytes of RAM, and solid-state drives measuring in terabytes, are comparable in computational might to high-end servers sold just a few years ago. We can leverage this computational power to run virtual machines on even our laptops, as well as to process large datasets.

Digital Computation 2

In this chapter, we look at the elements of modern digital computation. The fundamental physical unit of computation is the transistor. The fundamental unit of information is the bit. Modern digital computers work by making use of three kinds of information: data, instructions, and pointers, which are used to keep track of the data and instructions in a computer's mass-storage devices and memory.

2.1 Fundamentals of Computation I: Transistors, Logic Gates, and Moore's Law

2.1.1 Transistors and Moore's Law

> The fundamental physical unit of computation is the transistor.
> Transistors can be wired together to do binary logic and arithmetic operations.
> CPU cores contain very large arrays of transistors to perform a wide array of operations.
> The transistor count of CPUs over time has followed Moore's Law. In today's personal computers, this has resulted in more cores per CPU.
> **In general, operations implemented by hardware are faster than software implementations; however, software is more flexible than hardware.**
> Software is what allows a hardware virtual universal Turing machine (vUTM) like our laptops and desktops to become many different Turing machines, including another vUTM.

> It's hardware that makes a machine fast. It's software that makes a fast machine slow.
>
> —Craig Bruce

Figure 2-1 Vacuum tube.
Public domain. 1952

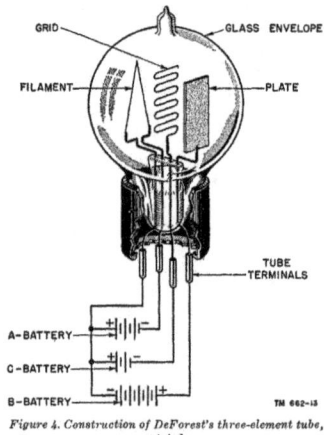

Figure 2-2 Transistor.
Image by author

2.1.2 The Transistor Is the Fundamental Physical Unit of Computation

The fundamental physical unit of computation in modern computers is the transistor. The transistor was rediscovered (or reinvented) in 1947 by a team at Bell Labs that included William Shockley (and for which William Shockley and two others would be awarded the Nobel Prize in 1956). Shockley gets special mention here not only for his seminal work on the transistor, but also for having started his own lab, Shockley Semiconductor Laboratory, and gathering into his lab some of the best and brightest people in electronics at that time—including Gordon Moore and Robert Noyce, who would go on to co-found Intel.

Transistors serve two functions in electronic circuits. They can amplify signals (as they did, e.g., in transistor radios that replaced vacuum-tube radios throughout the 1950s and 1960s), or they can switch electronic signals on and off (which is their function in computation).

The first electronic devices used in computers to switch signals on and off were vacuum tubes—the ENIAC contained 17,468 vacuum tubes. However, during the nuclear arms race in the 1950s and 1960s, the need to make missile guidance systems and avionics packages as small and lightweight as possible motivated the switch from vacuum tubes to transistors. Later, in the Space Age, the same constraints to make electronic systems as small and lightweight as possible meant that transistors were used in place of vacuum tubes in US satellites and crewed spacecraft.

The next major step in the physical miniaturization of computers came with the invention and implementation of integrated circuits (ICs). Jack Kilby of Texas Instruments, who won the 2000 Nobel Prize for his contributions in the development of ICs, described an integrated circuit in 1959 as "a body of semiconductor material...wherein all the components of the electronic circuit are completely integrated."

In 1957, Moore, Noyce, and others convinced Sherman Fairchild to create Fairchild Semiconductor, where they created and perfected the manufacture of silicon-based transistors. Silicon, the stuff of sand, was vastly cheaper than germanium, at that time the most common material used in semiconductor and transistor manufacture. Noyce's push for the use of silicon in the manufacture of transistors and semiconductors led to the company's financial success. But switching to silicon wasn't the company's only innovation. In 1959, Jean Hoerni developed the planar process for creating transistors in ICs that makes today's CPUs—with their vast arrays of billions of transistors uniformly arranged (as NAND gates)—possible.

But we're getting ahead of ourselves by about 40 years when we speak about billions of transistors on a single chip. First things first—as in the first silicon IC. Fairchild Semiconductor created this, too. It was an IC consisting of four transistors. The year was 1960.

Alas, the good times at Fairchild Semiconductor were not to last forever.

In 1968, over issues of leadership and vision, Moore and Noyce left Fairchild Semiconductor and founded Intel Corporation.

In 1971, Intel created the first commercially produced microprocessor, the 4-bit Intel 4004 CPU. It had 2,250 transistors. Intel followed the 4-bit CPU with its first 8-bit CPU, the Intel 8008, in 1972. The 8008 had 3,500 transistors.

Intel improved on the 8-bit CPU when it released the Intel 8080, which had 6,000 transistors. The 8080 would be used in many hobbyist microcomputers, which heralded the Age of Personal Computers. The year was 1974.

2.1.3 Transistors Are Organized into Logic Gates

Computation in modern computers is done via Boolean logic. Transistors are connected together into units called logic gates, which perform Boolean logic operations on input. Even adders, circuits that underlie arithmetic operations in the cores of CPUs, are made up of logic gates. (Please see Table 2-1.)

The logic gate that is used in most CPUs is the NAND gate. NAND gates have a property called "functional completeness," meaning that with only NAND gates, one can build circuits to perform any Boolean function. Circuits in modern computers that are made of logic gates include computer memory, as well as the registers and the arithmetic and logic units (ALUs) in the cores of CPUs.

Again, arithmetic on a CPU is performed via logic gates.

Table 2-1 Several logic gates, their schematic symbols, Boolean algebraic expressions, and truth tables. Logic gates are connected together to perform arithmetic and logical operations in CPUs. NAND gates are the most commonly used logical gates in CPUs. Diagram by author

Name	Logic Gate	Logic Expression	Truth Table
AND	(A, B → C)	$A \wedge B$	A B C 0 0 0 0 1 0 1 0 0 1 1 1
OR	(A, B → C)	$A \vee B$	A B C 0 0 0 0 1 1 1 0 1 1 1 1
NAND	(A, B → C)	$\neg (A \wedge B)$	A B C 0 0 1 0 1 1 1 0 1 1 1 0
NOR	(A, B → C)	$\neg (A \vee B)$	A B C 0 0 1 0 1 0 1 0 0 1 1 0

2.1.4 Moore's Law

In 1965, Gordon Moore, cofounder of Intel Corp., made the observation that roughly every two years, the number of transistors in a given area of IC chips doubles. This observation has been extended to include the speed, mass, volume, and cost of computation devices—again, roughly every two years, speed doubles while, mass, volume, and cost of computation devices are cut in half.

Although in 2015 Gordon Moore has said he sees this rate of technological progress reaching saturation and although there has indeed been a slowdown in these exponential rates of growth and diminishment, an adjusted Moore's Law still holds true.

This means that each generation of CPU increases the total number of transistors in the CPU.

2.1.5 The Transistor Budget

Transistor count has affected the evolution of microprocessor architectures in fundamental ways. For example, any CPU design begins with an engineering study to indicate how large the silicon die will be, and at what size

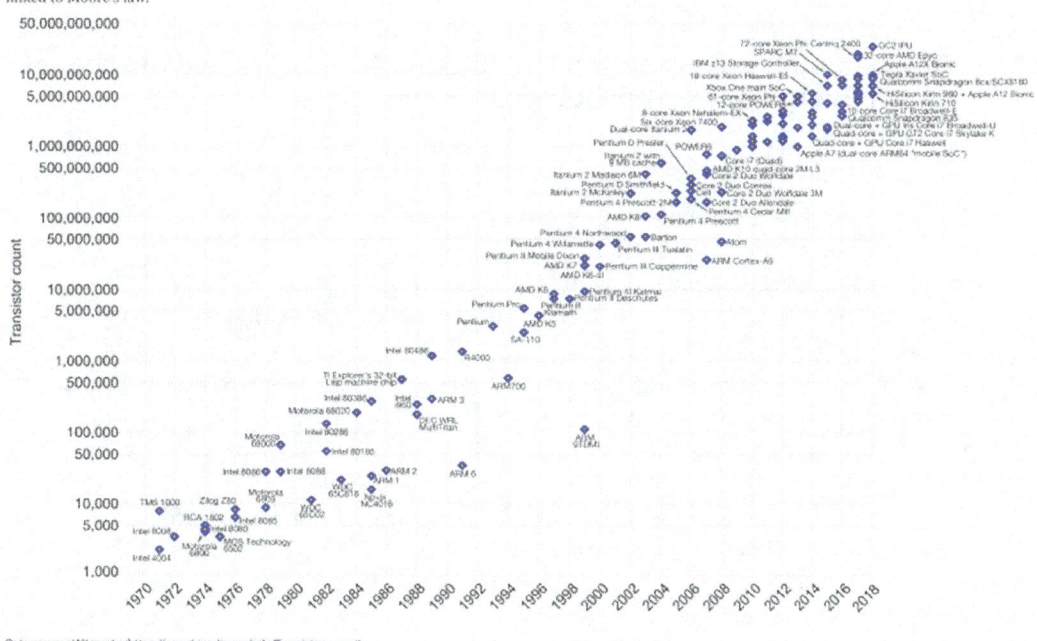

Figure 2-3 Transistor count over time. Creative Commons (Figure 2.3. Max Roser, Hannah Ritchie and Edouard Mathieu (2023)—"What is Moore's Law?" Published online at OurWorldinData.org. Retrieved from: https://ourworldindata.org/moores-law.)

the transistors will be fabricated. This gives a maximum transistor count for the die long before any of the actual die layout has been performed.

After the total number of transistors is known, those transistors are parcelled out to the various component functions that make up a CPU: so many transistors go to the cache, so many go to the registers, so many go to implementing machine instructions and so on. Subsystem design teams guard these 'transistor budgets' as jealously as governments or corporations guard their financial budgets.

The eventual CPU design is always a compromise between the features the designers want to 'buy' and the limitations of the transistor budget they are given to shop with. If you ask a CPU designer why one particular feature didn't make it into the final silicon, the answer is almost invariably, 'We didn't have the transistor budget for it.'

—Eben Upton*

Transistor budgets determine what functionality gets hardwired into a CPU. As total transistor counts have increased from generation to generation of CPUs, successive generations have been able to do more—and do it faster—than the CPUs of previous generations.

One example relevant to our studies was the integration of the floating-point unit (FPU) into Intel CPUs starting with the i486DX processor, released in 1992. Before then, researchers had the choice of processing floating-point numbers (floats) on the CPU using microcode, or adding a second chip—the FPU—onto the system board. The FPU significantly sped up calculations, as all floating-point operations were hardwired into it, but FPUs were expensive.

---

* Eben Upton *et. al. Learning Computer Architecture with Raspberry Pi*. John Wiley and Sons. 2016. p.95.

Increasing transistor counts made integrating the FPU into the CPU possible. Today, everyone using a personal computer gets to do floating-point operations at hardware-level speeds.

2.2 Fundamentals of Computation II: Bits, Boolean Logic, and the Digital Age of George Boole and Claude Shannon

> The fundamental unit of information is the bit.
> The bit has only two states: 0 or 1, off or on, false or true.
> As ones and zeros, bits can represent numbers in base-2.
> Computers use base-2, or the binary number system, to do logic and arithmetic operations.
> Humans use a base-10, or the denary number system.
> Physically, magnetic polarity, voltage differences, and light pulses represent bits in the storage, transmission, and computation of bits.
> The Digital Age depends on our ability:
>
> 1) To represent the phenomenological world with bits (analog-to-digital conversion)
> 2) To move bits around efficiently (digital communication)
> 3) To perform logic operations on bits (digital computation)
> 4) To transform digital data to analog data (digital-to-analog conversion)

2.2.1 George Boole

George Boole was a self-taught English mathematician. He thought of his work in logic as a way to symbolize the expression of pure thought.

After Boole's untimely death, his work was treated largely as a philosophical curiosity.

As a graduate student at MIT, Claude Shannon, known today as the Father of the Digital Age, was introduced to Boole's work on symbolic logic in a philosophy class he took over the summer.

Then, after working as a summer intern in 1937 at Bell Labs, where he was exposed to real-world engineering problems in communications, including the growing ad hoc complexity in the circuit layouts of phone routing switches at relay stations, Shannon began to realize that Boolean algebra might be applied to simplify those layouts, as well as the circuit layouts of a machine he was working with at MIT.

Shannon recognized that Boole's work had real-world applications with regard to the electromechanical relays used by AT&T to create temporary, dedicated circuits between the phones of callers and the phones of those being called.

As Shannon explained:

> It is not so much that a thing is "open" or "closed," the "yes" or "no" that you mentioned. The real point is that two things in series are described by the word "and" in logic, so you would say this "and" this, while two things in parallel are described by the word "or"...There are contacts which close when you operate the relay, and there are other contacts which open, so the word "not" is related to that aspect of relays...The people who had worked with relay circuits were, of course, aware of how to make these things. But they didn't have the mathematical apparatus of the Boolean algebra.*

---

* Jimmy Soni & Rob Goodman. *A Mind At Play: How Claude Shannon Invented the Information Age*. Simon and Schuster. 2017. p.38.

These revelations became the basis of Shannon's master's thesis in 1937. Boolean algebra would subsequently become integral to circuit design, as well as the logic of all modern electronic digital computers.

A symbolic analysis of relay and switching circuits by Claude Shannon. Master's Thesis, MIT, Department of Electrical Engineering. 1940.

Figure 2-4 MIT makes Claude Shannon's master thesis available as a publicly accessible, free download. Click or scan the QR code to go to the download page. https://dspace.mit.edu/handle/1721.1/11173

George Boole had envisioned that his algebra would be imminently practical for thought. I imagine he would have been deeply disappointed to learn that for many years, it had been relegated to the status of a philosophical curiosity.

Thanks to Claude Shannon, Boole's work spread from philosophy classes to engineering classes. It is the foundation of circuit design. And today, many people with just a passing knowledge of how computers work have at least heard of Boolean logic.

2.2.2 Claude Shannon

Claude Shannon wasn't finished; and he certainly hadn't yet peaked.

Shannon earned his Ph.D. in mathematics in 1940. Between then and when he published *The Mathematical Theory of Communication* in Bell Labs' *Bell System Technical Journal* in 1948, he worked in cryptography and communications during WWII at Bell Labs. He later said his insights into communication theory and cryptography developed simultaneously.

> The work on both the mathematical theory of communications and the cryptology went forward concurrently from about 1941. I worked on both of them together and I had some of the ideas while working on the other. I wouldn't say one came before the other — they were so close together you couldn't separate them.[‡‡]

—Claude Shannon

The Mathematical Theory of Communication provides a rigorous treatment on the conveyance of information from sender to receiver through a channel, which may or may not be noisy. The information conveyed may be discrete (like that from a teletype or a telegraph) or continuous (like that over an analog radio signal). In the work, Shannon considers such subjects as "Entropy Loss in Linear Filters"[*] for continuous information and "A Discrete Channel and its Capacity".[†]

The Mathematical Theory of Communication has since become the basis for all modern digital communication, earning Claude Shannon the sobriquet "Father of the Digital Age."

[‡‡] David Kahn. *The Codebreakers: The Story of Secret Writing*. Scribner. 1996. p.744.

[*] Claude Shannon & Warren Weaver. **The Mathematical Theory of Communication**. The University of Illinois Press: Urbana. 1949. pg 60.

[†] *op. cit.* pg 44.

[W]e're living in the information age. It's Shannon whose fingerprints are on every electronic device we own, every computer screen we gaze into, every means of digital communication. He's one of these people who so transform the world that, after the transformation, the old world is forgotten.

—Author James Gleick
The New Yorker[‡]

2.3 Fundamentals of Computation III: Data, Instructions, and Pointers

The three kinds of information in modern digital computers	
	Definition and examples
Data	Text files, image files, sensor data, datasets
Instructions	Applications to create, manipulate, transform, and delete data
Pointers	Information that says where the on mass-storage devices and in memory the data and instructions reside

There are just three kinds of information in modern digital computers:

1) **Data**: This includes text files, multimedia files, multimedia video streams over the network, emails, and, of course, datasets. For the purposes of this class, we will restrict our discussion primarily to datasets.
2) **Instructions**: These are instructions to the CPU that tell it what to do to the data. Think programs. The programs we will write are instructions to our machines telling them how to manipulate or transform the data in our datasets.
3) **Pointers**: These are pieces of information that the operating system and CPU use to keep track of the locations of data and instructions on the mass-storage devices or in memory. These locations are called **addresses**.

Table Of Contents
Chapter One..1
Chapter Two..11
Chapter Three...19
Chapter Four...32

Figure 2-5 Pointers in the analog world. In a table of contents, chapters are mapped to page numbers. The page numbers tell where the chapters begin. Page numbers here serve as pointers

---

[‡] Siobhan Roberts. "Claude Shannon, Father of the Digital Age, Turns 1100100". The New Yorker. April 30, 2016. Online article fetched 6 Oct 2024.

2.3 Data, Instructions, and Pointers

2.3.1 Headline 1

Lorem ipsum dolor sit amet, consectetuer adipiscing elit. Ut purus elit, vestibulum ut, placerat ac, adipiscing vitae, felis. Curabitur dictum gravida mauris. Nam arcu libero, nonummy eget, consectetuer id, vulputate a, magna. Donec vehicula augue eu neque. Pellentesque habitant morbi tristique senectus et netus et malesuada fames ac turpis egestas. Mauris ut leo. Cras viverra metus rhoncus sem. Nulla et lectus vestibulum urna fringilla ultrices. Phasellus eu tellus sit amet tortor gravida placerat. Integer sapien est, iaculis in, pretium quis, viverra ac, nunc. Praesent eget sem vel leo ultrices bibendum. Aenean faucibus. Morbi dolor nulla, malesuada eu, pulvinar at, mollis ac, nulla. Curabitur auctor semper nulla. Donec varius orci eget risus. Duis nibh mi, congue eu, accumsan eleifend, sagittis quis, diam. Duis eget orci sit amet orci dignissim rutrum.

2.3.2 Headline 2

Nam dui ligula, fringilla a, euismod sodales, sollicitudin vel, wisi. Morbi auctor lorem non justo. Nam lacus libero, pretium at, lobortis vitae, ultricies et, tellus. Donec aliquet, tortor sed accumsan bibendum, erat ligula aliquet magna, vitae ornare odio metus a mi. Morbi ac orci et nisl hendrerit mollis. Suspendisse ut massa. Cras nec ante. Pellentesque a nulla. Cum sociis natoque penatibus et magnis dis parturient montes, nascetur ridiculus mus. Aliquam tincidunt urna. Nulla ullamcorper vestibulum turpis. Pellentesque cursus luctus mauris.

2.3.3 Headline 3

Nulla malesuada porttitor diam. Donec felis erat, congue non, volutpat at, tincidunt tristique, libero. Vivamus viverra fermentum felis. Donec nonummy pellentesque ante. Phasellus adipiscing semper elit. Proin fermentum massa ac quam. Sed diam turpis, molestie vitae, placerat a, molestie nec, leo. Maecenas lacinia. Nam ipsum ligula, eleifend at, accumsan nec, suscipit a, ipsum. Morbi blandit ligula feugiat magna. Nunc eleifend consequat lorem. Sed lacinia nulla vitae enim. Pellentesque tincidunt purus vel magna. Integer non enim. Praesent euismod nunc eu purus. Donec bibendum quam in tellus. Nullam cursus pulvinar lectus. Donec et mi. Nam vulputate metus eu enim. Vestibulum pellentesque felis eu massa.

Story 3 continued on page **B6**

Figure 2-6 Another real-world analog of pointers. In this case, pointers are used to join fragments of the same article in a newspaper. The piece of information at the end of a fragment that says where the next fragment begins (as in Story 3 here) is a **pointer**

As programmers, our interest in computer architecture focuses mostly on the CPU and system memory and their interactions. Data and programs must be stored in memory before they can be accessed by the CPU. Bits move between the CPU and memory using a system bus, which in this diagram has been further broken down to the address bus, the data bus, and the control bus (Figure 2-7).

Both CPU and memory use the data bus to move data and program instructions between them. Pointers are used to keep track of the data and instructions in memory. They move along the address bus.

Signals used by the CPU and memory to coordinate traffic over the system bus use the control bus.

The details of how data and programs can stored in the same memory for access by the CPU were first worked out by the inventors of ENIAC, John Mauchly and J. Presper Eckert, in the design of their second all-electric computer, the EDVAC.

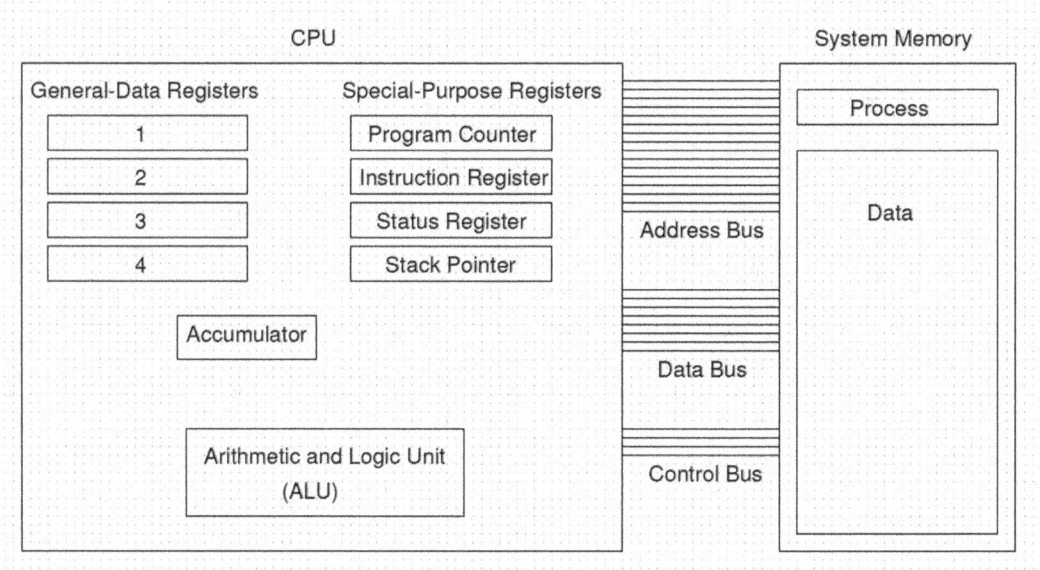

Figure 2-7 The vUTM made real: a simplified general-purpose computer. —Diagram made with **xcircuit** by author

2.4 Code and Data: Cycles of Fetch, Decode, and Execute, Over and Over

The core of a CPU executes instructions and processes data.

At its simplest, a core contains data registers to hold the data, an instruction register to hold the next instruction to be executed, and an arithmetic and logic unit (ALU) where the data is processed.

The core contains general data registers to hold ints, chars, and bools, and floating-point registers to hold floats.

Ints and floats are processed differently in separate parts of the core. When they are combined arithmetically—for example, when an int is added to a float—the int becomes a float, and the operation is done in the FPU part of the core.

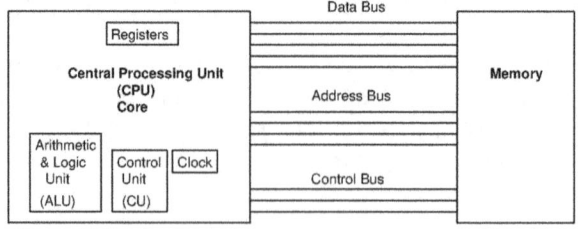

Figure 2-8 A hypothetical microcomputer. "The *central processor unit* CPU, where calculations and logical operations take place, contain a limited number of storage locations called *registers*, a high-frequency clock, a control unit, and an arithmetic logic unit (ALU)."   —Kip Irvine, *Assembly Language For x86 Processors, 7th Edition*

2.4 Fetch, Decode, and Execute

- The *clock* synchronizes the internal operations of the CPU with other system components.
- The *control unit* (CU) coordinates the sequencing of steps involved in executing machine instructions.
- The *arithmetic logic unit* (ALU) performs arithmetic operations such as addition and subtraction and logical operations such as **AND**, **OR**, and **NOT**.

—ibid. p.33

> The memory of a modern digital computer holds programs and data.
> The CPU fetches data from memory, along with instructions from programs that tell the CPU how to process the data.
> The CPU sends data that is to be saved to memory.
> This interaction between the CPU and memory requires pointers to keep track of the data and instructions in memory.

Clock Each operation involving the CPU and the system bus is synchronized by an internal clock pulsing at a constant rate. The basic unit of time for machine instructions is a *machine cycle* (or *clock cycle*). The length of a clock cycle is the time required for one complete clock pulse. In the following figure, a clock cycle is depicted as the time between one falling edge and the next:

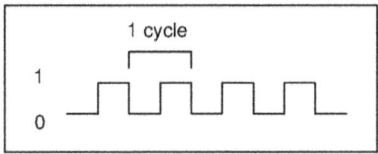

A machine instruction requires at least one clock cycle to execute, and a few require in excess of 50 clocks...Instructions requiring memory access often have empty clock cycles called *wait states* because of the differences in the speeds of the CPU, the system bus, and memory circuits.

—ibid. p.34

The fetch-decode-execute cycle in the core of a CPU:

1. First, the CPU has to **fetch the instruction** from an area of memory called the *instruction queue*. Right after doing this, it increments the instruction pointer.
2. Next, the CPU **decodes** the instruction by looking at its binary bit pattern. The bit pattern might reveal that the instruction has operands (input values).
3. If operands are involved, the CPU **fetches the operands** from registers and memory. Sometimes, this involves address calculations.
4. Next, the CPU **executes** the instruction, using any operand values it fetched during the earlier step. It also updates a few status flags, such as Zero, Carry, and Overflow.
5. Finally, if an output operand was part of the instruction, the CPU **stores the result** of its execution in the operand.

We usually simplify this complicated-sounding process to three basic steps: **Fetch**, **Decode**, and **Execute**. An *operand* is a value that is either an input or an output to an operation. For example, the expression $Z = X + Y$ has two input operands (X and Y) and a single output operand (Z).

—ibid. p.35

Kip Irvine. *Assembly Language For x86 Processors, 7th Edition*, Pearson. 2015. p.33.

Chapter Summary

Modern digital computers use transistors arranged into logic gates to execute instructions and process data. They do this by moving data and instructions from memory to registers in the cores, executing the instructions on the data, then moving processed data back to memory. These actions are continual and incredibly fast. Although we are creatures of perception and reaction times measured in milliseconds (thousandths of a second), these machines that serve us execute their instructions over and over in microseconds (millionths of a second) and nanoseconds (billionths of a second).

Operating Systems 3

An operating system is software that manages a computer's hardware while providing application writers a consistent interface to the hardware. Early computers had no operating systems. Many modern microcontrollers have no operating systems. Operating systems are practical only on machines with enough memory and compute cycles to support them, and yet, they have become an indispensable part of personal computers. They allow application writers to write applications that run on a specific operating system, instead of writing applications that run on very specific assemblages of hardware. So in exchange for memory and compute cycles, operating systems allow an application to run on many computers made up of quite varied components.

> It's hardware that makes a machine fast. It's software that makes a fast machine slow.
> —Craig Bruce

3.1 Operating Systems and Linux

An operating system is software that manages a computer's resources, which greatly simplifies an application programmer's job in writing applications that run on the computer.

The OS provides a standard, consistent interface to the hardware for application writers. This means that, more or less, an application writer can write an app meant to run on an OS, and it will run on all machines that have that OS installed.

(Not all computers have operating systems. Examples include microcontrollers that lack the memory to hold an operating system.)

Applications are binary files not meant to be human-readable. Rather, they are machine code files meant to be executed directly by the CPU so that they run as fast as possible. Examples include Microsoft Word, Mozilla Firefox, and the Python interpreter.

Generally, OS writers provide application writers with the means through code to interface with the OS, allowing applications standard ways to access computer hardware, regardless of hardware manufacturer or the special functionality of the hardware.

OS writers also provide documentation to hardware manufacturers, showing them how to interface their hardware optimally to the OS. Hardware manufacturers use this information to write device drivers.

Table 3-1 An operating system is a layer of software that manages the hardware of a computer and is designed to provide a standard interface for application writers

3 layers of modern digital computers
Apps and OSs are both software
Applications
Operating system
Hardware

This standardization also benefits a user of the applications, as—for example—a user of a modern graphical display computer knows how each window and each menu bar of each application behave.

3.1.1 A Brief History of Operating Systems, with an Emphasis on UNIX

> At some point I realized I was three weeks from an operating system.
> —Ken Thompson, principal creator of UNIX*

The operating system of a computer is a set of software that manages the computer's hardware resources and provides a standard, consistent interface to the hardware for application writers (programmers who write compiled programs) (Table 3-1).

The first computers did not have operating systems. Programmers had to write their programs to interface directly with computer hardware and peripherals. The first operating system used on production systems was written for IBM's first commercial scientific computer, the IBM 704. The year was 1956.

The advantages of standardizing a consistent interface for application writers became quickly apparent. Chief among these is the speed at which programmers could develop applications. Soon, operating systems proliferated, with each major computer vendor offering its own operating system for the machines it was selling.

Soon, computer sellers and buyers realized that a single operating system for all computers would make the cost of application development even cheaper, as an application written on one computer could run on another with few changes, provided both computers ran the same OS. This was the motivation behind the development of MULTICS, first announced in 1965.

MULTICS and a slightly older operating system called CTSS (1964), both products of MIT, were designed for interactive sessions with programmers and users. According to Kernighan, "[m]ost operating systems in that era were 'batch processing.' Programmers put their programs on punch cards (this was a long time ago!), handed them to an operator, and then waited for the results to be returned, hours or even days later."[†]

The punch card symbolizes batch processing, where programmer and user have no interaction with a program while it's executing.

Interactive sessions, where the programmer or user sat at a terminal and interacted directly with a computer, at that time were still considered innovative. The creators of UNIX would make their operating system interactive.

Another innovation of MULTICS incorporated into UNIX was having the operating system keep track of information about files on mass-storage devices. This freed programmers and users from

---

[*] Brian Kernighan. *UNIX: A History and a Memoir*. Kindle Direct Publishing. 2020. p.33.
[†] *ibid* p.30.

having to provide this information themselves to programs or the operating system. In UNIX, this information is held in *i-nodes*.

Also, in UNIX, a file is "simply a sequence of bytes. Any structure or organization of the contents of a file is determined only by the programs that process it; the filesystem itself doesn't care what's in a file. That means that any program can read or write any file. This seems obvious in retrospect, but it was not always appreciated in earlier systems..."[†]

So the UNIX writers would innovate and borrow innovations, as they conceived of, then wrote, UNIX. Their motivation arose in part from their appreciation of where MULTICS was heading.

As recounted by Dennis Ritchie of Bell Labs[‡], the Bell Labs people who were part of the MULTICS consortium realized that MULTICS was doomed to failure (essentially, death by committee), and the Bell Labs people—Ken Thompson and Dennis Ritchie chief among them—started sketching out a replacement for MULTICS, one that would keep what they thought were some of the best parts of CTSS and MULTICS.

The result was UNIX, whose name Ritchie admits was "a somewhat treacherous pun on MULTICS." The motivation of the Bell Labs team to get around to finally implementing their replacement for MULTICS was the desire to play a game called "Space Travel" on a machine with "an excellent display processor."[‡‡]

Thompson started by implementing the filesystem, then worked out other parts of the operating system.

The year was 1969.

UNIX quickly grew in popularity, especially in academic institutions. It is the inspiration, if not the basis, for the most popular operating systems today, including Microsoft's MS-DOS, which, contrary to popular myth, was not written by Bill Gates, but by Tim Paterson—as a hobby! Paterson had learned UNIX while a student at university, and his OS included many of the command names used in UNIX.

The Age of Personal Computers started with the release of the 16-bit IBM Personal Computer in 1981. IBM chose to use in its PCs 16-bit Intel CPUs (central processing units, the primary logic and arithmetic chips in computers). This choice resulted in Intel's quickly becoming the world's largest CPU manufacturer, displacing IBM. And although IBM was also the world's largest OS provider at the time, it chose to license for use in these PCs an operating system compatible with Intel's 16-bit CPU. This choice resulted in Microsoft's quickly becoming the world's largest OS provider, again displacing IBM.

In 1991, Finnish graduate student Linus Torvalds released Linux, an operating system that he wrote from scratch modeled on UNIX and designed to run on Intel Personal Computer CPUs. Torvalds invited other OS programmers to help him improve Linux. From the start, Torvalds made Linux free to use and free to alter.

As such, as it grew in popularity, it posed a threat to vendors of UNIX, who charged license fees. The 1990s saw Linux grow and mature as it overcame primarily legal challenges from UNIX vendors. UNIX programmers became Linux programmers.

Today Linux has largely supplanted UNIX.

[†] Kernighan, Brian. **ibid.** p.62.

[‡] Ritchie, Dennis. "The Evolution of the UNIX Time-sharing System," 1984. https://www.bell-labs.com/usr/dmr/www/hist.html

[‡‡] *ibid.*

3.2 The UNIX/Linux Filesystem

> UNIX/Linux benefits from filesystem innovations made in MULTICS.
> MULTICS implemented a hierarchical filesystem.
> MULTICS managed and tracked the properties of files, instead of requiring users to do so.
> UNIX/Linux does both of these. The UNIX/Linux filesystem is organized as a **tree**, which is a structure in **graph theory** that has a single, central node at the top called the "root."
> The nodes of this tree are either directories or files. The root is a directory. Directories are traversable. Files and empty directories are the leaves of the tree.
> New volumes can be mounted at arbitrary nodes in the filesystem, allowing (potentially) unlimited filesystem expansion.

```
$ stat .bash_history
File: .bash_history
Size: 360141          Blocks: 712        IO Block: 4096   regular file
Device: 252,1         Inode: 106180322   Links: 1
Access: (0600/-rw-------)  Uid: ( 1000/    user)   Gid: ( 1000/    user)
Access: 2025-03-29 14:54:14.790619004 -0500
Modify: 2025-03-29 07:44:23.653484927 -0500
Change: 2025-03-29 07:44:23.653484927 -0500
Birth: 2024-11-01 14:18:29.646727902 -0500
```

Figure 3-1 File info maintained by the operating system and printed by the Linux *stat* command

An innovation carried over by the creators of UNIX and incorporated now into all desktop operating systems is to have the operating system keep track of critical information about files in the filesystem.

In *UNIX: A History And A Memoir*, Brian Kernighan mentions someone reminded him how awkward it was just to create a file on a disk on another system at the time:

> The Honeywell TSS system required you to enter a subsystem to create a file disk. You were asked about 8 questions: initial size of file, maximum size, name, device, who could read it, who could write it, etc. Each of these had to be answered interactively. When all the questions had been answered, the operating system was given the information; and, likely as not, something was mistyped and the file creation failed. That meant you got to enter the subsystem again and answer all the questions again. It's no wonder that when a file finally got created, the system said 'SUCCESSFUL!' ‡‡

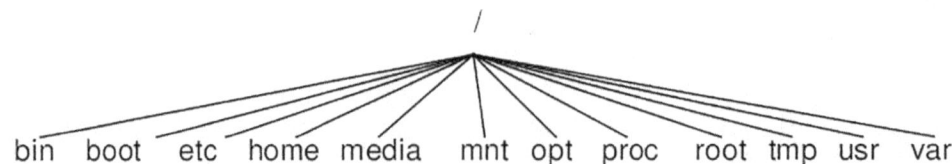

Figure 3-2 The UNIX/Linux filesystem is a tree structure

---

‡‡ *ibid.* p 65.

The topmost level is called the root. When you include the filename, the path from the root to every file in the system is unique.

The hierarchical filesystem structure is a MULTICS innovation.

3.3 The Memory Manager and Process Scheduler

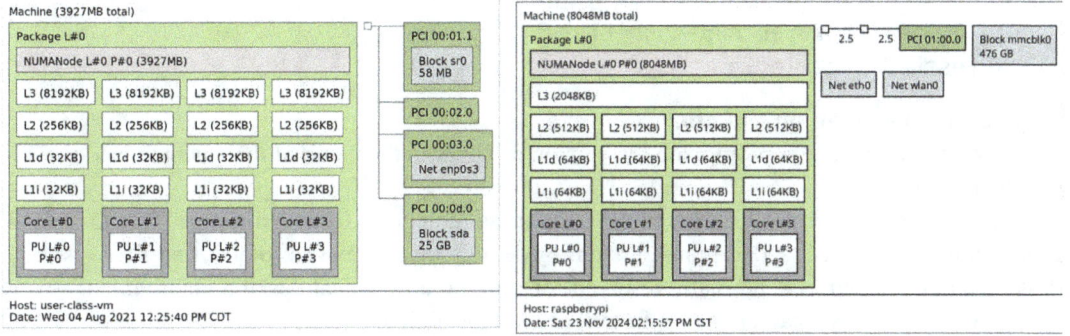

Figure 3-3 Output of the Linux command **lstopo** run on a quad-core VM on an Intel host (left) & an ARM machine (right)

The diagrams above show the hardware that we will mostly concern ourselves with as programmers: the CPU cores and the system memory.

The mass-storage devices (**Block sda** in the Dell and **Block mmcblk0** in the raspi) hold copies of the programs and data. When a program is launched, a copy of the ones and zeroes that make up the program on the mass-storage device is written into memory (**NUMANode** in the diagrams). A copy of a program in memory is called "a process." Data associated with the program that is in the mass-storage device may also be copied into memory.

A program must be loaded into memory before it can be run. Data must be loaded into memory before it can be processed.

Program execution and data processing take place in the cores of the CPU.

The operating system's memory manager and process scheduler work together to move program instructions into the cores for execution and to move data between the memory and the cores for processing and saving.

In the diagrams, the L caches lie between the cores and the memory. ("L" means "level.") The L caches are tiny SRAM chips that hold already-used instructions and data for quick retrieval to the cores if needed again—quicker than if fetched from memory.

The parts of an operating system that manage the critical hardware components of a computer are all together called "the kernel"—while the software that lets us most directly interact with the kernel is called a "shell." The parts of the kernel that interest us most are the **memory manager** and the **process scheduler**.

The memory manager keeps track of whether assignable memory is used (allocated) or free. It determines how memory is allocated to each process: how much and when.

The process scheduler determines which process runs, on which core it runs, and when. It can pause a running process for a process with a higher priority, and it can move a running process to another core, or even move it to the back of the running queue.

The memory manager and process scheduler work together to move the data and instructions in our programs back and forth between memory and CPU cores.

3.4 Working with Datafiles in Linux

```
Ubuntu 24.10 linux-testbed-45gb tty3
linux-testbed-45gb login: _
```

TTY terminal window on Ubuntu.
Displayed above the logon prompt are the version of Ubuntu, the name of the machine, and the TTY session number.

Above is a recreation of a TTY (teletype) terminal session on an Ubuntu machine. True to its UNIX roots, Linux offers text-based terminal sessions by default, though for ease of use, one TTY session on desktop Linux machines is normally reserved for running a graphical desktop environment—which the hardcore Linux user can opt not to install, or to uninstall later.

TTY stands for "teletype" or "teletypewriter," an electromechanical machine with a keyboard like a typewriter's by which human operators communicated with mainframe and miniframe computers. Operators typed out their statements on the keyboards.

As the operators typed, the teletypes printed their statements on continuous-feed paper. Hitting **RETURN** or **ENTER** terminated the statements, which were then converted to electrical signals and sent to the computers by cables for interpretation and execution, while the teletypes advanced the paper one line and returned the carriage.

After the computers processed operators' statements, they would send their output, if any, by cables to the teletypes, for the operators to read the responses; then the teletypes advanced the paper one line and returned the carriage, to await more input from the operators—or more output from the computers.

Operators could capture the histories of their sessions, which the teletypes punched out on paper tape. (The paper tape reader/writer was usually on the left-hand side of the QWERTY keyboard.) If operators wished to pick up a session later, they could feed the paper tape of that earlier session into their teletypes, which read the information encoded in the punch holes of the tape and sent that information to the computers for processing.

Figure 3-4 **Wikipedia teletype article.** In *UNIX: A History and a Memoir*, Brian Kernighan mentions that the teletype used by Ken Thompson and Dennis Ritchie was much like the Model 33 that is the topic of this article. Click or scan image to go to article. https://en.wikipedia.org/wiki/Teletype_Model_33

UNIX was created years before graphical user interfaces (GUIs), or even monitors.* Though graphical desktop environments are widely used on Linux systems, text-based processing is still done using command-line tools.

Not only are these tools written to run optimally (which means as small and fast as possible), they use less memory and fewer compute cycles than graphical tools that perform the same tasks.

Furthermore, all work done on high-performance compute clusters (HPCCs, or supercomputers), and most work done on remote Linux machines, is done in text-based terminal sessions.

For these reasons, when working on text-based datafiles, command-line tools are preferred.

1) To the furthest extent possible in UNIX/Linux, everything is treated like a file.
2) To the furthest extent possible in UNIX/Linux, all files are human-readable. There are exceptions, of course, for example, binary files (applications) and relational database files.
3) To the furthest extent possible in UNIX/Linux, datafiles are structured one record per line. The newline character is the record delimiter, and new records are appended to the bottom of the datafiles. Consider, for example, log files.

3.5 An Introduction to the Process Scheduler

Before a program can run, it must be loaded into memory.

The copy of a program in memory is called a **process**.

As a process is loaded into memory, it is assigned an ID number, called the **Process ID**, or PID.

The process scheduler of an operating system decides which processes run and when.

As your processes run, especially long term, you may notice that the scheduler will interrupt them to run processes with a higher priority. This is normal.

Processing datasets requires coordination between the memory manager and process scheduler in moving the data and the instructions to process the data between the memory and the cores of a machine's CPU.

Chapter Summary
As soon as computers became powerful enough to hold the software layer that we call "an operating system," operating systems were written to make the job of application writers easier, as well as to allow an application to run on computers made up of different hardware but with the same operating system installed on them. Even now, some computational machines, like microcontrollers, do NOT have operating systems; but most do. Understanding the interplay between an OS's memory manager and process scheduler helps programmers understand how computers execute their instructions to process datasets.

---

* The Xerox Alto is the first computer designed to have a graphical user interface. It was introduced in 1973, just four years after the inception of UNIX. It was too expensive to mass-produce; however, technological innovations introduced in the Alto (including a graphical desktop, a trashcan icon, incorporation of Doug Engelbart's mouse, and a WYSIWYG word processor) inspired Steve Jobs to create first the Lisa then the Macintosh.

Introduction to Bash

4

Bash is an application that allows users to interface with a computer's operating system. Bash has its own programming language and includes an interpreter, allowing users to write and run scripts to automate tasks. In this introduction, we will look at some of the Bash tools used to automate working with datasets.

4.1 The Bash Shell

> A **shell** is an application that allows users to interface with a computer's operating system. A shell is what users are presented with when opening a terminal session with a computer. Within a shell, users can open files, launch applications, and process or modify data. Some scientists and engineers do much, if not all, of their data processing within a shell. The most popular shell in Linux is the Bash shell, released in 1989.

```
username@ubuntu-machine:~$
```

The default prompt in the Bash shell. Your **username** on the computer comes first, separated by an "@" from the name of the machine that you're logged into. After the full colon is the path to your working directory (Bash uses a tilde (~) as shorthand to mean your home directory, whose absolute path in this example is /home/user). The dollar sign ($) signifies that in this Bash session, you are a normal user.

The shell is a command-line interpreter that provides users with an interface to a computer's operating system.* A user enters a text command in the shell; and if the command is well-formed—that is, free of grammar, spelling, and punctuation errors—the shell interpreter executes it. In general, a shell is the most direct interface to the OS most users will have.

---

* The name "shell" is a play on words.
The kernel is the set of software that makes up the core of the operating system.
The word "kernel" also refers to the center of a seed, which is surrounded by a shell.
Software shells are applications that give most users their most direct access to the operating system's kernel.

The most popular shell in Linux is Bash.[†] The Bash shell first came out in 1989, and on most Linux systems, it is the default shell.

Shells have their own scripting languages, and some researchers prefer to work on their datasets using only the shell and tools that they can execute on the command line (such as **vim** and **gawk**).

4.2 Changing the Bash Prompt

I wish to start by showing you how, without fuss or explanation, we can modify the Bash command-line prompt during a session, then restore it (Figure 4-1).

I find it sometimes useful to shorten the prompt so that I have almost all of the space on the command line to write on.

A Bash environment variable named **PS1** holds a string value that defines the prompt.

We will save that string as the value in a new variable we'll create called **TEMP**, then we'll change the value of PS1 to ' > ', where the close angle bracket has one space to both its left and right.

Finally, we will restore the prompt to its default value.

As you will see, the changes we'll make take effect immediately.

```
username@ubuntu-machine:~$
username@ubuntu-machine:~$ TEMP=$PS1 # we invoke a bash variable
username@ubuntu-machine:~$ # by pre-pending a $ to its name
username@ubuntu-machine:~$ PS1=' > ' # we change the value of
username@ubuntu-machine:~$ # the PS1 variable
 > # ...and changing the value changes the prompt!
 >
 > # let's restore the prompt to its default value...
 > PS1=$TEMP
username@ubuntu-machine:~$ # and it's back!
```

Figure 4-1. Changing the Bash prompt—twice!

In this lesson, we learn several facts about working on the Bash command line:

1) We can modify the values of Bash environment variables, customizing our experience working in Bash.
2) In Bash, by convention, all variable names are uppercased.
3) In Bash, we write assignment statements (in which we create and instantiate variables) without spaces between the variable name on the left-hand side, the assignment operator (which in other contexts we call the equal sign), and the value on the right-hand side.
4) In Bash, when we invoke a variable by name, we prepend the name with a dollar sign.
5) We can annotate our Bash statements with notes and comments by starting them with a hash (or pound) symbol. (Annotating statements with keywords can make them easier to look up in Bash history, as we shall see later.)

[†] A system may come with more than one shell installed. To temporarily switch shells, on the command line, type the name of another installed shell, then press ENTER.
The current default shell for MacOS is **zsh**. To switch to Bash shell for the duration of a session, the MacOS user just needs on the command line to type: **bash** ENTER.

In later lessons, we will learn more about Bash variables, as well as how to search the history of our Bash sessions.

To ensure our session is saved to the Bash history file, we must close the session gracefully. To do that in Bash, on the command line, type:

exit enter

4.3 Navigating Bash History and the LINUX Filesystem

> Every desktop/laptop OS uses hidden files and folders. The names of hidden files and folders start with a dot (.)
>
> A hidden text file called .bash_history resides in each user's home directory on a Linux system when the user uses Bash.
>
> When a Bash session is quit gracefully, Bash appends the Bash statements entered by the user during the session to the .bash_history file.
>
> Users have access to the contents of their Bash history files from the Bash command line:
>
> 1) They can scroll through their histories using the keyboard up ↑ and down ↓ arrows.
> 2) They can do a reverse-i-search by pressing **Ctrl** **r** while the Bash terminal window has the focus, then entering a search substring.
> 3) They can pipe the output of the history command to grep, which outputs lines that contain a match, like this: **history | grep some-search-string**.
>
> HINT: To prevent a statement from being appended to the Bash history file, just prepend the statement with a space.[a]
>
> ---
> [a]The Bash command **egrep** is deprecated.
> "egrep" stands for "extended grep."
> Writing regular expressions in extended grep is easier than in regular grep.
> To use the functionality of extended grep, we now write: **grep -E**.

Before we turn our attention to datafiles, let's work with some common commands and shortcuts in Bash and maybe pick up a little more LINUX along the way.

We already know that by default, when we launch a Bash session, Bash sets our home directory as our working directory.

```
username@ubuntu-machine:~$ pwd # print working directory
/home/username
```

Figure 4-2. pwd: print working directory

Your **working directory** is the directory in which you are currently working. When you enter the pwd command, Bash returns the **absolute path** of your working directory. The absolute path always starts with the slash (/) and shows the location of your working directory in the filesystem starting at the top of the filesystem or root. An absolute path is unambiguous.

The line also contains a comment, which is set off from the Bash statement, or command, by a hash sign (#). The interpreter scans our input on the command line character by character, from left to right, and when it reaches the hash sign, it stops, ignoring everything that follows.

The comment will be preserved in the Bash history. This means you can annotate your commands, or add keywords to make finding the line in searches easier.

In the figure above, we note that the line has three parts: the prompt, a command, and a comment. We are commenting our commands because the comments will be preserved in the Bash history file, allowing us to review or use them later.

Let's consider the output of the pwd command: /home/user. In Bash, there are two ways to define paths to files and folders in the filesystem:

1) With **absolute paths**, which always begin with a slash (/) that denotes the top of the filesystem (called the root). An absolute path shows the full path to a file or folder from the root down. Absolute paths are unambiguous.
2) With **relative paths**, which don't begin with a slash and which show the paths to files and folders relative to the working directory.

```
username@ubuntu-machine:~$ ls # list directory contents
Desktop Documents Downloads Music Pictures Public Videos
```

Figure 4-3. ls: list directory contents

In modern Linux systems with graphical desktop environments, home directories when created are populated with directories like Desktop, Documents, and Downloads.

We list the contents of our working directory with the **ls** command. In the figure above, directories within our working directory are colored blue.

We change our working directory with the **cd** (change directory) command. Let's cd relative to our working directory:

```
username@ubuntu-machine:~$ cd Desktop # change working directory
username@ubuntu-machine:~/Desktop$ # to Desktop
username@ubuntu-machine:~/Desktop$ # note that Desktop is one level deep
username@ubuntu-machine:~/Desktop$ # relative to working dir
username@ubuntu-machine:~/Desktop$ cd # now to go home
username@ubuntu-machine:~$
```

Figure 4-4. cd: change directory

With no argument following, **cd** returns users to their home directories.

If a path is given as an argument, without starting with a slash, the path is interpreted as being relative to the working directory. Note that the prompt is updated to show the new working directory.

cd by itself always returns you to your home directory, no matter where you are in the filesystem.

Reminder: Comments are written to Bash history where they can be accessed later. You can add keywords to Bash statements as comments, then search your Bash history for those statements by keywords.

And now that we've worked a (very) little in the Bash shell, let's end our session so that our input is written to the Bash history file. With the focus on the terminal window, on the keyboard, press: ⎡Ctrl⎤ d.

(You can also use the Bash command **exit**.)

4.3 Navigating Bash History and the LINUX Filesystem

Ctrl d signals to the system "no more input." Inserting a **Ctrl** d ends the session gracefully. Among other actions, it lets Bash write the contents of the session to its history file.

Now that we've gracefully closed our session, let's open a new one. Launch the terminal app, and at the Bash prompt, type: **hist** **tab** **return**.

Notice what happened. After you typed the first few letters of the word "history," pressing **tab** lets Bash complete the word. We call this feature **tab**-completion. It lets us speed up input as we type Bash statements. Please make an effort to use **tab**-completion as much as you can. It will really speed up how quickly you work on the command line!

```
username@ubuntu-machine:~$ history
1    pwd # print working directory
2    ls # list directory contents
3    cd Desktop # change working directory
4    # to Desktop
5    # note that Desktop is one level deep
6    # relative to working dir
7    cd # now to go home
8    history
```

Figure 4-5. The Bash **history** command. By default, the last 1000 lines of input on the Bash command line are saved to a hidden file in your home directory called .bash_history. The history of your Bash sessions is searchable, and you can easily rerun Bash commands with a few keystrokes

To rerun a previous command, you need only type **!nnn**, where **nnn** is the line number of the command in the Bash history. Using the history output in the figure above, to rerun **cd** Desktop, on the command line, type: **!3** **return**. This is really useful when you've composed a long Bash statement that you need to run again and again.

(And if you don't want a Bash statement saved to the Bash history file, just start the statement with a **space**. In other words, instead of typing **cd** **return**, type: **space** **cd** **return**.)

We have more than one way to search the history of our Bash sessions.

With the focus on the terminal window, type: **ctrl** r. The **reverse-i-search** prompt appears:

```
(reverse-i-search)`':
```

This tool allows you to search your Bash history in reverse—that is, starting with your most recent commands and ending with your oldest. In this example, we are searching for a specific instance in which we executed the **cd** command. We enter **cd** at the prompt, and **reverse-i-search** returns the most recent line that contains the substring "cd".

```
(reverse-i-search)`cd': cd # now to go home
```

If we press **RETURN** now, that line would be executed; however, we are searching for another line in our history that contains "cd". To continue the reverse search, type again: **ctrl** r.

```
(reverse-i-search)`cd': cd Desktop # change working directory
```

For this example, let's assume this is the line we want. Now press **RETURN**, and the line is executed.

```
username@ubuntu-machine:~$ cd Desktop  # change working directory
username@ubuntu-machine:~/Desktop$
```

Another way we can search Bash history is by using the Bash pipeline—which we're going to see a lot of—with the string search tool **grep*** matches strings in files and prints the lines that contains the matches, while the Bash pipeline (|)† lets us redirect the output of one command as input to another command.

Let's say we want to see all the commands in our Bash history that have the string "cd" in them. If we run the **history** command, the output is all the lines in our Bash history. However, if we pipe the output of the history command to **grep**, to match only lines that have "cd" in them, we get the output we want:

```
username@ubuntu-machine:~/Desktop$ history | grep cd
    3  cd Desktop  # change working directory
    7  cd
   14  cd Desktop  # change working directory
   15  history | grep cd
username@ubuntu-machine:~$
```

Please note that the **grep** command colors the matching substrings on each line, making it easier for you to verify that the line does indeed contain a match.

4.4 Files in LINUX

> 1) To the furthest extent possible in UNIX/Linux, everything is treated as a file.
> 2) To the furthest extent possible in UNIX/Linux, all files are human-readable. There are exceptions, of course, for example, binary files (applications) and relational database files.
> 3) To the furthest extent possible in UNIX/Linux, datafiles are structured one record per line (in tabular datafiles, that's one record per row). The newline character (\n) is the record delimiter, and new records are appended to the bottom of the datafiles.

Roughly, we can divide the files we work with into two types: those that hold instructions (programs and scripts) and those that hold data. When we type a Bash command like **cd**, we are actually invoking a program file by its name, **cd**, and when we hit ENTER or RETURN, it runs with whatever options and arguments we've added on the command line passed into it.

Programs and executable scripts that we can invoke on the Bash command line just by their names are in directories whose absolute paths are in the string value of a Bash environment variable called **PATH**.

```
username@ubuntu-machine:~$ echo $PATH
/usr/local/sbin:/usr/local/bin:/usr/sbin:/usr/bin:/bin:/usr/games:/usr/local/games
```

---

* **grep** stands for "globally search for a regular expression and print matching lines".

† |, the symbol known as the vertical tab, and on American keyboard layouts is found on the far-right key on the second row.

4.4 Files in LINUX

We can see the contents of PATH's string value by echoing it to **STDOUT**.

Note that when we invoke a Bash variable, we prepend its name with a dollar sign ($). The string in this example is made up of absolute paths to directories named either **bin** or **sbin**, separated by full colons (:).

By convention, we place executable files (compiled programs and executable scripts) in directories named **bin** or **sbin**.

In the PATH string, we refer to the full colon (:) as the value **separator**. The separator tells the Bash interpreter where one value ends and the next begins.

When we invoke a Bash command, the Bash interpreter inspects the contents of these directories in sequence, starting with the leftmost one in the **PATH** string, looking for a file with a matching filename.

The first file with a matching filename that the interpreter finds is the one that the Bash interpreter executes.

```
username@ubuntu-machine:~$ cat say_hello_world

#!/bin/bash
echo "hello, world!"

username@ubuntu-machine:~$ ./say_hello_world
hello, world!
```

Figure 4-6. Example of an executable Bash script, as well as how to execute a program or executable script NOT in a directory listed in the PATH string

YOU DO NOT HAVE THIS FILE IN YOUR WORKING DIRECTORY.
This example is to read, not to do (not yet, anyway).

In this example, I use the **cat** command to print the contents of an executable Bash script I wrote called **say_hello_world**. The script is in my working directory.

I invoke the script to run by prepending its name with **dot-slash** (./).

We use the dot-slash to run compiled programs and executable scripts that are NOT in the directories listed in the Bash's **PATH** string.

Executable scripts allow us to automate tasks. We will soon learn how to write executable Bash scripts.

Our focus in this course will be primarily on files that hold text data. Let us turn our attention now to those.

To create text files, we start with two Bash commands that go together: one that lets us create empty directories and one that lets us create empty files:

mkdir -p dirName creates a directory in the working directory. The **-p** option creates nesting directories if they don't already exist.

touch fileName creates an empty file in the working directory.

ls -l outputs a long listing of the contents of the working directory. This includes file size in bytes, the owner and group of the file, and the read-write-execute permissions of the owner, group, and world. We can run this command on a single file to get this information on that file:

```
username@ubuntu-machine:~$ touch newFile
username@ubuntu-machine:~$ ls -l newFile

-rw-rw-r-- 1 user user 0 Jul 11 15:24 newFile
```

Figure 4-7. Creating a new file, then getting the long listing on it

The long listing shows the file owner—the first "user"—and the group—the second "user." It also shows the file size in bytes, "0," as well as the read-write-execute file permissions for owner, group, and world—read and write for owner, read and write for group, and read-only for everybody else.

echo 'someString' lets us print someString from the Bash command line. By default, it prints to **STDOUT**, standard out, which by default is the terminal. (We will end this chapter talking more about **STDIN**, **STDOUT**, and **STDERR**.)

Bash has redirection operators that let us redirect output into files. In this case, we will write the output of echo into newFile:

echo 'someString' > newFile

```
username@ubuntu-machine:~$ echo 'someString'

someString

username@ubuntu-machine:~$ echo 'someString' > newFile
username@ubuntu-machine:~$ ls -l newFile

-rw-rw-r-- 1 user user 11 Jul 11 15:24 newFile

username@ubuntu-machine:~$ cat newFile

someString
```

Figure 4-8. Here we redirect the output of the echo command into newFile using a single close angle bracket (>), which Bash uses as the redirection write operator. Note the changes in the long listing of newFile—its size and modification timedate string have changed

We can read the contents of a file to STDOUT using the cat command.

4.4.1 Clobbering a File

If we write another string to newFile, we overwrite the contents of the file.

```
username@ubuntu-machine:~$ echo 'anotherString' > newFile
username@ubuntu-machine:~$ cat newFile

anotherString
```

Figure 4-9. Clobbering a file

To overwrite accidentally the contents of a file is to "clobber" the file. In the example above, if we meant to overwrite the contents of **newFile**, well and good. However, if we thought we were appending **anotherString** to the existing contents of the file, then we have **clobbered** the file.

When overwriting the contents of a file is unintentional, we call it "clobbering." We have ways to avoid clobbering our files. The most common way is to remove write permissions on the files from those who have them, which is most often the owner and the group. Another way is to set the **noclobber** option of the Bash session.

To append to an existing file, we use two close angle brackets (») to redirect text into the file. The text is appended as a new line, thus:

```
username@ubuntu-machine:~$ echo 'testString' >> newFile
username@ubuntu-machine:~$ cat newFile

anotherString
testString
```

Figure 4-10. Appending to a text file

To append more text into a file, we use the » redirection operator.

If we remove write permissions on a file, we can neither write nor append to it; whereas if we set the **noclobber** option of the Bash session, we cannot write to an existing file, but we can append to it.

We will look at how to set permissions and set the noclobber option below.

I wish to end this section by pointing out that overwriting the contents of a text file can be useful. As an example, you may be using a text file as a scratch pad. You may want to clear its contents now and then. To do that, just start the command line with the redirection write operator, thus:

```
username@ubuntu-machine:~$ >newFile
username@ubuntu-machine:~$ cat newFile
username@ubuntu-machine:~$
```

Figure 4-11. Clearing the contents of a file

Begin the Bash statement with the redirection operator, and follow it immediately with the filename of the file you want to clear. Because the file is empty, the **cat** command has no output to send to the terminal.

4.4.2 Changing File Permissions

The files of datasets that you generate during experimental runs are the rawest datasets you'll have to work with. But it's also possible that more refined datasets generated by your colleagues will be in their rawest format (relative to your work). In either case, these first, primal datasets are your **exemplars**.

Perhaps except to annotate them with information that conveys their provenance, you should not make changes to your exemplars. In fact, as soon as you get these datafiles, you should make them read-only—and back them up.

You can set the read-write-execute permissions for owner, group, and world using the **chmod** command.

Using the chmod Command

```
username@ubuntu-machine:~$ ls -l newFile
-rw-rw-r-- 1 user user 0 Jul 11 15:24 newFile
```

Figure 4-12. The long listing of newFile, revisited

To understand changing permissions, we start by revisiting the long listing of newFile. The long listing gives the permissions that the owner, group, and world have on the file. The owner and group can read and write the file. Everybody else can only read the file. Restating the permissions of owner, group, and world on newFile:

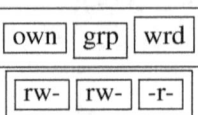

With Base-8 Numbers (Octals)

To understand how to set permissions using base-8 numbers, we start by observing that a bit (0 or 1) can serve as a flag; that is, if a setting has only two values, and if the setting is modifiable, we can change the setting with **set flag** or **clear flag** commands, or their equivalent.

For each user—owner, group, and world—three permissions on a file can be set or cleared: read, write, and execute. If we use flags to set and clear those permissions for each user, and order them as **"read-write-execute"**, then the string of flags showing that the owner, for example, has read and write permissions on a file, but no execute permission on the flag, becomes:

o:110 (or owner: read:yes, write:yes; execute:no)

The string of flags showing that the group has the same permissions on the file becomes:

g:110 (or group: read:yes, write:yes; execute:no)

And the string of flags showing that everybody else has read-only permission on the file becomes:

w:100 (or world: read:yes, write:no; execute:no)

Because these base-2 permissions take up only three positions each, we can convert them to base-8, which we can represent with natural numbers 0..7.

1	0	0

100 base-2 is 4 in octal.

0	1	0

010 base-2 is 2 in octal.

0	0	1

001 base-2 is 1 in octal.

Base-8, or octal, is represented by 3 consecutive base-2, or binary, values.

r	w	x

rwx read-write-execute permissions transposed on to octal values:

r	-	-

r - - read permission equals 4 in octal.

-	w	-

- w - write permission equals 2 in octal.

-	-	x

- - x write permission equals 1 in octal.

6	6	4

o g w owner and group have read+write (4+2) permissions.
world has read-only (4) permission.

o g w owner has read+write (4+2) permissions.
group has read-only (4) permission.
world has no (0) access permission.

o g w owner-group-world permissions set using octal values

And now we can modify the permissions on newFile:

chmod 644 newFile

```
username@ubuntu-machine:~$ chmod 644 newFile
username@ubuntu-machine:~$ ls -l newFile
-rw-r--r-- 1 user  user  0 Jul 11  15:34 newFile
```

Figure 4-13. Changing permissions on newFile using chmod + octal values

In this example, owner keeps read+write permissions (4+2), group gets read-only (4) permission, and world stays read-only (4).

We verify this using **ls -l** on the file.

4.4.3 Setting the Session noclobber Flag

In Bash, we can set an option for a session that prevents writing to existing files (clobbering) while permitting appending to those files.

We set this option using the **set** command, thus:

`username@ubuntu-machine:~$ set -o noclobber`

The **noclobber** option prevents us from accidentally overwriting a file (clobbering), but permits us to append to existing files.

This option is useful when you want to append records to a text file that contains a recordset while ensuring that existing files don't get clobbered.

And when you want to reset the noclobber flag for the session, do this:

`username@ubuntu-machine:~$ set +o noclobber`

Note that to reset the flag, we prepend **+** to the **o** (for **option**).

4.5 Character Encoding and Text File Formats

If it wasn't documented, it didn't happen.

Datasets are the foundation of STEM research. Ensuring the accuracy, integrity, and preservation of data captured in experiments is a primary responsibility of the experimenter. This makes every experimenter a data steward, as well as a data custodian, of the data collected in experiments.

Ensuring the accuracy of the data as it's captured in an experiment is beyond the scope of this discussion, which we will confine to the choice of character encodings and file formats for the text data and the text files on which the data is recorded. In general, the rule of thumb for character encoding is "The simpler, the better," and for file format is "The flatter, the better."

Use only universal character encodings. Currently, these are ASCII and UTF-8 (See Table 4-1 for the ASCII character set).

Table 4-1 ASCII. ASCII stands for "American Standard Code for Information Interchange." Based on the English alphabet, it encodes 128 characters (95 of them printable) in seven bits. Note that it is void of diacritical marks or special characters, and so even for other languages that make up their alphabets with Roman characters but have special characters or diacritical marks, ASCII, strictly speaking, cannot render messages in those languages orthographically correctly. Nevertheless, the preference today is to use ASCII for the recording, transmission, and archiving of text datasets

Bin	Hex	Char	Desc	Bin	Hex	Char	Bin	Hex	Char	Bin	Hex	Char
0000 0000	00	NUL	(null)	0010 0000	20	space	0100 0000	40	@	0110 0000	60	`
0000 0001	01	SOH	(start of header)	0010 0001	21	!	0100 0001	41	A	0110 0001	61	a
0000 0010	02	STX	(start of text)	0010 0010	22	"	0100 0010	42	B	0110 0010	62	b
0000 0011	03	ETH	(end of text)	0010 0011	23	#	0100 0011	43	C	0110 0011	63	c
0000 0100	04	EOT	(end of transmission)	0010 0100	24	$	0100 0100	44	D	0110 0100	64	d
0000 0101	05	ENQ	(enquiry)	0010 0101	25	%	0100 0101	45	E	0110 0101	65	e
0000 0110	06	ACK	(acknowledge)	0010 0110	26	&	0100 0110	46	F	0110 0110	66	f
0000 0111	07	BEL	(bell)	0010 0111	27	'	0100 0111	47	G	0110 0111	67	g
0000 1000	08	BS	(backspace)	0010 1000	28	(	0100 1000	48	H	0110 1000	68	h
0000 1001	09	TAB	(horizontal tab)	0010 1001	29	)	0100 1001	49	I	0110 1001	69	i
0000 1010	0A	LF	(NL line feed, new line)	0010 1010	2A	*	0100 1010	4A	J	0110 1010	6A	j
0000 1011	0B	VT	(vertical tab)	0010 1011	2B	+	0100 1011	4B	K	0110 1011	6B	k
0000 1100	0C	FF	(NP form feed, new page)	0010 1100	2C	,	0100 1100	4C	L	0110 1100	6C	l
0000 1101	0D	CR	(carriage return)	0010 1101	2D	-	0100 1101	4D	M	0110 1101	6D	m
0000 1110	0E	SO	(shift out)	0010 1110	2E	.	0100 1110	4E	N	0110 1110	6E	n
0000 1111	0F	SI	(shift in)	0010 1111	2F	/	0100 1111	4F	O	0110 1111	6F	o
0001 0000	10	DLE	(data link escape)	0011 0000	30	0	0101 0000	50	P	0111 0000	70	p

Binary	Hex	Char	Binary	Hex	Char	Binary	Hex	Char	Binary	Hex	Char
0001 0001	11	DC1 (device control 1)	0011 0001	31	1	0101 0001	51	Q	0111 0001	71	q
0001 0010	12	DC2 (device control 2)	0011 0010	32	2	0101 0010	52	R	0111 0010	72	r
0001 0011	13	DC3 (device control 3)	0011 0011	33	3	0101 0011	53	S	0111 0011	73	s
0001 0100	14	DC4 (device control 4)	0011 0100	34	4	0101 0100	54	T	0111 0100	74	t
0001 0101	15	NAE (negative acknowledge)	0011 0101	35	5	0101 0101	35	U	0111 0101	35	u
0001 0110	16	SYN (synchronous idle)	0011 0110	36	6	0101 0110	56	V	0111 0110	76	v
0001 0111	17	ETB (end of transmission block)	0011 0111	37	7	0101 0111	57	W	0111 0111	77	w
0001 1000	18	CAN (cancel)	0011 1000	38	8	0101 1000	58	X	0111 1000	78	x
0001 1001	19	EM (end of medium)	0011 1001	39	9	0101 1001	59	Y	0111 1001	79	y
0001 1010	1A	SUB (substitute)	0011 1010	3A	:	0101 1010	5A	Z	0111 1010	7A	z
0001 1011	1B	ESC (escape)	0011 1011	3B	;	0101 1011	5B	[	0111 1011	7B	{
0001 1100	1C	FS (file separator)	0011 1100	3C	<	0101 1100	5C	\	0111 1100	7C	|
0001 1101	1D	GS (group separator)	0011 1101	3D	=	0101 1101	5D	]	0111 1101	7D	}
0001 1110	1E	RS (record separator)	0011 1110	3E	>	0101 1110	5E	^	0111 1110	7E	~
0001 1111	1F	US (unit separator)	0011 1111	3F	?	0101 1111	5F	_	0111 1111	7F	DEL

Use the simplest character encoding that sufficiently captures the data. Prefer ASCII.
Avoid proprietary file formats. This includes Microsoft Excel.
Use file formats that offer the greatest interoperability among different platforms and applications.
For archiving, datafiles should be unencrypted and uncompressed.

For long-term archiving, a copy schedule to new media that falls well within the lifetime of the current storage medium should be made and adhered to.

4.6 The UNIX Philosophy: An Introduction

> Rule of Modularity: Write simple parts connected by clean interfaces.
> Rule of Clarity: Clarity is better than cleverness.
> Rule of Composition: Design programs to be connected to other programs.
> Rule of Simplicity: Design for simplicity; add complexity only where you must.
> Rule of Silence: When a program has nothing to say, it should say nothing.
> Rule of Repair: When you must fail, fail noisily and as soon as possible.
> Rule of Optimization: Prototype before polishing. Get it working before you optimize it.
> Rule of Diversity: Distrust all claims for the "one true way".

—Eric S Raymond, *The Art of UNIX Programming*
This is a subset of the published rules.

In form and function, Linux is a direct descendant of UNIX. As such, it inherits the UNIX philosophy. We will not only see this as we work in Linux, but we will also be taking advantage of it.

Eric S. Raymond writes:

> The UNIX philosophy is not a formal design method...It is pragmatic and grounded in experience. It is not to be found in official methods and standards, but rather in the implicit half-reflexive knowledge, the *expertise* that the UNIX culture transmits.

As we work first in Bash, then Python, I will ask you to recall any one of these rules to justify in part what we are doing, or why a program behaves the way it does.

For now, I would like to direct your attention to the last two, the first of which I will paraphrase as: "Get it working before you worry about it."

Get your code running doing what it's supposed to do; and when you've got that, you've got a rough draft. After you've got your rough draft, worry about making it better.

And as for the last rule: Do not fall in love with a single Bash tool, or with one way to solve a general problem. To do so is to cut yourself off from possibilities that can lead to improvements. Always look for a better solution, a simpler solution, one that runs faster, or is easier to maintain.

Raymond, Eric S. *The Art of UNIX Programming*. Addison-Wesley. 2004. pp. 11–25.

Raymond, Eric S. *op. cit.* pg. 11.

4.7 The Bash Interpreter

> Bash has its own **interpreter**.
>
> An interpreter is an application that first reads a human-readable statement; and if it is well-formed—that is, free of grammar, spelling, and punctuation errors—it then puts the statement in a language the machine understands; then the machine executes it.
>
> This interpreter not only allows us to run Bash scripts.
>
> It also allows us to run commands while using Bash interactively.
>
> A Bash session environment is set by the values of environment variables. An example of a Bash environment variable is **PATH**, which we've already seen.
>
> Users can change the values to customize their Bash session.
>
> The Bash interpreter also allows us to create and use variables during a session. It uses file-like objects in memory called **symbol tables** to keep track of variables—at a minimum their names, and the positions of their values in memory.

4.7.1 Variables

Variables in programming language statements can be thought of as analogous to variables in algebraic statements as algebra was introduced to us in middle school—that is, as placeholders for values in the math statements. Hence, we might be given a table like the one on the left, in which we're asked to replace x in $y = x^2$ with the values in the x-column, one at a time, each time yielding a new value for—or *updating*—y.

x	y
0	
1	
2	
3	
4	
5	
6	
7	
8	
9	

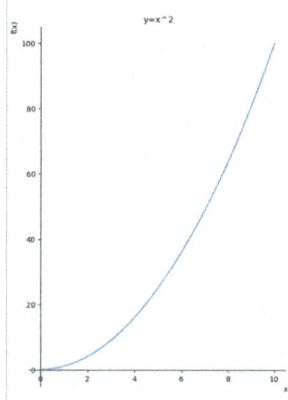

Find values of y for the values of x where $y = x^2$.

A plot of $y = x^2$. Drawn using SymPy.

Figure 4-14 Variables

We might even have been shown a plot of $y = x^2$ like the one on the right as an aid.

> Variables in programming language statements are made up of a *name*, or *symbol*, or *lexeme*, and a value.
>
> We create, or instantiate, variables using *assignment statements*—for example:
>
> **y = 1**, or
>
> **y = x**2** # ** is the exponentiation operator and means "raise to the power of."
>
> In both examples, the equal sign is the *assignment operator*, and on the left-hand side (LHS) of the assignment operator is the name of the variable we want to create. In the first example, the right-hand side (RHS) is a simple value, and we set the value of *y* to 1. In the second example, the interpreter evaluates the expression on the right-hand side, **x**2**. *x* must already have been created and have a value assigned to it. That value replaces *x* in the expression, which is then evaluated; and the value that results is the value assigned to *y*.
>
> To avoid ambiguity, when read aloud, avoid using "equals" for the assignment operator. I prefer "takes the value of" or "becomes," instead. Hence, example 1 is "y takes the value of 1," and example 2 is "y takes the value of x raised to the power of 2."

4.7.2 The Bash Environment

To work properly, when Bash launches a session, it needs "to know" certain facts like the username of the person running the session, as well as the absolute paths to the directories on the computer that hold applications and executable scripts. Altogether, these facts are called the Bash environment, and they are stored as values to variables in session memory. Because they are variable values, they are modifiable.

To see the variables of your current Bash environment, as well as their values, on the command line, enter **env** and pipe the output to **less**:

env | less

Press the SPACEBAR to advance through the output one screenful at a time.

Press q to quit.

Note that by convention, Bash variable names are ALL CAPS. We invoke Bash variables by prefixing a dollar sign ($) to their names. To see the value of a variable, we echo the variable name:

echo $PATH

The value of the Bash environment variable PATH is a string containing the absolute paths to the directories holding applications and scripts. We can launch any application or script whose directory is in the PATH string value just by typing its name on the command line and hitting RETURN. As soon as we hit RETURN or ENTER, the Bash interpreter searches through the directories in the PATH string in the order they are listed for the file whose name matches the command we've entered on the command line.

As soon as a match is found, that file—which is an application or an executable script—is loaded into memory, then executed (in the case of executable scripts, the application associated with the script is loaded into memory, and it runs the script).

Note that the order of the full paths to the directories matters. The Bash interpreter searches the directories in order and runs the first match it finds. This means that other files whose names match in directories listed later in the PATH string won't be run.

Writing Bash Scripts Using Bash Environment Variables
We can use Bash environment variables in our scripts. Because environment variables like USERNAME and HOME vary from user to user, using Bash environment variables whenever we can in our scripts means our collaborators can run them with few, if any, changes.

4.7.3 The Bash Interpreter

An interpreter is an application that reads human-readable instructions that are normally written in text files called scripts, then interprets them into machine instructions for the machine to execute. Bash has an interpreter, which allows programmers to write scripts to automate tasks that can be run in Bash.

In Linux, many installation scripts used to install applications are written in Bash.

4.7.4 The Symbol Table and Variables

> An essential function of a compiler is to record the variable names used in the source program and collect information about various attributes of each name. These attributes may provide information about the storage allocated for a name, its type, its scope (where in the program its value may be used), and in the case of procedure names, such things as the number and types of its arguments, the method of passing each argument (for example, by value or by reference), and the type returned.
>
> The symbol table is a data structure containing a record for each variable name, with fields for the attributes of the name. The data structure should be designed to allow the compiler to find the record for each name quickly and to store or retrieve data from the record quickly.
>
> Entries in the symbol table contain information about an identifier such as its character string (or lexeme), its type, its position in storage, and any other relevant information. Symbol tables typically need to support multiple declarations of the same identifier within a program.*
>
> —Alfred Aho

Although the quote discusses symbol tables as used by compilers, symbol tables are used by interpreters, as well, to keep track of variables and other objects used during a session. Think of symbol tables as the short-term memory of Bash and Python interpreters of items (and their attributes) that persist only for a session.

The Bash interpreter keeps track of variables through a data structure (for now, think of it as being a file-like object) in session memory called "a symbol table." For each variable you create, Bash creates an entry in the symbol table that has at a minimum the variable name (called "the symbol") and a pointer to the starting address in memory where the value of the variable is stored.

---

* Alfred Aho et al.. *Compilers: Principles, Techniques, and Tools, 2d Edition*. 2018. pp.11 & 85.

When an interpreter scans a statement that contains a variable name, it does a lookup in the symbol table for that name. If it finds it, the interpreter fetches the value in memory associated with the variable, replaces the variable name in the statement with the value, then evaluates the statement.

4.8 Some Bash Tools for Working with Datafiles

file: Returns file's text encoding
ls -l: Returns long listing of file's attributes
wc: Returns line, word, and byte count of file
head: Returns first ten lines of file
tail: Returns last ten lines of file
cat -vet: Returns file contents, displaying whitespace tab as ^I and newline character as $
cut: Returns specified fields or columns
grep -E: Extended grep: returns lines containing matching pattern
gawk: GNU awk: utility to reformat data easily
sed: Stream editor
shuf: Returns uniformly random lines in file, by default without replacement
sort: Returns lines of file in sorted order, by default alphanumeric sort
tr: Translate: deletes or substitutes characters from STDIN, sends result to STDOUT
uniq: Returns a single instance of identical, contiguous lines
vim: Improved vi: a text editor

For decades, computer users worked primarily, if not exclusively, with text data. Before computers became powerful enough to make graphical desktop environments practical, users entered commands from the keyboard, and computers responded with text output.

Such is the history of UNIX and even early Linux.

As a result, UNIX/Linux now has a rich set of command-line tools for working with text data, tools optimized to run very fast. With a few Bash text-manipulation commands, we can do as much, and faster, as we can with a Python script.

An introduction on working with digital datafiles on modern computers should start with reminders to the reader. First reminder: All information in a modern digital computer is either **data** (like the data in our datafiles), **instructions** (which for our purposes means instructions to the machine on what to do with the data in our datafiles), or **pointers** (which keep track of the data and instructions in the computer's mass-storage device and memory).

Second reminder: The information in a modern computer is binary. It can be thought of as consisting of only ones and zeros. The smallest unit of information is a single one or zero, called a "bit." In computers, bits are grouped and manipulated in lengths that correspond to natural-number exponents of base-2 (i.e., 2^n). Strings four bits in length are called a "nibble," strings eight bits in length are called a "byte," strings of 16 bits are called a "word," of 32 bits are called a "32-bit word," and of 64 bits, a "64-bit word." The table below summarizes this:

String lengths of 1s and 0s				
Length	2^n	Name	# States	Notes
1	0	bit	1	x^0 for any x equals 1
1	1	bit	2	the bool datatype
3	3	octet	8	
4	4	nibble	16	hexadecimal (0-9)(A-F): a common format for representing binary strings
8	8	byte	256	1st hobbyist computer OSs (1970s)
16	16	word	65536	1st IBM PC OS (1981)
32	32	32-bit word	4294967296	4 GB, the limit for addressing memory in 32-bit OSs
64	64	64-bit word	$1.844674407 \times 10^{19}$	current data and address lengths

A third reminder: Much of the data that researchers use (like the characters used to print English strings) has no "natural" correlation to strings of ones and zeros. For example, no arrangement of eight bits "naturally" corresponds to the lowercase letter "a." The assignment of which eight bits means "a" and which means "b" is arbitrary and so must be agreed to by the members of the data-sharing community.

Although many character-encoding standards exist, only two should be used for now in the creation of datafiles: ASCII and UTF-8. This ensures that anybody in the world in possession of a modern computer should be able to open and read the contents of the datafiles.

So much for information on modern digital computers. Now let's talk specifically about working with datafiles on UNIX/Linux systems.

Finally, a fourth reminder:

> 1) To the furthest extent possible in UNIX/Linux, everything is treated like a file.
> 2) To the furthest extent possible in UNIX/Linux, all files are human-readable. There are exceptions, of course, for example, binary files (applications) and relational database files.
> 3) To the furthest extent possible in UNIX/Linux, datafiles are structured one record per line. The newline character is the record delimiter, and new records are appended to the bottom of the datafiles.

These facts influence how we process datafiles on Linux systems, and they influence the design and behavior of the command-line tools we use to process datafiles. For example, when we search for a text string in a file using the grep tools, by default they return the entire line in which a match is found—and because the record separator in text files by default is the newline (\n) character, a match returns the entire record.

This means you can do a text search on a recordset in one text file and easily redirect the resultset to another file in which the records and their order in the dataset will be preserved.

As researchers, you will generate datasets, or work with the datasets of others. In either case, the datasets in your possession will be valuable, perhaps even irreplaceable. The first copy of a dataset in your possession should be considered the **exemplar**. The exemplar is the data in your possession in its rawest form. Ideally, you should not alter it one bit; practically, however, you should probably annotate it just enough to provide provenance.

A common problem with datasets that get shared is the lack of provenance. Who made the dataset? Where was it made? When was it made? What equipment was used? What known factors influenced the quality of the data? The answers, added to the dataset (often at the top of the file), provide important information not only for the original researcher, but for those who use or analyze the data later.

(And don't worry about how to strip descriptive data from the top of a dataset when you want to work with just the dataset. We can do that rather easily with the Bash **tail** command.)

It is critical that you have a backup scheme in place for regularly backing up your files. When deciding how often you should back up your files, you should ask yourself how much work you are willing to lose. As a rule, you should consider running a full backup of the contents of your home directory weekly and incremental backups daily.

(A Bash tool that I use to make backups is **rsync**.)

There are other steps you should take to protect your datafiles. Only when datafiles are being created or annotated, do they need to be writeable. Therefore, once you have received a datafile from a colleague or finished generating a datafile in an experimental run, you should make it read-only.

In UNIX/Linux, file and folder permissions are **read**, **write**, and **execute**, and we set them for **owner**, **group**, and **world**. By setting all to read-only on our datafiles, we prevent them from being accidentally overwritten, or clobbered.

However, if you are generating a datafile, you do not want to set it read-only. Doing so will prevent new records from being appended to the bottom of the datafile. Rather, you want to set your Bash session to allow appending to existing files while preventing clobbering them.

You can do this with the Bash statement **set -o noclobber**. If you set this option for the current Bash session, you'll still be allowed to append to files in the session, but you can't clobber any files. To reset this option, change the dash in the statement to a plus sign, like this:

set +o noclobber.

4.9 The General-Purpose Bash Commands *time* and *watch*

time and **watch** are special Bash commands in that we open other commands within them, and they either return how long those commands take to run to completion (**time**) or rerun those commands at a set interval, allowing us to track their progress as they run to completion (**watch**).

```
$ time apt dist-upgrade
```

To find out how much time it takes to run the command **apt dist-upgrade**, we invoke it as an argument of the Bash **time** command. In this specific instance, **apt update** has reported that 91 packages can be upgraded

```
real      10m48.185s
user      2m41.656s
sys       1m1.745s
```

Figure 4-15. Output of the **time** command after **apt dist-upgrade** has run

Of the three timings, we are generally most interested in the first one, which is also known as **wallclock time**, or how much time it took **apt dist-upgrade** to run to completion.

Programs that determine how much time it takes processes to run are called "profilers." **time** is an example of a simple profiler.

We will discuss profilers more when we get into Python programming.

```
$ watch df
```

To rerun a command at a set interval in order to get regular outputs as updates, we invoke it as an argument of the Bash **watch** command. In this specific instance, we invoke the **df** (disk free) command as an argument of watch, which is useful if we want to watch as a mounted partition fills up as we move data into it.

```
Every 2.0s: df                   ubuntu-machine: Sun Aug 29 16:06:56 2021

Filesystem    1K-blocks      Used Available Use% Mounted on
tmpfs            402092      1356    400736   1% /run
/dev/sda3      25151748  21308740   2542324  90% /
tmpfs           2010452         0   2010452   0% /dev/shm
tmpfs              5120         4      5116   1% /run/lock
tmpfs              4096         0      4096   0% /sys/fs/cgroup
/dev/sda2        524272      5340    518932   2% /boot/efi
tmpfs            402088       104    401984   1% /run/username/1001
```

Figure 4-16. The output of **watch df** on the virtual machine *ubuntu-machine*

Note that **watch** updates (or reruns) the output of the **df** command every two seconds.

The **watch** command is useful when you want to keep an eye on the progress of a long-running program. In this specific instance, we could keep an eye on how much space is available on **/dev/sda3** while copying data into it (perhaps via **rsync**).

We halt **watch** by entering: CTRL c .

4.10 The Bash Pipeline

> In Bash, the vertical bar (|) is called "the pipe." The pipe allows a user to redirect the output of one command as input for a second command. Compound Bash statements that are made of pipes are called "pipelines." Pipelines can be of any length.

Pipes are perhaps the single most striking invention in Unix. A pipe is a mechanism, provided by the operating system and made easily accessible through the shell, that connects the output of one program to the input of another. The operating system makes it work; the shell notation to use it is simple and natural; the effect is a new way of thinking about how to design and use programs.*

Before a program can run, it has to be loaded into memory. Before data can be processed, it has to be loaded into memory.

---
* Brian Kernighan, *UNIX: A History and a Memoir*, 2020. p.67.

The operating systems of our personal computers come with many applications that can be run on the command line to manipulate data and text. In UNIX/Linux, we call these "software tools"; and in general, each software tool does a single, specific task. This is in keeping with a design philosophy of programming that is called "the Unix philosophy."

You can find many articles on the Internet devoted to the Unix philosophy. One in fact is a Wikipedia article on that philosophy:

The Unix Philosophy on Wikipedia. Click or scan image to go to article.
https://en.wikipedia.org/wiki/Unix_philosophy

We have already talked about two and encountered one of the rules in this design philosophy. The one that we've encountered is The Rule of Silence: **"When a program has nothing to say, it should say nothing."**

In other words, if a program executes with no errors, it should show, say, or print nothing.

The programmers who wrote the software tools that we use in our Bash pipeline follow perhaps one rule in writing their programs, The Rule of Composition: **"Design programs to be connected to other programs."** And in using their software tools in Bash pipelines, we are perhaps following yet another rule, The Rule of Modularity: **"Write simple parts connected by clean interfaces."**

In UNIX/Linux, the pipe provides us with a clean interface.

The germ idea that motivated creation of the pipe:

> Summary—what's most important.
> To put my strongest concerns in a nutshell: 1. We should have some ways of coupling programs like garden hose—screw in another segment when it becomes necessary to massage data in another way.*

In 1964, Doug McIlroy of Bell Labs imagined a way of connecting programs together "like garden hose" that would allow data to flow between them.

Garden-hose idea meets pipe implementation. "Ken" is Ken Thompson, who designed and implemented the first version of UNIX in 1969:

> Doug wanted to allow arbitrary connections in a sort of mesh of programs, but it was not obvious how to describe an unconstrained graph in a natural way, and there were semantic problems as well: data that flowed between programs would have to be queued properly, and queues could explode in an anarchic connection of programs. And Ken [Thompson, inventor of Unix] couldn't think of any real application anyway.
> But Doug continued to nag and Ken continued to think. As Ken says, "One day I got this idea: pipes, essentially as they are today." He added a pipe system call to the operating system in an hour; he describes it as "super trivial" given that the mechanisms for I/O redirection were already there.
> Ken then added the pipe mechanism to the shell, tried it out, and called the result "mind-blowing."[†]

```
ls |# list working directory contents, followed by pipe
wc -l # word count command. -l option returns line count only.
```

Figure 4-17. Documenting your pipeline is important!

---

* *Ibid.* p.68.

[†] *Ibid.* p.68.

Here is how you add end-of-line comments:

cmd1-pipe-hash-comment-newline-cmd2-pipe-hash-comment-newline-etc

Note: There is no trailing pipe in a pipeline. The last command ends the pipeline.

4.11 Some Advice for Writing Bash Scripts and Pipelines

As with expository writing, strive for a programming style that is simple, clear, and direct.

1. Before writing, think. Some programmers start coding after hearing what a program should do. This is wrong and is generally expensive behavior—wastefully expensive.
Have a specific goal in mind. Make a plan.

> In preparing for battle I have always found that plans are useless, but planning is indispensable.
> —Dwight D. Eisenhower

Likely, your working code will not look much like what you envisioned when you started, but the planning is indispensable. After all, you are trying to get a machine to do what you want it to do using a limited set of commands.

Write out what you want the machine to do. Articulate it. If you don't know where to begin, begin by answering these two questions: What is your input? And what do you want the output to be?

2. Go slow. Put your script together only a few statements at a time, or your pipeline only one statement at a time.

> Bugs happen, and they happen all the time. Debugging is a normal part of development. The more statements you add to a script or pipeline before running to test, the more time you will spend debugging your code. And the relationship between number of lines written at one time and time to debug is not linear.

Add your new command (with options), then rerun your script or pipeline. Verify that the output of the new command is what you expected. If it's not, you have a choice:

1) Find out why and fix.
2) Find another command or option that will render the output you need.
3) While developing, keep in mind The Rule of Diversity: **Distrust all claims for "one true way"**.

Here it's worth quoting Eric Raymond at length:

> Even the best software tools tend to be limited by the imaginations of their designers. Nobody is smart enough to optimize for everything, nor to anticipate all the uses to which their software might be put. Designing rigid, closed software that won't talk to the rest of the world is an unhealthy form of arrogance.
> Therefore, the Unix tradition includes a healthy mistrust of "one true way" approaches to software design or implementation. It embraces multiple languages, open extensible systems, and customization hooks everywhere.[‡]

In other words, avoid falling in love with one software tool. (Don't try to do *everything* in **perl**—or even in **python**.) In Bash, there can be several tools to perform the same task. My advice, in general: use the one that's easiest to use and whose implementation is easiest to read and understand. The exception: a tool that runs significantly faster than others should be preferred—but then, the onus will be on you to learn the faster tool and how it works!

Once you have the Bash statement that gives you what you want, add a pipe and move on to the next command.

[‡] Eric S. Raymond, *The Art of UNIX Programming*, 2004. p.24.

3. Use Internet resources to find the best command or commands to do the job.

Almost probability=1, you are not the first person who is trying to solve a specific problem with the tools at hand for the kind of data you're working with.
stackoverflow.com and other sites are valuable resources for finding viable, even elegant, solutions.
4. Corollary to 3: Be open to new, even better, options. For example, you may be looking for a solution that implements **perl**, only to find a simpler one—one that's easier to read and understand—in **gawk**. If you find a better solution to the one you came up with, use it.
—And don't hesitate to give proper attribution. That's how the open source community works.
5. Corollary to 4: Do NOT simply copy-and-paste someone else's solution, then move on. As a programmer, you are always learning new ways of doing things. The new way may be an algorithm with a better time efficiency than the one it's replacing, or it may be a command that is easier to understand. In any case, STUDY the solution. Google it, read the man pages on it; play with it.
And once you understand it, comment your understanding in the script or pipeline.
6. I/O is expensive. To the furthest extent possible, avoid redirecting intermediate results to text files on mass-storage devices. To the furthest extent possible, keep the data moving between commands in memory. Redirect to text files only when you must preserve intermediate resultsets.
7. Use a lint program to find programming and stylistic errors in your Bash scripts. The lint program we use in class is **shellcheck**. As the lint program finds problems with your code, fix them.

```bash
 #!/bin/bash

# example of a bash script interactive loop
# this is an infinite loop that prompts for input
# each time the loop runs, the input is used as the name for a directory
# that's created in the working directory
# an empty string as input drops the interpreter out of the loop

while true; do # statements on the same line are separated by ;
    read -p "please give project name: " PROJ
    # nest the escape condition within the loop
    if [[ "$PROJ"=="" ]] # compare with empty string
    then
        break # drop out of the loop
    fi

    # now do the repetitive task
    mkdir $PROJ
done
echo "and now we're out of the loop!"
```

Figure 4-18. A Bash script with issues. We'll run this script through the linter **shellcheck** to see what problems it can find

```
shellcheck bash_interactive_script
In bash_interactive_script line 1:
 #!/bin/bash
^-- SC1114: Remove leading spaces before the shebang.

In bash_interactive_script line 11:
```

4.11 Some Advice

```
            read -p "please give project name: " PROJ
            ^--^ SC2162: read without -r will mangle backslashes.

In bash_interactive_script line 13:
    if [[ "$PROJ"=="" ]] # compare with empty string
              ^-- SC2077: You need spaces around
                          the comparison operator.
              ^-- SC2140: Word is of the form
                          "A"B"C" (B indicated).
                          Did you mean "ABC" or "A\"B\"C"?

In bash_interactive_script line 19:
    mkdir $PROJ
          ^---^ SC2086: Double quote to prevent globbing
                          and word splitting.

Did you mean:
    mkdir "$PROJ"

For more information:
    https://www.shellcheck.net/wiki/SC1114 -- Remove leading
                                spaces before the ...
    https://www.shellcheck.net/wiki/SC2077 -- You need spaces around
                                the compar ...
    https://www.shellcheck.net/wiki/SC2140 -- Word is of the form
                                "A"B"C" (B in...
```

Figure 4-19. **shellcheck** exposes issues with the script. Hyperlinks take the programmer to a wiki where entries give each flagged problem more explanation

Figure 4-20 If you need more info to understand the issue and suggested fix, **shellcheck**'s authors maintain a wiki in which they go into more depth. Click on the image to go to the shellcheck site

```bash
#!/bin/bash

# example of a bash script interactive loop
# this is an infinite loop that prompts for input
# each time the loop runs, the input is used as the name for a directory
# that's created in the working directory
# an empty string as input drops the interpreter out of the loop

while true; do # statements on the same line are separated by ;
    read -pr "please give project name: " PROJ
    # nest the escape condition within the loop
    if [[ "$PROJ" == "" ]] # compare with empty string
    then
        break # drop out of the loop
    fi

    # now do the repetitive task
    mkdir "$PROJ"
done
echo "and now we're out of the loop!"
```

Figure 4-21. The same Bash script with issues fixed

Finally, keep in mind that your research will result in at least two sets of text files that you can present to those who review your work: (1) the datasets, from raw data to published results, and (2) your scripts and pipelines, which document how you transformed your raw data into the published results.[§]

In the next part of this book, we will be working (finally!) at the console on the Bash command line to write pipelines and executable scripts.

Please make sure that you have access to a Linux machine to work on and that you have cloned a copy of the **intro_to_programming** repo on GitHub into your home directory.

Chapter Summary

The most popular shell in UNIX/Linux (and MacOS) is Bash. In this chapter, we have looked at navigating the Linux filesystem. We have worked with text files through Bash, and we have learned how to get basic info about those files, as well as how to set their permissions. We have learned about the pipe and how to pipe the output of one command as input into another command. Finally, we have learned about running our scripts through linters to help find and fix problems in the scripts.

[§] Later, as we learn Python, we will generate a third set of text files that you can present to reviewers: unit test files, which show which tests you run to ensure your code gives correct results.

5. Bash: Combining Commands and Variables to Make Pipelines and Scripts to Process Data

In the last chapter, we were introduced to the Bash shell. In this chapter, we will look at how to write Bash pipelines and scripts to automate common tasks, including finding and extracting info from datasets.

5.1 Introduction to vim and the Bash script: How to Make an Executable Script That Runs on the Command Line and Takes Arguments

"**vim**" means "improved vi," a powerful text editor that is the default editor in IPython. **vim** has several modes. We will use two to write and edit our scripts: the command mode and the edit mode.

To make a script executable, do these three steps:

1) Put a shebang ("hash-bang," or #!) on the top line of the Bash script.
2) Change the file's permissions to include **executable** for owner, group, or world.
3) Move the script into a folder whose absolute path is in the Bash PATH environment variable string.

```
#!/bin/bash

PROJPATH=$HOME/project
PROJ=$1

mkdir -p $PROJPATH/$PROJ/data/raw
mkdir -p $PROJPATH/$PROJ/data/processed

mkdir -p $PROJPATH/$PROJ/figure/exploratory
mkdir -p $PROJPATH/$PROJ/figure/final

mkdir -p $PROJPATH/$PROJ/script/raw
mkdir -p $PROJPATH/$PROJ/script/final

mkdir -p $PROJPATH/$PROJ/text/readme
mkdir -p $PROJPATH/$PROJ/text/text_of_analysis
```

Figure 5-1. The script we're writing in vim

To demonstrate the versatility of Bash scripts, we start with a script that creates a project filesystem. This Bash script takes the name of a project off the command line and uses it to build a filesystem for the project in a directory in the home directory called "project."

Advantages of using scripts include automating repetitious tasks, executing tasks faster than humans can manually, and ensuring that a pattern (like the layout of project filesystems) is repeated without error.

Note the order in which the Bash interpreter executes each line in the script: it starts at the top, executes the first line, then the second line, then the third line, and so on, until it reaches the end of the script.

We call the order in which a machine executes instructions in a program or script the **control flow**. We say that the lines in this script are executed **sequentially**, or that the flow is **sequential**. Perhaps unsurprisingly, the most common order of instruction execution in programs is sequential. We will look more closely at control flow in our introduction to algorithms and our introduction to programming.

```
vim makeProjectFS
```

Creating a text file in our home directory called "makeProjFS"

We start by invoking **vim** on the Bash command line and passing the name of the file we want to make as an argument.

Figure 5-2 Opening a new file in vim

In **vim**, we will work in only two modes: **command** mode and **edit** mode.

vim always starts in command mode. If ever you don't know which mode you're in, hit ESC.

5.1 Making Executable Bash Scripts I

Hitting ESC will always put you in **command** mode.

Please note that the cursor is at the start of the first line. As we write in **vim**, the cursor shows us the position of our next character. The next few figures will be screenshots to show you what you will see in the vim window, including the cursor. Later, the focus will be on coding, and the cursor will not be shown.

Please note the bottom line. In command mode, **vim** puts information to the user on the bottom line.

The tildes (~) between the top and bottom lines signify nothing is written into these lines, which is the case when we open an empty file.

```
▮
~
~
~
-- INSERT --                              0,1            All
```

Figure 5-3 Entering the edit mode in vim

We can enter the **edit** mode in **vim** in one of two ways: by pressing either lowercase a (for "append") or lowercase i (for "insert").

In this case, we'll press i to insert text.

Please note that **vim** lets us know on the informational line that we're in **edit** mode because of the - - **INSERT** - - alert.

We can now write into our text file.

```
#!/bin/bash▮
~
~
~
-- INSERT --                              1,12           All
```

Figure 5-4 Writing the hash-bang (shebang) line at the top of our executable script

The shebang includes the absolute path to the application that will run the executable script when we invoke the script by itself on the Bash command line.

This is a Bash script, so the Bash interpreter will run it; hence, we put the absolute path to the Bash interpreter in the **shebang**.

Please note that on the informational line, **vim** tells us the position in the text file of our cursor; in this case, line 1, column 12.

```
#!/bin/bash
~
~
~
:w!▮
```

Figure 5-5 Writing our edits to disk and staying in vim

To save our edits, we return to **command** mode by pressing ESC.

On the bottom line, we enter **command** input by pressing the full colon key : (or SHIFT ; on keyboards with US layout). To tell **vim** that we want to write our edits to disk, we enter lowercase w, and to tell **vim** "nothing follows" or "that is all," we add an exclamation point !.

Once we've entered : w !, we hit ENTER or RETURN.

```
#!/bin/bash

# initialization
PROJPATH=$HOME/project
PROJ=rat
~        ~              ~
-- INSERT --            5,9            All
```

Figure 5-6. Writing the initialization lines

We continue editing our script by pressing lowercase a to append (which enters **edit** mode and moves the cursor one space to the right).

To keep our home directory tidy, we'll write all of our project filesystems into a subdirectory called "project."

Most scripts, programs, and algorithms require some kind of set up before execution of the main code begins. We call this set up "initialization."

In keeping with good programming practices, we'll denote in our code the initialization section.

Please note that in our first assignment statement, we are making use of the Bash environment variable **HOME**, whose value is the absolute path to the user's home directory.

Please note that in our second assignment statement, we're using the string literal "rat." It is normal when developing code to use dummy values that we'll replace later with the values we'll want to use in production. This keeps the number of free variables low and aids in quickly debugging issues that arise during development.

Now to show you how to show line numbers and how to move your cursor to the start of whichever line you need to go to. First, press ESC to enter **command** mode. Second, press : s e t SPACEBAR n u ENTER. That is, in command mode, you are **set**ting line **nu**mbering.

```
1 #!/bin/bash
2
3 # initialization
4 PROJPATH=$HOME/project
5 PROJ=rat
~
~
~
:set nu                                    5,8            All
```

Figure 5-7. Turning on *line numbering* in vim

Numbering lines in scripts can be useful in moving the cursor quickly to whichever line you need to edit.

For example, if you need to move the cursor to line 3, then in command mode, you press : 3 ENTER.

5.1 Making Executable Bash Scripts I

Likewise, if you want to move the curse to the top of the file, then in command mode, you press :｜1｜ENTER .

Finally, if you want to move to the bottom of the file, then in command mode, you press :｜$｜ENTER .

To turn off line numbering, we enter :｜s｜e｜t｜SPACEBAR｜n｜o｜n｜u｜ENTER .

Write the changes to disk and quit **vim**: press :｜w｜q｜ENTER to write edits to disk and quit; finally, on the Bash command line, rerun: **vim makeProjectFS**.

```
#!/bin/bash

# initialization
PROJPATH=$HOME/project
PROJ=rat
~
~
~
"makeProjectFS"  5L,62B                    5,8       All
```

Figure 5-8. Syntax highlighting in vim

Syntax highlighting color-codes the words in our script, enhancing the readability of the code and helping us catch common bugs.

We reenter **edit** mode by pressing ｜a｜ for "append," placing the cursor one position to the right.

```
#!/bin/bash

# initialization
PROJPATH=$HOME/project
PROJ=rat

# main program
mkdir -p $PROJPATH/$PROJ
~
~
~
-- INSERT --                                9,25      All
```

Figure 5-9. Using yank(copy)–paste to speed things up

All of our Bash statements in the main part of our script start the same. Let's copy–paste that part seven times to speed things along.

With the cursor at the end of the **mkdir** line (as far as we've written it), press ｜ESC｜ to get to **command** mode.

To copy the entire line that the cursor is on, press ｜y｜ for "yank" twice—｜y｜｜y｜—then to paste the line as copied, press ｜p｜.

We now have one copy of the **mkdir** line. Press [p] six more times to finish with eight **mkdir** lines.

```
# main program
mkdir -p $PROJPATH/$PROJ
mkdir -p $PROJPATH/$PROJ
mkdir -p $PROJPATH/$PROJ
mkdir -p $PROJPATH/$PROJ
mkdir -p $PROJPATH/$PROJ
mkdir -p $PROJPATH/$PROJ
mkdir -p $PROJPATH/$PROJ
mkdir -p $PROJPATH/$PROJ
                                    15,1            All
```

Figure 5-10. Eight copies of mkdir line so far

Save your work with **:w!**, move the cursor up with the [↑] key to the start of the first **mkdir** line, and move the cursor to the end of the line by pressing the dollar sign [$] ([SHIFT] [4] on keyboards with US layout).

With the cursor at the end of the first **mkdir** line, press [a] to enter **edit** mode with append, then complete the line.

Press the [↓] key to go to the end of the next line. Finish it. Repeat.

```
# main program
mkdir -p $PROJPATH/$PROJ/data/raw
mkdir -p $PROJPATH/$PROJ/data/processed
mkdir -p $PROJPATH/$PROJ/figure/exploratory
mkdir -p $PROJPATH/$PROJ/figure/final
mkdir -p $PROJPATH/$PROJ/script/raw
mkdir -p $PROJPATH/$PROJ/script/final
mkdir -p $PROJPATH/$PROJ/text/readme
mkdir -p $PROJPATH/$PROJ/text/text-of-analysis
-- INSERT --                        16,1            All
```

Figure 5-11. All the mkdir statements completed

If we save the script and run it now, it'll create a project filesystem for a project named "rat," which for now is what we want it to do.

Let's make sure that it does that before we finish the script.

Save your edits to disk and quit **vim** by first entering **command** mode by pressing [ESC], then writing our edits to disk and quitting by pressing [:][w][q][ENTER].

On the Bash command line, enter:

bash makeProjectFS [ENTER]

If the script runs without error, Bash won't report anything.

To see if the project filesystem has been created, enter:

tree project [ENTER] .

Figure 5-12 tree returns a tree-like display of a directory's contents. Displayed here is a project filesystem, in which the project name is "rat"

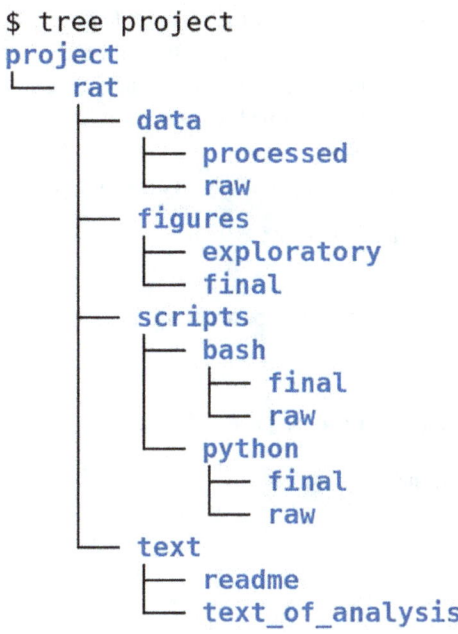

```
$ tree project
project
└── rat
    ├── data
    │   ├── processed
    │   └── raw
    ├── figures
    │   ├── exploratory
    │   └── final
    ├── scripts
    │   ├── bash
    │   │   ├── final
    │   │   └── raw
    │   └── python
    │       ├── final
    │       └── raw
    └── text
        ├── readme
        └── text_of_analysis

17 directories, 0 files
```

While in development, it is important to constantly test your code, to ensure that it behaves as expected.

To delete the project filesystem so we have a "clean slate" to develop on, on the Bash command line, we can type:

```
$ rm -rf ~/project/ # remove directory with recursion and force options
```

Let's finish making the script executable. Once it's executable, we can invoke it like we do Bash commands like **ls** or **cd**—that is, by itself.

First, we chmod the file, enabling the execute bit for whomever (owner, group, or world) should be able to execute it. Let's see what the file's current permissions look like:

```
$ ls -l makeProjectFS
-rw-rw-r-- 1 user user 393 Jul  6 15:39 makeProjectFS
```

We want to preserve the current permissions, adding only the execute bit for owner. To do this, we enter:

```
$ chmod 764 makeProjectFS
# owner:read+write+execute (4+2+1), group:read+write (4+2); world:read-only (4)

$ ls -l makeProjectFS
-rw-rw-r-- 1 user user 393 Jul  6 15:39 makeProjectFS
```

Figure 5-13. Setting the execution bit for script owner

Now that we've added the **shebang** to the top line of the script and set the execution bit so the script owner can execute the script simply by invoking it on the Bash command line, our last step is to put the script into a directory whose absolute path is in our **PATH** string.

Because normal users cannot move files into system directories, we are prohibited from moving our executable script into the currently listed directories in **PATH**; however, in Ubuntu, if we create a directory in our home directory called "**bin**," on boot the system will add the absolute path of that bin directory to our **PATH** string!

1) Make a bin directory in our home directory:

    $ mkdir ~/bin

2) Reboot your Ubuntu system:

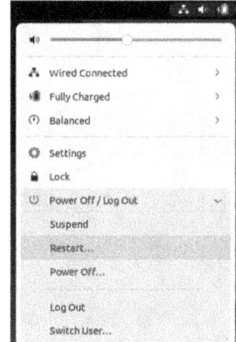

Figure 5-14 Rebooting an Ubuntu system from the graphical desktop environment

Move your mouse to the upper right-hand corner of the desktop and left-click in the icons there, and a drop-down menu should appear. Click the **Power Off/Log Out** option, and you should be presented with more options.

Choose **Restart…**

A popup **Restart** window will appear, with buttons to CANCEL and RESTART.

Choose RESTART

Log back in to your system, launch a terminal window, and enter:

$ echo $PATH
/home/user/bin:/usr/local/sbin:/usr/local/bin:/usr/sbin:/usr/bin:/sbin:/bin

Figure 5-15. PATH string prepended with absolute path to the bin directory in our home directory

Remember: The Bash interpreter searches in sequence for a matching filename to the name we enter on the command line, starting with the directory listed first in the **PATH** string, then moving to the directory listed second, and so on.

In other words, the Bash interpreter will always search the directory where we put our executable scripts and compiled programs before it searches anywhere else.

5.1 Making Executable Bash Scripts I

Next, we move our executable script into our **bin** directory:

```
mv makeProjectFS ~/bin/
$ makeP
```

Figure 5-16. Now, if on the Bash command line we type the first few letters in the name of our executable script, then hit TAB , the name should complete

```
$ makeProjectFS
```

makeProjectFS TAB-completes.
This means that the Bash interpreter "sees" the file in your home bin directory.
Hit ENTER to ensure the script runs without error.
After **makeProjectFS** runs, on the command line, enter:

```
$ tree project
```

A twig-and-leaf representation of the "rat" project filesystem should be displayed.

Now we want to modify our executable script so that it takes the name of a new project passed in as an argument on the command line and uses the name in setting up a project filesystem.

Bash assigns the string values in a Bash statement to numeric variables $0..$9. The space (which you create when you press the SPACEBAR) serves as a separator between elements in a Bash statement.

The name of the command or executable script is assigned to **$0**. In this specific example, that would be **makeProjectFS**, and if we were to make a project name an argument on the command line—for example, **makeProjectFS mouse**—then "mouse" would be assigned to **$1**.

Within our script, we can use Bash's numeric variables to refer to the elements in the Bash statement where we invoke the script by name.

This means that by making a simple change in the second assignment statement in our executable script, we can make it take an argument as the project name when it creates the project filesystem.

```
# initialization
PROJPATH=$HOME/project
PROJ=$1 # take the argument off command line as project name
```

Figure 5-17. Modifying assignment statement #2 in vim

By assigning variable **PROJ** the value that's assigned to numeric variable **$1**, we pass into our script the string value of the argument for use in our script.

Yes, it's that simple.
After the executable scripts runs, we run:

```
$ tree project
```

to verify that the mouse project filesystem has been created.

Please note that in developing our executable script, we followed a cycle of write-test-write-test.
In general, you should write no more than a few lines, test, then write a few more lines, and test. Frequent testing helps you catch bugs early and fix them.

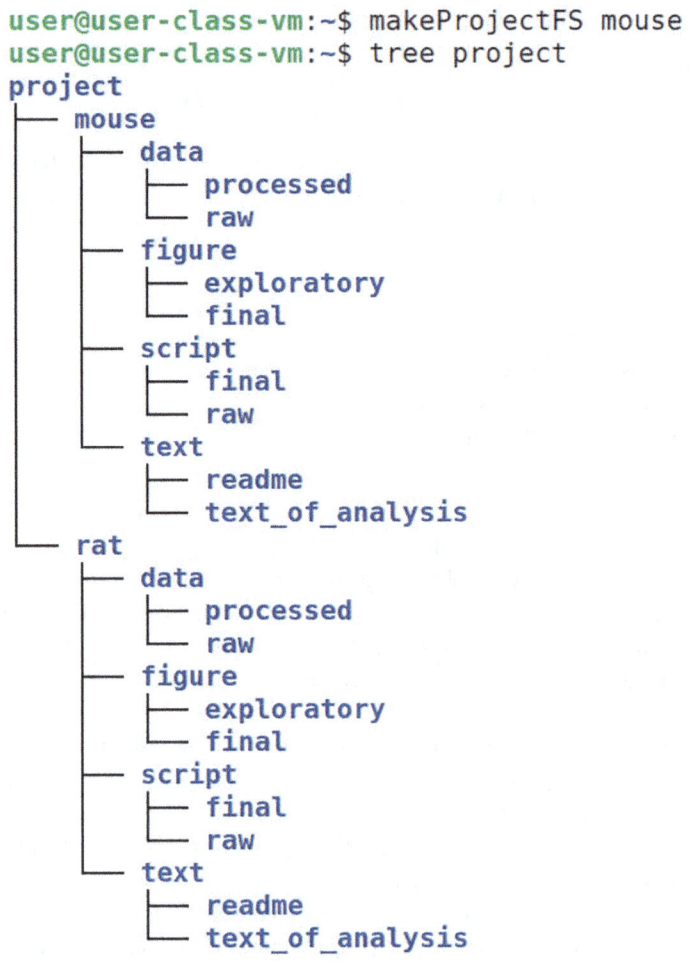

Figure 5-18 Executing makeProjectFS with a project name as argument

5.1.1 Linting Our Executable Script

Finally, running our code through a linter can help us catch grammar, spelling, punctuation, and style errors that we may have missed. The errors we make are the hardest for us to see and fix—we didn't write that error intentionally so of course it doesn't look wrong to us!

If the Bash interpreter keeps throwing an error while trying to process your code, and you can't figure out why, try running your code through a linter to see if the linter can find the problem. It will also offer suggestions on how to fix it—and those suggestions may be better than your own fixes!

Finally, linters can help us learn best practices. This hearkens directly back to the fact that linters may offer better suggestions to improve your code than anything you've thought up.

5.1 Making Executable Bash Scripts I

```
$ shellcheck ~/bin/makeProjectFS

In /home/james/bin/makeProjectFS line 9:
mkdir -p $PROJPATH/$PROJ/data/raw
         ^--------^ SC2086 (info): Double quote to prevent globbing and word splitting.
                    ^----^ SC2086 (info): Double quote to prevent globbing and word splitting.

Did you mean:
mkdir -p "$PROJPATH"/"$PROJ"/data/raw
```

Figure 5-19. Linting our script with shellcheck

Shellcheck recommends double-quoting each invocation of our user variables.

```
$ sed 's|$PROJPATH|"$PROJPATH"|g' ~/bin/makeProjectFS
#!/bin/bash

# initialization
PROJPATH=$HOME/project
PROJ=$1 # take the argument off command line as project name


# main program
mkdir -p "$PROJPATH"/$PROJ/data/raw
mkdir -p "$PROJPATH"/$PROJ/data/processed
mkdir -p "$PROJPATH"/$PROJ/figure/explo$1ory
mkdir -p "$PROJPATH"/$PROJ/figure/final
mkdir -p "$PROJPATH"/$PROJ/script/raw
mkdir -p "$PROJPATH"/$PROJ/script/final
mkdir -p "$PROJPATH"/$PROJ/text/readme
mkdir -p "$PROJPATH"/$PROJ/text/text-of-analysis
```

Figure 5-20. Using sed to find-and-replace

If we are in the script with **vim**, we can run this find-and-replace.

But we can use **sed** on a file we don't have open to do the find-and-replace.

The pattern used is: **s/find/replace/**. The **s** means "substitute." **find** can be a string literal or a regular expression. The **g** means "global," which means replace all instances in each line of the file.

Because double quotes are part of the **replace** string, we use vertical bars (|) as our separator.

sed prints to STDOUT. This lets us inspect the changes before we modify the file.

```
$ sed -i 's|$PROJPATH|"$PROJPATH"|g' ~/bin/makeProjectFS
```

sed with the inplace option (-i) modifies the file.

Our edit is applied to the script.

Now we do the same with the second variable, then rerun shellcheck on our script.

DO NOT TAKE SHORTCUTS! MAKE SURE TO INSPECT THE EDITS BEFORE YOU APPLY THEM TO YOUR SCRIPT!

```
$ sed -i 's|$PROJ/|"$PROJ"/|g' ~/bin/makeProjectFS
```

sed -i modifies instances of the second variable

Rerunning **shellcheck** ~/**bin/makeProjectFS** returns nothing, meaning that the linter has found no more issues with our script.

Time to move on.

5.1.2 Review

A program is a file on the hard drive. We invoke, or launch, a program by writing its filename on the command line.

For example, "pwd" is a file named "pwd" in /bin. When we type "pwd" on the command line and hit RETURN or ENTER, Bash searches the directories listed in its PATH string in order until it finds a file named "pwd." It then loads a copy of the file, which is an application, into memory (at which time we refer to it as a process); and the computer runs the program.

The output, if any, is sent to STDOUT.

We can write Bash and Python scripts and configure them to run in Bash-like applications. It requires we do three things:

1. Making the script executable (by setting the execution bit for owner, group, or world)
2. Writing the shebang on the first line of the script (it contains the absolute path to the application that will execute the script)
3. Moving the script into a directory whose path is in the PATH string

In this chapter, we created a bin directory in our home directories and added its path to our PATH strings. We can now put our executable Bash and Python scripts (even compiled apps!) in the directory to run them off the command line as we do Bash commands.

5.2   tr Command: Translate or Delete Characters

UNIX is the answer, but only if you phrase the question very carefully.
—Anonymous

5.2.1   A Bash Pipeline Spellchecker

Figure 5-21 In a video made by Bell Labs in 1982 called "The Unix Operating System," Brian Kernighan demonstrates how shell commands and scripts can be piped together to create a spellchecker. Scan or click the QR code to go to the video on YouTube. https://www.youtube.com/watch?v=tc4ROCJYbm0

We'll make our own spellchecker pipeline.

5.2 The tr Command

```bash
#!/bin/bash

# initialization
DICT=/usr/share/dict/american-english

# test if personal dictionary exists
# if not, create it
if [ -e ~/my_dict ]; then
MYDICT=~/my_dict
else
touch ~/my_dict # create an empty file
MYDICT=~/my_dict
fi

tr -d '[:punct:]' | # delete punctuation
tr -s ' ' '\n' | # replacing spaces with newline characters
sort | # alphabetically sort the words in the input string
uniq| # remove multiple instances of the same word
egrep -xvf $DICT | # compare entire lines, return complement,
                   # run against dictionary file
tr '[:upper:]' '[:lower:]' | # replace all uppercase letters with lowercase equiv.
egrep -xvf $DICT | # remove common words that are uppercased in input string
egrep -xvf $MYDICT # remove entries in our personal dictionary file
```

Figure 5-22. The finished version of the pipeline we will develop

We echo or pipe into this pipeline a string or text file. The commands in the pipeline process the text piped to them.

The **grep** commands let pass only words in the stream that do NOT exist in the dictionary files.

Finally, the pipeline sends those words to STDOUT.

The difference between the script we're writing now and the project filesystem script we wrote is that our first script was essentially a single command, **mkdir**, repeated over and over, while this one takes data into a pipeline and transforms it step by step using several different commands.

In the first script, we did not have to worry much thinking about the order in which the commands are executed; in this script, we do.

Key here to understanding how to achieve the specification of what our script should do is understanding the datafile—the dictionary file.

```
$ wc -l /usr/share/dict/american-english
104334 /usr/share/dict/american-english
```

Figure 5-23. wc command with line count option

wc means "word count." With a file as argument and no options, **wc** prints three numbers: line count, word count, and byte count of the file.

With the -l option, **wc** prints only the line count.

```
$ tail /usr/share/dict/american-english
zoos
zorch
zucchini
zucchini's
zucchinis
```

```
zwieback
zwieback's
zygote
zygote's
zygotes
```

Figure 5-24. tail: print last lines of a file

Keeping in mind that, to the further extent possible in UNIX/Linux, each line in a text file is a record, we see that the dictionary file is made up of words, one to a line.

In other words, each record in the dictionary file holds one word.

We can consider all the words in the dictionary file as belonging to a set called the "set of american-english words," and we want to find all the words in the input string of words that have no match in this set. The set of all words that are not in the "set of american-english words" is called that set's complement.

Figure 5-25 The tr command

tr - translate or delete characters

- **arguments** :
  - -c : use the complement of SET
  - -d : delete characters in SET
- **escape sequences** :
  - \b : backspace
  - \f : form feed
  - \n : new line
  - \r : return
  - \t : horizontal tab
  - \v : vertical tab
- **sets** :
  - [:alnum:] : all letters and digits
  - [:alpha:] : all letters
  - [:blank:] : all horizontal whitespace
  - [:cntrl:] : all control chars
  - [:digit:] : all digits
  - [:graph:] : all printable chars, not including space
  - [:lower:] : all lower case letters
  - [:print:] : all printable chars, including space
  - [:punct:] : all punctuation chars
  - [:space:] : all horizontal or vertical whitespace
  - [:upper:] : all upper case letters

Note that the **tr** command makes extensive use of sets and their complements to work.

Sets are used quite a bit in processing datasets for proving existence ("Is there at least one red supergiant among these stars?") or showing group membership ("Show me all cats more than 3 years old that are due for a rabies booster."); and computers are efficient working with sets.

So what we want the computer to do is print the members of the complement to the "set of american-english words" that are in the input string.

This attention to vocabulary is intentional. If we need help at any step in developing this script, we need to describe what we're trying to do in the same words that programmers use who post solutions on sites like **stackoverflow**.

So now we have a clearer idea of what we want to do: we want to transform the input string of words into a recordset of words, structured like the recordset of words in the american-english dictionary file. This way the two sets of words can be compared.

From this comparison, we want all the words in the input that are NOT in the american-english recordset in our resultset.

The **grep** tools have options to output the lines that have NO match in a file of PATTERNS (using the -x, -v, and -f options). All we have to do is transform the input string of words before invoking our grep tool.

```
$ find /usr -name american-english 2>/dev/null
/usr/share/dict/american-english
```

Figure 5-26. Using the *find* command to verify the existence and path of the *american-english* file

Please note the arguments that we pass into **find**, as well as the redirection: (1) where in the filesystem to start searching (/ is the topmost level, or root); (2) the name of the folder or file we're looking for; and (3) we use the number mapped to STDERR (2), to redirect warnings and errors to **/dev/null**, known as the **"bit bucket"**.

find by default can be chatty as it warns us when we don't have permission to access directories that it's trying to access (using our permissions), and there are many directories that we as normal users cannot access in a computer's filesystem. We're not interested in the warnings, just in the matches; hence, not to be overwhelmed by all the warnings, we'll redirect them to the bit bucket.

We redirect messages that we don't want to save or be bothered with to the bit bucket.

All that the computer will print out to us are the matches.

You should see the absolute path to the american-english dictionary file in /usr, and if you don't—not to worry: one is in your **intro_to_programming** repo.

In our executable script, we will create a variable whose name is DICT and whose value is the absolute path to the american-english dictionary. We will invoke the variable as an argument passed into the **egrep** command at the end of the pipeline.

Now let's start coding.

```
vim ~/bin/spellcheck.sh
```

Creating our new executable script in our home bin directory

By adding the suffix **.sh**, we signal to **vim** that we're writing a Bash script, and **vim** enables syntax highlighting for Bash scripts.

```
#!/bin/bash

# initialization
DICT=/usr/share/dict/american-english
```

Figure 5-27. We start by writing the parts that we know we need

```bash
#!/bin/bash

# initialization
DICT=/usr/share/dict/american-english

echo "At Bell Laborotories, UNIX systems privide more timesharing
ports than all other systems combined." # echo
```

Figure 5-28. For development, we will echo the same string into the pipeline

The misspells are intentional; they are the words that our spellcheck script should catch.
If we run the script now, it will simply echo the string to STDOUT.

```bash
#!/bin/bash

# initialization
DICT=/usr/share/dict/american-english

substr1="At Bell Laborotories, UNIX systems privide more timesharing"
substr2="ports than all other systems combined."
substr="${substr1} ${substr2}"
echo "${substr}" # echo into pipeline
tr -d '[:punct:]' # delete punctuation
```

Figure 5-29. Remove punctuation from the input string

Please note that by placing one statement on a line, followed by the pipe and #, we can comment each statement in our pipeline.

Now we should test our script by running it to ensure that all punctuation has been removed from the string.

```
$ bash ~/bin/spellcheck.sh
At Bell Laborotories UNIX systems privide more timesharing
ports than all other systems combined
```

Figure 5-30. Verifying that punctuation has been removed from the input string

```bash
#!/bin/bash

# initialization
DICT=/usr/share/dict/american-english

echo "At Bell Laborotories, UNIX systems privide more timesharing
ports than all other systems combined." |# echo into pipeline
tr -d '[:punct:]' |# delete punctuation
tr -s ' ' '\n' # replace spaces with newline chars
```

Figure 5-31. Substitute spaces in the input string with newline chars

5.2 The tr Command

In a way, this is the most critical statement.

Now each word is on its own line, just like in the dictionary file.

However, given the rules of English orthography, the first word in every sentence is capitalized, and common words are sometimes capitalized (as when they are part of an official noun phrase, as in "Federal Bureau of Investigation").

For these words to be matched to their counterparts in the dictionary file, uppercase letters must be lowercased.

```
$ bash ~/bin/spellcheck.sh
At
Bell
Laborotories
UNIX
systems
privide
more
timesharing
ports
than
all
other
systems
combined
```

Figure 5-32. Verifying that spaces have been replaced with newline chars in the input string

```
#!/bin/bash

# initialization
DICT=/usr/share/dict/american-english

echo "At Bell Laborotories, UNIX systems privide more timesharing
ports than all other systems combined." |# echo into pipeline
tr -d '[:punct:]' |# delete punctuation
tr -s ' ' '\n' |# replace spaces with newline chars
tr '[:upper:]' '[:lower:]' |# replace uppercase with lowercase chars
sort # sort the lines alphabetically
```

Figure 5-33. Substitute uppercase chars with lowercase equivalents and alphabetically sort the lines

```
$ bash ~/bin/spellcheck.sh
all
at
bell
combined
laborotories
more
other
ports
privide
```

```
systems
systems
than
timesharing
unix
```

Figure 5-34. All words are now lowercased and sorted alphabetically

Note that "systems" appears twice, and they are grouped contiguously.

```bash
#!/bin/bash

# initialization
DICT=/usr/share/dict/american-english

echo "At Bell Laborotories, UNIX systems privide more timesharing
ports than all other systems combined." |# echo into pipeline
tr -d '[:punct:]' |# delete punctuation
tr -s ' ' '\n' |# replace spaces with newline chars
tr '[:upper:]' '[:lower:]' |# replace uppercase with lowercase chars
sort |# sort the lines alphabetically
uniq |# return a single instance of identical contiguous lines
grep -E -xvf "$DICT" # x: match whole lines, v: select non-matching lines
```

Figure 5-35. uniq and grep -E have been added, completing the pipeline

When run, our script should return any words NOT in the dictionary file.

```
$ bash ~/bin/spellcheck.sh
laborotories
privide
timesharing
unix
```

Figure 5-36. All words in the input string but NOT in the dictionary file

Looks good although correctly spelled words are in the list.

We could add them to the dictionary file, or we could add them to a personal dictionary file, then run the output through it.

In any case, all that's left to do is set the execution bit, rename the file, shellcheck it (and incorporate any improvements it suggests), and finally remove the string literal so that we can pipe any string into the script.

```
$ mv ~/bin/spellcheck.sh ~/bin/spellcheck
$ chmod 764 ~/bin/spellcheck # make executable for owner
$ shellcheck ~/bin/spellcheck
$
```

Figure 5-37. Renaming script, setting the execution bit for owner, linting the script, and making shellcheck's suggested change

Make sure to test your script after making these changes and to fix anything that breaks. In this case, shellcheck has no suggestions to make.

```bash
#!/bin/bash

# initialization
DICT=/usr/share/dict/american-english

tr -d '[:punct:]'         |# delete punctuation
tr -s ' ' '\n'            |# replace spaces with newline chars
tr '[:upper:]' '[:lower:]' |# replace uppercase with lowercase chars
sort                      |# sort the lines alphabetically
uniq                      |# return a single instance of identical contiguous lines
grep -E -xvf "$DICT"      # x: match whole lines, v: select non-matching lines
```

Figure 5-38. Removing the string literal used during development; executable script now takes any text piped into it as input

To delete an entire line in **vim**, make sure your cursor is over the line; then in **command** mode, type: [d][d].

Make sure to save your changes with: [:][w][q]

```
$ echo "At Bell Laborotories, UNIX systems privide more timesharing
ports than all other systems combined." | spellcheck
laborotories
privide
timesharing
unix
```

Figure 5-39. Spellcheck configured so we can pipe text into it

You can pipe a text file into **spellcheck** (using **cat**).

Please note what this means. We can write executable scripts and embed them in Bash pipelines. You can use **spellcheck** over and over in different scripts, saving you from having to write the code whenever you need to implement a spellchecker (provided of course that it meets whatever specifications are set forth for those other projects!).

Can We Do Better?

Don't stop with your first draft.
    — Kernighan and Plauger, The Elements of Style

Just because we've developed a script that meets specs doesn't mean that we've necessarily finished. True, our code may do everything we need it to do, and we're the only ones who'll ever use it. We automate in order not to waste people's time—including our own.

However, it may be the case that because of flaws and limitations in our rough draft, our script cannot handle new tasks that come up.

Kernighan and Plauger, *The Elements of Style, 2d Edition*. McGraw Hill. 1978. p.54.

Consider, for example, that as written, all words in the input string are lowercased. This means that proper nouns that are in the dictionary file would be output with the misspelled words. In our example input string, "UNIX" is such a word. It turns out that a small change to the existing pipeline will ensure that words in the input string with capital letters will match words in the dictionary file with the same capital letters.

But also consider, too, that words in the input string not in the dictionary file will be output with the misspelled words. In our example input string, "timesharing" is such a word. Again, with a small change to our existing pipeline, we can add a second dictionary file to filter correctly spelled words in the input string that aren't in the american-english file.

Let's add the commands to take care of the first issue, then add the commands to take care of the second one.

```
#!/bin/bash

# initialization
DICT=/usr/share/dict/american-english

tr -d '[:punct:]' |# delete punctuation
tr -s ' ' '\n' |# replace spaces with newline chars
sort |# sort alphabetically
uniq |# return single instance of identical records grouped contiguously
grep -E -xvf "$DICT" # x: match whole lines, v: select non-matching lines
tr '[:upper:]' '[:lower:]' |# replace uppercase with lowercase chars
grep -E -xvf "$DICT" # x: match whole lines, v: select non-matching lines
```

Figure 5-40. Spellcheck invoking *grep* twice

Output words are first run as-is against the dictionary file.

This filters out from the output proper nouns, initializations and acronyms, and all-caps words like "UNIX." Then the words piped out from the first *grep* statement are lowercased before being piped into the second *grep* statement.

```
#!/bin/bash

# initialization
DICT=/usr/share/dict/american-english
MYDICT=~/my_dict

tr -d '[:punct:]' |# delete punctuation
tr -s ' ' '\n' |# replace spaces with newline chars
sort |# sort alphabetically
uniq |# return single instance of identical records grouped contiguously
grep -E -xvf "$DICT" # x: match whole lines, v: select non-matching lines
tr '[:upper:]' '[:lower:]' |# replace uppercase with lowercase chars
grep -E -xvf "$DICT" # x: match whole lines, v: select non-matching lines
grep -E -xvf "$MYDICT" #
```

Figure 5-41. Spellcheck invoking a second dict file

5.2 The tr Command

This dictionary file is maintained by the user and holds legitimate words not in the system dictionary.

The user can append new words to this dictionary on the Bash command line, thus:

```
echo new_word >> $MYDICT
# test if personal dictionary exists
# if not, create it
if [ -e ~/my_dict ]; then
    MYDICT=~/my_dict
else
    touch ~/my_dict # create an empty file
    MYDICT=~/my_dict
fi
```

Figure 5-42. If my_dict does NOT exist, create it

There is one problem with running the script as-is in Figure 5-41, and that's if *my_dict* doesn't already exist, it will throw an error. We call the code we write to handle errors and warnings "error-trapping." To handle this error, we test if the file exists, and if it doesn't, to create it.

5.2.2 A DOS to Linux Files Converter

One difference between Linux-generated and Microsoft-generated text files is that Linux uses the newline character (\n) to end lines while Microsoft uses carriage-return/linefeed (CRLF, \r on Linux systems) to do so.

In the datafile directory of our repo, we have an example of a Windows-generated datafile, one record per line, but using CRLF as the record separator.

```
$ ls -lh datetime_windows_unicode_crlf_dataset.txt
-rw-rw-r-- 1 user user 57K Jan 18 13:42 datetime_windows_unicode_crlf_dataset.txt
$ wc datetime_windows_unicode_crlf_dataset.txt
0    4041  57561 datetime_windows_unicode_crlf_dataset.txt
```

Figure 5-43. Getting stats on our Windows-generated text file

This example is in the datafile directory of our repo.

Note that we get back good size-of-file info when we use the **ls** command, but seemingly nonsensical info when we use the **wc** command. (Zero lines? Huh?)

The issue is that Linux systems by default do not read CRLF characters in strings as line delimiters.

```
    $ tr -s '\r' '\n' < datetime_windows_unicode_crlf_dataset.txt\
> FIXED_datetime_windows_dataset.txt
    $ wc FIXED_datetime_windows_dataset.txt
    2021  4041  57561 FIXED_datetime_windows_dataset.txt
```

Figure 5-44. Using *tr* to replace \r with \n

Note the redirection arrows. Essentially, this statements reads the contents of the first file into the **tr** command, which replaces all CLRF EOL characters with \n characters and writes out result to a second file.

That done, when we get the word count of the output file, we find that the file has 2022 lines.

```
$ head FIXED_datetime_windows_dataset.txt
ID,datetime,DOW,dow
43346,9/24/2012 16:10,MON,1
43346,9/25/2012 18:47,TUE,2
43346,9/26/2012 20:35,WED,3
43346,9/27/2012 19:58,THU,4
43346,9/28/2012 16:26,FRI,5
43346,9/29/2012 17:27,SAT,6
43346,9/30/2012 19:37,SUN,7
43346,10/1/2012 17:55,MON,1
43346,10/2/2012 18:12,TUE,2
```

Figure 5-45. The first ten lines of the datafile

Now that the dataset is in a file with line separators that Linux processes, we can work on its records with our tools.

5.3 Extracting and Analyzing Data from Datafiles Using Bash Pipelines

A computer lets you make more mistakes faster than any other invention — with the possible exceptions of handguns and Tequila.

— *Mitch Ratcliffe*

```
#!/bin/bash

# initialization
WEBLOG=$1

# implementation
gawk '{print $1}' $WEBLOG |# extract column one from each record in the log file
sort |# collect identical ip addresses in contiguous blocks for counting
uniq -c |# return single instance of each ip addr with count
sort -nr |# sort count numerically in reverse order
head # return first 10 lines (top 10 web browser)
```

Figure 5-46. The finished version of the pipeline we will develop

This executable script takes the path to a web log as its argument, extracts the ip addresses of the machines whose browsers are logged connecting to the web server, and finds the 10 with the highest hit counts in the web log.

In this chapter, we'll craft an executable script to extract information from our first kind of datafile, a log file.

As we'll see, working with datafiles always starts with gathering metadata on the data within the files, as well as gathering summary statistics on the datafiles themselves. We'll write our script making use of this information.

Imagine being given this specification for a script:

SPECIFICATION: Given a web log from a web server as input, find the ip addresses of those browsers accessing the server's sites with the highest hit counts. Return the top 10.

5.3 Extracting and Analyzing Data

A web hit is a request for a file from a web server. The web page that you read on your web browser can be made up of the contents of many files on a web server, not least of which is the file that tells your browser how to put the contents of those files together to render a web page.

The web log records each hit.

A specification is (often) general guidance of what our code should do, what it should take for input, and what it should return for output.

Let's start by making a datafile directory into our home directory, then copying a web log from our repo into it.

```
$ mkdir ~/datafile && cp repo/intro_to_programming/datafile/web_log2.log
                                  ~/datafile
```

Making a datafile directory and copying a file from our repo into it

Please note the double ampersand (&&). This is an operator that connects the two Bash statements logically in this way: **iff** (if and only if) the first statement completes successfully, execute the second statement.

```
$ head -3 datafile/web_log2.log
120.37.226.197 - - [01/Feb/2015:04:37:26 -0600] "GET /surge/?p=290 HTTP/1.1"
200 25995 "-" "Mozilla/4.0 (compatible; MSIE 6.0; Windows NT 5.1; SV1;
Mozilla/4.0 (compatible; MSIE 6.0;
Windows NT 5.1; SV1) ; .NET CLR 2.0.50727 ; .NET CLR 4.0.30319)"
120.37.226.197 - - [01/Feb/2015:04:37:32 -0600]
 "POST /surge/wp-comments-post.php
HTTP/1.1" 302 - "http://w3.biosci.utexas.edu/surge/?p=290"
"Mozilla/4.0 (compatible;
MSIE 6.0; Windows NT 5.1; SV1; Mozilla/4.0 (compatible; MSIE 6.0;
Windows NT 5.1; SV1) )"
157.55.39.207 - - [01/Feb/2015:04:37:37 -0600] "GET
/prc/Sabal/images/SAMXM-sdlngs-TADI2-fall02.jpg HTTP/1.1"
200 57013 "-" "Mozilla/5.0 (compatible; bingbot/2.0;
+http://www.bing.com/bingbot.htm)"
```

Figure 5-47. Using *head* to print the first three lines of the log to STDOUT

In this web log, each record is a line, the record separator is the newline char (\n), and the separator between items in each record is the space. Hence, each record spans two-and-a-half lines in the display.

Each record records a hit (**GET** statement in the first record, **POST** statement in the second record, and **GET** statement in the third), and each record begins with the IP address of the visitor to the web server.

It is the IP addresses of the visitors that we're interested in, given the specification.

```
$ wc -l datafile/web_log2.log
144151 datafile/web_log2.log
```

Figure 5-48. Getting the record count with *wc -l*

In the timespan covered by the web log, there are roughly 144,000 hits.

A cursory scan of the first 25 records show what you probably already intuitively know: not all the hits for a single IP address are contiguous—that is, they are not grouped together in the web log. As one browser at one IP address is pulling files from the web server, others are making their own requests.

Given the specification, our script, taking the contents of the web log as input, should extract the first element of each record—the IP addresses of the visiting web browsers—sort them so they are contiguous, get the counts of the contiguous identical IP addresses, then sort those counts.

Please note that this plan depends on knowing what we can do with data in Bash.

When you have an idea of what needs to be done at some step in a Bash pipeline—but you don't know how to do it in Bash—it's time to Google Stack Overflow and those other helpful sites.

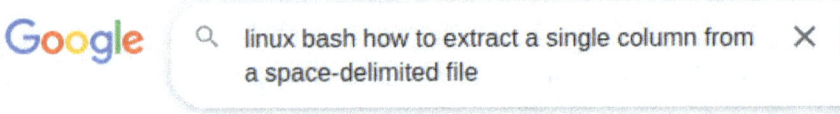

Figure 5-49 Search engines, and Q&A websites for computer programmers and systems administrators like *Stack Overflow*, are our friends

Note that the combination gets us fastest to our answers when we know how to phrase the question.

Note also that the first answer returned is not always the best, nor is it necessarily relevant or applicable to our situation. Please read the answers, even those in small print.

Because there is no single best tool in UNIX/Linux to solve a problem or a class of problems, if offered choices, I recommend going with the one that is simplest, easiest to understand, or the one that makes the most sense to you.

For this specific problem, two tools recommend themselves: **cut** and **gawk**.

Either will do.

In this exercise, I will use **gawk**. Its default record-element delimiter is the space.

```
$ gawk '{print $1}' datafile/web_log2.log | head
120.37.226.197
120.37.226.197
157.55.39.207
157.55.39.155
66.249.79.47
157.55.39.207
157.55.39.207
66.249.79.47
66.249.79.47
68.180.229.27
```

Figure 5-50. gawk in action

5.3 Extracting and Analyzing Data

awk (and its descendant **gawk**) is a programming language designed to extract and format text. It was first released in 1977.

Its authors designed it to be easy to use by non-IT people.

In **awk**, curly braces are used to enclose blocks of code. **awk** indexes on 1. Numeric variables ($1, $2, $3, etc.) map to items on a line; hence, $1 refers to the first item in each record of the web log. Statements in **awk** are separated by semicolons (;) and they in turn are enclosed in single quotes, and this is what is passed into the **awk** interpreter.

In this instance, there is only one statement, and it is passed into a **gawk** interpreter.

gawk interprets this single instruction, telling our machines that for each record in the log, return only the first element on the line.

```
$ gawk '{print $1}' datafile/web_log2.log | sort | uniq -c | tail
25 99.7.97.109
19 99.8.57.4
14 99.88.241.91
 1 99.88.246.41
 1 99.8.90.67
 2 99.89.129.197
 1 99.89.55.54
 9 99.93.99.166
 1 99.97.113.173
30 99.99.156.143
```

Figure 5-51. Our pipeline up to *uniq -c*

In our last script, we used the **uniq** command to return a single instance from each grouping of identical contiguous items. In this script, we use it return that AND the count of how many items are in the group.

Please note that in the output, the count is the first element in each record, while the IP address is the second.

Many Bash commands that we use for working on datasets (where each line is a record) by default act on or with the first element in each line. **sort** is an example.

By placing the count first, **sort -n** will sort each record numerically by count, which is what we want.

```
$ gawk '{print $1}' datafile/web_log2.log | sort | uniq -c | sort -nr | head
2015 157.55.39.203
1994 10.201.0.19
1878 68.180.229.27
1620 66.249.79.47
1620 128.125.245.75
1609 66.249.79.63
1573 66.249.79.55
1475 157.55.39.52
1447 100.43.85.13
1441 207.46.13.22
```

Figure 5-52. The fully developed pipeline

At this point, we are ready to write our pipeline into a text file and turn that text file into an executable script.

We need to remember that we pass in the web log's path as an argument on the Bash command line, and no script should go into production without documentation and testing.

```
#!/bin/bash

WEBLOG=$1

gawk '{print $1}' datafile/web_log2.log | sort | uniq -c | sort -nr | head
~
~
~
-- INSERT --                                              5,75           All
```

Figure 5-53. Starting the script

We create the script by typing on the command line:

$ vim ~/bin/getHitCount

In the **edit** mode, we write the shebang, an assignment statement that assigns the argument string, which is the path to the weblog, to a meaningful name (WEBLOG), and we paste in the pipeline we developed on the Bash command line.

Write changes to disk and quit. : w q

```
#!/bin/bash

WEBLOG=$1

gawk '{print $1}' $WEBLOG |# extract ip addrs from weblog
sort |# sort ip addrs
uniq -c |# get hit count for each visitor in weblog
sort -nr |# sort by count in desc order
head # print top 10 visitors by count
~
~
~
-- INSERT --                                              9,38           All
```

Figure 5-54. Finishing the script

5.3 Extracting and Analyzing Data

We reopen the file in **vim** and note the syntax highlighting.

Now we edit the pipeline, putting each command in the pipeline on its own line.

We remember to replace the literal path string with the variable name on line one, and we remember to add comments.

Write changes to disk and quit.

```
$ mv getHitCount ~/bin
$ chmod 744 ~/bin/getHitCount
$ getHitCount datafile/web_log2.log
2015 157.55.39.203
1994 10.201.0.19
1878 68.180.229.27
1620 66.249.79.47
1620 128.125.245.75
1609 66.249.79.63
1573 66.249.79.55
1475 157.55.39.52
1447 100.43.85.13
1441 207.46.13.22
```

Figure 5-55. Making our script executable and testing it

Looks good.

As a last step, let's lint our code and make any suggested changes.

```
$ shellcheck ~/bin/getHitCount
In /home/james/bin/getHitCount line 5:
gawk '{print $1}' $WEBLOG |# extract column 1 from weblog
                  ^-----^ SC2086 (info): Double quote to prevent
                          globbing and word splitting.
Did you mean:
gawk '{print $1}' "$WEBLOG" |# extract column 1 from weblog
For more information:
https://www.shellcheck.net/wiki/SC2086 -- Double quote to prevent globbing ...
```

Figure 5-56. Linting getMaxHitCount

Well, this is easy to fix with **sed**: **sed 's|$WEBLOG|"$WEBLOG"|g' bin/getMaxHitCount**.

If the output looks good, write the edit into the script with **sed** using the **-i** option, then remove the write bit from the script.

Finished.

5.4 gawk: How Many Named Stars Are There?

Figure 5-57 The **awk** programming language was first implemented in 1977

The authors of **awk**—Aho, Weinberger, and Kernighan, all of Bell Labs—used the first letters of their last names to name their collaboration.

Above is the cover of the book they wrote, meant to serve as a manual of sorts.

Figure 5-58 gawk was written intended to provide users with a version of **awk** that's easier to use than the original. Click the image or scan to go to the **gawk** manual homepage. https://www.gnu.org/software/gawk/manual/

In this image from the International Astronomical Union (IAU), we see **Aldebaran**, **Betelguese**, and **Rigel** labeled by their proper names. Most known stars lack proper names.

SPECIFICATION: Given a star catalog whose records show proper names for those stars that have them, find out how many stars in that catalog have proper names.

5.4 How Many Named Stars?

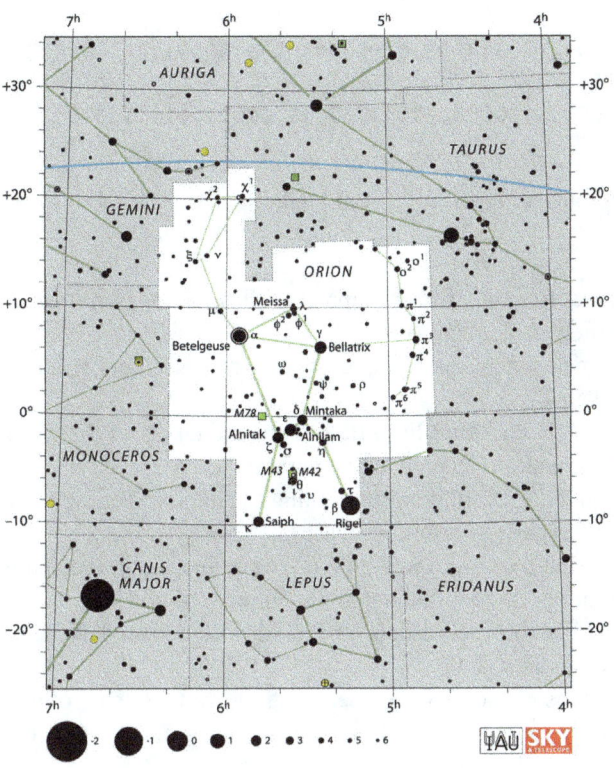

Figure 5-59 Named stars in Orion and adjacent constellations. Credit: IAU and Sky & Telescope, Creative Commons. Click the image to go to the image on the IAU site. https://www.iau.org/public/images/detail/ori/

```
$ cp repo/intro_to_programming/datafile/hygdata_v41.zip  ~/datafile/
$ zcat ~/datafile/hygdata_v41.zip | head -4
"id","hip","hd","hr","gl","bf","proper","ra","dec","dist","pmra","pmdec","rv",
"mag","absmag","spect","ci","x","y","z","vx","vy","vz","rarad","decrad",
"pmrarad","pmdecrad","bayer","flam","con","comp","comp_primary","base","lum",
"var","var_min","var_max"
0,,,,"","",Sol,0.0,0.0,0.0,0.0,0.0,0.0,-26.7,4.85,G2V,0.656,0.000005,0.0,
0.0,0.0,0.0,
0.0,0.0,0.0,0.0,0.0,"","","",1,0,"",1.0,"",,
1,1,224700,,"","","",0.00006,1.089009,219.7802,-5.2,-1.88,0.0,9.1,2.39,
F5,0.482,
219.740502,0.003449,4.177065,0.00000004,-0.00000554,
-0.000002,0.0000156934097753,
0.01900678824815125,-0.0000000252103114,-0.000000009114497,"","",Psc,1,1,"",
9.638290236239703,"",,
2,2,224690,,"","","",0.000283,-19.49884,47.9616,181.21,-0.93,0.0,9.27,
5.866,K3V,0.999,
45.210918,0.003365,-16.008996,-0.00000007,0.00004213,-0.0000002,
0.0000739611451172,
-0.34031895245171123,0.0000008785308705,-0.000000004508767,"","",Cet,1,2,"",
0.39228346253952057,"",,
3,3,224699,,"","","",0.000335,38.859279,442.4779,5.24,-2.91,0.0,6.61,
```

```
-1.619,B9,-0.019,
344.552785,0.030213,277.614965,0.00000392,0.00001124,-0.00000486,
0.0000876262870725,
0.6782223625543176,0.0000000254042369,-0.000000014108078,"","",And,1,3,"",
386.9011316551087,"",,
```

Figure 5-60. Copying our compressed hygdata datafile and using *zcat* to extract and read contents into pipeline

zcat is useful for extracting data from compressed files, saving us from having to uncompress files in order to work with their contents in Bash.

A dataset whose elements are arranged in rows (each row is a record) and columns (or dimensions) is known as a tabular dataset.

Please note that line 1 is the **label line**. It contains the labels of the columns in the dataset. Too often, it is the only documentation attached to a dataset.

Many of the labels in a dataset may mean nothing to anybody but the researchers who created the dataset, or other domain experts—in this case, astronomers.

In this case, we note that the values in a record are comma-separated and that columns in a record with no values hold either nothing in the field or an empty string. Either can be read as "no value."

We note that column 1 in this recordset is labeled **id**, which is used as the unique identifier for each record, and **id** indexes, or starts, at 0.

Finally, for the purposes of meeting the specification, we note that column 7 of record 0 contains the string **Sol**, which is the proper name of our nearest star, and the label corresponding to column 7 is **"proper"**.

This is the column that holds the data we're interested in.

```
$ zcat ~/datafile/hygdata_v41.zip | gawk -F',' '{print $7}' | head
"proper"
Sol
""
""
""
""
""
""
""
""
```

Figure 5-61. Working with what we already know, *gawk*'s *print* values in a specific column

In the last dataset, the web log file, the field separator was the space. In this dataset, it is the comma (,).

The default field separator in **gawk** is the space. We tell the **gawk** interpreter that the field separator in this dataset is the comma with the **-F** option, following it immediately with the separator—which in this case is the comma.

We pipe the output to **head** to limit output to the first 10 records.

From this, we see that we need to configure the pipeline—or commands currently in it—to drop the label line so column 7 label is not mixed in with the data and to not include empty strings in the output.

5.4 How Many Named Stars?

```
$ zcat ~/datafile/hygdata_v41.zip | tail -n +2 | gawk -F',' '{print $7}'\
| head
Sol
""
""
""
""
""
""
""
""
""
""
```

Figure 5-62. Dropping the label line using *tail*

We can remove comment lines and label lines at the top of a datafile using the **tail** command. As an option—note the plus (+) sign—we specify which line tail should start reading the datafile; in this case, at line 2.

```
$ zcat ~/datafile/hygdata_v41.zip | tail -n +2 |\
gawk -F',' '{print length($7)}' | head
3
2
2
2
2
2
2
2
2
2
```

Figure 5-63. Investigating how to not print lines with empty strings

Note that an empty string has a length (2) and that there could be stars whose proper names are two letters long.

I consider empty strings marking instances of no proper names, but no quotes enclosing proper names, to be a flaw in how the data in column 7 is rendered.

The process of cleaning data so we can work with it is known as "data wrangling" or "data munging," and it is a normal activity in working with datasets.

In this case, we can use **sed** to clean the data.

```
$ zcat ~/datafile/hygdata_v41.zip | tail -n +2 | sed -e 's/""//g' |\
gawk -F',' '{if (length($7) == 2) print $7}'
$
```

Figure 5-64. Embedding a *sed* statement to remove empty strings ("") from the dataset

To verify that the empty strings have been removed from the data, we test for length 2 in column 7.
The pipeline returns the empty set.
This result also tells us that there are no stars with proper names of length 2.
Now we can finish our pipeline.

```
$ zcat ~/datafile/hygdata_v41.zip | tail -n +2 | sed -e 's/""//g' |\
gawk -F',' '$7{print $7}' | wc -l
465
```

Figure 5-65. Pipeline that answers "How many named stars are in our star catalog?"

Note the restructuring of the **gawk** statement. The value of the first instance of **$7** behaves as a Boolean value: that is, if the field is empty, it is false, and the instruction in the curly braces is not executed; however, if there are any characters in the field, it is true, and the instruction is executed.

This is not a pipeline that we'll use multiple times so we have no need to make it into an executable script.

It does show that we can query our datasets with short pipelines.

5.5   Getting Resultsets from Bash Queries

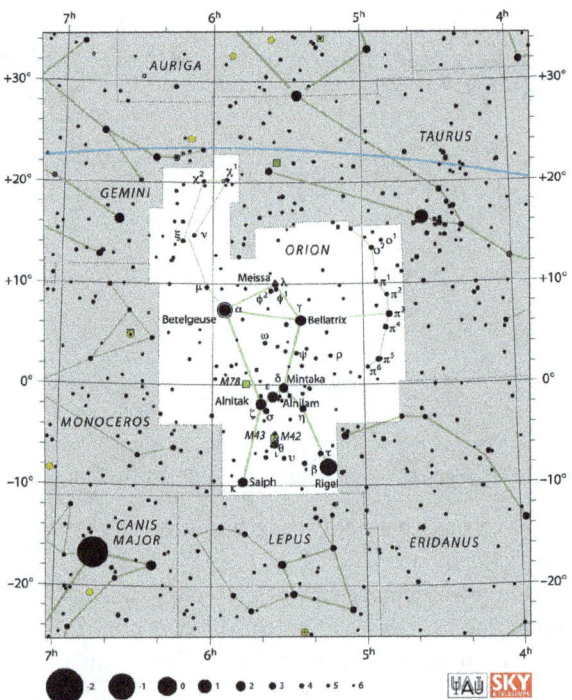

Figure 5-66 The constellation **Orion**. Credit: IAU and Sky & Telescope, Creative Commons. Click the image to go to the image on the IAU site.
https://www.iau.org/public/images/detail/ori/

The International Astronomical Union (IAU) recognizes 88 constellations and sets the borders between them.

The IAU abbreviation for Orion is **Ori**.

Please note that there are many stars within the borders of Orion that do not belong to the set of stars used to draw the constellation.

```
$ zcat ~/datafile/hygdata_v41.zip | grep Betelgeuse
27919,27989,39801,2061,"","58Alp Ori",Betelgeuse,5.919529,
7.407063,152.6718,27.33,
10.86,21.0,0.45,-5.469,M2Ib,1.5,3.189296,151.364387,19.682142,-0.0000198,
```

5.5 Getting Resultsets

```
0.00002068,0.00001074,1.5497291183713153,0.12927763169419373,
0.0000001324995789,
0.000000052650765,Alp,"58",Ori,1,27919,"",13415.28798266127,Alp,0.571,0.281
```

Figure 5-67. The record for α Orionis, or Betelgeuse, in our star catalog

Often when extracting a subset from a set of text records, we do so by finding string patterns shared by the records we're selecting for that are not in the other records.

```
$ zcat ~/datafile/hygdata_v41.zip | sed -e 's/""//g' |\
gawk -F',' '$30~/Ori/{print}' | wc -l
1977
$ zcat ~/datafile/hygdata_v41.zip | grep Ori | wc -l
1977
```

Figure 5-68. Double-checking results

There are times when we want to see if we get the same result using a different query. In the first pipeline, after determining that **con** (for "constellation") is column 30, we can anchor our literal search string to column 30 (the tilde serves as the anchor); any matches MUST have **Ori** in column 30.

In the second pipeline, **Ori** can appear anywhere in a record for that record to match.

In either case, 1977 records make up the resultset. And in either case, we frame our query to return the record count of the resultset.

```
$ zcat ~/datafile/hygdata_v41.zip | sed -e 's/""//g' |\
gawk -F',' '$7{print}' | grep Ori |\
gawk -F',' '{ if ($14 < 2.5) print $7}'
Rigel
Bellatrix
Mintaka
Alnilam
Alnitak
Saiph
Betelgeuse
```

Figure 5-69. Return all named stars in Orion with apparent magnitudes less than 2.5

Although we work with Python **pandas**, which makes querying our datasets much easier, we should observe that we now have all the basics on hand to craft such queries using Bash pipelines.

Note that the sequence of commands in the pipeline matters.

In this example, we print ALL records that have a proper name in column $7, piping them to select only those that have the string "Ori" in them, and finally pipe those into a second **gawk** statement to select records of stars whose apparent magnitude in column $14 is brighter than 2.5 (the bigger the magnitude, the dimmer the star):

```
$ gawk -F, '{ if (\$14 < 2.5) print}' > resultset
```

Then we rerun the pipeline.

5.5.1 Advanced Subject: Format Printing

Referring back to the image of Orion, however, we note that the stars we're interested in all have Greek letter designations—Betelgeuse is α Orionis, Rigel is β Orionis, etc.

In the 28th field of each record is a three-letter abbreviation for the Bayer Greek letter—α is **Alp**, β is **Bet**, etc.

We will shape our query to return the named stars with their Greek letter designations and sort them by apparent magnitude, brightest on top and dimmest on bottom.

To print the dimensions of each record in the order we want, as well as control the format in which they are printed, we will make use of the format print function **printf**(). Note how we invoke it in the pipeline below. The first argument passed into the printf() function is a string setting the print directives for the values to be printed out. The remaining arguments passed into the function are the column numbers from which the values for each record are taken, in the order in which we want them printed out.

In this case, that order is as follows: the apparent magnitude of the star (column 14), its Bayer Greek letter (column 28), the three-letter constellation abbreviation of the constellation it's in (column 30), and the star's proper name (column 7).

A record is printed out only if the star has a proper name and is in the constellation of Orion (Ori).

```
$ zcat ~/datafile/hygdata_v41.zip | sed -e 's/""//g' |\
gawk -F',' '$7{printf("%5s\t%s %s\t%s\n", $14, $28, $30, $7)}' |\
grep Ori | sort -n
0.18        Bet Ori     Rigel
0.45        Alp Ori     Betelgeuse
1.64        Gam Ori     Bellatrix
1.69        Eps Ori     Alnilam
1.74        Zet Ori     Alnitak
2.07        Kap Ori     Saiph
2.25        Del Ori     Mintaka
2.75        Iot Ori     Hatysa
3.19        Pi-3 Ori     Tabit
3.39        Lam Ori     Meissa
```

Figure 5-70. Named stars of Orion, sorted by apparent magnitude and listed with their Greek letter designation

> Friendly reminder: The higher the apparent magnitude, the dimmer the star.
>
> Please note the new **gawk** statement, which uses a print formatted function, printf().
>
> Format printing is a standard C library function, and the need/ability to control the formatting of printouts dates back to early UNIX.
>
> In this case, all values are handled as strings (**%s**), and apparent magnitude is tab-separated (**\t**) from the Bayer Greek letter, which is separated from the constellation abbreviation by a space, which itself is tab-separated from the star's proper name. (**\n** is the newline character.) The values come from columns 14, 28, 30, and 7, in that order.
>
> **sort**, as you may remember, operates on the first element of each record; hence, the resultset is sorted by apparent magnitude, with the brightest star at the top.

5.6 How to Make an Executable Script That Prompts Users for Input

> To make a script interactive so that it prompts the user for input:
>
> 1) Place the prompt for input within an infinite loop.
> 2) Test the input for the condition to drop out of the infinite loop (this is commonly an empty string).
> 3) If the condition is met, BREAK out of the loop. For simple scripts, this signals the end of script execution.
> 4) If the condition is not met, the script executes instructions within the infinite loop using the new user input.
>
> Once the machine finishes executing these instructions, the program counter returns to the top of the infinite loop, and the user is prompted for new input.

```bash
#!/bin/bash

# an infinite loop. in this example, only the user's input of an empty string
# --- essentially, hitting RETURN instead of entering a project name when
# prompted --- will cause the program counter to leave the while loop.

while true; do # two statements on the same line are separated by a semicolon
# here, "do" marks the start of the while loop's block of code,
# while "done" below marks the end of it.

# at the top of the loop, we prompt the user for input from the command line
# and assign the input string to the variable PROJ
# -p means "prompt"
# "read without -r will mangle backslashes." ---shellcheck
read -pr "please give a project name: " PROJ

# next, we test whether the user's input satisfies the condition
# to drop out of the infinite loop ---
# in other words, has the user hit ENTER or RETURN,
# (which generates the empty string),
# instead of entering a project name?
if [[ "$PROJ" == "" ]]
then
break # if the value of PROJ is the empty string, break out of while loop
fi

# otherwise, the user has entered a project name.
# here, we tell the bash interpreter to make a directory
# in the working directory with the project name as its name
mkdir "$PROJ"
```

```
done # end of while loop

echo "and now we're out of the loop!"
```

Figure 5-71. An interactive Bash script

This script uses an infinite while loop to keep prompting users for input, then the machine acts on the input. Once the users have no more input, they hit ENTER at the prompt (inputting an empty string).

The machine tests for empty strings. Once user input is the empty string, the machine executes a "break" to break out of the loop.

5.7 Datetime in Bash

Figure 5-72 UNIX time.
Scan or click the image to go to the Wikipedia article.
https://en.wikipedia.org/wiki/Unix_time

Time is a fundamental dimension in science and engineering. Phenomena evolve over time. In many plots in which time is a dimension, it is the domain (X) over which the values of other dimensions (Y) are plotted. Accordingly, it figures prominently in our understanding of the phenomenological world.

In the first UNIX systems, timedate was a 32-bit integer that included fractions of a second, with the start of the epoch being midnight 1 January 1971. However, including fractions of a second would result in a rollover of the 32-bit integer, marking the end of one epoch and start of the next, and a very short timespan (roughly two and a quarter years).

As a result, the datetime integer was recalibrated to hold only whole seconds, and a signed 32-bit integer can hold an epoch that spans 68 years before and after the start of the epoch, which today is midnight 1 January 1970.

Today, to overcome the $\pm$ 68 year limit, in many systems, timedate uses a 64-bit integer.

In Bash, the **date** command without arguments prints to STDOUT a datetime string representing the time kept on our machine.

```
$ date
Sun Mar  2 04:13:09 PM CST 2025
```

Invoking datetime with the *date* command

The **date** command sends to STDOUT a string representation of the signed 32 (or 64)-bit integer value holding a UNIX/Linux system's timedate.

This string can be one of a record's values as a system generates datasets.

```
$ date +"%Y-%m-%d %H:%M:%S %z"
2025-03-02 16:16:27 -0600
```

Modifying datetime string format with the string argument

We can control the format of the datetime string by using the **date** command with a string argument. See **man date** for more info.

```
$ cal
March 2025
Su Mo Tu We Th Fr Sa
                   1
 2  3  4  5  6  7  8
 9 10 11 12 13 14 15
16 17 18 19 20 21 22
23 24 25 26 27 28 29
30 31
```

Figure 5-73. Invoking the current calendar month with the Bash command *cal*

cal can be installed on a Debian/Ubuntu system with:
sudo apt install ncal

```
$ cal 1543
                              1543
      January                February                  March
Su Mo Tu We Th Fr Sa    Su Mo Tu We Th Fr Sa    Su Mo Tu We Th Fr Sa
 1  2  3  4  5  6              1  2  3                    1  2  3
 7  8  9 10 11 12 13     4  5  6  7  8  9 10     4  5  6  7  8  9 10
14 15 16 17 18 19 20    11 12 13 14 15 16 17    11 12 13 14 15 16 17
21 22 23 24 25 26 27    18 19 20 21 22 23 24    18 19 20 21 22 23 24
28 29 30 31             25 26 27 28             25 26 27 28 29 30 31

       April                    May                     June
Su Mo Tu We Th Fr Sa    Su Mo Tu We Th Fr Sa    Su Mo Tu We Th Fr Sa
 1  2  3  4  5  6  7              1  2  3  4  5                 1  2
 8  9 10 11 12 13 14     6  7  8  9 10 11 12     3  4  5  6  7  8  9
15 16 17 18 19 20 21    13 14 15 16 17 18 19    10 11 12 13 14 15 16
22 23 24 25 26 27 28    20 21 22 23 24 25 26    17 18 19 20 21 22 23
29 30                   27 28 29 30 31          24 25 26 27 28 29 30

       July                   August                  September
Su Mo Tu We Th Fr Sa    Su Mo Tu We Th Fr Sa    Su Mo Tu We Th Fr Sa
 1  2  3  4  5  6  7              1  2  3  4                       1
 8  9 10 11 12 13 14     5  6  7  8  9 10 11     2  3  4  5  6  7  8
15 16 17 18 19 20 21    12 13 14 15 16 17 18     9 10 11 12 13 14 15
22 23 24 25 26 27 28    19 20 21 22 23 24 25    16 17 18 19 20 21 22
29 30 31                26 27 28 29 30 31       23 24 25 26 27 28 29
30

      October                November                December
```

```
Su Mo Tu We Th Fr Sa   Su Mo Tu We Th Fr Sa   Su Mo Tu We Th Fr Sa
 1  2  3  4  5  6                 1  2  3                        1
 7  8  9 10 11 12 13    4  5  6  7  8  9 10    2  3  4  5  6  7  8
14 15 16 17 18 19 20   11 12 13 14 15 16 17    9 10 11 12 13 14 15
21 22 23 24 25 26 27   18 19 20 21 22 23 24   16 17 18 19 20 21 22
28 29 30 31            25 26 27 28 29 30      23 24 25 26 27 28 29
30 31
```

Figure 5-74. *cal* with a year as argument sends to STDOUT a calendar of the year

In 1543, Copernicus's *De revolutionibus orbium coelestium* and Vesalius's *Humani corporis fabrica* were published. Copernicus's work removed the Earth from the center of the cosmos, while Vesalius's work documented more than 300 corrections to the works of the ancient Roman physician Galen, effectively overthrowing a commonly held belief that ancient knowledge was superior to any knowledge a modern researcher could discover and proving that **Appeal to Authority** was indeed a fallacy.

For these achievements, some mark 1543 C.E. as the beginning of the Age of Science.

5.8   Introduction to Regular Expressions Using *grep -E*

> *A regular expression is a notation for specifying a pattern of text.*
> Brian Kernighan

We use strings to search for matching patterns of text every time we use an Internet search engine. Most of the time, it suffices to use a *string literal* in our searches. That is, we enter "cat"—*c-a-t*—into the textbox of our favorite search engine, and we expect *c-a-t* in the strings of our resultset.

Regular expressions expand our ability to define beyond literal strings the patterns of text we allow for a match.

I have found that the best way to teach what that means is by little explanation and more use of copious examples, using **grep -E** for casting our regular expressions and a dictionary file to search in for matches.

```
$ find /usr -name american-english 2>/dev/null
/usr/share/dict/american-english
```

Figure 5-75. Linux has dictionary files

To find the *american-english* dictionary file, we use the **find** command, starting at the root of the filesystem and searching by filename. Because the **find** command is noisy with error messages (letting us know that a regular user does not have permission to search certain directories), we redirect error messages (using **2>**) to the bit bucket, **/dev/null**.

Brian Kernighan. *UNIX: A History and a Memoir*. Kindle Direct Publishing. 2020. p73.

5.8 Regular Expressions

find returns the absolute path to the only match.

```
$ DICT=$(find /usr -name american-english 2>/dev/null)
$ echo $DICT
/usr/share/dict/american-english
```

Figure 5-76. Making the output of *find* the value of a variable called *DICT*

```
$ grep -E "cat" $DICT
```

And now let's make a regular expression in grep -E and run it

Regular expressions are enclosed in double quotes. A *string literal* is itself a regular expression. We start with **"cat"** and run it against our dictionary file. **egrep** returns each line in which a match occurs.

Figure 5-77 A few of the 923 matches

```
bobcat
bobcat's
bobcats
caricature
caricature's
caricatured
caricatures
caricaturing
caricaturist
caricaturist's
caricaturists
cat
cat's
cataclysm
```

A match must contain *c-a-t* contiguously and can occur anywhere in the line.

And now for the metacharacters. In regular expressions, the metacharacters take on a meaning different than they have in normal use.

The metacharacters: . ^ $ [ ] { } ( ) | * + ? \

```
$ grep -E "^cat" $DICT
```

Our first example uses the metacharacter called the "caret" (^)

In a regular expression, the caret anchors the regular expression to the start of a line. In other words, only lines that start with the regular expression match.

Figure 5-78 Here are some of the 195 matches

```
cat
cat's
cataclysm
cataclysm's
cataclysmic
cataclysms
catacomb
catacomb's
catacombs
catafalque
catafalque's
catafalques
catalepsy
catalepsy's
cataleptic
cataleptic's
cataleptics
```

Note how the anchor modifies the meaning of the regular expression. Only lines that start with *c-a-t* match.

```
$ grep -E "cat$" $DICT
```

Figure 5-79 We can also anchor a regular expression to the end of a line

```
Muscat
bobcat
cat
copycat
ducat
lolcat
muscat
polecat
pussycat
scat
tomcat
wildcat
```

The metacharacter to do that is the dollar sign ($). Note that there are far fewer matches in the dictionary file.

Let's open up what constitutes a match. Instead of matching only *c-a-t* anchored at the end of a line, let's match *c-any vowel-t* anchored at the end of a line.

```
$ grep -E "c[aeiou]t$" $DICT
```

Here, we use the square brackets as metacharacters

5.8 Regular Expressions

As metacharacters, the square brackets([ ]) enclose elements that define a **character class**. The square brackets contain the members of the character class. In the example above, we define the character class to contain the lowercase vowels. The regular expression, anchored to the end of a line, matches **c-any character in the character class-t**.

Any word that ends thus is in the resultset.

Figure 5-80 Some of the character class matches

```
haircut
illicit
implicit
lancet
licit
lolcat
mascot
```

```
$ grep -E "c[^aeiou]t$" $DICT
```

Figure 5-81 Regexes also allow us to specify a pattern that excludes characters

```
Brecht
Utrecht
Walpurgisnacht
Wehrmacht
acct
borscht
yacht
```

To do this, we use the ^ to create the **negated character class**.

To create the negated character class, we place the caret as the first character within the square brackets.

As you can see from the output, the regular expression, anchored at the end of a line, matches *c-any character not a vowel-t*. In the dictionary file, the only words that match end in *c-h-t*.

```
$ grep -E "^c.t$" $DICT
```

```
cat
cot
cut
```

Figure 5-82 We can create a regular expression that anchors to both ends of a line

In fact, the regular expression ^$ signifies an empty line.

Here, we use the period (**.**) as metacharacter. As a metacharacter, it matches any character except the newline character.

This regular expression reads "Anchor **c** to the start of a line, anchor **t** to the end of the line; and allow exactly one character between them."

Only three lines in the dictionary file match.

```
$ grep -E "^d..t$" $DICT
```

Figure 5-83 A series of dots

```
daft
dart
debt
deft
dent
dept
diet
dint
dirt
dolt
duct
duet
dust
```

Likewise, two **.**'s match any two contiguous characters between **d** anchored to the start of a line and **t** anchored to the end of the line.

```
$ grep -E "^d.{2}t$" $DICT
```

Figure 5-84 The curly braces as metacharacters allow us to quantify matches

```
daft
dart
debt
deft
dent
dept
diet
dint
dirt
dolt
duct
duet
dust
```

Here, we specify matching any two contiguous characters between **d** anchored to the start of a line and **t** anchored to the end of the line.

Note that the output is exactly the same as that of the previous example.

5.8 Regular Expressions

```
$ grep -E "(ing){2}$" $DICT
```

Figure 5-85 Several of the matches for *inging*

```
binging
bringing
clinging
cringing
dinging
flinging
fringing
hamstringing
hinging
impinging
```

The parentheses metacharacters are used for grouping. In this example, we group the string *ing* so that they are treated like a single character by the following quantifier. In other words, lines that contain *i-n-g-i-n-g* match.

Above are some of the 32 matches.

Other quantifiers used in regular expressions are these metacharacters:
? : Match zero or one times
* : Match zero or more times
+ : Match one or more times

```
$ grep -E "^(ul)+" $DICT
```

Figure 5-86 Several matches for *one or more grouped matches of (ul) at start of word*

```
ultrasound
ultrasound's
ultrasounds
ultraviolet
ultraviolet's
ululate
ululated
ululates
ululating
```

Here, we allow for a match to contain the letters **u-l** to occur to least once at the start of a word; hence, matches include **ultrasound**, **ultraviolet**, and **ululate**.

```
$ grep -E "spr(ing|ung)" $DICT
```

Figure 5-87 Several of the matches for *spring* OR *sprung*

```
Hertzsprung
Hertzsprung's
hairspring
hairspring's
hairsprings
handspring
```

The alternate metacharacter (|) matches either-or one character or another (or one group of characters or another).

In this example, the pattern matches *spr* anchored to the start of a line, followed by either *ing* or *ung*.

5.9 Words You Can Make on a Calculator

The array of seven-segment LEDs in calculators form "letters" from numbers when the array is turned upside down. The available "letters" are **B-E-h-I-L-O-S**.

The challenge is to create the regular expression that, when run against the American English dictionary file, returns all the words that can be made on a calculator.

In *UNIX: A History and a Memoir*, Brian Kernighan tells the story of someone at Bell Labs who, in 1972CE, asked if there might be a way, using the dictionary "on your computer" to find "what words [one] can make on [one's] calculator when [holding] it upside down?"

In turn, Kernighan asked, "What letters [can one] make when [holding the] calculator upside down[?]" The answer was "BEHILOS."

According to Kernighan, "Being in a research group, it felt good to be able to help someone who had a really practical problem... I turned to the keyboard and typed this command..."*

My challenge to you is: knowing what you now know about regular expressions, can you come up with a regular expression that generates a list of possible words from the american-english dictionary?

HINT: Use a character class, and anchor it to the start and end of the words in the american-english dictionary.

---

* Brian Kernighan. *UNIX: A History and a Memoir*. Kindle Direct Publishing. 2020. p72.

5.10 Regular Expressions, sed, and tr: Reformatting Records in a Dataset

```
>Unigene27342_All      size 239     gap 0  0%
CGGGATGCTCTTCGAATGGCCGGGCGGATCCTCCGAGCCAGGGGTGTTCTCGATAGTGCTCGGGTCGCTT
GTGCACTCTT
CCCCAAGTAGCTCTTGCAAGAAGCCCACTTGATTGTTCGTGGGCAAGTCCCCGAGATTAAGAAAAGCC
TCGAAACTGTTG
CCTTTCTCGACTTCTTCAATGAGGACCATCTCGCGACCACAAGTGACCTCTGCCTCATCAGCAGCACCA
GAGGTATCTT
```

Figure 5-88. A fasta record from our dataset

In the fasta format, the record separator is the right angle bracket (>) at the start of the record and is followed by the record's unique identifier. The first line is called the description line. The researcher decides what goes in this line.

The remaining lines are data lines. They are of fixed length.

Recall: To the furthest extent possible, in UNIX/Linux in datasets written to text files, each record is a line, and the record separator is the newline (\) character.

To work with recordsets with our Bash tools, we may find it easier to do so when each record is a line; hence, the motivation to reformat records like fasta records so each record occupies a single line.

```
# lines 4-7 to "linearize the sequences"
# from https://www.biostars.org/p/17680/ by Fr\'{e}d\'{e}ric Mah\'{e}
# Creative Commons License
zcat All-Unigene.fa.zip |# read fasta recordset in zipped file into memory
sed -E -e 's/(^>.*$)/#\1#/' |# use egrep; enclose 1st line in each
# record with hash marks
tr -d "\n" |# delete newline characters
tr "#" "\n" |# replace hash symbols with newline characters
sed -e '/^$/d' |# delete empty lines
tr -d "\n" |# delete newline characters --- fasta record separator (>)
# is in place
tr '>' "\n" |# replace > with newline characters
sed -e 's/%/% /' |# insert a space after the percent sign.
# space is field separator.
tr -s ' ' |# replace each sequence of a repeated character
# with a single occurrence.
sed -e '/^$/d' # delete empty lines
```

Figure 5-89. We extract a fasta recordset into this pipeline from a compressed file using zcat (Frédéric Mahé, Creative Commons. https://www.biostars.org/p/17680/)

Text files in general compress very well. A compressed text file can occupy as little as 50% space on our mass-storage device what the original, uncompressed file does. The data stays in memory for as long as it stays in the pipeline. As the data passes through a pipeline, we call it a **datastream**.

The stream editor **sed** allows us to modify the data while it passes through the pipeline. In this case, we use it together with **tr** to reformat records in the recordset from fasta format to one record per row.

The first **sed** command uses a regular expression to enclose the first line in each fasta-formatted record within hash marks (#). We will have an introduction to regular expressions later in the class.

The second **sed** command uses regular expression metacharacters ^ (start-of-line anchor) and $ (end-of-line anchor) with nothing between them to signify an empty line.

The third **sed** command substitutes any percent sign with a percent sign and space. We do this specifically to the All-Unigene.fa dataset because of where the percent signs are placed in the records, and we use spaces as field separators.

One problem that researchers sometimes confront is that one piece of software will write out the data from their experiments in a format that another piece of software cannot read.

There are variations of this problem. The data may be formatted in a way that makes it difficult for the researcher to work with. Or, the software itself may format data in a way that makes it difficult using the same software to work with the output dataset as input.

Software that reads data in one format and either reads it into a data structure or reformats it so that in either case it is easier to extract the data we're interested in is called a **"parser"**, and while as a rule, I recommend that researchers use parsers in published libraries (if they exist and are known to be good), sometimes researchers find that they need to write their own.

Now that we've had an introduction to regular expressions, we're ready to look at how this parser—a Bash pipeline—reformats fasta records into records that each one occupies a single line. We start by piping lines extracted from the zip-compressed file into the **sed** statement that follows.

```
$ zcat ~/datafile/All-Unigene.fa.zip | sed -E -e 's/(^>.*$)/#\1#/' | head -12
#>Unigene1_All    size   535     gap   0   0%#
ATCATTATTGATAGCAACAACAATCCGGAGCACTTCCTC
ACCACCAATCC
ATACTATGATTCTCGCGTTGTGGGTAAATATTGTGAGAAA
CGTGATCCTA
CCCTGGCAGTTGTAGCTTACAGGAGAGGACAATGTGATGATG
AACTCATC
AATGTTACGAATAAGAACTCTTTGTTCAAACTGCAGGCCAGA
TATGTAGT
TGAAAGGATGGACGGCGATCTGTGGGAAAAGGTTCTTACTCC
TGATAATG
CCTTTAGAAGACAGCTCATTGATCAAGTTGTGTCAACAGCTT
TGCCTGAG
AGTAAAAGCCCAGAGCAAGTTTCTGCTGCTGTTAAGGCTTTC
ATGACTGC
TGATCTTCCCCATGAATTAATTGAGCTTCTTGAAAAGATAGT
ATTGCAGA
ATTCAGCATTCAGTGGGAACTTTAATCTGCAAAACCTGCTTA
TCTTAACA
GCCATTAAAGCAGATCCAACTCGAGTTATGGATTACATTAAT
AGATTGGA
TAACTTTGATGGACCAGCTGTTGGTGAAGTGGCTA
```

Figure 5-90. First 12 lines from the compressed fasta recordset, run through a *sed* expression to find lines that match a regular expression and modify them by enclosing them with hash marks (#)

By printing only the first 12 lines, we capture only the first record from the All-Unigene.fa recordset.

5.10 Reformatting Records in a Dataset

```
(^>.*$)
```

Please note this regular expression in the *sed* statement in Figure 5-90

The parentheses are grouping operators, and the metacharacters within match lines that start with the close-angle bracket, followed by zero or more characters, to the end of the line.

```
#\1#
```

The second part of the substitution clause says essentially, "If a line matches this pattern, enclose it in hash marks."

And as we can see from the first record whose lines pass through the pipeline, this is exactly what happens:

```
#>Unigene1_All    size   535     gap  0   0%#
```

We can verify that the first lines of the fasta records are enclosed in hashes

The rest of the lines in each record so far remain unmodified.

```
tr -d "\n" |# delete newline characters
tr "#" "\n" |# replace hash symbols with newline characters
sed -e '/^$/d' |# delete empty lines
tr -d "\n" |# delete newline characters --- fasta record separator (>)
# is in place
tr '>' "\n" |# replace > with newline characters
```

Figure 5-91. The next five commands do sequential *deletions* and *replacements*

The first line shows the entire pipeline so far.

The second line shows the five commands that do sequential deletions and insertions, enlarged to make them easier to read:

The first command deletes all newline characters. This brings the data lines together into a single field.

The second command replaces the hashes surrounding the first line of each record with newline characters.

The third command deletes empty lines.

The fourth command deletes the newline characters that the second command put in.

And the fifth command replaces the fasta record separator with the newline character.

The transformation of records is almost complete.

```
Unigene1_All    size   535     gap  0   0%ATCATTATTGATAGCAACAACAATCCGGAGCACTTCCTCACC
```

At this point, almost everything looks right, but the percent field is not separated from the data field

Also, the separations between fields have more than one space.

The next two commands fix these issues.

```
sed -e 's/%/% /' |# insert a space after the percent sign.
# space is field separator.
tr -s ' ' |# replace each sequence of a repeated character with
# a single occurrence.
sed -e '/^$/d' # delete empty lines
```

Figure 5-92. Last three lines of our the fasta record reformatter

The first command puts a space between the percent sign (%) and the data field.
The second command replaces multiple contiguous spaces with a single space.
And the third command removes empty lines.

```
Unigene1_All size 535 gap 0 0% ATCATTATTGATAGCAACAACAATCCGGAGCACTTCCTCACCACCAATCCA
TACTATGATTCTCGCGTTGTGGGTAAATATTGTGAGAAACGTGATCCTACCCTGGCAGTTGTAGCTTACAGGAGAGGACAAT
GTGATGATGAACTCATCAATGTTACGAATAAGAACTCTTTGTTCAAACTGCAGGCCAGATATGTAGTTGAAAGGATGGACGG
CGATCTGTGGGAAAAGGTTCTTACTCCTGATAATGCCTTTAGAAGACAGCTCATTGATCAAGTTGTGTCAACAGCTTTGCCT
GAGAGTAAAAGCCCAGAGCAAGTTTCTGCTGCTGTTAAGGCTTTCATGACTGCTGATCTTCCCCATGAATTAATTGAGCTTC
TTGAAAAGATAGTATTGCAGAATTCAGCATTCAGTGGGAACTTTAATCTGCAAAACCTGCTTATCTTAACAGCCATTAAAGC
AGATCCAACTCGAGTTATGGATTACATTAATAGATTGGATAACTTTGATGGACCAGCTGTTGGTGAAGTGGCTA
```

Figure 5-93. First record of our recordset, reformatted

Now we can redirect the output of our pipeline to a text file named **reformatted_fasta_recordset** and work on it with our Bash tools and Python functions.

Please redirect the output to a file in your datafile directory called "**reformatted_Unigene.fa**."

5.11 Finding Approximate Matches with *agrep*

> Because changes happen in genomes—insertions, deletions, and substitutions of nucleotides—bioinformaticists rely on search tools that allow for **indels** and **substitutions** of a nucleotide search string to find regions of a genome they're interested in.
>
> **agrep** (*approximate* grep) is a tool that belongs to the **grep** family of tools. **agrep** matches text to a search string, allowing for insertions, deletions, and substitutions.

```
$ FASTA_FILE=~/datafile/reformatted_Unigene.fa
```

Creating a variable for the path to our reformatted fasta file

Assigning the path to the file is intended to enhance the readability of the *agrep* statements we'll be writing.

```
$ agrep -1 "GATTACAGATTACA" $FASTA_FILE
```

Our first *agrep* statement

In this case, the resultset contains records whose nucleotide strings match GATTACAGATTACA, allowing for a single insertion, deletion, or substitution.

Note that perfect matches are also allowed.

```
$ agrep -1 "GATTACAGATTACA" $FASTA_FILE | wc -l
42
```

Figure 5-94. Getting the count of records with approximate matches

So why have we chosen **GATTACAGATTACA** as our search string?

—Because we want to be able to see and verify the matches.

If you inspect the resultset of the **agrep** statement alone, it's hard if not impossible to find those matches.

```
$ agrep -1 "GATTACAGATTACA" $FASTA_FILE | grep -E "GATTACA"
```

Piping output of *agrep* into *grep*

However, if we pipe the resultset into **grep -E "GATTACA"**, grep colors the matching string literal. We can then inspect the nucleotides to the left and right of **GATTACA** to find the whole string that matches **GATTACAGATTACA** approximately.

GATTGCA**GATTACA**AACACGA

The *agrep* match in record Unigene148651

grep's coloring of the literal match GATTACA allows us to find and inspect *agrep*'s approximate match of GATTACAGATTACA.

In this case, the first GATTACA has a substitution ('G' for the second 'A').

GATTCA**GATTACA**TACT

The *agrep* match in record Unigene148349

agrep's approximate match of GATTACAGATTACA.

In this case, the first GATTACA has a deletion (the second 'A').

GATTGACA**GATTACA**CCATTAC

The *agrep* match in record Unigene63629

agrep's approximate match of GATTACAGATTACA.

In this case, the first GATTACA has an insertion.

agrep allows you to restrict matches to just insertions or deletions or substitutions, as well as how many changes are allowed in a match.

Please refer to **man agrep** for more info.

5.12 Write Once, Run Everywhere: Embedding Our Executable Scripts in Pipelines and Invoking Them in Other Scripts

We close this chapter with a section showing how you can build a code base efficiently.

We'll start by defining **foundational code** as code that reoccurs often in our code base, and we'll offer as an example code in a bioinformatics code base that, given a nucleotide string as input, tests to ensure that the string is made up entirely of letters that represent nucleotides. (Soon, as we start programming in Python, we will write just such a function.)

As you write your code base, you may find that you need to test often nucleotide strings to ensure they're clean. In fact, any nucleotide string passed into our code should be tested to ensure it's clean before it's processed further, **especially if it's being passed in by hand.**

In Bash, once you find yourself writing code to do a task for which you've already written code, it's time to consider making that code its own executable script, then invoking it wherever you need it, whether that's within a pipeline or another script.[†]

The concept of writing recurring code once as a function, module, or script, then invoking it wherever it's needed in our code base, is called **"write once, run everywhere"**, and it offers a couple of advantages.

The first is that it relieves us from having to repeat ourselves, sometimes seemingly endlessly. This kind of repetition risks inviting errors in the copies, or inconsistencies between all the different implementations in the code base.

The second is that it greatly simplifies code maintenance. If we find an issue in our implementation of the algorithm we're using—or if we learn of a functionally equivalent algorithm that is substantially faster or uses much less memory than the one we're using—we need only go to the one script or module or function that holds our implementation and make the changes there.

The fix or improvement immediately becomes part of all the scripts and pipelines in our code base that invoke it.[‡]

```
$ echo "this is a sillie test" > some_text_file
$ cat some_text_file | spellchecker
sillie
```

Figure 5-95. Using an executable script in a pipeline

In this example, we pipe the contents of a text file into our spellcheck script.

This demonstrates that we can embed the executable scripts we write into Bash pipelines.

In our next example, we will embed one executable script inside another. We start by making a copy of the **bash_interactive_script** and naming it **interact_mk_proj_fs**.

```
cp ~/bin/bash_interactive_script ~/bin/interact_mk_proj_fs
```

Using the *cp* command to create the *interact_mk_proj_fs*

By invoking *makeProjectFS* on the command line, we create only one project filesystem.

However, by invoking it within *makeProjectFS*, then invoking the first script on the command line, we can interactively input multiple project names, and for each project name we enter (until we hit RETURN), the computer will create a project filesystem.

[†] This example invites discussion of other topics, like how to start writing a code base, how to maintain your code base, etc.

It may be fair to say that many code bases begin unplanned and develop in fits and start from the bottom-up, and only once its growth starts to make it unmanageable, do those growing it start to consider imposing order and structure on it.

Substantial rewrites of the code—which we call "refactoring"—are part of this cleaning-up process.

It happens so often, it gets its own term.

[‡] Likewise, if we introduce an error or inefficiency in that single implementation, it immediately becomes part of all the scripts in our code base that invoke it.

This brings to mind the quote by Mitch Ratcliffe, **"A computer lets you make more mistakes faster than any other invention — with the possible exceptions of handguns and Tequila."**

For this reason, refactoring includes and requires extensive testing.

5.12 Write Once, Run Everywhere

```bash
#!/bin/bash

# initialization
PROJPATH=$HOME/project
PROJ=$1 # take the argument off command line as project name


# main program
mkdir -p "$PROJPATH"/"$PROJ"/data/raw
mkdir -p "$PROJPATH"/"$PROJ"/data/processed
mkdir -p "$PROJPATH"/"$PROJ"/figure/explo$1ory
mkdir -p "$PROJPATH"/"$PROJ"/figure/final
mkdir -p "$PROJPATH"/"$PROJ"/script/raw
mkdir -p "$PROJPATH"/"$PROJ"/script/final
mkdir -p "$PROJPATH"/"$PROJ"/text/readme
mkdir -p "$PROJPATH"/"$PROJ"/text/text-of-analysis
```

Figure 5-96. The executable script **makeProjectFS**

Figure 5-97 tree project to inspect the contents of the project folder in our home folder

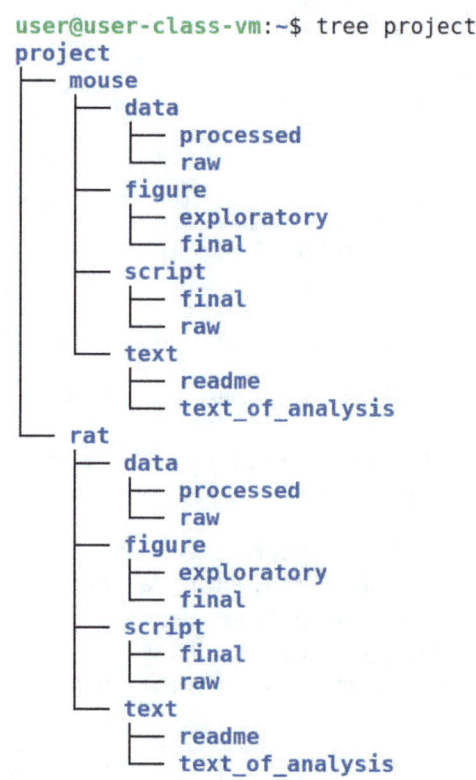

```bash
#!/bin/bash

# an infinite loop. in this example, only the user's input of an empty string
# --- essentially, hitting RETURN instead of entering a project name when
# prompted --- will cause the program counter to leave the while loop.

while true; do # two statements on the same line are separated by a semicolon
    # here, "do" marks the start of the while loop's block of code,
    # while "done" below marks the end of it.

    # at the top of the loop, we prompt the user for input from the command line
    # and assign the input string to the variable PROJ
    # -p means "prompt"
    read -p "please give a project name: " PROJ

    # next, we test whether the user's input satisfies the condition
    # to drop out of the infinite loop ---
    # in other words, has the user hit ENTER or RETURN,
    # (which generates the empty string),
    # instead of entering a project name?
    if [[ "$PROJ" == "" ]]
    then
    break # if the value of PROJ is the empty string, break out of while loop
    fi

    # otherwise, the user has entered a project name.
    # here, we tell the bash interpreter to make a directory
    # in the working directory with the project name as its name
    makeProjectFS "$PROJ"
done # end of while loop

echo "and now we're out of the loop!"
```

Figure 5-98. The executable script **interact_mk_proj_fs**

Note that on line 21, the script invokes our other executable script **make_proj_fs**, passing into it the project name the user enters on line 10.

```
$ interact_mk_proj_fs
please give project name: cat
please give project name: dog
please give project name:
and now we're out of the loop!
```

5.12 Write Once, Run Everywhere

Figure 5-99 Running *executing_interact_mk_proj_fs*, passing in *cat*, then *dog* as the arguments, then running *tree project* to inspect the result

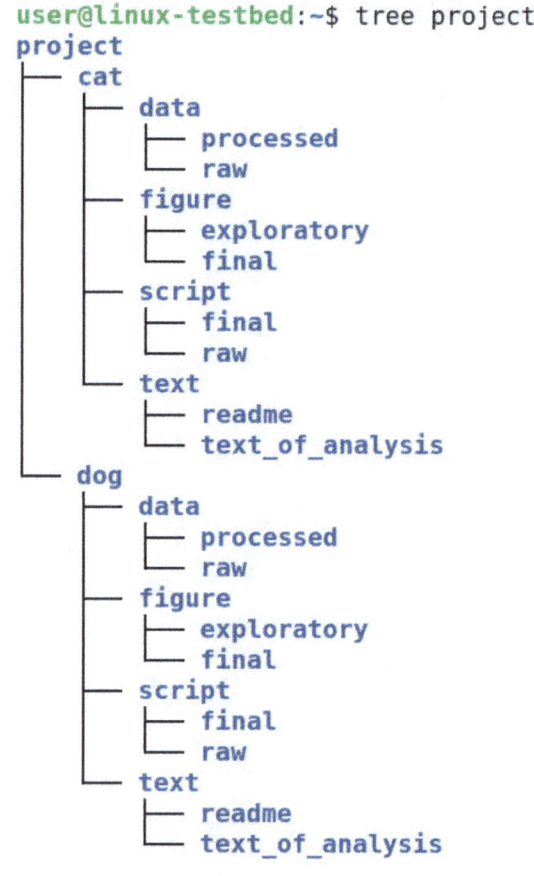

As we learn Python, we will apply this concept of "write once, run everywhere" as a basic part of our best programming practices.

Chapter Summary

Scientists and engineers find themselves doing repetitive tasks on computers that can be automated, especially when it comes to creating and processing datasets. Being at ease on the command line while working with your datasets extends your ability to work on those datasets beyond computers with graphical desktop environments. This includes being at ease working on supercomputers.

Algorithms and Coding 6

In the last chapter, we learned how to write Bash pipeline and scripts by making use of Bash commands. In this chapter, we go deeper into how programs are written by looking at algorithms. An algorithm is a set of instructions that solves a problem. Algorithms are found not only in math and programs, but also in magic tricks and recipes!

6.1 An Introduction to Algorithms

> An algorithm is a set of definite, specific instructions that solves a task. Through control flow, a programmer decides the order and number of times each instruction is executed.
>
> Examples of algorithms include recipes, instructions to tie knots, some magic tricks, and computer programs. In math, algorithms are often called "methods." Examples include least-squares method and Newton's method.
>
> Algorithms that are done manually are sometimes called manual or hand algorithms, to distinguish them from algorithms run by computers, which sometimes are called computer algorithms.
>
> Computer algorithms are often rendered in non-language-specific, informal descriptions called **"pseudocode"** that explain the instructions through math, logic, and natural language. Pseudocode rendering of algorithms is meant to aid reading comprehension of the algorithms.
>
> Computer programs are made from the implementations of algorithms in programming languages. The creators of these languages often have different design goals in mind as they write their languages. The ease of translating pseudocode into code in real programming languages depends very much on the programming language. Python by design was written to make transcribing pseudocode into Python code rather straightforward.

Figure 6-1 The story of algorithms runs through two great libraries—though not exclusively so (Top. O. Von Corven, *"The Great Library of Alexandria"*. 19th century. Public domain. Bottom. Yahyá al-Wasiti, Scholars at an Abbasid library in Baghdad. 1237. Public domain)

The first is the Great Library of Alexandria in Africa, established between 323 and 283 BCE, and the second is the Bayt al-Hikma of Baghdad in Asia, established between 754 and 775 CE.

In each case, the ambition of their founders was to collect in one place all knowledge then extant. Accordingly, each library attracted researchers from around the known world who endeavored both to master the knowledge in their disciplines and to extend their disciplines by contributing new knowledge.

One faculty researcher of the Great Library of Alexandria was Euclid (left), probably born in 325 BCE. His magnum opus, *Euclid's Elements*, covers geometry and number theory. It is in the *Elements*, Book VII, Propositions 1 and 2, that Euclid sets down a method for determining the greatest common

6.1 Algorithms

Figure 6-2 One famous faculty researcher of The Great Library of Alexandria and one famous faculty researcher of the Bayt al-Hikma (Joseph Durham, *Euclid*. Oxford University Museum of Natural History. Photo released into public domain by photographer. USSR commemorative stamp. *Muammad ibn Ms al-Kwrizm*. 1983. Not copyrighted IAW Article 1259 of Book IV of the Civil Code of the Russian Federation No. 230FZ of December 18, 2006)

divisor of two natural numbers, which today is known as Euclid's GCD algorithm. It is the oldest algorithm in production software today.

Al-Khwarizmi (right), born into a Persian family in 780 CE, worked as a faculty researcher in the Bayt al-Hikma. Around 820 CE, he produced separate math texts, one that codified and extended algebra (for which he is known as the Father of Algebra), and one that—extrapolating from the work of the Indian mathematician and astronomer Brahmagupta—provided methods for arithmetic calculations using the Hindu number system (which, because of the contributions of al-Khwarizmi and other Muslims, we know today as the Hindu-Arabic number system).

Al-Khwarizmi's works eventually made their way to Europe (chiefly through the Fibonacci's *Liber Abaci*), greatly influencing the adoption in Europe of the Hindu-Arabic number system—the base-10 number system, which includes ten digits, including one to represent zero, as well as base-10 positional notation. Along with the number system, Europeans adopted Al-Khwarizmi's methods of arithmetic computation. In math, algorithms are often called "methods."

For his work in systematizing methods of computation, Al-Khwarizmi is also known as the Father of Algorithms.

Although the word "algorithm" was first used in English around 1230 CE, it didn't take its modern meaning until the 19th century. The Ancients came up with the firsthand algorithms to solve math problems. The oldest algorithm used in production software is Euclid's Greatest Common Divisor algorithm, which Euclid described in *The Elements* circa 300 BCE.

6.1.1 Recipes as Algorithms

Considering recipes as algorithms makes a good introduction to understanding algorithms in general—both hand and computer algorithms. Recipes take raw ingredients as input and yield dishes, drinks, or desserts as output. Computer algorithms we will implement take nucleotide strings or numbers as input, for example, and return, say, amino acid strings or other numbers as output.

Most recipes transform their input to output by following steps in sequence: first do this, second do that; and finally apply finishing touches. Likewise, most existing computer code is sequential in structure.

However, some recipes have steps to perform if certain conditions hold true. One condition listed on many prepared food labels is the means of heating up the food: if by microwave, do this; if by stovetop, do that; and if by oven, do this and that. Until a student pointed these conditions out to me, my favorite condition to use applied to the baking of breads and cakes at high altitudes.

Likewise, in computer programs, we can use conditional branching to direct a computer to execute a block of code if some condition holds true. (We can do even more with conditional branching, as we shall soon see.)

Finally, some recipes have steps to perform again and again, until a condition changes. Examples include desserts, in which the cook is expected to perform the same steps on each of 12 cups of pudding.

In computer programs, instructions that are performed again and again until a condition changes are enclosed in loop structures. While other programming languages have several loop structures, Python has only two: the while-loop and the for-loop. The while-loop is the most general loop structure there is. It can be set up to behave like all the others. The for-loop is ideal for iterating* over a collection of countable items.

6.1.2 Definition of an Algorithm from *The Art of Computer Programming*

> Donald Knuth, *The Art of Computer Programming, Volume I: Fundamental Algorithms*:
> "Besides merely being a finite set of rules which gives a sequence of operations for solving a specific type of problem, an algorithm has five important features:
>
> "1) Finiteness. An algorithm must always terminate after a finite number of steps.
> "2) Definiteness. Each step of an algorithm must be precisely defined; the actions to be carried out must be rigorously and unambiguously specified for each case.
> "3) Input. An algorithm has zero or more inputs, i.e., quantities which are given to it initially before the algorithm begins.
> "4) Output. An algorithm has one or more outputs, i.e., quantities which have a specified relation to the inputs.

(continued)

---

* **iterate** [Latin *iterāre, iterāt-*, from *iterum*, again]
"*it · er · ate*": To say or perform again; repeat.
—*The American Heritage Dictionary of the English Language*, 5th Edition. Version 15.1.722. Houghton Mifflin Harcourt Publishing. 2025.

> "5) Effectiveness. An algorithm is also generally expected to be effective. This means that all the operations to be performed in the algorithm must be sufficiently basic that they can in principle be done exactly and in a finite length of time by a man using pencil and paper."

6.1.3 Control Flow

Programmers not only decide which instructions go into an algorithm, they also decide the order and number of times the instructions are executed.

We do this through *control flow*. We can think of the flow of execution of instructions in an algorithm as:

1) **Sequential**: In sequential flow, we start at the top, execute the first instruction there, then move down, executing each instruction in turn, one at a time. Most code is sequential in flow.

```
# example sequential flow
instruction statement #1
instruction statement #2
instruction statement #3
instruction statement #4
```
Figure 6-3. Sequential flow

Most program statements are written to be executed in sequence: the program counter starts at the top of the block of code and executes the first statement; when it completes, it executes the second statement; when it completes, it executes the third statement; and so on.

In most code, the flow of program execution is sequential.

2) **Branching**: We will consider only conditional branching. (Python lacks unconditional branching.) Conditional branching makes use of statements like *if* conditional *then*, *if* conditional *then else*, *if* conditional_1 *elif* conditional_2, and *if* conditional_1 *elif* conditional_2 *else* to control which instructions get executed if a conditional (or conditionals) evaluate as true.

```
# example conditional if-branch
if (conditional expression):
    instruction statement #1
instruction statement #2
instruction statement #3
instruction statement #4
```
Figure 6-4. Conditional branching. Case 1: **If-then.**

When a branch contains a single if-clause, once the program counter reaches the if-clause, the conditional expression is evaluated. If it evaluates true, then the if-clause's block of code (here,

---

Donald E. Knuth, *The Art of Computer Programming, Vol. I: Fundamental Algorithms.* Addison-Wesley. 1968. pp.4–6.

instruction statement #1) is executed. The program counter then exits the if-clause's block of code and resumes execution of the outer block of code.

Logically, if the conditional expression evaluates as true, instruction statement #1 in the example is executed, and whether the expression evaluates as true or false, instruction statements 2, 3, and 4 are then executed in sequence.

```
# example conditional if-branch
if (conditional expression A):
    instruction statement #1
if (conditional expression B):
    instruction statement #2
instruction statement #3
instruction statement #4
```

Figure 6-5. Conditional branching. Case 2: **Multiple if-then branches.**

When a conditional contains multiple if-clauses, once the program counter reaches the first if-clause, the conditional expression is evaluated. If it evaluates true, then the if-clause's block of code (here, instruction statement #1) is executed. The program counter then exits the if-clause's block of code and—in this case—executes the second conditional test. If it evaluates true, then the if-clause's block of code (instruction statement #2) is executed.

Logically, this branching allows multiple tests of the same value, and each time a test evaluates true, its block of code gets executed.

```
# example conditional if/else-branches
if (conditional expression):
    instruction statement #1
else:
    instruction statement #2
instruction statement #3
instruction statement #4
```

Figure 6-6. Conditional branching. Case 3: **If-then-else.**

When a branch contains an if-clause and an else-clause, once the program counter reaches the if-clause, the conditional expression is evaluated. If it evaluates true, then the if-clause's block of code (here, instruction statement #1) is executed. If the conditional expression evaluates false, then the program counter drops down to the else-clause, and its block of code (here, instruction statement #2) is executed. Logically, if the conditional expression evaluates as true, instruction statement #1 in the example is executed; if false, instruction statement #2 is executed; and whether the expression evaluates as true or false, instruction statements 3 and 4 are then executed in sequence.

```
# example conditional if/elif-branches
if (conditional expression A):
    instruction statement #1
elif (conditional expression B):
    instruction statement #2
instruction statement #3
instruction statement #4
```

Figure 6-7. Conditional branching. Case 4: **If-elif**

6.1 Algorithms

When a branch contains an if-clause and an elif-clause, the conditional expressions are evaluated in sequence. If an expression evaluates true, then its associated block of code is executed.

Once an if or elif's block of code is executed, the program counter drops out of the branch and resumes execution of the outer block of code.

Logically, if conditional expression A evaluates as true, instruction statement #1 in the example is executed; if conditional expression B evaluates as true, instruction statement #2 is executed; and in either case, as soon as the associated block of code is executed, the program counter then continues with instruction statements 3 and 4.

```
# example conditional if/elif/else-branches
if (conditional expression A):
    instruction statement #1
elif (conditional expression B):
    instruction statement #2
else:
    instruction statement #3
instruction statement #4
```

Figure 6-8. Conditional branching. Case 5: **If-elif-else**

When a branch contains an if-clause and an elif-clause, the conditional expressions are evaluated in sequence. If an expression evaluates true, then its associated block of code is executed. If none evaluate true, then the block of code of the else clause is executed.

Once an if or elif or else's block of code is executed, the program counter drops out of the branch and resumes execution of the outer block of code.

Logically, if conditional expression A evaluates as true, instruction statement #1 in the example is executed; if conditional expression B evaluates as true, instruction statement #2 is executed; and if neither is true, the else-clause's block of code is executed.

Finally, the program counter continues with instruction statement 4.

3) **Looping**: Python has two loop structures: the **for** loop and the **while** loop. The **for** loop keeps count of how many times it executes the instructions within the loop before it stops, and the **while** loop uses a conditional to decide whether it should execute the instructions with the loop (again).

```
# example 1 for loop
for valueVariable in someCollection:
    instruction statement #1
    instruction statement #2
instruction statement #3
instruction statement #4
```

Figure 6-9. for loop example 1

The program counter reads the for-clause, which includes a variable name that the interpreter will assign to each value, in turn, in the collection that the programmer wants the Python interpreter to iterate over.

For each value in the collection, Python will execute the for loop's block of code. In this example, for each value, Python will execute instruction statements 1 and 2 in sequence.

Once the block of code has been executed for each value in the collection, the program counter drops out of the for loop and continues executing statements in the outer block.

```
# example 2 for loop
for record in recordset:
    instruction statement #1
    instruction statement #2
instruction statement #3
instruction statement #4
```

Figure 6-10. for loop example 2

This example shows a typical use of the for loop. Here, the collection is our recordset, and as Python iterates over the recordset, it assigns a record as the value of the variable we are calling "record."

We use meaningful variable names in our code. Hence, it makes sense to name the variable holding each record "record."

Again, for each record in the recordset, Python executes instruction statements 1 and 2.

```
# example while loop
controlVar = someValue
while controlVar:
    instruction statement #1
    instruction statement #2  # the last statement modifies controlVar
                              # so that at some point controlVar
                              # evaluates as false
instruction statement #3
instruction statement #4
```

Figure 6-11. The while loop

The **while loop** is the most general loop structure. It can be made to behave like all other loop structures, including the for loop.

The block of code in a while loop runs each time the control expression or value evaluates as true. Therefore, for a while loop to run at least once, the control variable must be set before the program counter reaches the while-clause so that it evaluates in the clause as true.

The block of code associated with the while clause is then executed. In a well-formed while loop (to enhance readability), the last statement in the block should be the one that modifies the value of the control variable in some way so that eventually the control expression or value evaluates as false, at which time the program counter drops out of the loop, and executes instruction statements 3 and 4 in sequence.

6.1.4 Euclid GCD Algorithm

The Euclid GCD algorithm. Scan or click on the image to go to a lesson on YouTube on how to use the Euclid GCD algorithm. https://www.youtube.com/watch?v=JUzYl1TYMcU

Euclid, a faculty member/researcher of the Great Library of Alexandria, wrote his GCD algorithm into his most famous work, *The Elements*, about 2300 years ago. It is the oldest algorithm used in production software. Using only the remainders of integer division, it efficiently allows one to find the greatest common divisor of two integers.

```
$ bc
bc 1.07.1
Copyright 1991-1994, 1997, 1998, 2000, 2004, 2006, 2008,
2012-2017 Free Software Foundation
This is free software with ABSOLUTELY NO WARRANTY.
For details type `warranty'.
```

Figure 6-12. To understand how Euclid's GCD works, we'll do an example by hand

bc (basic calculator) is a UNIX/Linux command-line calculator.

```
88755 % 23973
16836
```

Figure 6-13. Among the basic arithmetic operators is the modulo operator

The modulo operator, or "mod," returns the integer remainder of the division of two integers. The typographical symbol that stands for the mod operator is the percent sign (%).

We can read the math statement in the example as "88755 mod 23973" or "88755 remainder 23973". Because the remainder is not zero (it is 16836), we have not yet reckoned the GCD of 88755 and 23973. We do not halt. (We continue executing the steps of the algorithm.)

```
88755 % 23973
16836
23973 % 16836
7137
```

Figure 6-14. Next step: Shift the numbers

23973 takes the place of 88755, and 16836 takes the place of 23973.

Our new arithmetic statement is: 23973 mod 16836. Their remainder is not zero (it is 7137). Hence, we do not halt. Shift the numbers. 7137 takes the place of 16836, and 16836 takes the place of 23973.

Our new arithmetic statement is: 16836 mod 7137.

Note that we are executing instructions in a loop, and at each end of a run through the loop, we inspect (or test) the remainder to determine whether we must run through the loop again.

```
16836 % 7137
2562
7137 % 2562
2013
2562 % 2013
549
2013 % 549
366
549 % 366
183
366 % 183
0
```

Figure 6-15. We keep running through the loop until we reach a remainder of zero

Zero signals that we drop out of the loop and halt. We have reached the end of the algorithm.
Our GCD is the last remainder generated before we reached zero—in this case, 183.
(To the ancient Greeks, who had no concept of zero, the remainder just disappeared, leaving them with the GCD.)

To quit **bc**, type: **quit** ENTER

```
$ factor 88755
88755: 3 5 61 97
$ factor 23973
23973: 3 61 131
```

Figure 6-16. We can use the Bash command-line tool factor to get the factors of 88755 and 23973

By inspection, we see they share only the primes 3 and 61.
3 * 61 = 183.

6.1.5 The Little Hummer Card Trick

> **Packet**: Four cards. At the start, they are all face-down, with the face card on the bottom.
> **Top card**: The card that is on the top of the packet at the time we execute the instruction.
> **Cut the packet**: Take cards off the top and put them on the bottom. In this trick, at each step in which we are told to cut the packet, we are free to choose how many cards to cut: 0, 1, 2, or 3.
> **Spread off top two cards**: Take off the top two cards together.

Figure 6-17 The little
hummer four-card packet

At the start of the trick, the packet is face-down, with the face card on bottom. We use a face card to more easily track that the algorithm works.

Figure 6-18 The little
hummer four-card trick
uses an algorithm to work

1) PUT TOP CARD ON BOTTOM.
2) TURN TOP CARD OVER, PUT BACK ON TOP.
$\left[\begin{array}{l}\text{3) CUT PACKET.} \\ \text{4) SPREAD OFF TOP 2 CARDS, TURN THEM OVER, PUT BACK ON TOP.}\end{array}\right]$ 2x
5) CUT PACKET.
6) TURN TOP CARD OVER, PUT ON BOTTOM
7) PUT TOP CARD ON BOTTOM.
8) TURN TOP CARD OVER, PUT BACK ON TOP

Note that steps 3 and 4 are in a loop that we do twice.

The variance is that we get to choose how many cards to cut at each step in which we're told to cut the packet.

If we follow the instructions exactly, when the algorithm halts, our face card will be facing one way, and our number cards will be facing the other way.

6.1.6 The Bubblesort Algorithm

Bubblesort is a famous algorithm; but because it performs so poorly, it is no longer used in production software.

Nevertheless, it is easy to set up, perform, and understand. Hence, we will use it on a small array of numbers to show how it sorts the numbers in the array.

As a demonstration, we will use three number cards to represent three numbers to be sorted in ascending order and a face card to represent a bool to track whether the array has changed.

A bool can have only one of two values: true or false. We will name this bool "hasChanged." When hasChanged is true, it will be face-up, and when hasChanged is false, it will be face-down.

Figure 6-19 There are many, many sorting algorithms

An array is a simple data structure. A data structure—using the words in the noun phrase to define it—is a way to structure data in memory for efficient access: read, update (or modify), add, or delete. The static array places its values contiguously, or side by side, in memory.

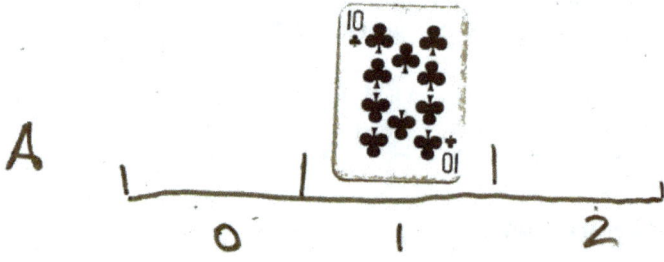

Figure 6-20 Generally, algorithms reference the elements of an array by their position in the array, or index

To read the second element in this array, named "A," we would write **A[1]**, and Python would return the value in that position, **10**.

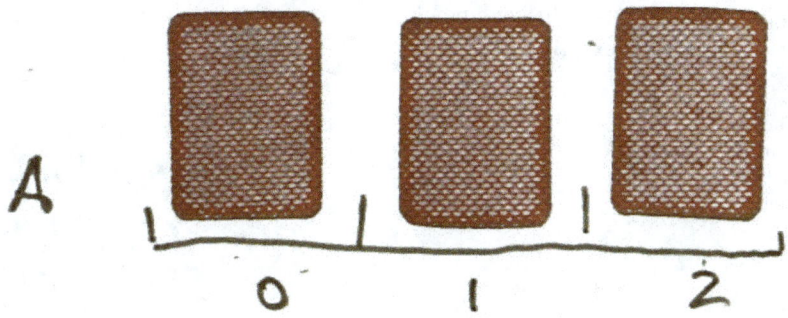

Figure 6-21 In fact, to anthropomorphize, the CPU doesn't "know" what values are in an array until it fetches them by array index and puts them into its data registers

For this reason, during this demonstration, we will keep the cards face-down until the CPU fetches them and puts them in its data registers to compare them (which in this algorithm it will do two at a time).

```
hasChanged = True
while hasChanged:
    hasChanged = False
    for 1 to (len(array) - 1):
        if (value at index) > (value at index+1):
            swap values
            hasChanged = True
```
Figure 6-22. The bubblesort algorithm in pseudocode

Note that the algorithm has two loops: an outer **while** loop and an inner **for** loop. For the algorithm to keep running, the bool "hasChanged" in the **while** statement must evaluate as true.

Because of this, it is necessary to initialize hasChanged as true.

Note that the first step after entering the **while** loop is to set hasChanged to false.

Figure 6-23 The *for* loop iterates through the array, one item at a time, from the first item to the next-to-last item

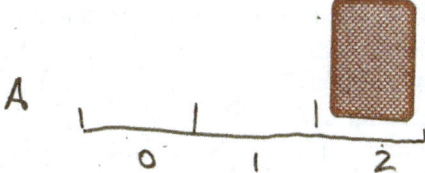

One by one, the item and its right-hand neighbor are moved into data registers and compared ("**if** (item **at** index) > (item **at** index + 1)").

Figure 6-24 The *for* loop iterates through the array, one item at a time, from the first item to the next-to-last item

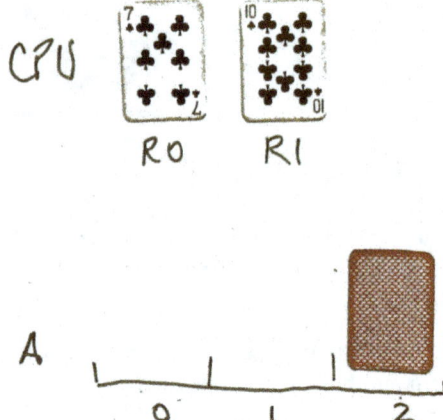

One by one, the item and its right-hand neighbor are moved into data registers and compared ("**if** (item **at** index) > (item **at** index + 1)").

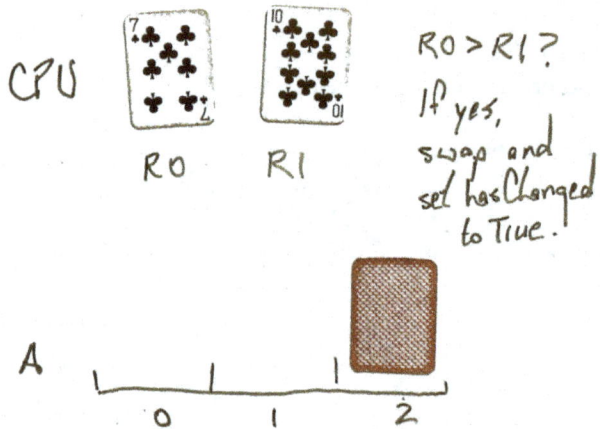

Figure 6-25 The values are compared

The values are compared; and if the left-hand value is greater than the right-hand value, two actions take place: the values are swapped in their positions in the array, and hasChanged takes the value of true.

You may have noticed that this algorithm needs to take several passes through the array to sort the items. It takes one pass through a sorted array. It is because of how many passes it needs through an array to sort it that this algorithm is no longer used in production software.

6.1.7 Notes on the Mystical History of Algorithms

As with mathematics and the sciences, the history of algorithms includes a mystical, pseudoscience aspect that continued up to the Age of Science—and beyond. Here we consider how the power and scope of algorithms narrowed over time from being able to generate new truths from a few axioms to not even being able to tell, using a general approach, whether another algorithm will eventually halt.

Figure 6-26 The Catalonian philosopher Ramon Llull (c.1232CE–c.1315CE). Click or scan the QR code to go to the Wikipedia article. https://en.wikipedia.org/wiki/Ramon_Llull

Llull's *Ars Magna* was the philosopher's attempt to generate all truths that could be known by starting with several statements as axioms; then by combining them in various ways, yield new truths.

Figure 6-27 The German polymath Gottfried Wilhelm Leibniz (1646CE–1716CE). Click or scan the QR code to go to the Wikipedia article. https://en.wikipedia.org/wiki/Gottfried_Wilhelm_Leibniz

Leibniz co-discovered The Calculus with Isaac Newton; and like Newton, he had a deeply mystical side. Inspired by Llull, Leibniz conceived of a "ratiocinator" and an "algebra of thought" by which one could arrive at truths—like who is right in a philosophical argument—mathematically.

By the end of the 19th century, mathematicians and philosophers had realized that the scope of what algorithms could do was much more modest than answering the ultimate question about life, the universe, and everything.

Figure 6-28 The German mathematician David Hilbert (1862CE–1943CE). Click or scan the QR code to go to the Wikipedia article. https://en.wikipedia.org/wiki/David_Hilbert

At the International Congress of Mathematicians, held in France in 1900 at the Sorbonne, Hilbert presented a list of ten problems for mathematicians to solve in the new century. The second problem encompasses the problem of decidability, which includes The Halting Problem.

The Halting Problem asks whether there exists a general algorithm that, given a program and its input, can determine whether that program will eventually halt or not.

Figure 6-29 The British mathematician Alan Turing (1912CE–1954CE). Click or scan the QR code to go to the Wikipedia article. https://en.wikipedia.org/wiki/Alan_Turing

Alan Turing proved in 1936 that no such general algorithm exists. In other words, the answer to The Halting Problem is: no.

6.2 An Introduction to Programming Style

Write clearly — don't be too clever.
　　　　　　　　　　　　　　—*Brian Kernighan & PJ Plauger*
　　　　　　　Rule #1 from The Elements of Programming Style

Make no mistake: rendering algorithms into code IS the business of programming.

But writing code is much more than implementing algorithms in a programming language. It includes writing and formatting our code in ways that make it easy to read and understand. The ideal—seldom achieved though we strive toward it—is that our code should be read and understood at a glance. It includes communicating to our users with messages that are easy for non-programmers to understand. Our messages should be tailored to our intended users—if they are STEM experts in a specific domain, our shared language should include domain-specific terms if appropriate. Remember: We want our users to understand what expected input is, what rendered output means, and what all error messages we write into our code mean.

Writing code also includes trapping errors—like bad input from our users—and handling those errors correctly. And it includes testing, testing, and testing our code to ensure it behaves as we intend it to—it processes expected input and handles errors correctly.

While that seems like a lot to a beginner, learning to program while keeping these requirements in mind—and implementing them into our work early on—inculcates in beginners good programming practices that will serve them well throughout their careers.

For this reason, our approach to teaching programming includes more than learning a programming language and implementing algorithms in that language.

> Always remain mindful that as a programmer, you are communicating to two audiences: users of your programs and other programmers.
> 　As in writing, in programming, we strive for a style that is simple, clear, and direct.
> 　And we document, document, document our code.

Simplicity is a great virtue but it requires hard work to achieve it and education to appreciate it. And to make matters worse: complexity sells better.
　　　　　　　　　　　　　　　　　　　　　　　　　　　Edsger Dijkstra

Kernighan and Plauger. *The Elements of Style, 2d Edition*. McGraw Hill. 1978. p2.

6.2 An Introduction to Programming Style

We begin to learn how to program with a brief discussion of what separates good programmers from bad, for much of what separates them is good programming habits. Many of the habits you acquire as you learn a craft, you acquire early on. By guiding your start in programming with good habits, we hope to save you much grief later unlearning bad habits, as well as keeping you in the company of good programmers.

> I like my code to be elegant and efficient. The logic should be straightforward to make it hard for bugs to hide... and performance close to optimal so as not to tempt people to make the code messy with unprincipled optimizations. Clean code does one thing well.
>
> —Bjarne Stroustrup
>
> Clean code is simple and direct.
>
> —Grady Brooch
>
> I could list all of the qualities that I notice in clean code, but there is one overarching quality that leads to all of them. Clean code always looks as if it were written by someone who cares.
>
> —Michael Feathers
>
> Quotes from *Clean Code: A Handbook of Agile Software Craftsmanship* by Robert C Martin.[a]
>
> [a] Robert C Martin. *Clean Code: A Handbook of Agile Software Craftsmanship*. Prentice Hall, 2009. pp. 7–8, 10.

6.2.1 Richard Hamming on Programming Style, As Told by Brian Kernighan

Richard Hamming was an American mathematician who worked on the Manhattan Project at Los Alamos and later at Bell Telephone Labs. Today, he is best known in computer science and telecommunications for Hamming codes, which detect and correct errors in strings of bits.

For his work on numerical methods and error-detecting and error-correcting codes, he received the Turing Award in 1968. Today, the IEEE has a Richard W. Hamming Award, whose recipients are cited for "exceptional contributions to information sciences, systems and technology."

> Dick was the person who started me writing books, which has turned out to be a good thing. He had a fairly low opinion of most programmers, who he felt were poorly trained if at all. I can still hear him saying, "We give them a dictionary and grammar rules, and we say, 'Kid, you're now a great programmer.'"[*]

According to Brian Kernighan, Richard Hamming had strong opinions about teaching how to program. His "dictionary and grammar rules" observation refers to teaching students the names of commands or functions, as well as how to string them together, with no mention of style.

> He felt that programming should be taught as writing was taught. There should be a notion of style that separated poor code from good code, and programmers should be taught how to write well and appreciate good style.[†]

As an aside: At the time Kernighan talked to Hamming on this subject, Kernighan was an intern at Bell Labs and a graduate student working toward his Ph.D. at Princeton.

---

[*] Brian Kernighan. *UNIX: A History and a Memoir*, 2020. pp.12–13.

[†] *ibid.*

He and I disagreed on how this might be accomplished, but his idea was sound, and it led directly to my first book, *The Elements of Programming Style*, which I published in 1974 with P.J. "Bill" Plauger, who was at the time in the adjacent office. Bill and I emulated Strunk and White's *The Elements of Style* by showing a sequence of poorly written examples, and explaining how to improve each of them.[‡]

The Elements of Programming Style uses Fortran as its implementation language. However, many of its style rules, including "Write clearly—don't be too clever," are applicable in all languages.

We will start our introduction to programming style by understanding that programmers must be effective communicators. You should design your code so that it is easy to read, easy to understand, and therefore easy to maintain.

All things being equal, a simple solution is preferable to a complex one. Writing programs can be compared to writing essays in several ways. For one, your first version of a working program should be thought of as a rough draft, and there is room for improvement.

Experienced programmers know how hard it can be for beginners to turn "a dictionary and some grammars rules" into a working program that meets specifications—after all, we all start as beginners.

And when you finally get your first programs running, you should be proud of your achievement.

But as beginners, you should also be aware that the first draft of working code is the equivalent of a rough draft; and as you gain experience, you will start looking for ways to improve your code—to make it faster, or simpler, or more readable.

> As we develop our code and implement our algorithms, we use meaningful names for our variables, functions, classes, and files. Code written thus is known as **"self-documenting code."**
>
> As we develop, we include comments in our code, as well as information to the users of our code like type hints—or, at a minimum, we comment in our code where we will insert user documentation.
>
> As we develop, we include whatever **error-trapping code** we know we must include to make our code robust—or, at a minimum, we comment where we will insert our error-trapping code, including what needs to be trapped. This includes **garbage filters** to catch and handle bad input.
>
> In **test-driven development (TDD)**, we write unit tests to test our code **BEFORE** we develop our code. We use the specification of what our code should do, as well as whatever example for input/output that we're given, to guide us in our writing of the tests. Then we develop our code toward clearing the errors that our unit tests throw and continue to do so until our code passes all tests.

Chapter Summary

Algorithms + data structures = programs. Niklaus Wirth, the creator of the Pascal programming language, wrote this in 1975 C.E. Algorithms are the very essence of programming. Finding algorithms that solve problems efficiently is an always active field of research in computer science.

[‡] *ibid.*

Floating-Point Numbers   7

Finding patterns and relationships in quantitative data collected in or gleaned from experiments is a common activity in STEM research. In this chapter, we will consider floating-point numbers datatype used in Python in modern digital computers, focusing on their accuracy and precision.

7.1 Floating-Point Numbers

> **What You Need to Know**
> Because memory and data registers are not infinite in size, calculations using numbers with fractional parts are subject to approximate results.
> Additionally, the numbers themselves, as they change from base-10 to base-2 and back again, are subject to issues affecting their accuracy and precision.
> STEM professionals, dependent as they are on using quantitative data, must especially be sensitive to the accuracy and precision of the data they collect and compute with.
> Numerical analysts develop algorithms to minimize the errors that arise in numerical computations.
> The IEEE754 was developed as a portable standard to minimize errors and reliably handle exceptions in numerical computations.
> Other strategies to deal with the issues of accuracy and precision of fixed-size data include use of arbitrary-precision math algorithms and computer algebra systems, both of which are included in SciPy (mpmath and SymPy, respectively).

> Significant discrepancies [between the computed and the true result] are very rare, too rare to worry about all the time, yet not rare enough to ignore.
> —William Kahan, chief architect of the IEEE754 specification for implementing floating-point numbers.

Figure 7-1 Scan or click on the image to go to the Wikipedia article on numerical analysis.
https://en.wikipedia.org/wiki/Numerical_analysis

Figure 7-2 Representative base-10 number

In this TI-59 calculator display, we are shown a signed 6-digit mantissa, as well as a signed exponent.

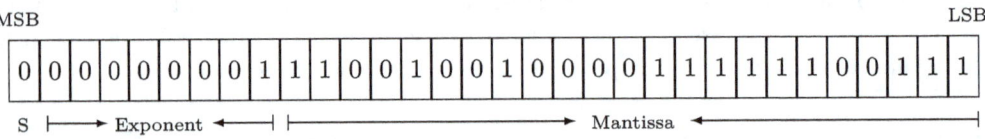

Figure 7-3 A 32-bit floating-point register holding the value of 3.14159_{10}

MSB means "most significant bit," while **LSB** means "least significant bit." **S** means "sign of mantissa": **0** is positive, and **1** is negative.

```
$ python
Python 3.12.3 (main, Jun  1 2024, 15:42:43) [GCC 11.4.0] on linux
Type "help", "copyright", "credits" or "license" for more information.
>>> import sys
>>> sys.float_info
sys.float_info(max=1.7976931348623157e+308, max_exp=1024, max_10_exp=308, min=2.2250738585072014e-308, min_exp=-1021, min_10_exp=-307, dig=15, mant_dig=53, epsilon=2.220446049250313e-16, radix=2, rounds=1)
>>>
```

Figure 7-4 Getting info on your system's floating-point numbers. Click on the image to go to online article at python.org. https://docs.python.org/3/library/sys.html

When we invoke the Python interpreter on the Bash command line, once the interpreter launches, it presents an interactive shell.

Python's interactive shell is primitive. For this reason, other interactive shells for Python are available. SciPy's interactive shell is **ipython**, and that is the one we'll mostly use.

sys is a built-in module that, according to the docs on python.org, "provides access to some variables used or maintained by the interpreter and to functions that interact strongly with the interpreter."

7.1 Floats

To make the module's objects and functions available to us, we have to **import** the module into our session.

sys.float_info returns a named tuple containing "low-level information about the precision and internal representation [of floats]. The values correspond to the various floating-point constants defined in the standard header file float.h for the C programming language."

With few exceptions, humans work with numbers in base-10, whereas modern digital computers store and manipulate numbers in base-2. When working with natural numbers $\mathbb{N}$, converting from base-10 to base-2 and back is straightforward.

To extend the set of natural numbers $\mathbb{N}$ into the integers $\mathbb{Z}$, commonly the leftmost bit (most significant bit, or MSB) is designated the sign bit, and negative binary numbers are reckoned by an algorithm called "two's complement."

Regardless of which base we're working in (base-2, base-3, base-10, etc.), dividing one integer by another yields rational numbers, the set of which is designated by $\mathbb{Q}$.

Also regardless of base, the result from dividing one integer by another yields either of the following:

(a) An integer
(b) A number with a fractional part that terminates
(c) A number with a pattern of digits in the fractional part that repeats infinitely

Which rational numbers $\mathbb{Q}$ have fractional parts that terminate and fractional parts with repeating patterns of digits depends on which base you're doing your math in.

For example, $(1/3)_{10}$, or one-third in base-10, as a decimal fraction is a repeating pattern of 3s, that is, $(0.333\ldots)_{10}$, whereas in base-3, the fractional part terminates $(0.1)_3$.

Likewise, $(1/10)_{10}$, or one-tenth in base-10, as a decimal fraction terminates; that is, it is $(0.1)_{10}$, whereas in base-2, $(1/10)_{10}$, $(0.000110011001100110011\ldots)_2$, has a pattern of ones and zeroes ($\overline{0011}$) that repeats infinitely.

Because the length of floating-point registers is fixed, this results in an approximation of $(1/10)_{10}$ in our computers' internal representation of it, and this inaccuracy in turn affects the accuracy of computer calculations using $(1/10)_{10}$.

```
>>> .1 + .1 + .1 == .3 # is the LHS equal to the RHS?
False
>>> round(.3, 17)
0.3
>>> round(.1 + .1 + .1, 17)
0.30000000000000004
```

Figure 7-5 Demonstrating how the inaccuracy of the computer's internal representation of $(0.1)_{10}$ affects computation

This demonstration shows that if you simply compare floats in conditional branching or looping, the computer may not follow the branch or terminate the loop.

Care must be taken when working with floats.

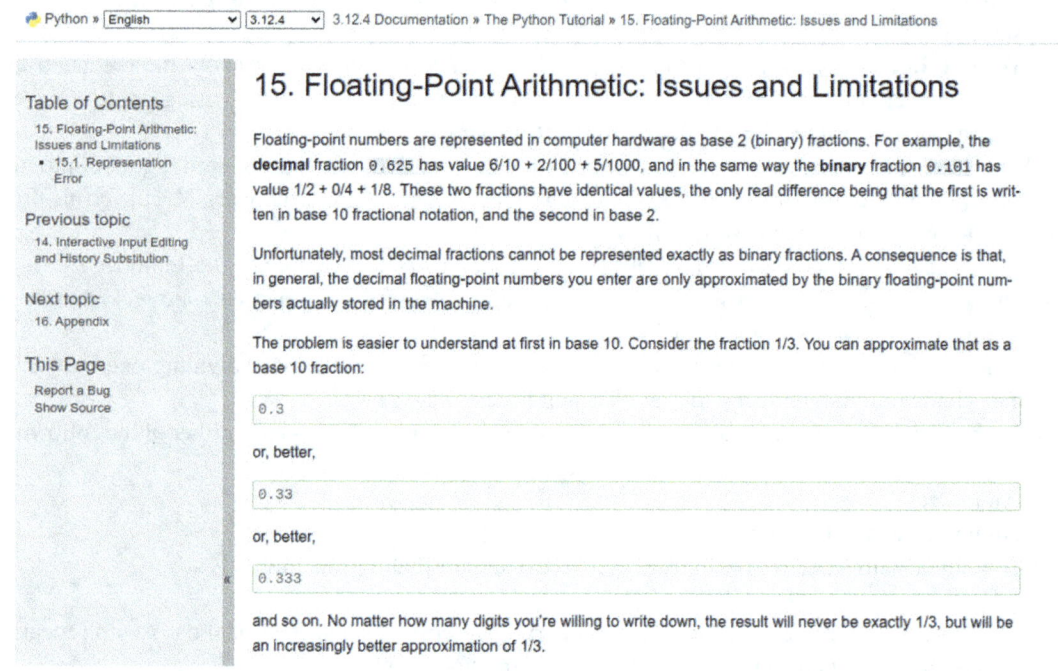

Figure 7-6 Floating-point arithmetic: issues and limitations. Click on the image to go to online article at python.org. https://docs.python.org/3/tutorial/floatingpoint.html

python.org devotes a chapter on the issues of accuracy and precision regarding **floats**.

7.2 Working with Floats: Rules of Thumb

7.2.1 If Possible, Algebraically Work Through Your Problem as Far as You Can in a Computer Algebra System (Like SymPy), and Substitute Numbers for Variables Only in the Final step(s)

7.2.2 Never Round Intermediate Results: Round End Results At Least To The Accuracy Of The Input Floats

7.2.3 If Possible, Re-arrange Calculations Using Floats And Integers So Integers Are Brought In At The End

7.2.4 Round When Comparing Floats: Use Only As Much Accuracy As Needed Or Warranted By The Accuracy Of The Input Floats

7.2.5 Do Not Use Floats If Integers Will Suffice

7.2.6 Do Not Represent Floats In Text Form In Files Or As Strings Unless Absolutely Necessary

7.2.7 If Working With Large Numbers, Rescale, If Possible, To Map To Values Closer To One

7.2.8 Subtracting Two Nearly Equal Numbers Results In A Large Loss Of Precision And Generally Should Be Avoided

7.2.9 Use Care When Assuming Associativity

In[1] the last sections of this chapter, we'll look at an alternative to using floats, as well as a tool to help us improve the accuracy of expressions we write using floats as input.

We start by looking at *mpmath*.

7.3 Arbitrary Precision Math with *mpmath*

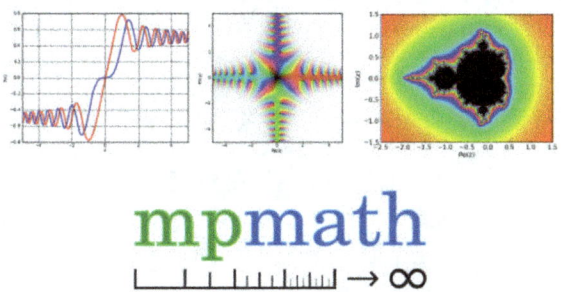

Figure 7-7 Website of *mpmath*. Click on the image to go to the website. https://mpmath.org/

mpmath is installed with **SymPy**, but can be installed stand-alone.

From the mpmath website:

mpmath can be used as an arbitrary-precision substitute for Python's float/complex types and math/cmath modules, but also does much more advanced mathematics. Almost any calculation can be performed just as well at 10-digit or 1000-digit precision, with either real or complex numbers, and in many cases mpmath implements efficient algorithms that scale well for extremely high precision work (mpmath.org. https://mpmath.org/).

mpmath uses internal binary representations of numbers stored in system memory as **bigints** to do its calculations, and results are represented as base-10 numbers. You can set the precision of numbers

---
[1] Items 5–9 taken from *Numbers and Computers, 2d Edition* by Ronald T. Kneusel. Springer, 2017. pp. 130–131.

in your calculations either by the number of bits or by the number of decimal places. By default, **mpmath** precision is set to 53 bits, or 15 decimal places. **It is important that, if you are using** *mpmath* **for extended precision in your calculations, you set the desired precision of the results as an initialization step.** Failure to do so will almost certainly lead to inaccurate results.

```
>>> from sys import float_info
>>> from mpmath import mp, fac
>>> # note mant_dig (mantissa length in base-2) & dig (mantissa length in base-10)
>>> float_info
sys.float_info(max=1.7976931348623157e+308, max_exp=1024, max_10_exp=308,
min=2.2250738585072014e-308, min_exp=-1021, min_10_exp=-307, dig=15, mant_dig=53,
epsilon=2.220446049250313e-16, radix=2, rounds=1)
>>> mp.dps = 78 # normally, users adjust precision by base-10 digits of precision
>>> int(fac(69))
171122452428141311372468338881272839092270544893520369393648040923257279754140647424000000000000000000
>>> print(mp) # note prec (bit length) & dps (mantissa length in base-10 digits)
Mpmath settings:
  mp.prec = 262              [default: 53]
  mp.dps = 78                [default: 15]
  mp.trap_complex = False    [default: False]
```

Figure 7-8 An *mpmath* example

mpmath has its own floating-point implementation, and it stores its numbers in binary in system memory as **bigints**. Nevertheless, it has its own issues regarding accuracy and precision.

For more, please read the documentation on the **mpmath** site.

7.4   Improving the Accuracy of Floating-Point Calculations with *Herbie*

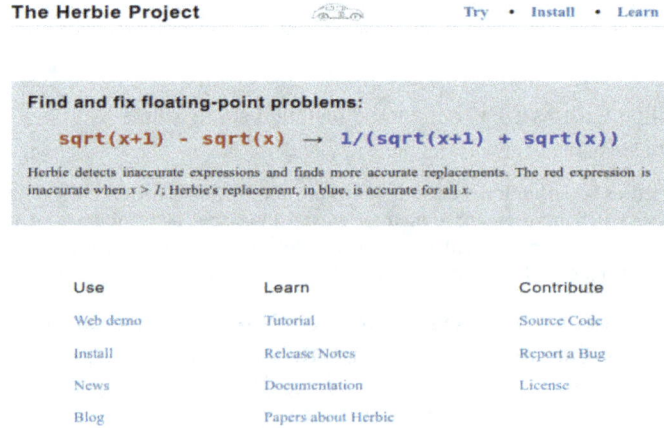

Figure 7-9   Website of *herbie*. Click on the image to go to website. https://herbie.uwplse.org/

herbie requires **rust** and **racket** to compile.

7.4 herbie

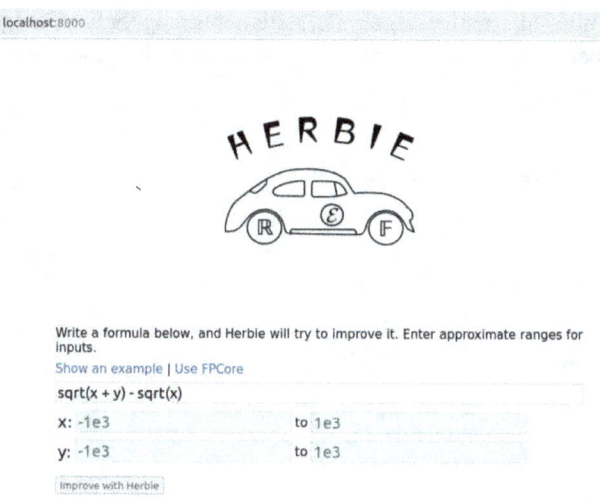

Figure 7-10 *herbie* running through a web interface on laptop

Once *herbie* is installed and the absolute path to the **racket** bin directory has been added to your PATH, you can launch it on the command line with: **herbie web**.

In the web interface, you pass in your algebraic equation with variables that will take floats, and you pass in the possible numeric ranges of the floats; then you click the button **Improve with Herbie**.

Figure 7-11 The top of *herbie*'s result page

herbie has found nine alternative algebraic statements, algebraically equivalent to the one we input. Over the number ranges for the variables we've provided, the most accurate two minimize inaccuracies quite significantly.

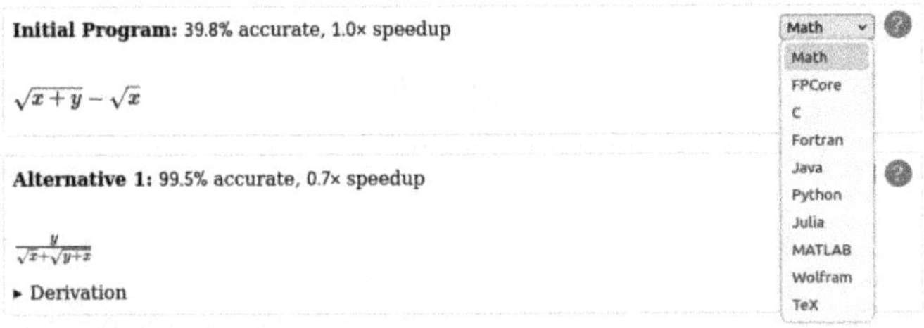

Initial Program: 39.8% accurate, 1.0× speedup

$$\sqrt{x+y} - \sqrt{x}$$

Alternative 1: 99.5% accurate, 0.7× speedup

$$\frac{y}{\sqrt{x} + \sqrt{y+x}}$$

▸ Derivation

Figure 7-12 The bottom of *herbie*'s result page

herbie enumerates the alternatives.

Not only that, *herbie* offers rewrites of the algebraic expressions in a drop-down menu.

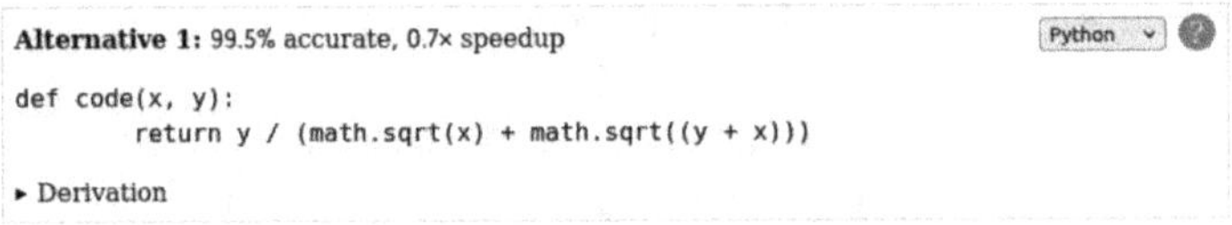

Alternative 1: 99.5% accurate, 0.7× speedup

```
def code(x, y):
        return y / (math.sqrt(x) + math.sqrt((y + x)))
```

▸ Derivation

Figure 7-13 *herbie*'s implementation of its most accurate alternative in Python

In coding this, you should remember to ensure that input for **x** and **y** lie within the ranges you provided.

Chapter Summary

System memory and data registers, being finite in length, result in a loss of accuracy and precision in floating-point numbers, or **floats**. The IEEE754 standard for floating-point arithmetic is designed to minimize the inaccuracies and imprecisions that arise in multiple calculations so that the approximate results remain accurate. STEM researchers who take care in the calculations of their float data can ensure, or even improve, the accuracy of their results.

Introduction to Python   8

The creator of Python, Guido van Rossum, designed Python to be easy to learn and easy to start using productively. And he made it free. Python can be learned and put to use in the lab and at the bench after one semester of instruction. This, plus the enthusiastic support of STEM researchers who've developed the libraries for it that are all together known as "SciPy," makes Python the general programming language of choice in the STEM community. In this chapter, we will learn about the Python interpreter and the IPython interactive shell.

8.1 Python Primer

> Python is an easy to learn, powerful programming language. It has efficient high-level data structures and a simple but effective approach to object-oriented programming. Pythons elegant syntax and dynamic typing, together with its interpreted nature, make it an ideal language for scripting and rapid application development
>
> —From *The Python Tutorial* on https://docs.python.org

Guido van Rossum wrote Python with the two design goals in mind: to make it easy for adults to learn and put to use.

He succeeded.

Within the 36-classroom hours of a single fall or spring class, a researcher can learn enough Python to write functions or scripts that automate tasks at the bench or allow them efficiently to process their data or their lab's data.

And nine or so of those classroom hours are spent getting familiar with using the Bash shell on Linux systems!*

---

* As you will quickly see, we do a fair amount of learning how to program on the terminal using Bash tools. The result is that students can work as comfortably and productively at the terminals of remote supercomputers as they can on the graphical tools in the graphical desktop environments of their laptops and desktops.

© James R. Derry 2026
J. R. Derry, *Introduction to Programming for Researchers*,
https://doi.org/10.1007/979-8-8688-1615-4_8

8.1.1 Python Comes with Built-Ins: Built-In Functions, Built-In Datatypes and Collections, and Built-In Modules

A	E	L	R
abs()	enumerate()	len()	range()
aiter()	eval()	list()	repr()
all()	exec()	locals()	reversed()
anext()			round()
any()	F	M	
ascii()	filter()	map()	S
	float()	max()	set()
B	format()	memoryview()	setattr()
bin()	frozenset()	min()	slice()
bool()			sorted()
breakpoint()	G	N	staticmethod()
bytearray()	getattr()	next()	str()
bytes()	globals()		sum()
		O	super()
C	H	object()	
callable()	hasattr()	oct()	T
chr()	hash()	open()	tuple()
classmethod()	help()	ord()	type()
compile()	hex()		
complex()		P	V
	I	pow()	vars()
D	id()	print()	
delattr()	input()	property()	Z
dict()	int()		zip()
dir()	isinstance()		
divmod()	issubclass()		_
	iter()		__import__()

Figure 8-1 Python's built-in functions. Click on the text image above to go to online documentation at **python.org**. https://docs.python.org/3/library/functions.html

Python instruction statements are made up of reserved words, or functions, or a combination of the two.

Built-in Types

The following sections describe the standard types that are built into the interpreter.

The principal built-in types are numerics, sequences, mappings, classes, instances and exceptions.

Some collection classes are mutable. The methods that add, subtract, or rearrange their members in place, and don't return a specific item, never return the collection instance itself but None.

Figure 8-2 Python built-in types. Click on the image to go to online documentation at **python.org**. https://docs.python.org/3/library/stdtypes.html

The principal built-in types we'll use are bools, numerics, the string, the list, the dictionary, the tuple, and the set.

8.1 Intro to Python

Table 8-1 Some Python built-in collections

Python collections

Collection	Abbr	Enclosure	Ordered	Mutable	Items
String	str	' ', " "	YES	NO	index/value
List	list	[ ]	YES	YES	index/value
Dictionary	dict	{ }	NO	YES	key/value
Tuple	tuple	( )	YES	NO	index/value
Set	set	{ }	NO	YES	keys only

Python collections can be thought of as high-level data structures (or abstract datatypes that, as objects, also contain their own methods, attributes, and overloaded operators).

Python collections organize in memory data and other Python collections(!) in ways that allow efficiently four operations:

(1) Read a value (the most commonly performed operation)
(2) Add a value
(3) Update a value
(4) Delete a value

Note that immutable collections forbid adding, updating, and deleting values—and yet, they're still useful!

Python by design is a modular language, meaning that the interpreter contains only core functionality. To extend its functionality, we import modules that contain specialized objects and functions.

8.1.2 Python Comes with a Built-In Error-Reporting Module Called the Traceback

The Traceback deserves special mention, especially since you're going to see it a lot as you write and run Python statements. The Traceback helps you find and fix errors in the Python you write and maintain.

In this example, we invoke a variable that we have not created and instantiated with an assignment statement. The Python interpreter searches its symbol table for variables by name when they're invoked. In this case, no entry for a variable named *testVar* exists in the symbol table, hence the *NameError* listed on the last line.

Finding and fixing bugs when an interpreter or compiler throws cryptic or even no warning or error messages can be a hard, frustrating slog. In Python, the Traceback is your friend, given the useful information that it provides for finding errors and understanding them.

Python Module Index

__future__	*Future statement definitions*
__main__	*The environment where top-level code is run. Covers command-line interfaces, import-time behavior, and `` `__name__ == '__main__'` ``.*
_thread	*Low-level threading API.*

a

abc	*Abstract base classes according to :pep:`3119`.*
aifc	**Deprecated:** *Read and write audio files in AIFF or AIFC format.*
argparse	*Command-line option and argument parsing library.*
array	*Space efficient arrays of uniformly typed numeric values.*
ast	*Abstract Syntax Tree classes and manipulation.*
asynchat	**Deprecated:** *Support for asynchronous command/response protocols.*
asyncio	*Asynchronous I/O.*
asyncore	**Deprecated:** *A base class for developing asynchronous socket handling services.*
atexit	*Register and execute cleanup functions.*
audioop	**Deprecated:** *Manipulate raw audio data.*

b

base64	*RFC 4648: Base16, Base32, Base64 Data Encodings; Base85 and Ascii85*
bdb	*Debugger framework.*
binascii	*Tools for converting between binary and various ASCII-encoded binary representations.*
bisect	*Array bisection algorithms for binary searching.*
builtins	*The module that provides the built-in namespace.*
bz2	*Interfaces for bzip2 compression and decompression.*

Figure 8-3 Python built-in modules. Click on the image to go to online documentation. https://docs.python.org/3.13/py-modindex.html

```
In [1]: testVar
---------------------------------------------------------------------------
NameError                                 Traceback (most recent call last)
Cell In[1], line 1
----> 1 testVar

NameError: name 'testVar' is not defined
```

Figure 8-4 An example of an error invoking the *Traceback*

8.1.3   The IPython Interactive Shell I

Figure 8-5 The IPython interactive shell. Click or scan the QR code to go to the IPython site, which includes online documentation. https://ipython.org/

8.1 Intro to Python

We start our introduction to Python in the IPython interactive shell.

The IPython interactive shell was created and developed by the Colombian physicist Fernando Pérez, currently a faculty researcher at UC Berkeley.*

IPython is the interactive shell of the SciPy software stack. We will use it in this book and course. On the Bash shell, launch IPython:

```
$ ipython
```

When IPython launches, it displays a header that includes the version of the Python interpreter that you're interacting with, as well as the version of IPython. The prompt In [1]: with flashing cursor signals that the Python interpreter that backends the IPython session is ready for input:

```
$ ipython
Python 3.13.2 (main, Feb  8 2025, 12:42:06) [GCC 11.4.0]
Type 'copyright', 'credits' or 'license' for more information
IPython 8.32.0 -- An enhanced Interactive Python. Type '?' for help.

In [1]:
```

An instance of the Python interpreter is running behind this interactive shell. Python statements that you enter on the command line are parsed one at a time; and if the statements are well-formed—that is, free of grammar, spelling, and punctuation errors—they are then passed on for further processing, until they are interpreted into instructions for the machine to execute. Output, if any, is printed on the following line.

Let's start with something simple, the arithmetic statement **1 + 1**

```
In [1]: 1 + 1
Out[1]: 2
```

When we hit RETURN, we are marking the end of the statement. The parser reads the statement as string input. It scans the line of characters left to right, character by character; and because there are no errors, the statement is passed on for evaluation.

And what does this involve at the level of memory and the CPU? The numbers and the instructions to add them and handle the output are stored in memory and manipulated as strings of ones and zeros. Because the numbers are ints (integers), each number is moved into a general data register on a CPU core, an instruction to add the contents of the two registers is executed (with the result stored in one of the registers); finally, the instruction is executed to move the result to STDOUT for display in base-10.

As you can see, in executing even simple statements in a high-level programming language, the computer does a lot of work "under the hood" that we don't see or have to think about. This work is itself the execution of yet more code. When we write and implement our own code, we are leveraging the code of others. From Python to the microcode of controllers on our system boards and the CPU, it's code all the way down.

(And yes, it sometimes amazes even the experts that it all works as well as it does, given the complexity of all the interworking parts.)

---

* The Python interpreter has its own interactive shell. However, that interactive shell lacks functionality, making it unsuitable for anything beyond the simplest uses.

```
In [2]: type(2)
Out[2]: int

In [3]: type(2.)
Out[3]: float

In [4]: type(2j)
Out[4]: complex
```

Figure 8-6 There are three numeric datatypes that you can work with using out-of-the-box Python: integers (*int*), floating-point numbers (*float*), and complex numbers (*complex*)

Here, we use the built-in function **type**() to identify the datatype of the numbers. Note that by appending a decimal point to an int, we render it a float.

Ints are whole numbers. Floats can have fractional parts. But because computer memory is finite, **all** floats—even the ones that represent irrational numbers like π, e, $\sqrt{2}$—are rational numbers. That is to say, they terminate. It is this fundamental limitation of numeric computation on computers that motivated the creation of computer algebra systems like **SymPy**.

Floats have other issues that STEM researchers who use them must be aware of. We will consider one at the end of this section.

```
In [5]: type(True)
Out[5]: bool

In [6]: type(False)
Out[6]: bool
```

Figure 8-7 The simplest datatype is the **bool**, which has only two states: true or false

```
In [7]: 7 < 5
Out[7]: False

In [8]: 5 < 7
Out[8]: True
```

Figure 8-8 The Python interpreter can evaluate mathematical expressions

When it tests an equality or inequality, it returns a **bool**.

```
In [9]: 'a' in 'sack'
Out[9]: True

In [10]: 'a' in 'truck'
Out[10]: False
```

Figure 8-9 The Python interpreter can also evaluate whether an item is in a collection

Here, we ask the interpreter to determine if "a" is in two different strings.

Python follows the **IEEE754** technical standard for handling floating-point numbers and their operations (click the boldfaced hyperlink to go to the Wikipedia article on IEEE754).

```
In [11]: .1 + .1 + .1 == .3
Out[11]: False
```

Figure 8-10 In Python, *.1 + .1 + .1* does *NOT* equal *.3*, as we can see in this example

While floating-point numbers are very useful in STEM research, they do come with their own issues and caveats. We looked at these more in-depth in **Chapter 7**. You should be familiar with these issues and caveats if your research data is quantitative—especially if that data must undergo extensive processing.

(Click the boldfaced hyperlink to go to Chapter 7.)

8.1.4 In Python, Everything Is an Object

In Python, everything is an object. Here, we use "object" to mean "object" as in "object-oriented programming language."

Rather than provide a definition of objects, for now, I wish to point out several features of objects that we can make immediate use of as beginners:

(1) **Methods and attributes:** A **method** is a function bound to an object. An attribute is data that describes the object. In Python, we invoke a method or attribute by appending it after the object name with a dot (.).
(2) **Method chaining:** We can chain methods together. The object that the methods transform or modify does so in the order that the methods are chained.
(3) **Operator overloading:** By **operator**, we mean an operator like the arithmetic operators (+, -, *, /). In Python, we can overload these operators so that they do more than work on numbers—in Python, the addition and multiplication operators are overloaded to work on strings!
(4) Each instance of an object in session memory carries with it its own copy of all the methods and attributes available to it. This means that a Python string, for example, needs to occupy much more memory than its equivalent C string.

```
int.
     as_integer_ratio()  denominator   mro         to_bytes
     bit_length          from_bytes    numerator
     conjugate           imag          real
```

Figure 8-11 Methods and attributes bound to integer objects in Python

In IPython, we can bring them up by typing: **int.** followed by ⎡TAB⎤

```
list.
     append()  copy()    extend()  insert()  pop()      reverse()
     clear()   count()   index()   mro()     remove()   sort()
```

Figure 8-12 Methods and attributes bound to lists in Python

"Method" is the word used to describe a function bound to an object. Like functions, methods may or may not take arguments.

```
str.
 capitalize()    expandtabs()    isalpha()        isnumeric()      ljust()        replace()       rstrip()        title()
 casefold()      find()          isascii()        isprintable()    lower()        rfind()         split()         translate()
 center()        format()        isdecimal()      isspace()        lstrip()       rindex()        splitlines()    upper()
 count()         format_map()    isdigit()        istitle()        maketrans()    rjust()         startswith()    zfill()
 encode()        index()         isidentifier()   isupper()        mro()          rpartition()    strip()
 endswith()      isalnum()       islower()        join()           partition()    rsplit()        swapcase()
```

Figure 8-13 Methods and attributes bound to strings in Python

Strings are frequently used in programming—to communicate with users, to read the contents of text files into memory, to write data out to text files. This may explain the large number of methods bound to Python strings.

```python
In [12]: with open('datafile/reformatted_Unigene.fa') as inFile:
   ...:     # in the next line, we chain methods
   ...:     LoS = inFile.read().splitlines()
   ...:     # the first method, .read(), reads the contents
   ...:     # of the file into session memory as a single string.
   ...:     # the second method, .splitlines(),
   ...:     # is a string method that splits the string
   ...:     # along newline characters, and puts the lines
   ...:     # in order into a list.
   ...:     # the result is that the file's contents are held
   ...:     # in memory as a list-of-strings, or LoS
```

Figure 8-14 Method chaining

Method chaining allows us to tell the Python interpreter how to work on an object several steps at a time. Without chaining, in this example, we would have had to tell the Python interpreter in a nested function or across several statements we want the machine to read the file contents into memory as a single string, then tell the interpreter we want the machine to split that single string along newline characters into a list of strings.

```python
In [13]: # in python, the addition operator (+)
   ...: # is overloaded for strings.
   ...: # the overloaded operator is called
   ...: # the concatenation operator.
   ...: 'hello ' + 'world'
Out[13]: 'hello world'
```

Figure 8-15 In Python, we can overload operators

In Python, we can overload operators so that they behave differently than they were originally designed to do. For example, the addition operator was originally designed to add numbers.

In Python, the addition operator has been overloaded to concatenate strings. When used this way with strings, we say that we are concatenating strings, and we call the operator the **concatenation operator**.

Chapter Summary

Unlike Fortran and R, programming languages designed for use by STEM researchers, Python is a general programming language. It was designed by its creator, Guido van Rossum, to be easy for adults to learn and easy for beginners to start putting it to use. This has made it very popular within the STEM community, and researchers have written a comprehensive software stack called "SciPy" to enhance Python's usefulness to STEM researchers. Even as we learn Python, we will also learn how to use SciPy software and libraries for working with datasets.

Using Python As a Calculator 9

In the last chapter, we were introduced to the Python interpreter. We often think of interpreters in terms of programming. However, Python and the SciPy libraries can all together be used as a powerful scientific graphing calculator. The IPython interactive shell or Jupyter notebook (both created by Fernando Pérez) can make your desktop, laptop, or tablet your go-to device for quick, easy, and sometimes specialized calculations.

> On the IPython interactive shell or in Jupyter notebooks, Python can be used as a calculator. The Python and SciPy communities offer free, open source, and powerful libraries that provide researchers with tools to supplement or even replace graphing and scientific calculators.
> (Of course, Python is a general-purpose programming language, meaning you can do so much more with it!)
> In this chapter and the next few, we will look at what you can do with Python as a calculator.

9.1 Datetime I: Duration of the COVID-19 Pandemic

As noted in the Bash chapter on datetime, time is a fundamental dimension in science and engineering. Phenomena evolve over time. In many plots in which time is a dimension, it is the domain (X) over which the values of other dimensions (Y) are plotted. Accordingly, it figures prominently in our understanding of the phenomenological world.

On March 11, 2020, the World Health Organization (WHO) characterized the COVID-19 outbreak as a pandemic. On May 5, 2023, the WHO declared an end to the global Public Health Emergency (PHE) for COVID-19.

Although it is difficult to mark the end of a pandemic, for our purposes, we will take these dates as marking the start and end of the pandemic.

Given that, how many days was the COVID-19 outbreak considered a pandemic?

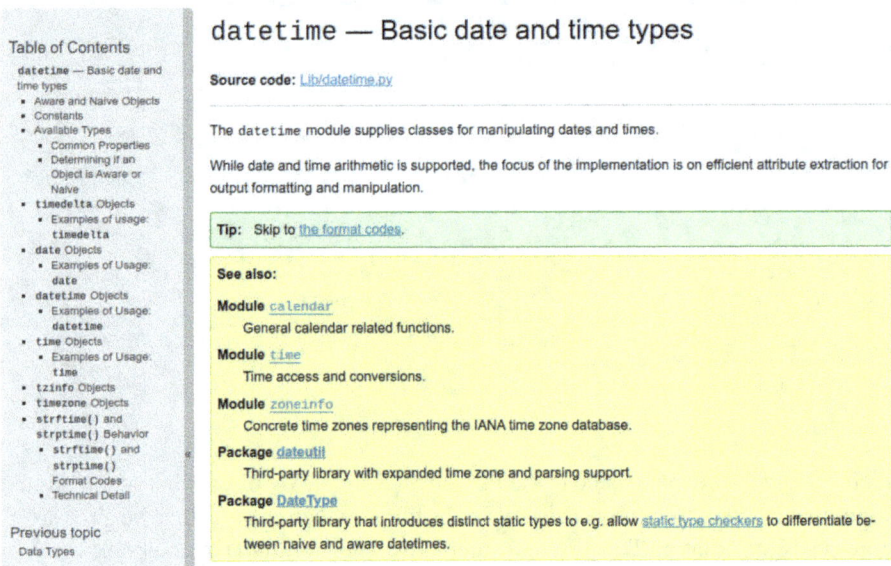

Figure 9-1 Click the image above to go to the online documentation at **python.org** on the **datetime** module. https://docs.python.org/3/library/datetime.html

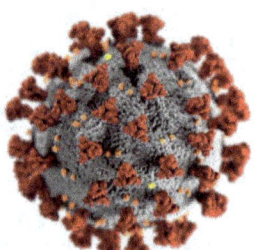

Figure 9-2 This illustration, created at the Centers for Disease Control and Prevention (CDC), reveals ultrastructural morphology exhibited by coronaviruses. Credit: Alissa Eckert, MSMI, Dan Higgins, MAMS. Public domain. https://phil.cdc.gov/details.aspx?pid=23312 Click the image above to go to the Wikipedia article on the COVID-19 pandemic. https://en.wikipedia.org/wiki/COVID-19_pandemic

```
In [1]: from datetime import date

In [2]: date1, date2= date(2020, 3, 11), date(2023, 5, 11)

In [3]: (date2 - date1).days
Out[3]: 1156
```

Figure 9-3 Calculating the number of days between the start and end of the COVID-19 pandemic

Note that straight entry of Python statements does not allow for comments.

```
In [1]: from datetime import date
   ...: # enter dates into date() function
   ...: # as three integers: (year, month, day)
   ...: # start: March 11, 2020
   ...: # end: May 11, 2023
In [2]: date1, date2= date(2020, 3, 11), date(2023, 5, 11)
   ...: # return difference in days
In [3]: (date2 - date1).days
Out[3]: 1156
```

Figure 9-4 Annotations and comments inserted into the input

Often, to comment and save space in the screenshots, I refine and reformat the IPython input and make the figure I present.

But like everybody, I input the statements as they appear in Figure 9-3, and I redo the input later.

In other words, don't try to input the statements as they appear in this figure; rather, input them as they're input in the previous figure.

9.2 Datetime II: Solving Date Problems

Out of curiosity, Danny Harris wants to know how many days old he is. He was born on March 29, 2007. He also wants to know on which day of the week he was born.

```
In [1]: from datetime import date
   ...: ''' enter dates into date() function
   ...:     as 3 integers: (year, month, day).
   ...:     date.today() returns a date object
   ...:     for the current day
   ...: '''
   ...: date1, today = date(2007, 3, 29), date.today()
   ...: # return difference in days
   ...: print((today - date1).days)
   ...: # print specifies '%A' returns day of week
   ...: print(date1.strftime('%A'))
6554
Thursday
```

Figure 9-5 Calculating the number of days from *today* and day-of-week

Again, there are just four statements you have to enter into the interactive shell:

from datetime import date
date1, today = date(2007, 3, 29), date.today() # multi-assignment statement
(today - date1).days # entered into its own input cell, outputs without print()
date1.strftime('%A') # no need to invoke print() here, either.

Now Danny wants to know on which date he was twice as old as his brother, who was born on June 10, 2010.

```
In [2]: bro_birthdate = date(2010, 6, 10)
   ...: difference = bro_birthdate - date1
   ...: # returns the date when danny was twice
   ...: # as old as his brother
   ...: date1 + (2 * difference)
Out[2]: datetime.date(2013, 8, 22)
```

Figure 9-6 Calculating the date when Danny was twice as old as his brother

9.3 Heat Loss

In the *Owner's Handbook and Programming Guide* for the HP-41C*, a heat loss problem is given as a sample problem to render into a program:

> Most conventional home water heaters are cylindrical in shape, and you can easily calculate the heat loss from such a water heater. The formula
>
> $$q = hAT$$

where	$q =$ the heat loss from the water heater (Btu per hour)
	$h =$ the heat-transfer coefficient
	$A =$ the total surface area of the cylinder
	$T =$ the temperature difference between the cylinder surface and the surrounding air

> For our example let's assume you have a 52-gallon cylindrical water heater and you wish to determine how much energy is being lost because of poor insulation . In initial measurements, you found an average temperature difference between the heater surface and surrounding air of 15 degrees Fahrenheit. The surface area of the tank is 30 square feet and the heat transfer coefficient is approximately 0.47 .

Instead of rendering this problem into a program, we will modify the specification to render simultaneously in a single statement the answers for all the temperature differences given:

15°F, 22°F, 65°F, 38°F, 27°F; and 45°F

In this sample, we will put all the temperature differences into an array, and the answers will be given in another array.

---

* Hewlett Packard. *The HP-41C Alphanumeric Programmable Scientific Calculator: Owner's Handbook and Programming Guide*. Hewlett Packard. 1979. pp.8–11.

9.4 Python As Calculator

We will solve the problem using **numpy**'s **array** function in the **ipython** interactive shell:

```
In [1]: # importing numpy's array function into the session
   ...: from numpy import array # importing numpy's array function into the session

In [2]: # using a multiple assignment statement
   ...: # to create the input variables in the heat-loss equation
   ...: h, A, T = .47, 30, array([15, 22, 65, 38, 27, 45])

In [3]: # calculating and printing the value of q
   ...: q = h * A * T; print(q)
[211.5 310.2 916.5 535.8 380.7 634.5]
```

Figure 9-7 Calculating simultaneously all the values for heat loss, given the temp diffs in the sample problem

The astute reader will observe that in the multiple assignment statement, the values of our input variables were both scalars (dimensionless numbers) and an array of scalars; yet in the calculation, we did not distinguish between them, nor signify to the Python interpreter that we were executing a linear algebra operation (multiplying a vector by scalars).

We could replace the value of T with a scalar, then execute the same math statement $q=hAT$ without making any changes to it.

numpy makes use of special data registers in the cores of CPUs called single-instruction, multiple data—or SIMD— registers, which apply an operation on data of identical datatype simultaneously. **numpy** makes using SIMD registers transparent to the user, as this example shows.

In fact, **numpy** makes working with tabular datasets easy, especially if your goal is to work with the quantitative data in the datasets as column or row vectors, as we shall see later in this book.

9.4 Find the GC Content Percentage of a Nucleotide String

Figure 9-8 The GC ratio within a genome can vary greatly. Scan or click the QR code above to go to the Wikipedia article on GC content. https://en.wikipedia.org/wiki/GC-content

Regions in a genome that are high in GC content typically include many protein-coding genes; hence, bioinformaticists have an interest in finding and mapping them.

```
nuclStr = 'gattacagattaca'
nuclStr = nuclStr.lower()
gc_content_per = 100 * (nuclStr.count('g') + nuclStr.count('c')) / len(nuclStr)
print(f'{gc_content_per:4.2f}%')
```

Figure 9-9 Our first example takes a string as input and uses assignment statements and string methods **str.lower()** and **str.count()** as part of the data processing

Finally, we use a format string—f' '—to format the floating-point number before printing it using the **print**() function.

Let's break this solution down line by line.

```
nuclStr = 'gattacagattaca'
```

This is an assignment statement.

We use assignment statements to create and instantiate variables.

In this instance, *nuclStr* is the name (or symbol) of the variable, and *'gattacagattaca'* is the value of the variable.

We call the equal sign ('=') **the assignment operator**; and to avoid confusion, when we read the assignment operator aloud, we say "takes the value of."

In this instance, we read the assignment statement aloud thus:

"nuclStr takes the value of 'gattacagattaca' ".

Could we have written our solution without the use of variables? Yes.

We could have used the string literal "gattacagattaca" wherever you see *nuclStr* in the solution, and you would have gotten the same answer. However, by using variables in our solution, if we need the GC content percentage of other nucleotide strings, we only need to update the value of nuclStr once, in the assignment statement, whereas; if we used string literals only, we'd have to modify our solution with new values in several places, which is not only tedious, but can easily lead to clerical errors (typos).

Best to use variables everywhere we can.

```
nuclStr = nuclStr.lower()
```

The *str.lower()* method.

We've added this line so that we can update the value of nuclStr with uppercase nucleotide strings, as well as lowercase ones.

This assignment statement updates the value of *nuclStr* by rendering all characters lowercase, then assigning the resulting string as the new value of the variable.

We need to do this because of the calculation line that comes next, where we ask the Python interpreter to count all lowercase instances of the letters "c" and "g."

If we didn't lowercase the input string, we'd have to take into account uppercase letters in the input string some other way to ensure a correct answer. Note that because our solution doesn't require returning the nucleotide string, we don't have to worry about preserving its original case.

Lowercasing the input string simplifies our solution.

```
gc_content_per = 100 * (nuclStr.count('g') + nuclStr.count('c')) / len(nuclStr)
```

The assignment statement in which the GC content percentage is calculated.

The calculation is performed on the right-hand side (**RHS**) of the statement, then the value that our machine gets assigned to the variable.

We will invoke the variable in the next line.

```
print(f'{gc_content_per:4.2f}%')
```

Displaying the result.

This little line is probably going to require more explaining than the rest of the lines put together.

Let's start with **format printing**. Format printing allows us to control how data is presented, both on the screen and the printed page. For tabular data, we can specify how wide each column should be, as well as how many digits to the right of the decimal point of each value in a column of floating-point numbers should be printed.

Python 3.6 introduced **f-strings** (f" ") to simplify making and using format-print strings. Note that we create an f-string by prepending an *f* to a string.

In f-strings, we enclose the variables we invoke with curly braces; and if we want to control how the variable's value is printed, we add a **print directive**, separated from the variable name with a full colon.

The print directive in this statement says: we are printing a float—hence, the *f* at the end of the directive—that we want four spaces to be allocated to the printing of the value and that we want only two digits to the right of the decimal point to be printed.

The rendered float is followed by a percent sign.

9.5 Stoichiometry with SymPy

†

Chemistry student Ilayda Gökkr has learned how to balance chemical equations by hand. Now she wants to do it by **SymPy** on her Google tablet. The answers she'll get will be rational fractions; for now, she will calculate their proportional whole numbers by hand.

SymPy, or "symbolic Python," is a full-featured **computer algebra system**, or CAS, that allows us to work with symbolic mathematics.

The Equation to Solve The teacher has shown his students how they can use CAS-capable calculators to balance chemical equations using linear algebra. Essentially, a chemical equation to be balanced can be solved as a linear algebra equation in the form $\mathbf{Ax} = \mathbf{b}$, in which matrix $\mathbf{A}$ and the vector $\mathbf{b}$ are given and the vector $\mathbf{x}$ is the unknown to solve.

Now Ilayda writes out in her notebook the steps to follow.

$$P_4 + Cl_2 \longrightarrow PCl_5$$

Step 1 Annotate the chemical equation with the coefficients to solve. These will make up a vector in the linear algebra equation called $\mathbf{x}$.

$$x_1 P_4 + x_2 Cl_2 \longrightarrow x_3 PCl_5$$

Step 2 Write out the rows of the matrix in the linear algebra equation, one element in the chemical equation per row. The coefficients to solve, x_1, x_2, and x_3, are now the labels of the matrix's columns. Ilayda writes in each column how many times each element appears in that position in the chemical equation.

---

† P. K. Andersen and G. Bjedov. "Chemical stoichiometry using MATLAB". Purdue University. 1997.
This paper gives several examples showing how to apply the linear algebra expression $\mathbf{Ax} = \mathbf{b}$ to balance chemical equations.
As you will see by the end of this section, you can follow the instructions in this paper on any CAS with linear algebra capabilities (including calculators) to balance chemical equations.

$$P = 4\,x_1 + 0\,x_2 \longrightarrow 1\,x_3$$
$$Cl = 0\,x_1 + 2\,x_2 \longrightarrow 5\,x_3$$

Step 3 Ilayda rewrites the expressions as homogenous equations, with zero on their right-hand side (RHS).

$$4\,x_1 + 0\,x_2 - 1\,x_3 = 0$$
$$0\,x_1 + 2\,x_2 - 5\,x_3 = 0$$

Step 4 Now she writes the matrix **A** from the coefficients on the left-hand side (LHS). The matrix has two equations with three unknowns.

$$\begin{bmatrix} 4 & 0 & -1 \\ 0 & 2 & -5 \end{bmatrix}$$

Step 5 Her teacher has told her that the matrix must be square and nonsingular. To complete the system, Ilayda adds a third equation, with an arbitrary value for the last unknown. Now the matrix is complete.

$$\begin{bmatrix} 4 & 0 & -1 \\ 0 & 2 & -5 \\ 0 & 0 & 1 \end{bmatrix}$$

Step 6 Vector **b** is made up of the values on the right-hand side (RHS) of the homogenous equations.

$$\begin{bmatrix} 0 \\ 0 \\ 1 \end{bmatrix}$$

Ilayda now has everything she needs to balance the equation using **Ax = b** in **SymPy**.

Figure 9-10 Ilayda has installed **SymPy** and **IPython** through **pip** on **pydroid** on her Google tablet. Scan or click the QR code above to go to the pydroid site. https://pydroid.app/

9.5 Balancing Chemical Eqns

```
$ ipython
```

Now she launches **IPython** through the terminal on **pydroid**.
IPython front ends an instance of Python.

```
Python 3.11.4 (main, Sep 30 2023, 10:54:38) [GCC 11.4.0]
Type 'copyright', 'credits' or 'license' for more information
IPython 9.0.2 -- An enhanced Interactive Python. Type '?' for help.

In [1]: from sympy import init_session

In [2]: init_session()
IPython console for SymPy 1.13.3 (Python 3.11.4-64-bit) (ground types: python)

These commands were executed:
>>> from sympy import *
>>> x, y, z, t = symbols('x y z t')
>>> k, m, n = symbols('k m n', integer=True)
>>> f, g, h = symbols('f g h', cls=Function)
>>> init_printing()

Documentation can be found at https://docs.sympy.org/1.13.3/


In [3]: x1, x2, x3 = symbols('x1 x2 x3')

In [4]: A, b, x = Matrix([4, 0, -1, 0, 2, -5, 0, 0, 1]).reshape(3, 3),\
   ...:            [0, 0, 1], (x1, x2, x3)

In [5]: system = A, b

In [6]: from sympy.solvers.solveset import linsolve

In [7]: [ans] = linsolve(system, x); print(ans)
(1/4, 5/2, 1)
```

Figure 9-11 On a Bluetooth keyboard connected to her tablet, Ilayda initializes **SymPy** and defines the scalars of vector **x**: **x1**, **x2**, and **x3**

She defines A, b, and x in **Ax = b**; she imports **SymPy**'s **linsolve** function; and finally, she sets up and solves the problem.

Note that **SymPy** returns fractions in the form of **p/q**.

Let's take a look at each line in turn.

```
In [1]: from sympy import init_session

In [2]: init_session()
IPython console for SymPy 1.13.3 (Python 3.11.4-64-bit) (ground types: python)

These commands were executed:
```

```
>>> from sympy import *
>>> x, y, z, t = symbols('x y z t')
>>> k, m, n = symbols('k m n', integer=True)
>>> f, g, h = symbols('f g h', cls=Function)
>>> init_printing()
```

Documentation can be found at https://docs.sympy.org/1.13.3/

Figure 9-12 Initialization takes place in the first two lines

In general, it is considered bad practice to import everything from a library; however, **SymPy** is an exception.

```
In [3]: x1, x2, x3 = symbols('x1 x2 x3')
```

After the import, the SymPy symbols() function is used to create the several SymPy variables representing the scalars of the vector x.

Note that a string with the variable names is passed into the **symbols**() function and that the names in the string are space-delimited. They could also be comma-delimited.

```
In [4]: A, b, x = Matrix([4, 0, -1, 0, 2, -5, 0, 0, 1]).reshape(3, 3),\
   ...:           [0, 0, 1], (x1, x2, x3)
```

There's a lot going on in this assignment statement.

Let's take it a little at a time.

First, note that this is a **multiple assignment statement**. Three variables are being created and instantiated in a single statement. **Python** allows this, which can be convenient.

Second, note how matrix **A** is entered by hand—as a one-dimensional list, which then gets reshaped into a 3 × 3 matrix with the **.reshape**() method for Matrix objects. This is the preferred (and easy) way to enter matrices by hand.

Third, the backslash at the end of the first line is used escape the newline character, allowing us to write this single statement over two lines.

(And we can write a very long statement over multiple lines by inserting backslashes at the ends of all but the last line.)

Finally, the values for the vectors **b** and **x** are entered.

Note that all values are comma-separated—both the collections, as well as the items within them.

```
In [5]: system = A, b

In [6]: from sympy.solvers.solveset import linsolve

In [7]: [ans] = linsolve(system, x); print(ans)
(1/4, 5/2, 1)
```

Figure 9-13 Finally, Ilayda solves Ax = b with linsolve()

Note that the variable name **ans** is enclosed by the square brackets of a list on the LHS of the assignment statement. **linsolve**() returns a **SymPy** collection called a **FiniteSet**; if the LHS is not modified, the tuple in this FiniteSet cannot be directly accessed; and it is the tuple of fractions that is the **ans**.

The tuple of fractions is what Ilayda wants.

This line holds two Python statements, separated by a semicolon (;). Many older programming languages use semicolons to end statements. While Python allows semicolons, best practices in Python code layout means that most of the time they are not needed.

As a final step, by hand Ilayda will find the lowest common denominator of the three fractions and use it to calculate the smallest natural numbers that have the same proportions as the fractions.

We will see how to do this in SymPy later in Section 10.12. Click the hyperlinked text if you wish to jump now to that chapter.

9.6   Ideal Gas Law

Figure 9-14 Dimensional analysis involves tracking physical dimensions and units of measurement while performing calculations. Scan or click the QR image above to go to the Wikipedia article. https://en.wikipedia.org/wiki/Dimensional_analysis

Figure 9-15 Pint is a Python package to define, operate and manipulate physical quantities: the product of a numerical value and a unit of measurement. Scan or click the QR image above to go to the online documentation. https://pint.readthedocs.io/en/stable/

Working in engineering and natural sciences often involves working with mathematical expressions whose variables or values are physical dimensional quantities. As STEM students, we are taught to keep track of these dimensions, as well as their units of measurement, as we calculate with the quantities, if only to ensure that the result is in the dimension(s) and unit(s) of measurement we seek.

Pint is a Python library that lets us keep track of dimensions and units of measurement as we run our calculations.

In freshman science textbooks, undergraduate students are given problems that requires dimensional analysis to solve.

The example below deals with the ideal gas equation **PV = nRT**.

> An American balloon company sells a balloon that is 36" in diameter. The company claims that the balloon has a gas capacity of 4.4 cubic feet. Given that this is the volume of the balloon at 78°F and that the internal pressure is 1.008 bar, how many grams of helium is in the balloon?
> Use R = 0.0821 * liter * atm / (mol * K).

```
In [1]: import pint
   ...: ur = pint.UnitRegistry()
   ...: Q_ = ur.Quantity  # to work with temperatures
```

```
In [2]: # aligning the units with those of the given R
   ...: P = (1.008 * ur.bar).to('atm')
   ...: V = (4.4 * ur.cu_ft).to('liter')
   ...: T = Q_(78, ur.degF).to('degK')

In [3]: R = 0.0821 * ur.liter * ur.atm / (ur.mol * ur.degK)

In [4]: # now that we've aligned P, V, and T with R,
   ...: # we can solve for n, which is the quantity of moles
   ...: n = P * V / (R * T)
   ...: n # show n
Out[4]: <Quantity(5.0542303, 'mole')>

In [5]: # finally, solve for grams of helium,
   ...: # as required in the problem statement
   ...: g_He = n * (4 * ur.g / ur.mol)
   ...: g_He # show quantity of grams of helium
Out[5]: <Quantity(20.2169212, 'gram')>

In [6]: # return a value of g_He to 3 significant digits
   ...: # note that we are rounding the fractional part of g_He
   ...: sigFigs, numDigInt = 3, 2 # 2 digits in the integer part
   ...: round(g_He, (sigFigs - numDigInt))
Out[6]: <Quantity(20.2, 'gram')>
```

Figure 9-16 A cleaned-up session of how we might use pint in ipython to solve the example ideal gas law problem above

A subproblem involves representation of the final answer. We save rounding for the final step, and if we are using the built-in Python function **round()** to round the integer part of the answer, our **ndigits** argument can be **None**, 0, or a negative value.

In our example, to calculate **ndigits**, we define two variables, sigFigs and numDigInt, which holds the number of digits in the integer part of the answer.

```
In [7]: g_He.magnitude # getting the scalar
Out[7]: 20.216921201727043

In [8]: g_He.units #...the units...
Out[8]: <Unit('gram')>

In [9]: # ...and the dimensionality
   ...: print(g_He.dimensionality)
[mass]
```

Figure 9-17 Finally, *pint* allows us to extract from a physical quantity its magnitude (or scalar), units of measurement, and dimensionality

9.7 Work Performed by Expanding Gas

At the end of Chapter 1, "Thermodynamic Systems," Enrico Fermi in his book *Thermodynamics* poses this problem:

> 4. Calculate the work performed by 10 grams of oxygen expanding isothermally at 20°C from 1 to .3 atmospheres of pressure (Enrico Fermi. *Thermodynamics*, Dover Publications. 1956. p.10.).

On the preceding page, he gives us the equation we need:

$$L = \frac{m}{M} \cdot R \cdot T \cdot log\left(\frac{p_1}{p_2}\right) \tag{9-1}$$

All that is left for us is to choose which value of the gas constant R to use. (Dr. Fermi offers two: one using ergs, the other using calories.) We choose ergs.

```
In [1]: from math import log
   ...: import pint
   ...: ureg = pint.UnitRegistry()
   ...: Q_ = ureg.Quantity # to convert temperature

In [2]: m = 10 * ureg.gram
   ...: M = 32 * ureg.gram / ureg.mole
   ...: p_1 = 1 * ureg.atm
   ...: p_2 = .3 * ureg.atm
   ...: T = Q_(20, ureg.degC).to('degK')
   ...: # backslash lets us write a single
   ...: # long statement over two lines
   ...: R = 8.314 * 10**7 * ureg.erg\
   ...:     / (ureg.mole * ureg.degree_Kelvin)

In [3]: # formula as written by fermi
   ...: L = (m / M) * R * T * log(p_1 / p_2)

In [4]: # output is a string
   ...: print(f"{L:.3e}")
9.170e+09 erg
```

Figure 9-18 Problem 4 in Chapter 1, posed by Enrico Fermi in *Thermodynamics*

Solved using **pint** and Python with built-in **math** module.
Note the print directive in the format print statement: **.3e**.
The print directive says, "Print in scientific notation, and print 3 digits after the decimal point."

9.8 Acceleration of Sun on Earth

The gravitational acceleration of the sun on the Earth can be found with:

$$\frac{G \cdot m}{r^2} \tag{9-2}$$

where:

G is the gravitational constant, **m** is the mass of the sun, and **r** is the distance of the Earth from the sun.

Use

$$G = \frac{6.6743 \cdot 10^{-11} \cdot m^3}{kg \cdot s^2} \tag{9-3}$$

$$m_{sun} = 1.989 \cdot 10^{30} \cdot kg \tag{9-4}$$

$$r_{earth} = 1.496 \cdot 10^{11} \cdot m \tag{9-5}$$

Find the acceleration of the sun on the Earth in $\frac{meters}{second^2}$ to four significant digits.

```
In [1]: import pint
   ...: ur = pint.UnitRegistry()

In [2]: # create and instantiate the variables
   ...: G = 6.67430e-11 * (ur.meter**3 / (ur.kilogram * ur.second**2))
   ...: m_sun = (1.989 * 10**30 * ur.kilogram)
   ...: r_earth = (1.496 * 10**11 * (ur.m))

In [3]: # calculate and show
   ...: acc_sun = G * m_sun / r_earth**2; acc_sun
Out[3]: <Quantity(0.00593167462, 'meter / second ** 2')>

In [4]: # print in scientific notation (e) to 4 significant digits
   ...: # (1 integer digit + 3 fractional digits, followed by exponent)
   ...: # output is a string
   ...: f"{acc_sun:.3e}"
Out[4]: '5.932e-03 meter / second ** 2'
```

Figure 9-19 *f-strings* (available from Python 3.6 on) allow us to easily render the output in scientific notation to the number of significant digits specified

9.9 Sound Level

Figure 9-20 Table of examples of **sound pressure**. Scan or click the image to go to the Wikipedia article. https://en.wikipedia.org/wiki/Sound_pressure#Sound_pressure_level

In his freshman physics lab, Carlos Huerta has signed out a tone generator, a sound level meter, a meter ruler, and a laser ruler. His task is to take multiple readings with the decibel meter at fixed distances from the tone generator to form a dataset of sound level readings.

Before taking the readings, to find the ideal values he should get, Carlos uses the sound pressure formula

$$L = L_0 - 20 \cdot log_{10}(r/r_0) \tag{9-6}$$

where

$L_0 =$ the sound level in decibels near the tone generator
$r_0 =$ distance of the sound meter near the tone generator
$L =$ the sound level in decibels at a reference distance
$r =$ the reference distance

At 1 cm from the tone generator, Carlos records 110 dB on the sound level meter. His first reference distance, where he will take multiple readings, is 1 m. According to the sound pressure formula, what should the meter read in decibels?

```
In [1]: from math import log10
   ...: import pint
   ...: ur = pint.UnitRegistry()
   ...: Q_ = ur.Quantity # to work with decibels

In [2]: # create and instantiate the variables
   ...: Lo = Q_(110, ur.dB)
   ...: ro = 1 * ur.cm
   ...: r = 1 * ur.m

In [3]: # solve problem and display answer
   ...: L = Lo - Q_(20 * log10(r / ro), ur.dB); print(L)
70.0 delta_decibel
```

9.10 SymPy on Jupyter Notebooks

Figure 9-21 Jupyter notebooks use web technologies to provide a free Mathematica notebook-like tool for sharing not only code, but also images and audio-visual content. Scan or click the QR image above to go to the Jupyter website. https://jupyter.org/

In addition, widgets exist for Jupyter notebooks that allow researchers to create interactive content.

Figure 9-22 NumPy (Numeric Python) is SciPy's library that offers fast computation of numeric multidimensional arrays, called in NumPy ndarrays. Click or scan the QR image above to go to the NumPy website. https://www.numpy.org/

Figure 9-23 SymPy (Symbolic Python) is SciPy's computer algebra system, or CAS. Click the text image above to go to the SymPy website. https://www.sympy.org/en/index.html

SymPy allows researchers to manipulate mathematical expressions algebraically. Using SymPy in Jupyter notebooks allows output to be rendered in textbook format, thanks to the JavaScript library MathJax.

9.10.1 The Jupyter Notebook

```
$ jupyter notebook
```

Launching Jupyter notebook on the command line in Bash.

We launch Jupyter notebook in the topmost level of our notebook directory.

```
[I 2025-04-04 16:17:53.878 ServerApp] ipyparallel | extension was successfully linked.
[I 2025-04-04 16:17:53.878 ServerApp] jupyter_lsp | extension was successfully linked.
[I 2025-04-04 16:17:53.880 ServerApp] jupyter_server_terminals | extension was successfully linked.
[I 2025-04-04 16:17:53.883 ServerApp] jupyterlab | extension was successfully linked.
[I 2025-04-04 16:17:53.885 ServerApp] notebook | extension was successfully linked.
[I 2025-04-04 16:17:53.965 ServerApp] Serving notebooks from local directory: /home/user
[I 2025-04-04 16:17:53.965 ServerApp] Jupyter Server 2.15.0 is running at:
[I 2025-04-04 16:17:53.965 ServerApp] http://localhost:8888/tree?token=d2a1685d77f10f3f698bcdf011b6f6222ff1e9a3f9005b23
[I 2025-04-04 16:17:53.965 ServerApp]     http://127.0.0.1:8888/tree?token=d2a1685d77f10f3f698bcdf011b6f6222ff1e9a3f9005b23
[C 2025-04-04 16:17:54.012 ServerApp]

To access the server, open this file in a browser:
    file:///home/user/.local/share/jupyter/runtime/jpserver-3552-open.html
Or copy and paste one of these URLs:
    http://localhost:8888/tree?token=d2a1685d77f10f3f698bcdf011b6f6222ff1e9a3f9005b23
    http://127.0.0.1:8888/tree?token=d2a1685d77f10f3f698bcdf011b6f6222ff1e9a3f9005b23
```

Figure 9-24 As Jupyter launches, it sends info to STDOUT

9.10 SymPy on Jupyter Notebooks

Jupyter uses web technology to render notebooks. Jupyter launches an instance of a web server to serve us our notebooks.

If Jupyter does not launch your machine's default web browser to serve content, the informational lines show you how you can still get to the Jupyter home directory, which again is the directory that you launch Jupyter notebook in.

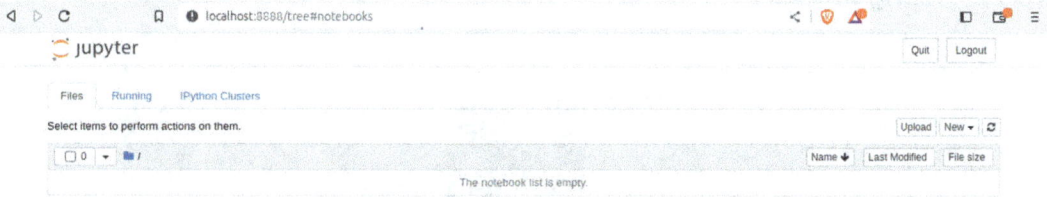

Figure 9-25 Jupyter opens a web browser in the working directory where we launched Jupyter notebook

This directory is empty, waiting to be filled with Jupyter notebooks.

We can create a new notebook by clicking on the $\boxed{\textbf{New}}$ button to the far right and selecting **Python 3 (ipykernel)**.

Now let's talk a bit about what we're looking at.

Figure 9-26 The computer scientist Tim Berners-Lee invented the World Wide Web in 1989 while working at CERN. Click or scan the image to go to the online article at CERN. https://home.cern/science/computing/birth-web

Berners-Lee's intent was to allow researchers to share their work digitally across many different computers. In this scheme, a web page is a combination of text and image files, laid out on the digital page just as they would be in a print research paper. But more than that, the page could contain hyperlinks, allowing researchers to open with just a click other online files of related content.

Figure 9-27 In the same spirit of allowing researchers to share their work collaboratively, the physicist Fernando Pérez created Jupyter notebooks using web technology. Click or scan the image to go to Dr Pérez's webpage at Berkeley. https://bids.berkeley.edu/people/fernando-perez

Jupyter notebooks allow researchers to share code, data, text, images, and audio-visual files, as well as to hyperlink to other online resources and render math output in textbook format (through MathJax).

IPython and Jupyter extensions allow parallel programming and the embedding of simulations and animations.

9.11 Falling Bodies

Figure 9-28 One of several articles on *gravity* in Wikipedia. The quadratic equation used in the example is in the **Equations** section of the article. Click or scan the image to go to the article *Equations for a falling body*. https://en.wikipedia.org/wiki/Equations_for_a_falling_body

In his Calculus I class, Freshman Ernesto Lopez encounters a problem in his textbook on falling bodies:

A weight is dropped from a height of 264.6 meters. In how many seconds does it hit the ground? What is its speed at the moment of impact? Ignore drag from air resistance.

The quadratic equation that returns height given time is:

$$-(1/2) * g * t^2 + v_0 * t + y_0 \qquad (9\text{-}7)$$

where

$$t = \text{time}$$
$$v_0 = \text{initial vertical velocity}$$
$$y_0 = \text{initial height}$$
$$g = \text{the gravitational acceleration at the surface of the Earth,}$$
$$\text{which for this problem we set at } 9.8 \text{ m/s}^2$$

Ernesto is enrolled in a STEM program in which students may use **computer** and **calculator algebra systems** for designated problems. This is one of them.

Having used Python in high school, Ernesto elects to use **SymPy** on **Jupyter notebook** on his laptop computer.

On the Bash command line, he enters:

jupyter notebook RETURN

which launches on Ernesto's laptop a small web server, an instance of the Python interpreter, and a webpage in the laptop's default web browser.

9.11 Falling Bodies

Figure 9-29 The homepage of *jupyter notebook*

The topmost level of the website is the directory in which jupyter notebook was launched. In this case, that's Ernesto's home directory.

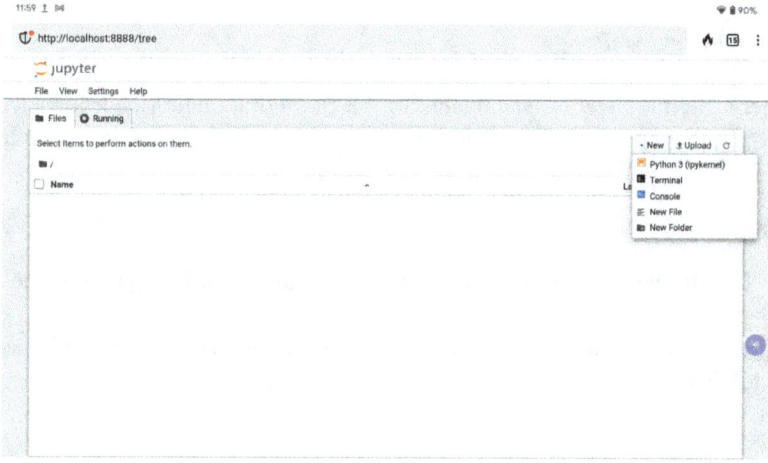

Figure 9-30 Opening a new webpage in jupyter notebook

Ernesto will use **SymPy** on a new page.

In the drop-down menu after clicking the $\boxed{\text{New}}$ button, he chooses **Python 3 (ipykernel)**.

Figure 9-31 A new jupyter notebook

By default, each cell is a computation cell.

```
from sympy import init_session
init_session()

IPython console for SymPy 1.13.3 (Python 3.13.2-64-bit) (ground types: python)

These commands were executed:
>>> from sympy import *
>>> x, y, z, t = symbols('x y z t')
>>> k, m, n = symbols('k m n', integer=True)
>>> f, g, h = symbols('f g h', cls=Function)
>>> init_printing()

Documentation can be found at https://docs.sympy.org/1.13.3/
```

Figure 9-32 Initializing *SymPy*

Ernesto enters the initialization statements in the first computation cell; then with the focus in this computation cell, he presses the key combo SHIFT ENTER, which sends the statements in the computation cell to the Python interpreter for processing.

```
g, v, t = symbols('g v t')
```

Reinitializing current SymPy variables and initializing a new one.

To keep the task as simple as possible, Ernesto decides to use the same variables as are used in the formula in his textbook.

```
# writing out the textbook formula,
# assigning it the variable name 'expr',
# and substituting variables in the formula with numeric values,
# which sets the problem up as it's stated in the textbook
expr = (-(1/2) * g * t**2 + v * t + y).subs({g:9.8, v:0, y:264.6})
```

Figure 9-33 Writing out the formula for evaluation

Here, Ernesto is writing out three distinct actions in a single statement:

(1) On the right-hand side of the assignment operator, he writes the formula.
(2) He uses the **.subs()** method to replace variables with numeric values.
(3) In this assignment statement, he assigns the formula as the value to a variable whose name is **expr**.

```
pprint(expr)
```

$264.6 - 4.9 \cdot t^2$

Figure 9-34 pprint() pretty prints the expression

Not really much to see here. But Ernesto is now ready to solve for *t*.

```
# first, ernesto uses sympy's general solver,
# which in this instance solves for t in the expression.
# taking the square root of a positive real yields
# positive and negative roots. for this falling body problem,
# only the positive root --- ans[1] --- has any meaning.
ans = solve(expr, t); print(ans)
```
[−7.34846922834953, 7.34846922834953]

Figure 9-35 Solving *expr* for *t*

SymPy has a family of solvers.

For a library to be added to the **SciPy** group of libraries, its developers must, to the greatest extent possible, use existing objects and collections. This enhances interoperability between libraries and keeps the learning curve for users to become familiar with the new library low.

Hence, this answer with two parts is returned in a list.
Ernesto can refer to either value by its index.

```
# according to the sympy docs, nsimplify()
# "attempts to find a formula that is
# numerically equal to the given input"
nsimplify(ans[1])
```

$3 \cdot \sqrt{6}$

Figure 9-36 nsimplify(), passing in the second value in the *ans* list

Knowing that many textbook writers expect the problems they put into their books to be solved by hand, Ernesto checks the **float** that is the answer by passing it into nsimplify() and seeing what gets returned.

In this case, the result is what a student using pencil and paper would get.

```
v = (g * t).subs({g:9.8, t:3*6**(1/2)}); print(v)
```

72.0149984378254

Figure 9-37 Calculating instantaneous velocity from *g* and *t*

Ernesto finishes this session by getting the answer to the second question. With these answers, he can verify the results he gets as he works to come to the second answer—the one of instantaneous velocity—through differentiation.

9.12   Spherical Trigonometry in Navigation

Assuming that the Island of Calypso is present-day Othonoi at 39°51′N 19°24′E, and given that Ithaca is at 38°22′N 20°43′E, find the **great-circle distance** (shortest route) Odysseus must cross to return to his wife.

Our plan: We will use **pint** to convert **dd°mm′ ss.s″** into decimal degrees, then use **numpy** to reckon the great-circle distance from the Island of Calypso to Ithaca.

Please note that because the latitude and longitude for each lie in the northern and eastern hemispheres, we will use positive angles for all.

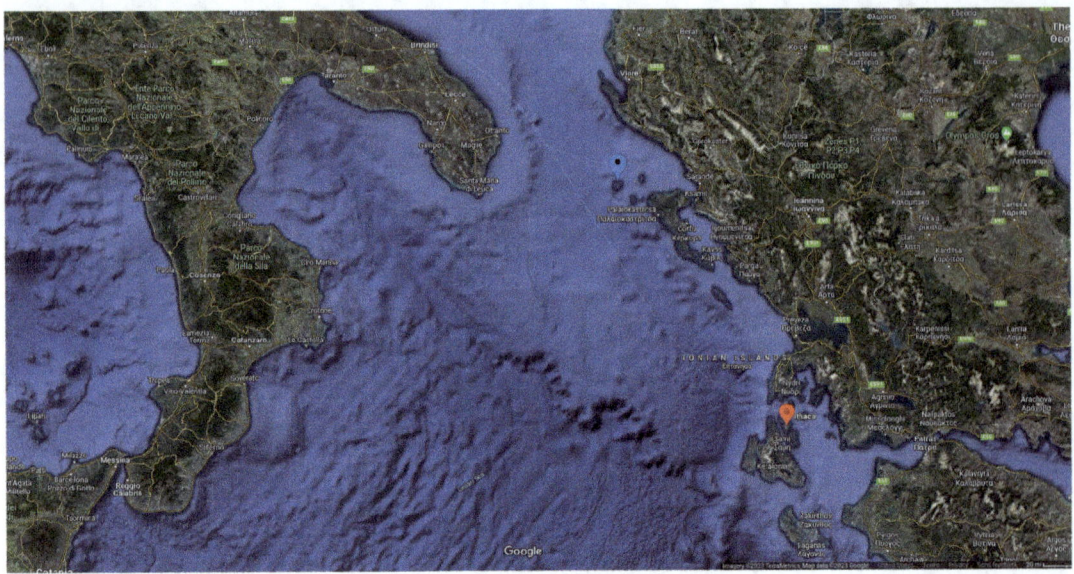

Figure 9-38 Odysseus is trapped on the Island of Calypso (where the blue Google pin is planted), where he pines away for his beloved wife Penelope in Ithaca (where the red Google pin is planted). Map from Google Earth

numpy's default angular unit is radians so we must convert the decimal degrees to radians in this great-circle distance formula:

$$\cos^{-1}[\sin(LAT_{calypso}) * \sin(LAT_{ithaca}) + \cos(LAT_{calypso}) * \cos(LAT_{ithaca}) \\ * \cos(LNG_{ithaca} - LNG_{calypso})] * (60 * nmiles/degree) \tag{9-8}$$

And then, we must take care to convert the radians we get back from taking the arc-cosine of the trig calculations into degrees before we multiply the result by the conversion factor of 60 nautical miles-per-degree.

Our result will be in nautical miles.

```
# initialization
# we start by importing the functions we need from numpy
# and creating an instance of the UnitRegistry()
from numpy import rad2deg, deg2rad, sin, cos, arccos
from pint import UnitRegistry
ur = UnitRegistry()

# now we enter the coordinates of the source
# (island of calypso) and destination (ithaca)
# pint renders h:m:s into decimal hours
LAT_calypso = (39 * ur.arcdeg) + (51 * ur.arcmin)
LON_calypso = (19 * ur.arcdeg) + (24 * ur.arcmin)
LAT_ithaca = (38 * ur.arcdeg) + (22 * ur.arcmin)
LON_ithaca = (20 * ur.arcdeg) + (43 * ur.arcmin)

# now we convert the coordinates into radians,
```

9.13 Introduction to Pandas

```
# which is the default angular unit in numpy
LAT_calypso, LON_calypso = deg2rad(LAT_calypso),\
deg2rad(LON_calypso)
LAT_ithaca, LON_ithaca = deg2rad(LAT_ithaca),\
deg2rad(LON_ithaca)

# next, we enter the great-circle distance formula
# given how long the RHS of the equation is,
# we break the formula across multiple lines
# using the backslash and aligning the parts
# to enhance readability
distance = rad2deg(arccos((sin(LAT_calypso) * sin(LAT_ithaca))\
 + (cos(LAT_calypso) * cos(LAT_ithaca)\
 *   cos(LON_ithaca - LON_calypso)))) \
 * (60 * ur.nautical_mile / ur.arcdeg)

distance
```

> 108.06502468948148 nautical_mile

```
# let's round to 4 significant digits
sigFigs, numDigInt = 4, 3
round(distance, (sigFigs - numDigInt))
```

> 108.1 nautical_mile

Figure 9-39 Breaking out his handy-dandy Python calculator complete with SciPy libraries, Odysseus reckons he is just 108 nautical miles from Penelope, as the crow flies

Getting home is doable, after all. Be of stout heart, Odysseus!

9.13 Climate Data

Adnane al-Rihab, who is majoring in climate system science at UT-Austin, is working with National Oceanic and Atmospheric Administration (NOAA) climate datasets. NOAA datasets are free to request and download.

As an example, he downloads historic daily weather data from Camp Mabry in Austin because the weather data in it goes back to June 1938.

We'll follow along as Adnane works with the his dataset in Python Pandas.

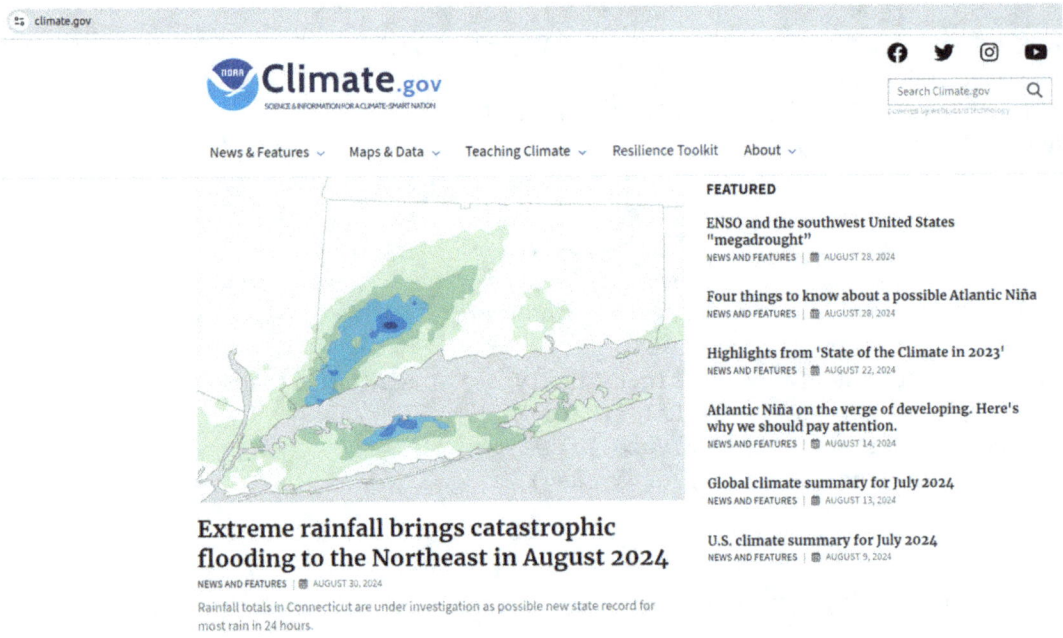

Figure 9-40 Our dataset comes from NOAA's *climate.gov* website. Click the image above to go to the site homepage. https://climate.gov

```
$ cp ~/repo/intro_to_programming/datafile/
AUSTIN_CAMP_MABRY_TX_US.weather_info_1938-2024_$GHCND\:USW00013958$.csv
 ~/datafile
```

Figure 9-41 We start by copying the Camp Mabry daily weather dataset from our repo into the dataset directory in our home directory

The filename is quite long; fortunately, we don't have to type it all out! Use TAB -completion, like this:

cp ~/**rep** TAB **intr** TAB **data** TAB **AUSTIN_CAMP_MABRY_T** TAB ~/**data** TAB

Then fill out the remainder of the Bash statement.

Once we have a copy of the dataset, we'll follow along with Adnane.

```
$ mv ~/datafile/AUSTIN_CAMP_MABRY_TX_US.weather_info_1938-2024_$GHCND\:USW00013958$.csv
 ~/datafile/camp_mabry.csv
```

Figure 9-42 Renaming the working copy of the datafile

9.13 Introduction to Pandas

Because the filename is so long, Adnane chooses to shorten it. Don't worry. The exemplar copy of the datafile will keep its name.

```
$ ls -lh ~/datafile/camp_mabry.csv
-rw-rw-r-- 1 user user 5.6M Mar  9 09:59 /home/user/datafile/camp_mabry.csv
$ wc ~/datafile/camp_mabry.csv
31498   296618 5829396 /home/user/datafile/camp_mabry.csv
$ head -2 ~/datafile/camp_mabry.csv
"STATION","NAME","DATE","ACMH","ACSH","AWND","DAEV","DAWM","EVAP","FMTM","FRGT",
"GAHT","MDEV","MDWM","MNPN","MXPN","PGTM","PRCP","PSUN","SN02","SNOW","SNWD",
"SX02","TAVG","TMAX","TMIN","TOBS","TSUN","WDF1","WDF2","WDF5","WDFG","WDFM",
"WDMV","WESD","WSF1","WSF2","WSF5","WSFG","WSFM","WT01","WT02","WT03","WT04",
"WT05","WT06","WT07","WT08","WT09","WT10","WT11","WT13","WT14","WT15","WT16",
"WT17","WT18","WT19","WT21","WT22","WV03"
"USW00013958","AUSTIN CAMP MABRY, TX US","1938-06-01",,,,,,,,,,,,,,,,"0.00",,,
"0.0","0.0",,,"91","72",,,,,,,,,,,,,,,,,,,,,,,,,,,
```

Figure 9-43 Getting Bash stats on the datafile

Following his training, Adnane starts by getting some basic info on the datafile, like its size in bytes and line count, and he checks whether the dataset includes a label line (it does).

Note that very little data was captured in June 1938, but the daily maximum and minimum temperatures were.

```
$ jupyter notebook
```

Launching *jupyter notebook*

Adnane wants to work on the dataset in **pandas**, and he may want to plot the dataset. Because **jupyter notebook** renders **pandas dataframes** in easy-to-read format and because of the plotting, he chooses to work in Jupyter notebook.

```python
%matplotlib inline
import pandas as pd

pd.set_option('display.max_columns', None)

df = pd.read_csv('~/datafile/camp_mabry.csv', \
parse_dates=True, index_col='DATE')
```

Figure 9-44 Initialization and reading datafile into *pandas dataframe*

After opening a new notebook, Adnane sets up the notebook for plotting and imports pandas in the first computation cell.

Because the records have lots of columns, and because pandas by default shows only the first and last few columns of records, Adnane specified that pandas shows max columns, which will allow all columns of a record to be printed.

Finally, he reads in the datafile. He wants the data to be indexed by date so he specifies that as an argument **index_col='DATE'**, where 'DATE' is the label of the date column.

Finally, dates are represented in strings, and strings are normally sorted in dictionary order. To ensure that the dates are properly sorted, Adnane sets the argument **parse_date=True**.

Note that in Python, the backslash (\) is used to break a statement over multiple lines.

Note that we should use meaningful names, and **df** is the conventional way to name a generic dataframe (it's used all the time in pandas examples), but Adnane is exploring the data now so the name is ok (for now).

df

DATE	STATION	NAME	ACMH	ACSH	AWND	DAEV	DAWM
1938-06-01	USW00013958	AUSTIN CAMP MABRY, TX US	NaN	NaN	NaN	NaN	NaN
1938-06-02	USW00013958	AUSTIN CAMP MABRY, TX US	NaN	NaN	NaN	NaN	NaN
1938-06-03	USW00013958	AUSTIN CAMP MABRY, TX US	NaN	NaN	NaN	NaN	NaN

Figure 9-45 Invoking the Camp Mabry dataframe

Pandas prints the first and last few records and all the columns. This allows Adnane to get the labels of the max temp and min temp columns, **TMAX** and **TMIN**, respectively.

(It takes a bit of scrolling to get to those columns!)

Note that the last item of this representation of the dataframe is its size: **31497 rows × 60 columns**. For now, Adnane just wants to work with TMIN and TMAX.

```
camp_mabry_daily_temps = df[['TMAX', 'TMIN']].copy(deep=True)
camp_mabry_daily_temps
```

9.13 Introduction to Pandas

	TMAX	TMIN
DATE		
1938-06-01	91	72
1938-06-02	94	67
1938-06-03	94	70
1938-06-04	90	68
1938-06-05	94	68
...	...	...
2024-08-20	106	79
2024-08-21	109	79
2024-08-22	107	79
2024-08-23	102	79
2024-08-24	99	77

31497 rows × 2 columns

Figure 9-46 Creating a dataframe with just min/max daily temps at Camp Mabry

Note that by using the dataframe.copy() method, and specifying columns (and their order), Adnane creates a new dataframe that holds just the dimensions he's interested in.

By passing in the **deep=True** argument, he is ensuring that this is a copy independent of the original.

Next, Adnane invokes the dataframe by name, just to make sure it looks good.

```
camp_mabry_daily_temps.agg(['min', 'max', 'mean', 'std'])
```

Figure 9-47 The dataframe.agg() method

	TMAX	TMIN
min	20.000000	-2.000000
max	112.000000	93.000000
mean	79.588596	58.433946
std	15.147684	14.623734

This method allows us to apply one or more aggregate functions to the data in the dataframe.

Note that we refer to the functions by their names as strings. Because they're passed into the method in a list, their order is preserved in the output.

Now Adnane wants to know which days had the highest and lowest TMAX and TMIN.

```
camp_mabry_daily_temps['TMAX'].idxmax()
```

```
Timestamp('2000-09-05 00:00:00')
```

```
camp_mabry_daily_temps['TMAX'].idxmin()
```

```
Timestamp('1962-01-10 00:00:00')
```

```
camp_mabry_daily_temps['TMIN'].idxmax()
```

```
Timestamp('1939-06-10 00:00:00')
```

```
camp_mabry_daily_temps['TMIN'].idxmin()
```

```
Timestamp('1949-01-31 00:00:00')
```

Figure 9-48 Getting dates with highest and lowest values of TMIN and TMAX

Because the dates serve as indices in this dataframe, querying which record by index has the max value in the TMAX column, Pandas returns the date.

Same with the other three queries.

```
camp_mabry_daily_temps.plot(figsize=[30, 3])
```

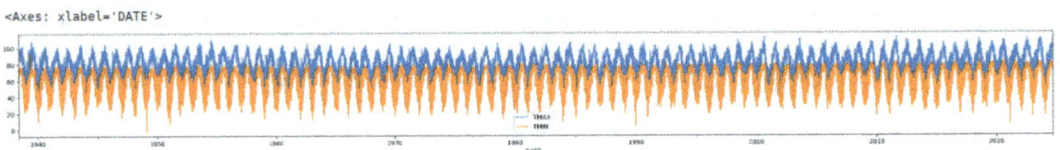

Figure 9-49 Plotting the data

Finally, Adnane plots the data.
The plot clearly shows the annual cycles.

To extend the *x*-axis across the width of the jupyter notebook, Adnane adjusts the height and width of the plot with the **figsize** named argument. Its value is a tuple containing width and height.

9.14 Digital Signals

Figure 9-50 Scan or click the image above to go to the Wikipedia article on digital signal processing

In her Digital Signal Processing class, Jacqueline Wang is being introduced to Fourier decomposition, which is used to decompose a signal wave to its component sine and cosine waves.

The example signal wave is:

$$\sin(2\pi \cdot (4t/5)) + \sin(2\pi \cdot 3t)/2 + \cos(2\pi \cdot t) \tag{9-9}$$

Because **Jupyter notebooks** provide a graphical interface for working with **SciPy** libraries, Jacqueline wants to use **SymPy** in a Jupyter notebook to plot the signal wave.

Jacqueline already has Python and standard SciPy libraries installed on her laptop. She starts by launching Jupyter notebook from the Bash command line:

```
$ jupyter notebook
```

After Jupyter notebook initializes, it opens a webpage in her laptop's default browser:

Figure 9-51 Homepage of Jupyter notebook

By design, Jupyter sets the directory that it's launched in as its top-level directory. Because Jacqueline launched it in her home directory, that is its top-level directory.

Figure 9-52 Creating a new notebook page

Jacqueline clicks the New button in the upper right-hand corner of the homepage. A drop-down menu appears. She chooses **Python 3 (ipykernel)**.

This creates a new notebook page and makes it the active page.

Figure 9-53 The first code cell in the notebook has the focus

In other words, the mouse cursor is in the code cell and blinking. Jacqueline can start typing into the cell immediately.

```
# initialization
from sympy import symbols, sin, cos, pi
from sympy.plotting import plot
t = symbols('t')
```

Figure 9-54 Importing the functions and constant needed from SymPy and creating the SymPy symbol used in the equation

9.14 Plotting with SymPy

It is normal when developing solutions, especially coded solutions, to make everything available from Python libraries, given that when we're developing we generally don't know what we'll need and what we won't.

However, this is a straightforward plot, and Jacqueline has experience working with SymPy.

Once she enters the statements into the code cell, with the cell still having the focus, she presses the key combination SHIFT + ENTER.

However, she could have also pressed the **Run** arrow in the menu bar.

```
signal = sin(2 * pi * (4/5) * t) + (1/2) * sin(2 * pi * 3 * t) + cos(2 * pi *t)
plot(signal, (t, 0, pi))
```

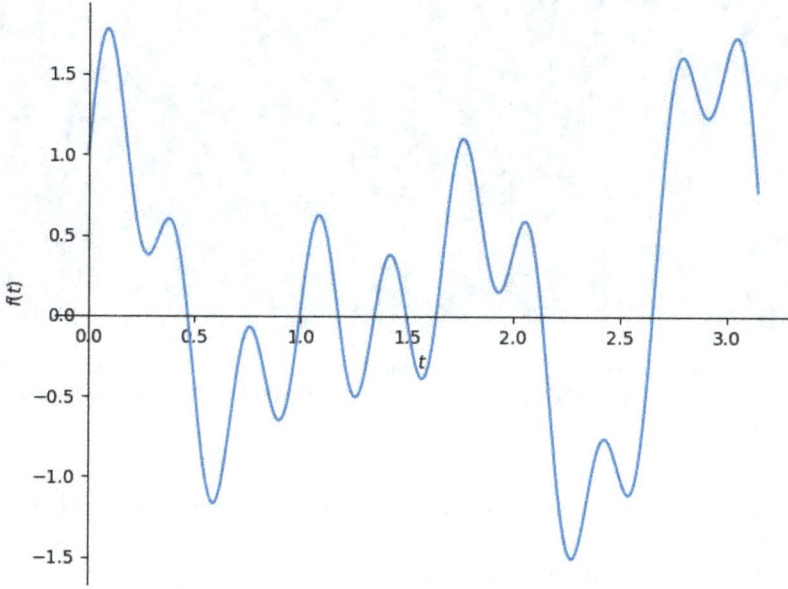

`<sympy.plotting.backends.matplotlibbackend.matplotlib.MatplotlibBackend at 0x7fe26c11e660>`

Figure 9-55 Plotting the signal

Jacqueline decides to write the expression defining the signal in one code cell (ending with the key combination SHIFT + ENTER), then plotting it in the next (and ending with the key combination SHIFT + ENTER).

This makes modifying the expression easier, as well as reading the plot statement easier.

9.15 Image-Driven Data Analysis: Flood Mitigation

Code and Lesson by Linchao Luo

Figure 9-56 NOAA Sea Level Rise Viewer, East Texas. Click the image to go to NOAA's online Sea Level Rise Viewer. https://coast.noaa.gov/slr/#/layer/slr/0/-10514776.461448252/3492100.3520282684/11/satellite/none/0.8/2050/interHigh/midAccretion

The UT-Austin lab of civil engineering Ph.D. student Linchao Luo is involved in a flood mitigation project in Southeast Texas.
His work is instrumental for data-driven decision-making.

What You Need to Know

Linchao's script returns **flooded area percentage** of the area bounded within a polygon that the user, using a mouse, draws on a map rendered on the computer screen.
To use:

(1) Run script on the command line or within the IPython interactive shell.
The script will direct your machine to render a NOAA High-Tide Flooding (HTF) tiff file into an interactive map on your computer display.
(2) Using your mouse, draw a polygon around the area of interest on the map.
(3) Your computer will reckon an estimate of how much of the bounded area is flood-prone and display it within the terminal or IPython interactive shell.
Please keep in mind that the image file is large and that it may take your computer a few moments to finish executing a command processing the data within the file or rendering the result on your display.

9.15 Image-Driven Data Analysis

Figure 9-57 By calculating metrics such as total flood extent, average flood depth, and the proportion of affected areas, Linchao provides critical insights for flood management and urban planning

Figure 9-58 NOAA Sea Level Rise Viewer data download page. Click the image to go to the download page. https://coast.noaa.gov/slrdata/index.html

Here you can download HTF files of the areas you are interested in finding the flooded area percentage of.

```python
import numpy as np
import matplotlib.pyplot as plt
from matplotlib.widgets import PolygonSelector

# shapely, rasterio, and pyproj
# render and allow manipulation of image
from shapely.geometry import Polygon, mapping
# https://shapely.readthedocs.io/en/stable/
import rasterio
# https://rasterio.readthedocs.io/en/stable/
from rasterio.features import geometry_mask
from rasterio.enums import Resampling
from pyproj import Transformer
# https://pyproj4.github.io/pyproj/stable/

import os
```

Figure 9-59 Working with image files requires specialized python libraries

The specialized libraries that Linchao uses were developed to work with geographical image files and to allow users to select regions within the images.

Rasterio ensures precise geospatial alignment and shapely manages and manipulates the polygonal boundaries.

Please go to the online documentation to learn more about each library.

```python
# Process the selected coordinates
if selected_coords:
    print("Selected coordinates:", selected_coords)
    
    # Check if coordinates are within raster bounds
    valid_coords = []
    for x, y in selected_coords:
        if (src.bounds.left <= x <= src.bounds.right) and \
           (src.bounds.bottom <= y <= src.bounds.top):
            valid_coords.append((x, y))
        else:
            print(f"Coordinate out of bounds: ({x}, {y})")
    
    # Proceed with the valid coordinates
    if valid_coords:
        polygon = Polygon(valid_coords)
        mask = geometry_mask([mapping(polygon)], \
                            transform=transform, \
                            invert=True, \
                            out_shape=data.shape)
        masked_data = np.ma.masked_array(data, mask=~mask)
        
        # Debugging step: Show how the mask looks
        print(f"Mask shape: {mask.shape}")
```

9.15 Image-Driven Data Analysis

```python
        print(f"Masked data shape: {masked_data.shape}")

        # Get unique values within the mask
        unique_values = np.unique(masked_data.compressed())
        print("Unique values in selected area:", unique_values)

        # Assume minimum non-zero value for flooding
        flooded_threshold = np.min(unique_values[unique_values > 0])
        print(f"Suggested Flooded Threshold: {flooded_threshold}")

        flooded_pixels_area = np.count_nonzero((masked_data > flooded_threshold)\
                                  & (~masked_data.mask))
        total_pixels_area = np.count_nonzero(~masked_data.mask)
        flood_percentage = (flooded_pixels_area / total_pixels_area) * 100 \
                    if total_pixels_area else 0

        print("Total Pixels in Selected Area:", total_pixels_area)
        print("Flooded Pixels in Selected Area:", flooded_pixels_area)
        print("Flooded Area Percentage: {:.2f}%".format(flood_percentage))

        # Display the original raster with the mask overlay
        plt.figure(figsize=(12, 8))
        plt.imshow(data, cmap="terrain", \
            extent=(src.bounds.left, \
                    src.bounds.right, \
                    src.bounds.bottom, \
                    src.bounds.top))
        plt.imshow(mask, cmap="gray", alpha=0.5, \
            extent=(src.bounds.left, \
                    src.bounds.right, \
                    src.bounds.bottom, \
                    src.bounds.top))
        plt.title("Raster with Selected Area Mask Overlay")
        plt.xlabel("Longitude")
        plt.ylabel("Latitude")
        plt.colorbar(label="Flood Depth")
        plt.show()
else:
    print("No area selected.")
```

Figure 9-60 Calculating flood statistics and displaying results

Calculating flood extent begins with applying a mask to the raster data and isolating the user-defined polygonal area selected in the previous step. By overlaying the mask on the downscaled raster, the analysis restricts calculations to the specified target region. Flood extent is determined by counting the number of pixels within the masked area where flood depth exceeds a threshold (e.g., > 0), representing flooding as added values to pixels. The printed results include the total number of pixels, flooded pixels, and the percentage of the area affected, providing quantitative insights into the flood impact.

Figure 9-61 Image rendered from tiff file

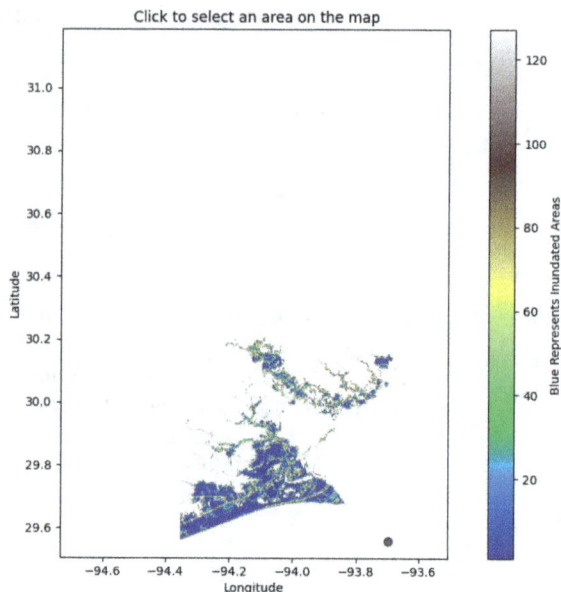

This image should appear when you run the script with the default tiff file.

Figure 9-62 Use your mouse and left-click to draw a polygon bounding your area of interest

Make sure to close the polygon!

Figure 9-63 Raster with selected area mask overlay

This shows the area of your selection.

```
Raster CRS: EPSG:4269
Raster Bounds: BoundingBox(left=-94.733776313, bottom=29.505426024, right=-93.507090859, top=31.18750342847437)
Selected coordinates: [(np.float64(-94.01296038304242), np.float64(29.86383699306018)), (np.float64(-94.01310580612387), np.float64(29.844048573982207)), (np.float6
4(-93.98706075454331), np.float64(29.828625247347905)), (np.float64(-93.97949459430761), np.float64(29.836773419909424)), (np.float64(-93.97964009738907), np.float6
4(29.86383699306018))]
Total Pixels in Selected Area: 326593
Flooded Pixels in Selected Area: 154586
Flooded Area Percentage: 47.33%
```

Figure 9-64 Printing out the calculation results

You'll find these results for your selection in the terminal window in which you invoked the script to run.

9.15 Image-Driven Data Analysis

Figure 9-65 Using drones to get higher-resolution images

NOAA image resolution is one pixel = 10×10 m square patch of land. To obtain higher resolution images at the sites of interest, Linchao's lab flies drones.

Chapter Summary

Although we think of Python as a programming language (which it is!), Python with the SciPy libraries makes a handy graphical scientific calculator.

Programming   10

In the last chapter, we worked through examples of how we can use Python and the SciPy libraries as a graphical scientific calculator. When we are solving problems one-off, this is fine. However, STEM researchers are often confronted with problems that they must solve over and over. Within the subject that is a focus of this book, that includes working with the same kind of datasets generated during the run of an experiment. In this case, we can vastly improve our efficiency and accuracy by automating tasks through programming. This is a long chapter that takes several class days to cover. But once we get through it, students have been acquainted with what it takes to make code production-ready.

Simple programming is a term we use to describe hand algorithms rendered into computer programs. In other words, actions that we do by hand, we turn into instructions for machines to do. Once we capture a hand algorithm as a program in a text file, we can have a machine execute it over and over on different data, including on all the records in a recordset.

An example of simple programming is converting the calculation for finding the percent GC content into a Python function that accepts a nucleotide string as input and returns the percent GC content as output.

As a function, we can invoke it whenever we need it. Furthermore, we can then embed the function into larger programs that make use of the GC content of a nucleotide string.

Invoking hand algorithms by function names, instead of having to rewrite the algorithms by hand every time we need them, is a primary advantage of simple programming.

But rendering hand algorithms into Python code will not be our only concern. Whenever you are hand-processing data, and the algorithms or data throw an error, you inspect the instructions and the data by eye and hand; and once you find the problem, if possible you fix it.

In each function, we will want to communicate to our users: what the function takes as input, what it returns as output, briefly what it does, and examples of how to use it.

Furthermore, we will want to communicate to other programmers through comments and self-documenting code how our programs work.

In our functions, we will instruct the machine to inspect the data to ensure the input is good before processing it. And we will want to automate testing our functions to ensure that for expected input, they yield expected output; while for bad data, we want to ensure our machines will let the users of our programs know immediately—and if possible, what the bad data is and where the bad data is in the input.

The code that ensures the input data is good, we call **garbage filters**, while the code that ensures functions yield expected output, given known input, we call **unit tests**.

We will learn how to write garbage filters and unit tests even as we communicate to users and programmers through documentation and comments and even as we learn how to implement our algorithms into Python code.

This is a fair amount to learn up front, but in fairness, we've already been commenting our Bash scripts, as well as manually testing them. So automating the testing, writing garbage filters, and implementing algorithms into Python code are our only new tasks. And as we do these tasks over and over and they become a habit, we will find that writing good, robust code becomes second nature.

Buckle up.

10.1 Our First Program: Of Functions, Modules, Garbage Filters, Tests, and Docstrings

We organize much of our code into functions and save them in text files called **modules**. This allows us to write our code once, then invoke it whenever we need it into our scripts and interactive sessions.

At a minimum, each function we write should include:

- A **function header** that includes **type hints**
- A **docstring** that describes to users what the function does and includes at least one example
- Code (we're calling **garbage filters**) that tests input to ensure that the input passed into the function is expected input and that handles bad input
- Code that **implements the algorithm** (the code that justifies writing the function in the first place)
- **comments** for programmers that explain what the code does

Our tools to ensure that our code is well-written and tested include:

- Pylint
- Unit tests

To write and edit our code, we will use tools that include:

- ipython
- vim
- sed

10.1 Our First Program: Of Functions, Modules, Garbage Filters, Tests, & Docstrings

> Type hints and docstrings are meant for the users of our functions, to help them understand what input is expected, as well as to understand what kinds of output our functions return, given good input.
>
> Comments in our code are meant for ourselves and other programmers who will maintain our code.
>
> We call code that ensures that only expected input is passed into our functions "garbage filters." Finally, the code that implements the algorithm is the code that processes expected input into desired output.
>
> As we start writing a function, we comment where we'll insert our docstring, our garbage filters (as well as what they'll test for), and our implementation of the algorithm.
>
> This provides us a framework to build on.
>
> As we develop our code, we will test and modify as necessary. Key to efficient and consistent testing is automating testing. Unit tests automate testing. In this chapter, we will start by using prewritten unit tests for the functions we'll be writing, and later, we will use a template to help us quickly create our own.

千里之行，始于足下。

Figure 10-1 A journey of a thousand miles begins with a single step

10.1.1 The Least Necessary to Write a Working Function

By design, Guido van Rossum made Python not only easy to learn, but also easy to start using productively. In this chapter, we will preview what it takes to write, save, and reuse a program in Python. In doing so, I hope to show you how easy it is to make a useful program, as well as save it in a way that lets us reuse it whenever we need it.

Although functional programming purists might balk at the statement that Python 3 is a functional programming language, it is more so than earlier versions of Python. In fact, making Python more so was one of Guido van Rossum's design goals for Python 3.

Wikipedia states: "functional programming is a programming paradigm where programs are constructed by applying and composing functions."

Let's see what that means in Python.

Please follow along in the IPython interactive shell.

In Python, we use the keyword **def** to tell the interpreter that we are creating a function. We follow that after a space with the name of our function, followed immediately by an open parenthesis, followed by the arguments by name that we want to pass into the function—the arguments are separated by commas—followed by the close parenthesis. We end the line with a full colon.

Our function header might look like this:

```
def testFunc(arg1, arg2)
```

An example function header.

At a minimum, the header needs the **def** keyword, function name, parentheses, and full colon.

Please note that the function name and the open parenthesis are concatenated—no spaces separate them.

A function does **NOT** need to take in arguments, nor return any values. Here is a complete, if trivial, working program:

```
def testFunc():
    pass
```

Our example function, modified.

A function need not take any arguments, and need not return any values.

In this example, the function's body of code contains a single statement: **pass**.

pass is a Python keyword that tells the interpreter, "Don't do anything here." It is like the **no-op** command (no operation) in other programming languages.

```
In [1]: def testFunc():
   ...:     pass
   ...:
```

Figure 10-2 Note that when we enter our definition of an example function that takes no arguments and returns no values, our Python interpreter accepts it without complaint

```
In [2]: testFunc()

In [3]:
```

Figure 10-3 Likewise, when we invoke it on the command line, our example function executes without the interpreter complaining

Of course, we pass nothing in, and nothing is returned.
Our example function does nothing.
Just like we designed it to do.

10.1.2 The Least Necessary to Write a Useful Function

Although our **testFunc()** is trivial, it demonstrates that a function does not need to take arguments, and it does not need to return values. That's because useful functions exist that do not take arguments, and useful functions exist that do not return values.

Now let's write a useful function.

Using one of our examples in the last chapter, where we processed data using Python as a calculator, let's write a function that takes a nucleotide string as its argument and returns the percent GC content (see Lesson 9.4).

10.1 Our First Program: Of Functions, Modules, Garbage Filters, Tests, & Docstrings

```python
def get_percent_gc_content(nuclStr):
    nuclStr = nuclStr.lower() # initialization
    return 100 * (nuclStr.count('g') + nuclStr.count('c')) / len(nuclStr)
```

Figure 10-4 Our first useful program

It is a function that takes a nucleotide string as input and returns the percent GC content.

Note that we give our function a meaningful name, just as we do the name of the argument. Giving our functions and variables meaningful names to enhance readability is referred to as "self-documenting code."

Please also note that we consider the first working copy of our program as a rough draft. We will be improving it in stages.

```
get_percent_gc_content('gattaca')
28.571428571428573
```

Figure 10-5 We immediately test our function to ensure that it works properly—in this case, that it returns the correct value for a nucleotide string

When testing, we should know beforehand what the return value or values should be for our test input.

Later, we will consider what it means to test our code thoroughly.

Our output is a float. Note how many digits there are to the right of the decimal point. As a rule, if your calculation is not rendering a final result, you do NOT round off. Because our function could be used in calculating intermediate results, we will leave the calculation within the function as is.

If we need to round off the output, we should round the return value—that is, for example, pass our function into Python's built-in **round**() function, like this:
round(get_percent_gc_cont('gattaca'), 2), which returns:
28.57.

And if the output is intended for human consumption only, we might consider embedding it in a format string, or **f-string**, to show that it is **percent** GC content, like this:
print(f"{get_percent_gc_content('gattaca'):4.2f}%"), which returns:
28.57%.

10.1.3 Documenting Our Function for Coders and Users

We're not yet finished working on our function.

We want to annotate our rough draft. It's not enough that we've made our code self-documenting by using meaningful function and variable names. We want to add comments to the code for the benefit of programmers who will read our code (possibly to maintain it) and to write guides and hints in the function's use for our users.

At this stage, commenting our code includes adding where we'll place our garbage filters, as well as what they'll test for, and where we'll put our implementation of the algorithm.

Put another way, we note in comments the layout of our code.

```python
def get_percent_gc_content(nuclStr):
    ''' docstring
    '''
    nuclStr = nuclStr.lower() # initialization
    # garbage filters
```

```
    # 1) assert that input is a string
    # 2) assert that symbols in string are nucleotides

    # implementation of algorithm
    return 100 * (nuclStr.count('g') + nuclStr.count('c')) / len(nuclStr)
```

Figure 10-6 Using comments as placeholders

Document your code. Code without documentation is incomplete.

Our functions and variables should have meaningful names that say what they are and what they do. Again, code that includes meaningful names for variables, functions, files, and other objects is called "self-documenting" code.

Know your Audience You should choose names that are meaningful to your users, who in many settings will be your collaborators and who are experts in the same domain as you. When your users are your collaborators, the names you use in your code should be the names you use at the bench.

In the rough outline of a function, we'll add an empty docstring and comments that serve as placeholders for where we'll write our garbage filters to test input to ensure it's the expected input, as well as where we'll write the implementation of our algorithm.

Note that the garbage filters and the implementation are laid out in the order they are executed: first we make sure that the input is expected input, then we let expected input continue to the implementation of the algorithm.

Our comments may include notes such as what our garbage filter should test for, as in this example. Used this way, comments serve first as reminders to ourselves, then as informational to those reading our code.

When we document our code, we are mindful that we are communicating to two different audiences: users of our code and the programmers who will maintain it. There may well be only one user of your code and only one programmer who's maintaining your code: you.

You still need to document your code. Think of it as doing your future self a favor, after you haven't used your code for a while, or after you haven't looked at it for a while.

For now, we will add comments to our code and provide type hints saying which datatype or collection is expected for input and which datatype or collection is returned as output; and we will provide a docstring that summarizes what our function does, as well as give examples in its use.

```
def get_percent_gc_content(nuclStr: str) -> float:
```

We start by adding type hints in the function header.

Type hints tell the users of our function what the expected datatypes or collections are for input, as well as what is returned for output.

In this example, the expected input is a string, and the return value is a float.
Type hints as a feature were added in Python 3.5. This means that you can add type hints only if your Python interpreter is 3.5 or later.

If you cannot enter type hints into the function header, you can instead write a type contract at the top of your docstring. In the case of our function, the type contract would look like this:

(str) -> float

which shows that the argument is of type "string" and the return value is of type "float."

```
def get_percent_gc_content(nuclStr: str) -> float:
    ''' Given a nucleotide string as input,
        return the percent g-c content.
```

```
            >>>get_percent_gc_content('gattaca')
            28.571428571428573
    '''
```

Figure 10-7 Next, we add a docstring

Docstrings are enclosed by either three single or three double quotes and are used to document code with multiline comments or info.

If you cannot add type hints to your function header, then you should start your docstring with a type contract.

Here, we provide a brief explanation of what our function does, taking care to mention both the argument and return values.

Next, we provide examples of that the user should get, using the given input.

```
def get_percent_gc_content(nuclStr: str) -> float:
    ''' Given a nucleotide string as input,
        return the percent g-c content.

        >>>get_percent_gc_content('gattaca')
        28.571428571428573
    '''
    nuclStr = nuclStr.lower() # initialization
    # garbage filters
    # 1) assert that input is a string
    # 2) assert that symbols in string are nucleotides

    # implementation of algorithm
    return 100 * (nuclStr.count('g') + nuclStr.count('c')) / len(nuclStr)
```

Figure 10-8 Our function documented for users and programmers

Type hints and docstrings are for the users; comments are for the programmers.

Documentation is often a matter of style and personal judgment. Comments should explain the code where you feel an explanation is necessary.

When commenting, be simple, clear, and direct. Don't skimp or be parsimonious.

There's even more work to do on this code. We need to test it for bad input, and at the top of the function, we need to handle the bad input. I call the error traps that handle bad input "garbage filters."

But for now, let's say that what we have is sufficient for a rough draft. We want to save our work.

Now we want to save our function so that we can recall it later when we need it, whether in a script or an interactive session.

This is where modules come in.

10.1.4 Saving Our Function to a Module

A **module** is a text file on our mass-storage device that holds the functions that we create. We save our working functions to a module; then, when we need them, we **import** the module into our script or session.

The way we are working with modules for now, our module must be in the same working directory as our script or our interactive session.

You have options for creating your first module and saving your function to it. For example, if you are in an IPython interactive session, you can use the magic **%edit** command, which invokes vi or vim by default. But for now, I will use vim in a Bash session to create the module, then I will copy and paste the function into my module. Finally, I will save the module to disk and quit vim.

If you are in an IPython interactive session, run the magic **%hist** command. Your function will be printed to STDOUT in a format that allows you to select all of it by mouse, then copy it.

In a Bash window in the same directory, type: **vim myModule.py**.

```
vim myModule.py
```

In Bash, we can create the module that we'll save our function in using vim.

An instance of vim will open in the command mode. Type lowercase **i** to enter the edit mode. We'll add a docstring to document our module, then paste our function into the window.

```python
''' this module holds the code we'll develop and use
    as we learn python.
'''
def get_percent_gc_content(nuclStr: str) -> float:
    ''' Given a nucleotide string as input,
        return the percent g-c content.

        >>>get_percent_gc_content('gattaca')
        28.571428571428573
    '''
    nuclStr = nuclStr.lower() # initialization
    # garbage filters
    # 1) assert that input is a string
    # 2) assert that symbols in string are nucleotides

    # implementation of algorithm
    return 100 * (nuclStr.count('g') + nuclStr.count('c')) / len(nuclStr)
```

Figure 10-9 In vim, we add a docstring to our module, then paste our function into it

Press ESC to escape edit mode and return to command mode, then type **:wq** to write your changes to disk and quit vim.

10.1.5 Autoreloading Edited Module Content to an IPython Session

If you are using the IPython interactive shell and you want to make edits to your module, you should run these two magic commands at the start of your session:

```
%load_ext autoreload
%autoreload 2
```

This will ensure that your edited code is read into session memory so the edited code can then be run and tested.

10.1 Our First Program: Of Functions, Modules, Garbage Filters, Tests, & Docstrings

To expose the functions in our module so we can invoke them in our script or session, we have to **import** our module.

In this example, on the command line of our IPython session, we might enter

import myModule

But this requires us to write out the module name every time we want to invoke a function in it.

We can call our modules by aliases in our scripts and sessions. This allows us to shorten the names we call them by; and in SciPy, many libraries are imported by aliases that are conventional—that is, they are used by everybody in the community. Hence, we should write:

import numpy as np
import pandas as pd
import matplotlib.pyplot as plt

```python
import myModule as mM
```

Here, we import myModule as mM.

Now, in our session, we will use **mM** to invoke our module.

```
In [1]: %load_ext autoreload

In [2]: autoreload 2

In [3]: import myModule as mM

In [4]: mM?
Type:           module
String form:    <module 'myModule' from '/home/user/myModule.py'>
File:           ~/myModule.py
Docstring:      this module holds the code we'll develop and use as we learn python.
```

Figure 10-10 Here, in an IPython session, we load autoreload and set autoreload to 2

This is so we can have any edits we make to our module loaded into session memory. Next, we import myModule into our session, then we invoke the module's documentation with a question mark.

Like our functions' docstrings, the docstrings we write into scripts and modules address our users.

```
In [5]: mM.get_percent_gc_content?
Signature: mM.get_percent_gc_content(nucl_str: str) -> float
Docstring:
(str) -> float # type contract
Returns the percent gc content of nucleotide string input.
### example ###
>>>get_percent_gc_content('gattacagattaca')
28.571428571428573
File:           ~/myModule.py
Type:           function
```

Figure 10-11 Now we get the documentation on our function, again by following its name with a question mark

Note that the type hints are in the signature line, and our docstring is presented to the user.
Finally, we test our code by passing in expected input; in this case, a clean nucleotide string.

```
In [6]: mM.get_percent_gc_content('gattaca')
Out[6]: 28.571428571428573
```

Figure 10-12 Users will often pass in the values we write in documentation examples, just to see if they get the same return values

As we learn how to program in Python, we will write our programs as much as we can in the form of functions, and we will save our functions to our module.

10.1.6 Writing Garbage Filters: Handling Bad Input

> **Error-trapping** is vital for writing robust code that processes data correctly.
> In out-of-the-box Python, we can trap the errors that Python throws in Tracebacks using **try...except**, and we can catch bad input passed into our functions and scripts using **assert** statements.
> If input does not pass our test in an **assert** statement, Python throws an **AssertionError** in a Traceback. We can add a message to the user whose input doesn't pass, explaining what is wrong with the input.

STEM researchers generate and process datasets whose records may be incomplete, contain errors, or are incorrectly formatted to be processed by some software in their pipelines. The causes of bad data are manifold, but two are: the technology generating the raw data and human error.

In this section, we will learn how to handle bad input using **assert** statements.

To write effective assert statements, we must be mindful of:

- The UNIX/Linux programming Rule of Repair:
  When you must fail, fail noisily and as soon as possible
- What constitutes good, or expected, input

The Rule of Repair requires that we test input into our functions and scripts as soon as possible. That means our garbage filters go to the top of our code, and that input is passed into them as soon as it is passed into our scripts or functions. The sooner, the better.

Taking into account what constitutes good, or expected, input means that we may have to write more than one test for each piece of input.

We need to write two garbage filter tests for input passed into our **get_percent_gc_content**() function, but the one that asserts that symbols in input strings be nucleotides requires that we learn a little more Python than we have so far. We will write our first garbage filter now, then add the second one as soon as we can.

10.1 Our First Program: Of Functions, Modules, Garbage Filters, Tests, & Docstrings

The simplest and most straightforward test we can apply to input is to ensure that it is the right datatype or collection, and the built-in function that allows us to do that is **isinstance**() (Click on the hyperlink to go to the entry on docs.python.org):

> **isinstance**(*object, classinfo*)
>
> Return `True` if the *object* argument is an instance of the *classinfo* argument, or of a (direct, indirect, or virtual) subclass thereof. If *object* is not an object of the given type, the function always returns `False`. If *classinfo* is a tuple of type objects (or recursively, other such tuples) or a Union Type of multiple types, return `True` if *object* is an instance of any of the types. If *classinfo* is not a type or tuple of types and such tuples, a `TypeError` exception is raised. `TypeError` may not be raised for an invalid type if an earlier check succeeds.

Figure 10-13 The entry for instance() on **docs.python.org**

```
testStr = 'hello, world!'

isinstance(testStr, str)
True
```

Figure 10-14 *isinstance()* in action

The function tests if a literal value or the value of a variable is an instance of the class we specify. It returns a **bool**: **True** if the value is of the type we specify; **False** otherwise.

"Assert statements are a convenient way to insert debugging assertions into a program."
—From **docs.python.org/3/reference/simple_stmts.html**

```
In [1]: testValue = 1.2

In [2]: assert isinstance(testValue, str), "input value must be a string"
-------------------------------------------------------------------------
AssertionError                            Traceback (most recent call last)
Cell In[2], line 1
----> 1 assert isinstance(testValue, str), "input value must be a string"

AssertionError: input value must be a string
```

Figure 10-15 *assert* statement in action

The **assert** statement has two parts. The first part is the test that must be passed for our code to keep processing the input. The second part is the message that becomes part of the **AssertionError** to explain to the user what is wrong with the input.

In this example, we set the value of the variable to be a float, while in the **assert** statement, we assert that the value must be a string. The result is an **AssertionError**.

After we add this assert statement to our function, this AssertionError is what users of our function will see if they try to pass a nonstring into the function.

```python
def get_percent_gc_content(nuclStr: str) -> float:
    ''' Given a nucleotide string as input,
        return the percent g-c content.

        >>>get_percent_gc_content('gattaca')
        28.571428571428573
    '''
    nuclStr = nuclStr.lower() # initialization
    # garbage filters
    # 1) assert that input is a string
    ### backslash at end of line below
    ### lets us write a long statement
    ### over multiple lines
    assert isinstance(nuclStr, str), \
        "argument must be a clean nucleotide string."
    # 2) assert that symbols in string are nucleotides

    # implementation of algorithm
    return 100 * (nuclStr.count('g') + nuclStr.count('c')) / len(nuclStr)
```

Figure 10-16 Inserting our *assert* statement as a garbage filter into our function in myModule

Once we've saved our changes, we test our function by invoking it in the IPython interactive shell, passing into it first good then bad input and making sure that the function behaves as expected.

Reminder: We have a second **assert** statement to write, but first we have to figure out how we're going to test each symbol in the nucleotide string to ensure that it is a valid symbol. (We'll do this presently; then we'll write the second garbage filter.)

10.1.7 Automating Testing Our Code Using Unit Tests

> **unit tests** let us automate testing our code.
> The word "unit" is intentionally ambiguous. A unit test can be run against a script, it can be run against a module of functions, or it can be run against a single function. For each case in turn, "unit" applies to "script," "module," or "function,"
> Put another way, we can write a unit test to test the functions in our module, or we can write a unit test to test just one function in our module.

Recall that even in our first days of writing Bash scripts and pipelines, we tested, tested, tested. In developing our solutions, we used input whose desired output we knew, and we constantly checked to ensure the output was taking the form or shape we desired.

Up to now, we've been testing manually only. Now, we're going to automate testing our code. We'll do that with unit tests. We'll start with prewritten unit tests, and later, we'll learn how to write our own unit tests.

```
$ cp ~/repo/intro_to_programming/unittests/unittest_get_percent_gc_content.py .
```

10.1 Our First Program: Of Functions, Modules, Garbage Filters, Tests, & Docstrings

Copy the unit test into the directory where your *myModule* is.
NOTE THE DOT AT THE END OF THE BASH STATEMENT ABOVE.
The dot in Bash is shorthand for your working directory.
Right now, this should be your home directory.

```
$ sed 's/FILE/myModule/g' unittest_get_percent_gc_content.py
```

We need to make a single change to the unit test file.
Run **sed** to replace **FILE** with **myModule**.
Inspect the output to STDOUT to ensure that **myModule** will be written into line 13, which immediately follows comment #1.

```
# 1. get the function to test or import the module to test.
from myModule import get_percent_gc_content
```

Figure 10-17 Verifying that *sed* has written *myModule* into the unittest file where it needs to go

If you see this: **from myModule import get_percent_gc_content**, you're golden. You're good to go.

```python
# 3. create a method for each garbage_filter test to perform.
def test_get_percent_gc_content_GF_1(self):
    ''' assert input must be a string
    '''
    with self.assertRaises(AssertionError):
        get_percent_gc_content(1.2)

# 4. create a method for each test to perform.
def test_get_percent_gc_content(self):
    result = get_percent_gc_content('gattacagattaca')
    # here, the test ensures that output of the function is indeed the expected output.
    self.assertEqual(result, 28.571428571428573)
```

Figure 10-18 Now is a good time to inspect the methods in code blocks #3 and #4 to see exactly what our unit test is testing for

In #3, I have written a test to ensure the garbage filter raises an assertion error when a nonstring object is passed into the function.

In #4, I have written a test to ensure that our implementation of the algorithm, when passed in good input, returns the correct output.

```
$ sed -i 's/FILE/myModule/g' unittest_get_percent_gc_content.py
```

Writing the substitution into the unittest file.
⎢↑⎥ puts the previous command executed on the Bash command line. ⎢CTRL⎥⎢a⎥ moves the cursor to the beginning of the line.
Use ⎢→⎥ to move the cursor into the space after **sed**, then type in **-i**. This writes the substitution in-place in the file.
Hit ⎢RETURN⎥ to make the change.

```
$ python unittest_get_percent_gc_content.py
.E
======================================================================
```

```
ERROR: test_get_percent_gc_content_GF_1 (__main__.Test_myModule.test_get
_percent_gc_content_GF_1)
assert input must be a string
----------------------------------------------------------------------
Traceback (most recent call last):
  File "/home/user/unittest_get_percent_gc_content.py", line 23, in tes
t_get_percent_gc_ content_GF_1
    get_percent_gc_content(1.2)
  File "/home/james/myModule.py", line 12, in get_percent_gc_content
    nuclStr = nuclStr.lower()  # initialization
    ^^^^^^^^^^^^^^^
AttributeError: 'float' object has no attribute 'lower'

Ran 2 tests in 0.000s

FAILED (errors=1)
```

Uh-oh. (Or maybe not.)

Getting errors (and fixing them) is normal while we develop our code.

Especially while you're learning to code, you should get used to getting error messages and learning how to read and understand them.

In this case, we are being told that when the unit test was testing our garbage filter that handles nonstring input, and that input, a float, was passed into the assignment statement that lowercases the input string; and it failed there.

CAUSE OF ERROR: The garbage filter is BELOW the initialization statement. It never gets to test for bad input before the initialization statement gets executed.

SOLUTION: Move the initialization statement BELOW the garbage filter.

```python
def get_percent_gc content(nucltStr: str) -> float:
    ''' Given a nucleotide string as input,
        return the percent g-c content.

        >>>get_percent_gc_content('gattaca')
        28.571428571428573
    '''
    # garbage filters
    #1) assert that input is a string
    ### backslash at end of line below
    ### lets us write a long statement
    ### over multiple lines.
    assert isinstance(nuclStr, str), \
        'argument must be a clean nucleotide string.'
    #2) assert that symbols in string are nucleotides

    nuclStr = nuclStr.lower()  # initialization
    # implementation of the algorithm
    return 100 * (nuclStr.count('g') + nuclStr.count('c')) / len(nuclStr)
```

Figure 10-19 Moving the initialization line just above implementation of the algorithm

10.1 Our First Program: Of Functions, Modules, Garbage Filters, Tests, & Docstrings

In command mode in **vim**, move the cursor to the start of the initialization line, type **dd** to delete the line, then move the cursor to the end of the blank line above the implementation comment line and press **p** for "paste." **vim** should paste the assignment statement just above the comment line. Now, write your changes to disk and quit: **:wq**

Rerun the unit test.

```
$ python unittest_get_percent_gc_content.py
..
======================================================================
Ran 2 tests in 0.000s

OK
```

According to our two tests, the function looks good.

The two dots after we run the unit test mean both tests pass. If one test threw an error, its dot would be a capital E, instead. And if one test failed, its dot would be a capital F, instead.

If we were given the expected input and output (**'gattaca'**) -> **28.571428571428573** as part of the specification, we could say that, as far as it goes, our code meets specs.

NB: There is a methodology for developing code called **"Test-Driven Development"**, or **TDD**, that makes extensive use of unit tests. In TDD, we write our tests first, then develop our code in a repeating cycle of **test-write-save** until we clear the errors and failures that the unit tests announce. **If we have written our tests to capture the specification(s) that we are to write to, then once we have passed all unit tests, we can say that our code meets specs.**

We will expand on this after the next lesson.

10.1.8 Linting Our Code with Pylint

> **Linting** our code catches grammar, spelling, and punctuation errors. Linters like **pylint** also make suggestions that encourage good stylistic and programming practices.

```
$ pylint myModule.py
************ Module myModule
myModule.py:20:0: C0303: Trailing whitespace (trailing-whitespace)
myModule.py:25:0: C0305: Trailing newlines (trailing-newlines)
myModule.py:1:0: C0103: Module name "myModule" doesn't conform to snake_case naming style (invalid-name)
myModule.py:5:27: C0103: Argument name "nuclStr" doesn't conform to snake_case naming style (invalid-name)
-----------------------------------------------------------------
Your code has been rated at 0.00/10 (previous run: 0.00/10, +0.00)
```

Figure 10-20 Running *pylint* the first time against myModule

Following our practice of doing what we find easiest, we will use **sed** to fix trailing whitespace and newlines and to change variable names to conform to snake_case naming style; and we will use **mv** to change the module name to conform to snake_case naming style.

```
$ sed -i '/^$/d' myModule. py
$ pylint myModule.py
************Module myModule
myModule.py:19:0: C0303: Trailing whitespace (trailing-whitespace)
myModule.py:1:0: CQ103: Module name "myModule" doesn't conform to snake _case naming
style (invalid-name)
myModule.py:4:27: C0103: Argument name "nuclStr" doesn't conform to snake case naming
style (invalid-name)
------------------------------------------------------------
Your code has been rated at 2.50/10 (previous run: 0.00/10, +2.50)
```

Figure 10-21 We start by deleting empty lines using: *sed -i '/^$/d' myModule.py*

By running **pylint** immediately afterwards, we see that the trailing newlines have been removed. Note also that our code's rating has improved.

```
$ sed -i 's/\s*$//g' myModule.py
$ pylint myModule.py
************Module myModule
myModule.py:1:0: C0103: Module name "myModule" doesn't conform to snake
_case naming style (invalid-name)
myModule.py:4:27: C0103: Argument name "nuclStr" doesn't conform to snake
case naming style (invalid-name)
------------------------------------------------------------
Your code has been rated at 5.00/10 (previous run: 2.50/10, +2.50)
```

Figure 10-22 Now we delete trailing spaces

```
$ sed -i 's/nuclStr/nucl_str/g' myModule.py
$ pylint myModule.py
************Module myModule
myModule.py:1:0: C0103: Module name ``myModule'' doesn't conform to snake
case naming style (invalid-name)
------------------------------------------------------------
Your code has been rated at 7.50/10 (previous run: 5.00/10, +2.50)
```

Figure 10-23 Next, we replace all occurrences in the file of *nuclStr* with *nucl_str*

pylint informs us that this is no longer an issue.
Note also that our code's rating has again improved.

```
$ mv ~/myModule.py ~/my_module.py
$ pylint my_module.py
------------------------------------------------------------
Your code has been rated at 10.0/10 (previous run: 7.50/10, +2.50)
```

Figure 10-24 Next, we rename *myModule.py*

pylint informs us that all issues it caught have been resolved.

Do be aware that we will have to modify our unit test file, updating the filename, to reflect this change.

We will do this next, then run the unit tests to ensure all is good.

```
$ sed -i 's/myModule/my_module/g' unittest_get_percent_gc_content.py
$ python unittest_get_percent_gc content.py
..
======================================================================
Ran 2 tests in 0.000s

OK
```

Figure 10-25 Now to update our unit test file to reflect the change-of-name of *myModule*

After making the change, we rerun the unit tests to ensure all looks good.

Don't forget that we have one more garbage filter that we're going to write for this function before we put it into production.

> **Afterword**
> Learning to program takes patience and persistence.
> Tools exist to make it easier, but even with those tools, it takes patience, persistence, and effort to learn how to program; even more so if your goal is to learn how to do it well.
> Remember: As a skillset, programming is made up of many different interconnected skills; and as a beginner, you are trying to develop all of them.
> Expect to make lots of errors while programming (and not just when learning how to program!).
> Especially grammar, spelling, and punctuation (GSP) errors.
> Even professional programmers make these kinds of errors—some all the time!
> What makes these errors especially frustrating is that it is hard for us to see our own errors.
> If you find yourself getting frustrated, take a break. Go do something else for a while. Come back to your project with fresh eyes.
> And sometimes, be prepared to start over.
> In my experience, the people who give up are the ones who lose patience with themselves, with the teacher, and with the subject, while the ones who go on to acquire the skillset are those who persist in spite of the frustrations and the setbacks.
> I believe that they are inspired to persist, and each may have a different inspiration.
> One student loved solving math puzzles; and as he worked with algorithms, he saw how related solving problems with algorithms was to solving math puzzles.
> Another student wanted to solve a specific problem his lab had in finding overlap in images from red, blue, and green channels taken of samples in electron microscopy—and somehow the lesson (later) about list comprehension in Python sparked an idea in him that he worked on and solved alone, writing for his lab before the session ended a Python script that solved their problem.
> I myself wanted to be more than just a user of other people's programs. I too wanted to write code to solve problems.
> So again, if you're finding getting started rough, be patient with yourself and the material, get your second wind; and start again.
> There's a reason you're here, which means there is a payoff once you pass this post.

10.2   Introduction to Programming I: Implementing Algorithms

> An interpreter like Python is analogous to a human interpreter, in that it understands the language we share with it—say, Python—in order to translate our instructions to the machine into a language the machine understands—ultimately, machine code.

> For our purposes, the instructions we write in our programs tell computers how to transform or reformat data.
> Our programs will include data structures in session memory for us to copy our data into.
> We say therefore that our programs consist of sets of instructions for a computer to execute on data, as well as the data structures that we copy our data into while working with it or:
> **Programs = Algorithms + Data Structures**

> Guido van Rossum wrote Python to be easy to learn and easy to write useful programs in. This includes implementations of algorithms in Python that are both easy to write and easy to read.

In this chapter, as we continue our introduction to programming, our focus will be on implementing algorithms in Python.

> *When you created [Python], did you consider the type of programmers it might have attracted?*
> **Guido:** Yes, but I probably didn't have enough imagination. I was thinking of professional programmers in a Unix or Unix-like environment. Early versions of the Python tutorial used a slogan something like "Python bridges the gap between C and shell programming," because that was where I was myself, and the people immediately around me. It never occurred to me that Python would be a good language to embed in applications until people started asking about that.
> The fact that it was useful for teaching first principles of programming in a middle school or college setting or for self-teaching was merely a lucky coincidence, enabled by the many ABC features that I kept—ABC was aimed specifically at teaching programming to nonprogrammers.
>
> —Interview with Guido van Rossum, creator of Python[*]

According to python.org, "Python is an interpreted, object-oriented, high-level programming language."

A high-level programming language is one that hides, or handles independent from the programmer, the low-level details of how statements are executed. The programmer loses control of code execution at a low level in exchange for statements that read more like pseudocode, or even a stilted variant of English.[†]

---

[*] *Masterminds of Programming: Conversations With the Creators of Major Programming Languages*, Edited by Federico Biancuzzi and Shane Warden. O'Reilly Media. 2009. pp. 26–27.

[†] **Pseudocode** is essentially a mix of math, logic, and a natural language like English, in which we can write algorithms in ways not specific to any programming language. Pseudocode is meant to be easily read and understood. Modern programming languages like Python that are designed to be easy to learn and easy to use are high-level languages whose statements tend strongly to resemble pseudocode.

10.2 Introduction to Programming I: Implementing Algorithms

Python programs are written and saved as human-readable text files called "scripts." "Interpreted" means that a program called an interpreter (in this case, a Python interpreter) reads the text files directly and the instructions in them, interprets them into machine code, then feeds that code to the computer for execution.

```
False       await       else        import      pass
None        break       except      in          raise
True        class       finally     is          return
and         continue    for         lambda      try
as          def         from        nonlocal    while
assert      del         global      not         with
async       elif        if          or          yield
```

Figure 10-26 Python reserved words as of Python version 3.13.0. Click the image to go to the reference page on the **python.org** site. https://docs.python.org/3/reference/lexical_analysis.html#identifiers

These identifiers are used as reserved words, or keywords of the language, and cannot be used as ordinary identifiers. They must be spelled exactly as written here.

These are the words we will use to write Python statements.

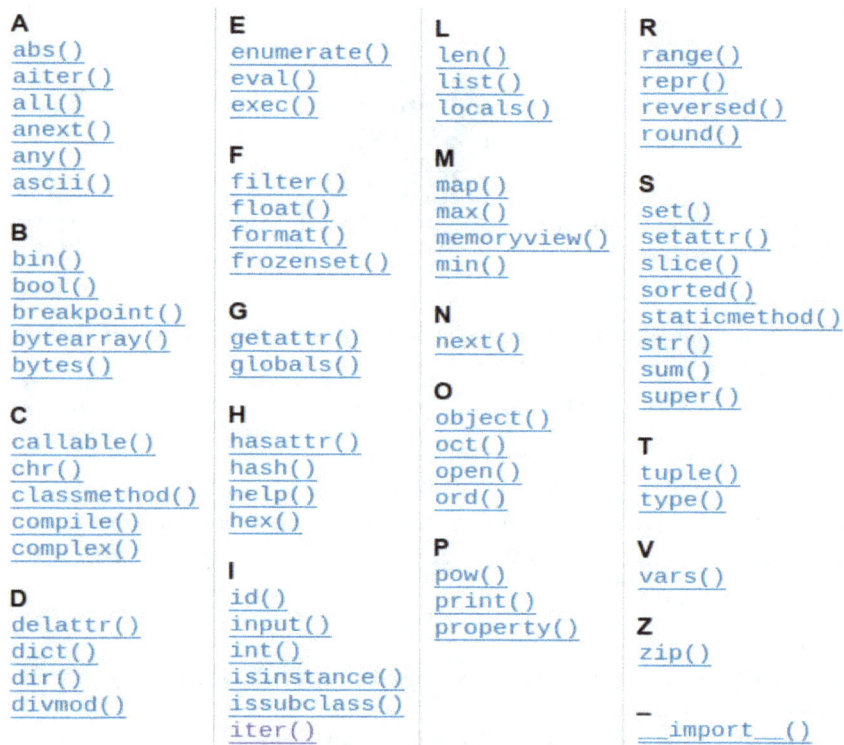

Figure 10-27 Python built-in functions as of Python version 3.13.0. Click the image to go to the reference page on the **python.org** site. https://docs.python.org/3/library/functions.html

In Python, invoking a function can also be a Python statement, for example: **print("hello, world!")**.

As with nested math functions, for example, **h(g(f(x)))**, the order of execution is innermost function first, and the return value of f(x) becomes the argument for the next innermost function—in this case, g()—then that function gets executed, and so on.

Hence, we read nested functions from innermost to outermost to understand what's going on in them.

Besides the built-in functions, Python offers hundreds more in its built-in modules; the SciPy community offers thousands more (also free!) for STEM researchers; and if that's not enough, Python makes it very easy for us to write our own!

> The order in which instructions are executed is determined by **control flow**.
> The order of execution can be (1) **sequential**, (2) **branching**, or (3) **looping**.
> When writing a program, the programmer decides, directly or indirectly, the order in which a machine executes the programmer's instructions.

10.2.1 The IPython Interactive Shell II

Figure 10-28 The IPython interactive shell. Click or scan the QR code to go to the IPython site, which includes online documentation. https://ipython.org/

Earlier, we introduced the IPython interactive shell. Now we continue our introduction to it as we learn how to program in Python.

We start by launching ipython in a Bash terminal session.

```
$ ipython
Python 3.13.2 (main, Feb  8 2025, 12:42:06) [GCC 11.4.0]
Type 'copyright', 'credits' or 'license' for more information
IPython 8.32.0 -- An enhanced Interactive Python. Type '?' for help.

In [1]:
```

Figure 10-29 The IPython interactive shell was created by physicist and programmer Fernando Pérez

It contains its own set of commands—called **magics**—that enhance its usefulness.

As we learn Python, we will also learn IPython magics.

10.2.2 Back to Python and Coding

Commonly used built-in collections

Python collections					
collection	abbr	enclosure	ordered	mutable	items
string	str	' ', " "	YES	NO	index/value
list	list	[ ]	YES	YES	index/value
dictionary	dict	{ }	NO	YES	key/value
tuple	tuple	( )	YES	NO	index/value
set	set	{ }	NO	YES	keys only

Earlier, we were introduced to some Python built-in collections. Now we will learn more about them, including how to use Python loop structures to step through the iterable collections.

We start by creating a string and assigning it as the value to a variable we'll call "testStr."

```
In [1]: testStr = 'hello, world'
```

A Python *assignment statement*.

We create variables and instantiate them using assignment statements.

The equal sign (=) is called **the assignment operator**. On the left-hand side (LHS) of the statement is the name we assign to the variable while on the right-hand side (RHS) is either the value or expression—whose value after it's evaluated—we assign to the variable.

Now that we've created the variable and instantiated it, we can invoke it in Python statements.

Referring to the table of Python collections, we observe that strings are ordered collections, that they cannot be modified once created (a property we call **immutable**), and that Python uses indices to reference values in strings (we say that the **items** in a string are **index/value pairs**).

```
In [2]: # we can now find the value at any position
   ...: # in a string by referring to its index
   ...: testStr[0]
Out[2]: 'h'
```

Figure 10-30 We enclose an index in square brackets immediately following a collection's name whose items are index/value pairs to reference the index's value

Python indexes on zero, which means it starts counting at zero. Hence, **testStr[0]** means the first position in **testStr**, and the statement, when executed, returns the value in that position, which is **'h'**.

Again, strings are immutable. This means that we cannot update a string's values once we've created the string.

```
In [3]: # if strings were mutable,
   ...: # this would be a legal statement...
   ...: testStr[0] = 'H'
```

```
TypeError                                 Traceback (most recent call last)
Cell In[3], line 3
      1 # if strings were mutable,
```

```
    2 # this would be a legal statement...
----> 3 testStr[0] = 'H'
```

`TypeError: 'str' object does not support item assignment`

Figure 10-31 The Python interpreter throws a *TypeError* when trying to update a value in a string

Please pay close attention to the contents of **Tracebacks** whenever Python throws them. They contain useful debugging info, including the line where the error was encountered and an explanation of what caused the error.

Here, we're being told that strings do not support item assignment, which means that strings' values cannot be updated.

```
In [4]: 'h' in testStr
Out[4]: True
```

Figure 10-32 The Python keyword *in* pulls double duty

As an operator in a simple statement, it tells the machine to test if a value is a member of a collection, as in this example.

The interpreter returns a bool.

```
In [5]: for letter in testStr:
```

The Python for-loop clause.

Here, **in** is part of the Python for-loop clause.

The for-loop is one of two loop structures in Python, the other being the **while** loop.

In this example, the for-loop directs the machine to iterate through testStr from start to end, and in the body of code below this clause, we'll tell the machine what to do with each value in turn.

Note the for-loop variable's name, 'letter'. We can name the for-loop variable anything we want (except Python keywords). As the machine iterates through the string, it assigns the variable whichever value it's currently at in the string; and we invoke the variable in the for-loop's block of code when telling the machine what to do to each value.

```
In [5]: for letter in testStr:
   ...:     print(letter)
   ...:
h
e
l
l
o
,
w
o
r
l
d
```

Figure 10-33 Here, we direct the machine to print the current letter as it iterates left to right through the string

```
In [6]: # first, we create a variable to test.
   ...: # when tested in the while statement,
   ...: # it must test True for the interpreter
   ...: # to enter the body of the while-loop
   ...: controlVar = 3

In [7]: while controlVar > 0:
   ...:     # in the body of the while-loop,
   ...:     # we tell the machine what to do
   ...:     # during each pass through it.
   ...:     # in the last statement, we modify
   ...:     # the value of the variable in a way
   ...:     # so that the expression in the while
   ...:     # clause eventually evaluates as False,
   ...:     # and the machine can drop out of the loop
   ...:     print(controlVar)
   ...:     controlVar -= 1
   ...:
3
2
1
```

Figure 10-34 The while loop is the more general loop construct

In fact, the while loop can be constructed to behave like any other loop construct, including the for loop.

10.3 Testing If Symbol in String Is Nucleotide

> **What You Need to Know**
> When an iterable collection is passed into the built-in **enumerate** function, it returns an enumerate object, itself an ordered collection, whose items are tuples, and the items of the tuples themselves are index, value pairs of the original collection.
> The **f-string**. f-strings were introduced into Python in version 3.6 to simplify writing and reading format print statements.
> **Backslashes are used to write long Python statements across two or more lines.** PEP 8 - Style Guide for Python Code says, "Limit all lines to a maximum of 79 characters."
> Here, the ESCAPE metacharacter (\) is used to escape the newline character, making long Python statements more readable by allowing programmers to write them across multiple lines, in keeping with Python's style guide.
> **Writing a long string as substring items within parentheses is one way to write long strings across two or more lines in Python code.**
> **For f-strings, simply write each substring as an f-string (prepend an *f* to each substring).**

In this section, we will write the second garbage filter for our **get_percent_gc_content**() function.

Specification: The garbage filter will test each symbol in a nucleotide string to ensure it is a nucleotide symbol. If a non-nucleotide is found, it and its index position in the string will added to a dictionary as index:value pairs. We assert that if the dictionary is empty, the nucleotide string is clean; otherwise, the interpreter throws an **AssertionError** printing the dictionary and its contents, thus showing users where to find the non-nucleotides in their strings, as well as what to look for.

Given its usefulness, we will write the garbage filter as a function that we can then import into any function in which we need to test if an input string is a clean nucleotide string, including the get_percent_gc_content() function. This is in keeping with the programming rule:

Write once, run everywhere.

To get the index:value pairs of the items in an ordered collection, we can use the built-in **enumerate**() function:

```
In [1]: enumerate('python')
Out[1]: <enumerate at 0x701674710db0>
```

Figure 10-35 Invoking the **enumerate**() function

Note that what the interpreter returns to the command line is an acknowledgement that an **enumerate** object has been created, as well as its starting address in memory.

enumerate objects are not meant to be viewed; rather, they are meant to speed up the execution of Python statements that use them.

```
In [2]: list(enumerate('python'))
Out[2]: [(0, 'p'), (1, 'y'), (2, 't'), (3, 'h'), (4, 'o'), (5, 'n')]
```

Figure 10-36 However, we can coerce an enumerate object into another ordered collection to see what its items are: tupled (**index, value**) pairs

```
In [3]: for item in enumerate('python'):
   ...:     print(item)
   ...:
(0, 'p')
(1, 'y')
(2, 't')
(3, 'h')
(4, 'o')
(5, 'n')
```

Figure 10-37 When we invoke *enumerate()* in a *for-loop* clause, the machine iterates over the tupled (index, value) pairs in the *enumerate* object

```
In [4]: for index, value in enumerate('python'):
   ...:     print(f"{index}: {value}")
   ...:
0: p
1: y
2: t
3: h
4: o
5: n
```

Figure 10-38 Finally, as the machine iterates over the tuples in the *enumerate* object, we can specify that we want it to work with the items in each tuple

10.3 Testing If Symbol Is Nucleotide

This is how we will use **enumerate()** in our new function.

```python
def ensure_clean_nucl_str(nuclStr: str) -> dict:
    ''' Given a nucleotide string as input,
        return a dictionary of index:value pairs
        of bad values in string.
        If nucleotide string is clean,
        return an empty dictionary.
        >>>ensure_clean_nucl_str('gattaxa')
        {5:'x'}
    '''
    #### garbage filter
    assert isinstance(nuclStr, str),\
        'input must be a string'

    #### implementation of algorithm
    ### initialization
    bad_values = {}
    for index, char in enumerate(nuclStr):
        if char not in 'acgtACGT':
            bad_values[index] = char

    return bad_values
```

Figure 10-39 Our new function.

We develop our function in its own text file. I prefer to name these scratch files after the functions in which I develop them; hence, I've written this function in a file called "ensure_nucl_str_clean.py."

After writing the function in **vim**, we save and quit.

Next, we run pylint against the file and correct any issues that pylint finds.

```
$ python unittest_ensure_nucl_str_clean.py
...
======================================================================
Ran 3 tests in 0.000s

OK
```

Figure 10-40 Unit testing our function

The first test tests the garbage filter.

Of the next two tests, one ensures that a clean nucleotide string as input returns an empty string while the other ensures that a nucleotide string with a single non-nucleotide as input returns a dictionary with an index:value pair showing position and value of the non-nucleotide as output.

Next chapter, when we start writing unit tests, we'll study the prewritten unit tests to see how they work. But for now, let's just stick with running the tests.

With the function linted and tested, we can copy and paste it into our module.

```python
def get_percent_gc_content(nucl_str: str) -> float:
    '''(str) -> float # type contract
        Returns the percent gc content of nucleotide string input.

        >>>get_percent_gc_content('gattacagattaca')
        28.571428571428573
    '''
    # garbage filters
    assert isinstance(nucl_str, str),\
        'input must be a clean nucleotide string'
    bad_values = ensure_clean_nucl_str(nucl_str)
    assert not bad_values,\
        f'bad values in string! check these index:value pairs\n{bad_values}'
    # initialization
    nucl_str = nucl_str.upper()
    # implementation of the algorithm
    return 100 * (nucl_str.count('G') + nucl_str.count('C')) / len(nucl_str)
```

Figure 10-41 Finally, we import our new function into any function that needs to use it as a garbage filter

Note that the second **assert** statement invokes the dictionary, and if there are items in the **bad_values** dictionary, an assertion error is thrown.

Note that the **f-string** of the **assert** statement is fairly long so we write it across two lines, one substring to a line, and enclosed in parentheses. If the assertion statement is thrown, the interpreter will concatenate the substrings into a single string message to the user.

10.4 Euclid GCD

> **What You Need to Know**
> Python supports **multiple assignment statements**. This allows the programmer to create and instantiate, or update, multiple variables in the same statement.
> Using the **bool** function, we can coerce values and collections into **bools**.
> All numeric values except zero evaluate as true. Zero evaluates as false.
> Collections that contain any items evaluate as true. Empty collections evaluate as false.
> As in other programming languages, the percent sign (**%**) serves as the **modulo**, or **remainder**, operator in integer division.

Before we implement the Euclid GCD algorithm in Python, we observe that Python supports multiple assignment statements:

```python
# here, we set the value natA to 53667 and natB to 25527
natA, natB = 53667, 25527
```

10.4 Euclid GCD

We observe that any number except zero coerced into a bool evaluates as true—and that zero alone evaluates as false:

```
bool(5) # coercing an int into a bool
True
bool(-5.) # coercing a float into a bool
True
bool(5j) # coercing a complex number
True
bool(0) # coercing zero into a bool
False
```

And we observe that in Python, as in many languages, the percent sign is used as the modulo, or remainder, operator in integer division.

```
# 5 mod 3, or what whole number remains
# after dividing 5 by 3
5 % 3
2
```

As a friendly reminder: the Euclid GCD algorithm works entirely with remainders. The remainder of an integer division is evaluated: if not zero, the divisor becomes the dividend and the new remainder becomes the divisor, and the remainder from *this* integer division is evaluated. The process continues until the remainder is zero, then we take the divisor of that integer division—the one where the remainder is zero—as our answer.

Now let's put this all together into Python code:

```
In [1]: # first we create and instantiate our variables
   ...: # as long as natB is NOT zero,
   ...: # the machine will keep executing the while loop
   ...: natA, natB = 53667, 25527
   ...: # while natB is NOT zero...
   ...: while natB:
   ...:     # use a multiple assignment statement
   ...:     # to shift/update the values
   ...:     natA, natB = natB, natA % natB
   ...: print(natA)
201
```

Figure 10-42 The Euclid GCD algorithm implemented in Python

After we create and instantiate the variables as an initialization, Python needs only two lines of code to implement the algorithm: a while clause and a multiple assignment statement in the while loop's block of code.

Before we write this algorithm into a function in our module, let's take a moment to consider how we might test for bad input. The input for this algorithm is two natural numbers greater than zero.

```
natA, natB = 53667, 25527
isinstance(natA, int) and (natA > 0) and isinstance(natB, int) and (natB > 0)
True
```

Figure 10-43 The compound logic statement that we'll use as a garbage filter

Note that both integer arguments undergo the same tests and that **and**-ing the tests together requires that all must be true, or the **assert** test fails.

Now, let's implement this algorithm, along with the garbage filter, in a Python function in a stand-alone text file, where we can lint it and run our unit tests against it.

```
def euclid_gcd(natA: int, natB: int) -> int:
    ''' Given two natural numbers greater than zero,
        return their greatest common divisor.
        FYI: two natural numbers are relatively prime
        when the return value is 1.
        >>>euclid_gcd(53667, 25527)
        201
    '''
    ##### garbage filter
    assert isinstance(natA, int) and (natA > 0)\
        and isinstance(natB, int) and (natB > 0),\
        'Both arguments must be ints greater than zero.'
    ##### implementation of algorithm
    while natB:
        natA, natB = natB, natA % natB
    return natA
```

Figure 10-44 *euclid_gcd()* function written into a stand-alone text file for linting and unit testing

Note that we include type hints and a docstring for our users, a garbage filter to catch and handle bad input, and comments for other programmers.

The code and comments that we add to make our code more robust and easier to read and use can be many lines more than the code needed to implement the algorithm.

If you're in the IPython interactive shell, you can open **euclid_gcd.py** on the command line using the IPython magic **%edit**. Type: **%edit euclid_gcd.py** RETURN .

The text file opens in **vim**.

When you've finished, save your changes and exit vim. You'll be back on the command line.

```
$ pylint euclid_gcd.py
************* Module euclid_gcd
euclid_gcd.py:4:15: C0103: Argument name "natA" doesn't conform to snake_case
naming style (invalid-name)
euclid_gcd.py:4:26: C0103: Argument name "natB" doesn't conform to snake_case
naming style (invalid-name)

------------------------------------
Your code has been rated at 6.00/10
```

Figure 10-45 Linting our new function

10.4 Euclid GCD

```
$ sed -i 's/natA/nat_a/g' euclid_gcd.py
$ sed -i 's/natB/nat_b/g' euclid_gcd.py
$ pylint euclid_gcd.py

-------------------------------------------------------------------
Your code has been rated at 10.00/10 (previous run: 6.00/10, +4.00)
```

Figure 10-46 Using *sed* to fix the issues

Pylint reports no more issues.

```
$ python unittest_euclid_gcd.py
..
===================================================================
Ran 2 tests in 0.000s

OK
```

Figure 10-47 Unit testing our new function

Looks good.
Now we copy our **euclid_gcd()** function in **myModule**.

Figure 10-48 We start in the *IPython* interactive shell by running two magic commands

```
In [1]: %load_ext autoreload

In [2]: %autoreload complete

In [3]: %edit myModule.py
Editing... done. Executing edited code...

In [4]: import myModule as mM

In [5]: mM.
         ensure_nuclStr_clean()
         euclid_gcd()
         get_percent_gc_content()
```

The first magic command tells the shell to load the **autoreload** module. The second instructs the shell to "Reload all modules every time before executing the Python code typed," including "any new objects in the module."

Note that when we return to the IPython interactive shell, it tests our code for grammar, spelling, and punctuation mistakes by running it. This is the best time to catch mistakes and present them to you, while the code is still fresh in your head.

If it does show a Traceback, make note of the error and line number, go back into your module with the **%edit** command, and fix the error. Wash, rinse, repeat until you've dealt with all the errors that IPython catches.

We import our module.
And now on the command line, we enter our module name, followed by a dot (.), then hit TAB.
IPython presents a drop-down menu with all the functions in our module.
Let's choose **euclid_gcd()** so we can test it with known values.

```
mM.euclid_gcd(53667, 25527)
201
```

```
# try two natural numbers that are relatively prime; for example, 27 and 8.
mM.euclid_gcd(27, 8)
1
```

Figure 10-49 Testing our new function with known good input/output

```
mM.euclid_gcd(27., 8)
```

Figure 10-50 Testing our new function's garbage filter with bad input

Python should throw an **AssertionError** in a Traceback that reads:
Both arguments must be ints greater than zero.
We will learn how to write our own **unit tests** later.

10.5 Converting Decimal Fractions into Binary

> **What You Need to Know**
> The **range()** function and the **range** object. "Range" in this context means an interval, as in the interval of a number line. The **range()** function returns an ordered collection of natural numbers.
>
>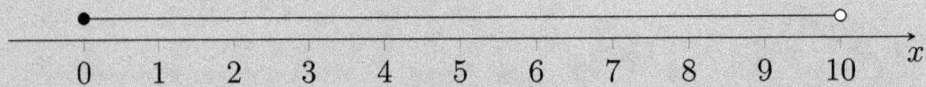
>
> **Figure 10-51** The interval, or *range*, of the natural numbers from zero (included) to ten (excluded)
>
> This, conceptually, is what you get when you write and run: **range(10)**.
> Another way that you may hear the range object described that results from running **range(10)** is that it holds the first 10 natural numbers, indexing on zero. When we execute **range(10)**, the Python interpreter outputs: **range(0, 10)** to acknowledge that it has created a range object with the endpoints zero (included) and ten (excluded).
> A number line interval that includes one endpoint but excludes the other is called "a half-open interval."
> By design, Python uses this half-open interval when creating range objects and slices (which we'll learn about later).
> You can change the small and big endpoints by passing in two **ints** into the **range()** function, which define the start and end of the half-open interval.

10.5 Converting Decimal Fractions into Binary

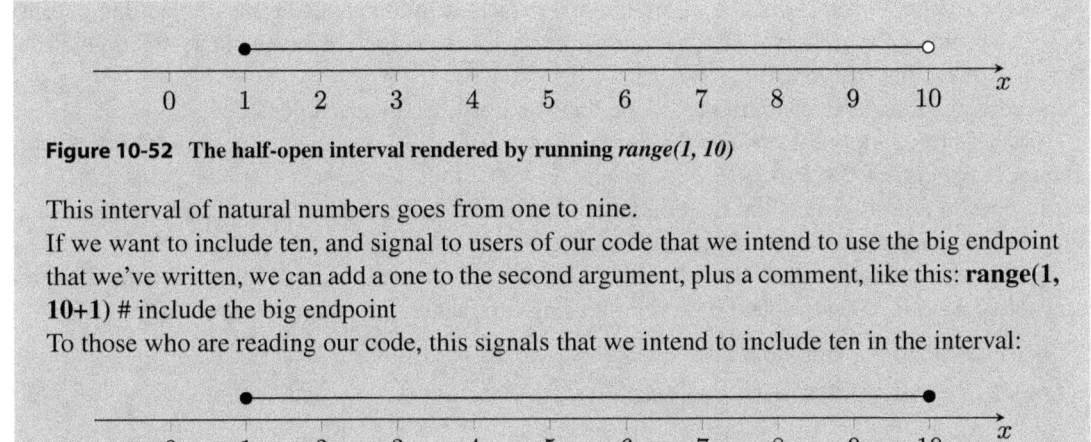

Figure 10-52 The half-open interval rendered by running *range(1, 10)*

This interval of natural numbers goes from one to nine.

If we want to include ten, and signal to users of our code that we intend to use the big endpoint that we've written, we can add a one to the second argument, plus a comment, like this: **range(1, 10+1) # include the big endpoint**

To those who are reading our code, this signals that we intend to include ten in the interval:

In Priyanka Bhakat's Introduction to Computational Chemistry course, the teacher shows the class a hand algorithm to convert positive decimal (base-10) fractions into binary (base-2) fractions. Now Priyanka refers to her notes on the lecture to implement the algorithm into a Python function that she can save in a module.

Table 10-1 Decimal fractions. Example: 0.126_{10}

Number	0.	1	2	6
Position	10^0	10^{-1}	10^{-2}	10^{-3}
		Tenths	Hundredths	Thousandths
Positional value		$1 \cdot 10^{-1}$	$2 \cdot 10^{-2}$	$6 \cdot 10^{-3}$

As the teacher decomposed the example decimal fraction in this table, (Table 10-1), he mentioned that—along with zero as a concept and a digit—ancient Indian mathematicians invented the positional notation that allows us to work easily with numbers in the ten-symbol (base-10) system that they came up with.

Then he mentioned that the positional notation works in other bases, as well, and he proceeded to show the class a binary fraction (Table 10-2).

Table 10-2 Binary fractions. Example: 0.101_2

Number	0.	1	0	1
Position	2^0	2^{-1}	2^{-2}	2^{-3}
		$\frac{1}{2}$	$\frac{1}{4}$	$\frac{1}{8}$
		One-half	One-quarter	One-eighth
Positional value		$1 \cdot 2^{-1}$	$0 \cdot 2^{-2}$	$1 \cdot 2^{-3}$

As the teacher decomposed the example binary fraction in this table, he mentioned that because base-2 has only two symbols—zero and one—in a way it is easier to reckon a binary fraction's value than it is a decimal fraction's:

1 means a positional value contributes to the final sum, while 0 means it doesn't.

(No need to multiply the positional values by more digits, like we have to for decimal fractions.) Hence, 0.101_2 is $\frac{1}{2} + 0 + \frac{1}{8}$, or $\frac{5}{8}$.

To convert a positive decimal fraction to a binary fraction, Priyanka's teacher said, we can use an algorithm that uses addition, or a very similar one that uses subtraction.

After a show of hands of whether he should show the algorithm using addition or subtraction, the teacher decided to show the class how to do it using subtraction.

Initialization: write a string to hold the positional values of the binary fraction. Write: '0.'

Step 1. Start with 2^{-1}. Subtract $\frac{1}{2}$ from decimal fraction. You will have 3 possible outcomes:

   a) 0. This positional value IS part of the answer; and there are NO more binary positional values in the answer. Append '1' to the binary fraction string and halt.
   b) A negative difference. This positional value is NOT part of the answer. Append '0' to the binary fraction string, add $\frac{1}{2}$ to the difference; and continue to next positional value, 2^{-2}.
   c) A positive difference. This positional value IS part of the answer. Append '1' to the binary fraction string and continue to next positional value, 2^{-2}.

Step 2. If you had (b) or (c), subtract $\frac{1}{4}$ from the decimal fraction you now have. You will have the same 3 possible outcomes you had in Step 1, except the fraction is now $\frac{1}{4}$, and the next positional value is 2^{-3}.

Step 3. Continue in the loop until you reckon as many positional values in the binary fraction as you want, or you reach (a) and halt.

The teacher then stepped through the algorithm to produce Table 10-3.

Table 10-3 Calculating binary fraction equivalent of decimal fraction. Example: 0.625_{10}

Bin frac	Dec frac	Pos Value	Diff	Step	Note
'10.'	.625	.5	.125	c	Append '1' to the binary fraction, shift difference to decimal fraction; update positional value
'0.1'	.125	.25	-.125	b	Append '0' to the binary fraction, restore decimal fraction to .125, update positional value to .125
'0.10'	.125	.125	0	a	Append '1' to the binary fraction and halt
'0.101'	HALT	HALT	HALT	HALT	Return binary fraction as answer

After reviewing her class notes, Priyanka decides to write her Python function implementing the addition algorithm. Knowing that binary rational fractions, like decimal rational fractions, can go on forever, she decides to limit how many binary positional values will be part of the answer. She'll set the default to 10 digits.

10.5 Converting Decimal Fractions into Binary

```python
def decFrac2binFrac(decFrac: float, numBinDigits: int = 10) -> str:
```

Although she's not yet ready to implement the algorithm, Priyanka decides on a name for her function, what it will take for arguments, and what it will return.

Before you try to implement an algorithm, you should have a specification for the implementation. If she has sample inputs/outputs, Priyanka can start writing the unit tests.

Priyanka starts reasoning out the algorithm.

Initialization:

(a) Write a string to hold the positional values of the binary fraction:
   bin_frac = '0.'
(b) Create and instantiate a float called 'running_sum':
   running_sum = 0.

To calculate any positional value within the binary fraction, she can use its position in the binary fraction, negated, and raised to the power of two:

$.5_{10} = 2^{-1}$
$.25_{10} = 2^{-2}$
$.125_{10} = 2^{-3}$
$.0625_{10} = 2^{-4}$

...and so on.

Hence, the Python statement that calculates the positional value for any position in a positive binary fraction is:

positional_value = 2-(position)**

Priyanka knows that by using a **for** loop, she can iterate position by position through the binary fraction, and at each position, she can calculate its positional value.

The algorithm, and its implementation, is starting to come into focus.

She can use a **range** object for the iteration. Hence:

for position in range(1, numBinDigits+1):
positional_value = 2-(position)** # update the positional value

Priyanka reasons that she can then add the **positional_value** to the **running_sum**, then compare that to the value of the decimal fraction to determine if the **positional_value** contributes to the binary equivalent of the decimal fraction.

She writes out her solution.

```python
def decFrac2binFrac(decFrac: float, numBinDigits: int = 10) -> str:
    '''
    
    '''
    # garbage filters
    # implementation of algorithm
    running_sum, binFrac = 0, '0.' # initialization
    for position in range(1, numBinDigits+1):
        pos_value = 2**-(position)
        running_sum = running_sum + pos_value
        if running_sum > decFrac:
            binFrac = binFrac + '0'
```

```
            running_sum = running_sum - pos_value
        else:
            binFrac = binFrac + '1'
    return binFrac
```

Figure 10-53 Priyanka's rough draft*

Note that the first working version is not a final version.

Priyanka still has to add garbage filters, user documentation, and unit tests. She may also want to add more comments in her code.

Then she'll need to lint it.

Garbage Filter: How to Assert That Only Positive Decimal Fractions Are Passed into Function

Priyanka knows she needs to ensure that only **floats** are passed into the function as **decFrac**, but how to ensure that those floats are only positive fractions?

If she can get just the fractional part of the float, then, if the float is just a fraction, when she subtracts the fractional part from it, she'll get zero. She can coerce the difference into a bool to test if the float is a positive fraction.

But how to get just the fractional part of a float?

After googling around, she learns that she has two options:

a. Use **modf()** in Python's built-in **math** module, which returns the fractional and integer parts of the float passed into it; or
b. Use the **mod** operator (%) with 1 as the divisor, or **n % 1**, which returns the fractional part of **n**.

Priyanka settles on using **b**.

```
# garbage filters
assert isinstance(decFrac, float),\
    'decFrac must be a positive fraction.'
# if decFrac is a positive fraction,
# the subtraction in the assert statement below
# yields zero. decFrac must be positive,
# so we negate the difference, making the zero True.
# other differences evaluate as False.
assert not decFrac - (decFrac % 1), \
    'decFrac must be a positive fraction.'
```

Figure 10-54 Priyanka's garbage filters for her function

Priyanka remembers the admonitions of her Introduction to Programming teacher, first among them:

Write clearly—don't be too clever.[†]

---

[*] A rough draft *could* be a final version, provided you are not sharing it with others and you do not intend to maintain it. If, however, you do intend to share and maintain it, then your rough draft is simply a working copy that is *still* in development.

[†] **"Write clearly — don't be too clever."**
Kernighan and Plauger. *The Elements of Programming Style, 2d ed*. 1978. pg 2.

10.5 Converting Decimal Fractions into Binary

She wonders if the second **assert** statement, as simple as it is, might qualify as at least a bit too clever.

Then she decides that the mathematical expression is simple arithmetic, and the interested programmer can quickly reason it out.

```python
# implementation of algorithm
# initialization
running_sum, binFrac = 0, '0.'

# iterate through the positions of
# the binary fraction. for each position,
# calculate its base-10 value, then test
# whether or not it contributes to the value
# of the decimal fraction.
for position in range(1, numBinDigits+1):
    pos_value = 2**-(position)
    if (running_sum + pos_value) > decFrac:
        # pos_value does NOT contribute
        # to decimal fraction
        binFrac = binFrac + '0'
    else:
        # pos_value contributes
        # to decimal fraction
        binFrac = binFrac + '1'
        # update running_sum
        running_sum = running_sum + pos_value
```

Figure 10-55 Priyanka edits her code and comments it

Priyanka considers her code a working draft, a piece of work that can be continually improved.

Additionally, she adds comments to explain her instructions to a machine so it renders the stringified binary fraction equivalent of a decimal fraction input.

```python
''' Given a positive fractional float as input,
    returns its base-2 equivalent as a string.
    A second argument is the number of digits
    in the binary fraction. The default is 10
    digits.

>>>decFrac2binFrac(.75)
'0.1100000000'
>>>decFrac2binFrac(.1, 20)
'0.00011001100110011001'
'''
```

Figure 10-56 Priyanka adds a docstring to explain her function to users

```
$ python unittest_decFrac2binFrac.py
......
======================================================================
Ran 6 tests in 0.000s

OK
```

Figure 10-57 Priyanka runs unit tests against her function

The unit tests ensure that the garbage filters work and that the implementation of the algorithm returns correct output, given expected output.

```
$ pylint decFrac2BinFrac.py


************* Module decFrac2BinFrac
decFrac2BinFrac.py:1:0: C0103: Module name "decFrac2BinFrac" doesn't conform to snake_case naming style (invalid-name)
decFrac2BinFrac.py:4:0: C0103: Function name "decFrac2binFrac" doesn't conform to snake_case naming style (invalid-name)
decFrac2BinFrac.py:4:20: C0103: Argument name "decFrac" doesn't conform to snake_case naming style (invalid-name)
decFrac2BinFrac.py:4:36: C0103: Argument name "numBinDigits" doesn't conform to snake_case naming style (invalid-name)
decFrac2BinFrac.py:28:17: C0103: Variable name "binFrac" doesn't conform to snake_case naming style (invalid-name)
decFrac2BinFrac.py:40:12: C0103: Variable name "binFrac" doesn't conform to snake_case naming style (invalid-name)
decFrac2BinFrac.py:44:12: C0103: Variable name "binFrac" doesn't conform to snake_case naming style (invalid-name)

-----------------------------------
Your code has been rated at 3.64/10
```

Figure 10-58 Priyanka writes her function to a text file, saves it, then runs pylint on it.

```
$ sed -i 's/decFrac2BinFrac/dec_frac_2_bin_frac/g' decFrac2BinFrac.py
$ sed -i 's/decFrac/dec_frac/g' decFrac2BinFrac.py
$ sed -i 's/numBinDigits/num_bin_digits/g' decFrac2BinFrac.py
$ sed -i 's/binFrac/bin_frac/g' decFrac2BinFrac.py
$ mv decFrac2BinFrac.py dec_frac_2_bin_frac.py
```

Figure 10-59 Priyanka fixes the issues enumerated by *pylint*

```
$ pylint dec_frac_2_bin_frac.py


------------------------------------
Your code has been rated at 10.00/10
```

Figure 10-60 Priyanka runs pylint a final time

Looking good, Priyanka!

10.5.1 The More You Know: Brahmagupta (598–668CE)

Brahmagupta is considered one of the best and most accomplished mathematicians and astronomers in history. His most famous work, Brahma-sphuta-siddhanta, dates to 628CE.

In it, Brahmagupta covers many subjects in astronomy and math, including the first clear description of the quadratic formula, and rules for using negative numbers, positive numbers, and zero.

The concept or invention of zero, as well as a symbol to represent it, first arose among Indian mathematicians hundreds of years before Brahmagupta; however, it was Brahmagupta's work that introduced this invention, as well as a number system that includes the negatives, to a wider audience—more specifically, mathematicians in the Islamic world.

Al-Khwarizmi (780–850CE) (re: Section 8.1, *An Introduction to Algorithms*) is known to have studied and built upon Brahmagupta's works in his own works, which describe algorithms for working in the base-10 number system invented by Indian mathematicians.

And it was mathematicians of the Islamic world who spread what Europeans would call the "Hindu-Arabic" number system throughout Asia, Africa, and Europe.

10.6 Introduction to Programming II: Unit Testing

> Unit tests are static tests conducted on isolated units of code (for our purposes, functions and scripts).
>
> We run unit tests while developing or maintaining code.
>
> In test-driven development, we start by writing tests, guided by the specifications of how the code should behave, then develop our functions or scripts, clearing the errors and failures our unit tests throw.
>
> We continue the test-develop-test cycle until all tests pass.

In this chapter, after we learn how to implement and run unit tests in Python, we will turn our current develop-algorithm-implement-test cycle on its head by following the methodology of test-driven development (TDD), in which we start by writing unit tests that implement the specification of the code we're tasked to write (including examples, if given, of good input/output), then developing our code in write-test-revise cycles until we clear all the errors and failures that the unit tests throw.

10.6.1 Unit Tests and Our unittest_template.py File

> Python comes with a built-in **unittest** module.
>
> The module requires that we write a class. When the code is run, it creates an instance of an object from the class.
>
> To simplify the process of writing unit tests, we have a **unittest_template.py**

(continued)

> **(continued)**
> To use it, we rename a copy of it, place the copy in the same directory as our module, then find and replace UPPERCASE keywords in the copy with names applicable to the module/function we want to test.
> We execute the unit tests by running the copy as a Python script on the Bash command line, for example:
> **python test_myModule_get_percent_gc_content.py**

```
$ cp ~/repo/intro_to_programming/unittests/unittest_template.py ~
$ cp ~/unittest_template.py ~/test_myModule_get_percent_gc_content.py
```

Figure 10-61 We start by copying the unittest template in our repo into our home directory

We copy twice: once to have a clean copy of the template on hand and once to rename the template to a name that shows what we're testing.

```python
import unittest

'''
this is a template of a unit test scirpt.
reference: https://docs.python.org/3/library/unittest.html
'''

'''
this template uses a FILE (module or script) and a function we created in class
to aid comprehension.
name your actual unit test script "test_<FILE WE'RE TESTING>.py"
'''

# 1. get the function to test or import the module to test.
from FILE import FUNC

# 2. create a class into which we pass the unit tests we want to perform.
class Test_FILE(unittest.TestCase):

    # 3. create a method for each garbage_filter test to perform.
    def test_GARBAGE_FILTER_1(self):
        ''' assert input must be a string
        '''
        with self.assertRaises(AssertionError):
            FUNC(BAD_ARG)

    # 4. create a method for each test to perform.
    def test_FUNC(self):
        result = FUNC(ARG)
        # here, the test ensures that output of the function is indeed
        # the expected output.
        self.assertEqual(result, RESULT)

# 5. we run the unit tests defined within the class.
```

10.6 Introduction to Programming II: Unit Testing

```
# we can modify verbosity level (default=1) to get more or less info
# as tests run.
#unittest.main(verbosity=2)


# 6. we set up our unit tests so we can invoke them off the bash command line
if __name__ == '__main__':
    unittest.main()
```

Figure 10-62 unittest_template.py

This template was designed to make using unit tests in out-of-the-box Python as easy as possible.

Note the UPPERCASE words in the file. We need only to replace them with words that apply to the file and functions we're working with now.

We keep a clean copy of the template on hand so we can copy/paste its parts into a working unit test script and modify the pasted-in parts as needed.

words to find and replace	
find:	replace with:
FILE	myModule
FUNC	get_percent_gc_content
GARBAGE_FILTER	GARBAGE_FILTER_get_percent_gc_content_1
GARBAGE_FILTER_2	GARBAGE_FILTER_get_percent_gc_content_2
ARG	'gattaca'
BAD_ARG	3
BAD_ARG2	'gxbbaea'
RESULT	28.571428571428573

Figure 10-63 Our first edit of *test_myModule_get_percent_gc_content.py*

We start by setting up unit tests for the first function we wrote into our module.

Note that we have two garbage filters for **get_percent_gc_content**(). We need to test each separately. We can **vim** into **test_myModule_get_percent_gc_content.py** to add the second garbage filter.

We can find and replace using different Bash tools, including **vim** or **sed**.

The advantage of **sed** is that we can use it to edit a text file without opening the file.

However, we will be in **vim** adding code for a second garbage filter so let's make our changes in **vim**.

```
# 3. create a method for each garbage_filter test to perform.
def test_GARBAGE_FILTER_1(self):
    ''' assert input must be a string
    '''
    with self.assertRaises(AssertionError):
        FUNC(BAD_ARG)
def test_GARBAGE_FILTER_2(self):
    ''' assert input must be clean
        nucleotide string
    '''
```

```
    with self.assertRaises(AssertionError):
        FUNC(BAD_ARG2)
```

Figure 10-64 test_myModule_get_percent_gc_content.py in vim

Here, we copy and paste the garbage filter method to create a second garbage filter; then we change the second one's UPPERCASE words just enough to ensure uniqueness.

```python
# 1. get the function to test or import the module to test.
from myModule import FUNC

# 2. create a class into which we pass the unit tests we want to perform.
class Test_myModule(unittest.TestCase):
```

Figure 10-65 The result of running *:%s/FILE/myModule/g* in command mode

In **vim**, we can find and replace all occurrences of a string while in the command mode by using: **%s/FIND/replace/g**

Let's find and replace the remaining UPPERCASE words, using the table above as a guide.

```python
    import unittest

    '''
    this is a template of a unit test scirpt.
    reference: https://docs.python.org/3/library/unittest.html
    '''
    '''
    this template uses a FILE (module or script) and a function we created in class
    to aid comprehension.
    name your actual unit test script "test_<FILE WE'RE TESTING>.py"
    '''

    # 1. get the function to test or import the module to test.
    from myModule import get_percent_gc_content

    # 2. create a class into which we pass the unit tests we want to perform.
    class Test_myModule(unittest.TestCase):

    # 3. create a method for each garbage_filter test to perform.
    def test_GARBAGE_FILTER_1(self):
        ''' assert input must be a string
        '''
        with self.assertRaises(AssertionError):
            get_percent_gc_content(3)
    def test_GARBAGE_FILTER_2(self):
        ''' assert input must be clean
            nucleotide string
        '''
        with self.assertRaises(AssertionError):
            get_percent_gc_content('gxbbaea')

        # 4. create a method for each test to perform.
        def test_get_percent_gc_content(self):
            result = get_percent_gc_content('gattaca')
            # here, the test ensures that output of the function is indeed
```

```
                   # the expected output.
           self.assertEqual(result, 28.571428571428573)
```

Figure 10-66 Result of find-replace substitutions on *test_myModule_get_percent_gc_content.py*

This unit test script is ready to run. Make sure to save changes to disk before quitting.

```
$ python test_myModule_get_percent_gc_content.py
...
====================================================
Ran 3 tests in 0.000s

OK
```

Figure 10-67 Output of the *unit test* script

The three dots signify that all three tests ran ok.

It's important to remember that your tests cover only the cases you're testing for. As you gain experience, you'll get better at figuring out what you need to test for and how to do so.

Now that we've written unit tests for our first function, let's make unittest files for the other two functions in our module. To keep it simple, we'll copy the unittest files we've already made for stand-alone euclid_gcd.py and ensure_nucl_str_clean.py, rename the copies by prepending **test_myModule_** to the filenames, then changing the names in the files on line 13 to **my_module**.

Save the changes, then run the tests.

```
$ python test_myModule_ensure_nucl_str_clean.py
...
====================================================
Ran 2 tests in 0.000s

OK
$ python test_myModule_euclid_gcd.py
...
====================================================
Ran 2 tests in 0.000s

OK
```

Last but Not Least

> Although we can run the unit tests for the functions in our module individually, eventually running all of them at a time gets cumbersome.
> We can write a Bash script to invoke each of the tests to run, then invoke the Bash script whenever we want to run the tests for all the functions in our script.

```
echo "##### unit testing ensure_nucl_str_clean"
python test_myModule_ensure_nucl_str_clean.py

echo "##### unit testing euclid_gcd"
python test_myModule_euclid_gcd.py

echo "##### unit testing get_percent_gc_content"
python test_myModule_get_percent_gc_content.py
```

Figure 10-68 Bash script to call the unit tests for all functions in myModule

The advantage of keeping each function's unit tests in a separate file is the ability to work on a function's unit tests without accidentally modifying the unit tests of the other functions.

10.7 Finding the Reverse Complement of a Nucleotide String

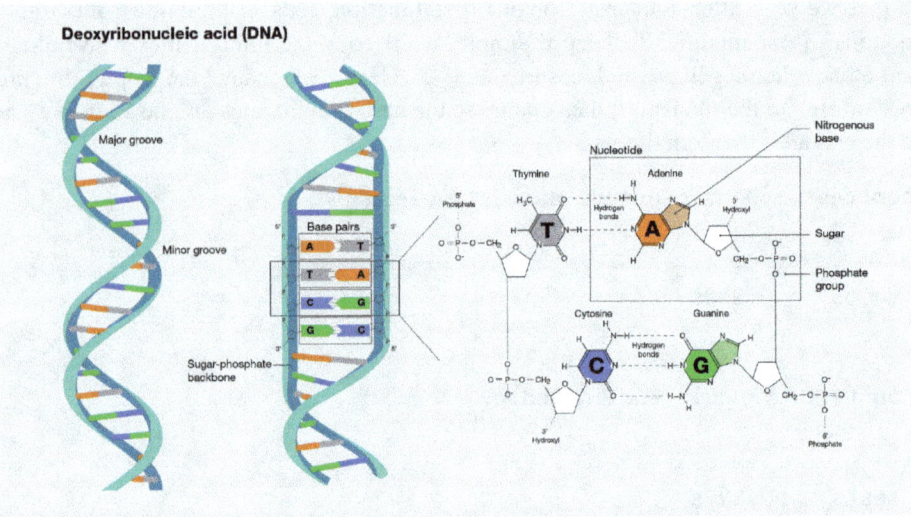

Figure 10-69 Segment of DNA. Source: National Institutes of Health (NIH). https://www.genome.gov/genetics-glossary/Deoxyribonucleic-Acid-DNA (National Human Genome Research Institute, NIH, DNA fact sheet, 24th August 2020. https://www.genome.gov/about-genomics/fact-sheets/Deoxyribonucleic-Acid-Fact-Sheet. Image URL: https://www.genome.gov/sites/default/files/media/images/2024-05/DNA_2024a.jpg)

Nucleotides along one strand bond to their complement nucleotides along the second strand. The nucleotides along one strand are read clockwise (CW) while their complements along the other strand are read counter-clockwise (CCW).

An arbitrary nucleotide string may contain active sites, or its reverse complement string may; hence, for an arbitrary nucleotide string, a bioinformaticist is also interested in finding its reverse complement.

We start by reminding ourselves that the for-loop lets us instruct the machine to iterate over a string, in order, one character at a time, and in the for-loop's block of code, instruct the machine to do something to each character in turn.

10.7 Finding the Reverse Complement of a Nucleotide String

So what we need now to output the reverse complement, given a nucleotide string as input, is:

a) for each nucleotide in the input string, return its complement; and
b) concatenate the complements into a string that is the reverse of the input string.

There is more than one way that we can tell the interpreter to do either step; but for now, we will discuss just one way to do each.

Let's start with returning the complement of a nucleotide. We can use a Python dictionary of nucleotide:complement pairs (as key:value pairs) to do this.

10.7.1 A Brief Introduction to the Python Dictionary

Referring to the table of Python collections, we see that the dictionary is unordered, mutable, and made up of key:value pairs. Keys must be unique.

Let's make a test dictionary to experiment with:

```
In [1]: testDict = {}

In [2]: testDict[1] = 3.141
   ...: testDict['a'] = 'hello'
   ...: testDict['zebra'] = [0, 1, 2]

In [3]: testDict
Out[3]: {1: 3.141, 'a': 'hello', 'zebra': [0, 1, 2]}
```

Figure 10-70 A dummy dictionary

In a dictionary, keys must be unique. Not every datatype or collection type can be used as keys, but strings and ints can; and as you can see, we can mix them.

```
In [4]: testDict['b'] = 'good-bye'
   ...: testDict['a'] = 'world'
   ...: testDict
Out[4]: {1: 3.141, 'a': 'world', 'zebra': [0, 1, 2], 'b': 'good-bye'}
```

Figure 10-71 We can add key:value pairs to a dictionary, and we can update the value of an existing key:value pair

```
In [5]: testDict['zebra']
Out[5]: [0, 1, 2]
```

Figure 10-72 We use a dictionary by passing a key into it

We get back the value associated with that key.

```
In [6]: 'b' in testDict
Out[6]: True

In [7]: 'world' in testDict
Out[7]: False
```

Figure 10-73 We can test for membership in a dictionary using the keyword *in*

Only keys are searched.
And now, back to getting the reverse complement of a nucleotide string.

```
In [8]: complDict = {'a':'t', 'c':'g', 'g':'c', 't':'a'}
```

Figure 10-74 A nucleotide:complement dictionary, where nucleotides are keys read in, and complements are the values returned, as in the example below

Please note that this dictionary's key:value pairs are all lowercase.

```
In [9]: complDict['c']  # we pass in 'c' as the key
Out[9]: 'g'

In [10]: complDict['t']  # we get back the complement
Out[10]: 'a'
```

Figure 10-75 Using the dictionary

Again, the keys are nucleotides we pass in, and the values are the complements that get returned. We pass a key into the dictionary, and the dictionary returns its associated value.

Now let's add this into a for-loop.

```
In [11]: nuclStr = 'acgt'

In [12]: for nucleotide in nuclStr:
    ...:     print(f"{complDict[nucleotide]}")
    ...:
t
g
c
a
```

Figure 10-76 Using a for-loop to return the complement of each nucleotide in a string

The next step is to concatenate these complements into a string in the reverse order in which they're output.

```
In [13]: outputStr = ''
In [14]: outputStr = outputStr + 'b'
    ...: print(outputStr)
b

In [15]: outputStr = outputStr + 'y'
    ...: print(outputStr)
by

In [16]: outputStr = outputStr + 'e'
    ...: print(outputStr)
bye
```

Figure 10-77 Here, we create a variable and instantiate it with an empty string

10.7 Finding the Reverse Complement of a Nucleotide String

Strings are immutable, but we can concatenate other strings to them. We combine an assignment statement with string concatenation to first concatenate a new letter to the right of the existing string, then make that the new value of the variable.

Here is how we can tell the interpreter to iterate over an input string and create an output string by concatenating the current letter to the right of an output string and setting that as the new value of the variable.

In this example, the interpreter is "writing forward" one letter at a time. How might we instruct it to write backwards, which is what we want it to do to create the reverse complement of an input nucleotide string?

```
In [17]: inputStr, outputStr = 'bye', ''
    ...: for letter in inputStr:
    ...:     outputStr = letter + outputStr
    ...:     print(outputStr)
    ...:
b
yb
eyb
```

Figure 10-78 Reversing an input string

The answer is: to reverse the string, we instruct the interpreter to concatenate the current letter **to the left** of the outputStr. Now let's tell the interpreter how to make the reverse complement from a nucleotide string.

```
In [18]: complDict = {'a':'t', 'c':'g', 'g':'c', 't':'a'}
    ...: nuclStr, outputStr = 'actg', ''
    ...: for nucleotide in nuclStr:
    ...:     # we pass the nucleotide into the dictionary
    ...:     # and concatenate the returned value
    ...:     # to the left of outputStr, then set
    ...:     # the concatenated string as the new value
    ...:     # of outputStr
    ...:     outputStr = complDict[nucleotide] + outputStr
    ...: print(outputStr)
cagt
```

Figure 10-79 Combining the complement dictionary with reversing the input string

```
In [19]: complDict = {'a':'t', 'c':'g', 'g':'c', 't':'a'}
    ...: nuclStr, outputStr = 'gattaca', ''
    ...: for nucleotide in nuclStr:
    ...:     outputStr = complDict[nucleotide] + outputStr
    ...: print(outputStr)
tgtaatc
```

Figure 10-80 Getting the reverse complement of another nucleotide string using the same instructions

Note that just like our Python implementation of the EuclidGCD algorithm, our reverse complement code uses a loop and an assignment statement. Given the creation of the complement dictionary, the Python implementation comes in at three lines of code—five when you count the initialization and print lines.

Not bad.

Now let's change the way we develop our code.

10.7.2 Developing Code by Test-Driven Development (TDD)

Let's start by writing our unit test, then develop our function in its own file. We know expected output **'tgtaatc'**, given sample input **'gattaca'**.

```
$ cp unittest_template.py unittest_rev_compl.py
$ touch rev_compl.py
```

Figure 10-81 We start our test-driven development by creating the files we need

One file for testing and one for development.

```
$ sed -i 's/FILE/rev_compl/g' unittest_rev_compl.py
$ sed -i 's/FUNC/rev_compl/g' unittest_rev_compl.py
$ sed -i 's/BAD_ARG/2.1/g' unittest_rev_compl.py
$ sed -i 's/ARG/"gattaca"/g' unittest_rev_compl.py
$ sed -i 's/RESULT/"tgtaatc"/g' unittest_rev_compl.py
```

Figure 10-82 Configuring *unittest_rev_compl.py*

```python
def test_GARBAGE_FILTER_1(self):
    ''' assert input must be a string
    '''
    with self.assertRaises(AssertionError):
        rev_compl(2.1)
def test_GARBAGE_FILTER_2(self):
    ''' assert input must be
        a clean nucleotide string
    '''
    with self.assertRaises(AssertionError):
        rev_compl('gattacx')
```

Figure 10-83 In *vim*, we copy/paste test_GARBAGE_FILTER_1 to make a second test

The second test will ensure a garbage filter is trapping dirty nucleotide strings.

```python
''' rev_compl.py
'''
def rev_compl(nucl_str: str) -> str:
    ''' Given a nucleotide string as input,
        return its reverse complement.
        Example:
        >>>rev_compl('gattaca')
```

10.7 Finding the Reverse Complement of a Nucleotide String

```
        'tgtaatc'
    '''
    # garbage filters
    # 1) ensure input is a string
    # 2) ensure input is a clean nucleotide str.
    # implementation of algorithm
    return
```

Figure 10-84 Starting the *rev_compl()* function in the *rev_compl* file

With just this much written and saved to the file, we start our test-driven development by running our unit tests against the function.

```
$ python unittest_rev_compl.py
FFF
======================================================================
FAIL: test_GARBAGE_FILTER_1 (__main__.Test_rev_compl.test_GARBAGE_FILTER_1)
assert input must be a string
----------------------------------------------------------------------
Traceback (most recent call last):
  File "/home/james/unittest_rev_compl.py", line 22, in test_GARBAGE_FILTER_1
    with self.assertRaises(AssertionError):
    ~~~~~~~~~~~~~~~~~~~~~~^^^^^^^^^^^^^^^^
AssertionError: AssertionError not raised

======================================================================
FAIL: test_GARBAGE_FILTER_2 (__main__.Test_rev_compl.test_GARBAGE_FILTER_2)
assert input must be
----------------------------------------------------------------------
Traceback (most recent call last):
  File "/home/james/unittest_rev_compl.py", line 28, in test_GARBAGE_FILTER_2
    with self.assertRaises(AssertionError):
    ~~~~~~~~~~~~~~~~~~~~~~^^^^^^^^^^^^^^^^
AssertionError: AssertionError not raised

======================================================================
FAIL: test_rev_compl (__main__.Test_rev_compl.test_rev_compl)
----------------------------------------------------------------------
Traceback (most recent call last):
  File "/home/james/unittest_rev_compl.py", line 35, in test_rev_compl
    self.assertEqual(result, "tgtaatc")
    ~~~~~~~~~~~~~~~~^^^^^^^^^^^^^^^^^^^
AssertionError: None != 'tgtaatc'

----------------------------------------------------------------------
Ran 3 tests in 0.001s

FAILED (failures=3)
```

Figure 10-85 Well, they told us everything's supposed to fail on the first run

I guess they were right.

Let's start fixing our function.

```python
''' rev_compl.py
'''
def rev_compl(nucl_str: str) -> str:
    ''' Given a nucleotide string as input,
        return its reverse complement.
        Example:
        >>>rev_compl('gattaca')
        'tgtaatc'
    '''
    # garbage filters
    # 1) ensure input is a string
    assert isinstance(nucl_str, str),\
        "Input must be a clean nucleotide string."
    # 2) ensure input is a clean nucleotide str.
    from my_module import ensure_nucl_str_clean
    bad_values = ensure_nucl_str_clean(nucl_str)
    assert not bad_values,\
        (f"nucleotide string at these positions "
         f"has bad values\n{bad_values}")
    # implementation of algorithm

    return
```

Figure 10-86 Because we've already worked with these garbage filters, we'll start with them

```
$ python unittest_rev_compl.py
..F
================================================================================
FAIL: test_rev_compl (__main__.Test_rev_compl.test_rev_compl)
--------------------------------------------------------------------------------
Traceback (most recent call last):
  File "/home/james/unittest_rev_compl.py", line 35, in test_rev_compl
    self.assertEqual(result, "tgtaatc")
    ~~~~~~~~~~~~~~~~^^^^^^^^^^^^^^^^^^^
AssertionError: None != 'tgtaatc'


--------------------------------------------------------------------------------
Ran 3 tests in 0.001s

FAILED (failures=1)
```

Figure 10-87 And now we're down to just having to implement the algorithm

```python
''' rev_compl.py
'''
from my_module import ensure_nucl_str_clean
def rev_compl(nucl_str: str) -> str:
```

10.7 Finding the Reverse Complement of a Nucleotide String

```python
    ''' Given a nucleotide string as input,
        return its reverse complement.
        Example:
        >>>rev_compl('gattaca')
        'tgtaatc'
    '''
    # garbage filters
    # 1) ensure input is a string
    assert isinstance(nucl_str, str),\
        "Input must be a clean nucleotide string."
    # 2) ensure input is a clean nucleotide str.
    bad_values = ensure_nucl_str_clean(nucl_str)
    assert not bad_values,\
        (f"nucleotide string at these positions "
        f"has bad values\n{bad_values}")
    # implementation of algorithm
    compl_dict, output_str =\
    {'a':'t', 'A':'T', 'c':'g', 'C':'G',\
     'g':'c', 'G':'C', 't':'a', 'T':'A'}, ''
    for nucleotide in nucl_str:
        output_str = compl_dict[nucleotide] + output_str

    return output_str
```

Figure 10-88 Adding the rev_compl algorithm

```
$ python unittest_rev_compl.py
...
----------------------------------------------------------------------
Ran 3 tests in 0.000s

OK
```

Figure 10-89 Finished

Now let's lint our code.

```
$ pylint rev_compl.py

----------------------------------------------------------------------
Your code has been rated at 10.00/10 (previous run: 8.89/10, +1.11)
```

Figure 10-90 Cool

A Few Words on Our Approach to Programming

Now that you've been through it, let's discuss for a moment our approach to learning how to program, which I concede is unorthodox.

But experience has taught me that motivated beginners who learn to program out of books in order to write code in the service of their labs or their research can have gaps in their knowledge or skillset that might prove expensive.

The fault is not theirs. An author wants or needs to make it easy for readers to follow along in the building of a webapp, for example, and so never shows how to make the webapp secure. Readers who deploy their own webapps on the Internet after reading the tutorial do so at their peril.

Likewise, researchers who learn—say—just enough out of programming books to write a script that processes datasets in a way their P.I.s determined their labs needed but that nobody else could figure out how to do are to be commended; but if they write their solutions in such a way that nobody else can understand them, much less maintain them, their code base may not last very long after the programmers move on, much to the frustration of their erstwhile colleagues.

I believe that beginning programmers should be taught that programming for the workplace requires more than just learning a programming language, and how to make machines perform certain tasks by telling them what to do in that language.

I believe they should be taught the importance of adopting a programming style that is simple, clear, and direct; they should be taught how to communicate to users of their code, as well as other programmers; they should be taught how to make their code robust; and they should be taught the importance of testing their code before putting it into production and immediately after conducting maintenance on it. All of this, in addition to learning how to implement algorithms in their chosen programming language to solve the problems they are motivated to solve.

Now that you've had a taste of it, I ask that you keep up caring about matters of good programming style and practice. How much you care will reflect in the quality of your code; and believe me, those who come to depend on your code will notice.

I don't promise you an easy row to hoe. But if you come to like or love programming, it can be very rewarding work.

Good luck.

10.8 Counting Symbols in a String

> **What You Need to Know**
> **error-trapping** and **exception handling** allow us to instruct machines to look for errors in data, as well as what to do when they find them.
> Python instructions designed specifically for trapping errors and handling exceptions include **assert** and **try...except**.
> **assert** terminates execution of a function or script by throwing an **AssertionError**.
> **try...except** allows execution to continue. If the machine encounters an error while **try**ing to execute a statement or a block of code, it then executes the code in the **except** block of code, in which the programmer tells the machine what to do in case an error is encountered.

In this lesson, we wish to write a function that takes an arbitrary string as input and returns a dictionary of **symbol:count** items. Please note that our specifications do NOT constrain which types of strings (as in nucleotide strings) or symbols (i.e., nucleotides) get passed in as input. Anything goes.

How might we write such a constraint-free function?
Answer: We make use of error-trapping.

10.8.1 Error-Trapping

If our code throws an error, we may not want processing to grind to a halt as the interpreter throws a Traceback to tell us or our users what failed.

Rather, we may want our interpreter to handle the error and keep processing the data. This is known as **exception handling**, and we have an example that happens to form the core of a useful algorithm—one that populates a dictionary with the symbols in an arbitrary string as keys, and sums of the occurrences of those symbols in the string as values.

To trap errors and handle exceptions, the Python language has a **try...except** compound statement.

In the **try** clause, we tell the machine which statement(s) we want it to execute, taking into account that we know that doing so can throw an error. In the case of the code we want to write, we want to use a dictionary to keep count of the symbols in an input string. Items in the dictionary are **symbol:count** pairs. However:

```python
symCntDict[symbol] = symCntDict[symbol] + 1
```

is the correct way to increment the count for an arbitrary symbol in the string, even though this statement throws a **KeyError** on the first instance of a symbol that the machine encounters in the string because the key does not yet exist in the dictionary!

We can instruct the machine to add a first instance of symbol:count pair to the dictionary when a KeyError is thrown, hence:

```python
try:
    symCntDict[symbol] = symCntDict[symbol] + 1
except KeyError:
    symCntDict[symbol] = 1
```

Before we update our code, I want to suggest a last edit.

The assignment statement **symCntDict[symbol] = symCntDict[symbol] + 1** will certainly do what we want it to; however, it is more idiomatic to write an assignment statement that increments by 1 as:

```python
symCntDict[symbol] += 1
```

I'm going to replace the old assignment statement with this one. However...
They are identical in what they do. If you find the old assignment statement easier to read, use it.

```python
def get_symbol_count(someStr: str) -> dict:
    ''' Given an arbitrary string as input,
        return a dictionary of symbol:count items,
        in which the symbols come from the string.
    '''
    assert isinstance(someStr, str),\
        "input must be a string."
    symbolDict = {} # initialization
    for symbol in someStr:
        try:
            symbolDict[symbol] += 1 # increment symbol count
        except KeyError:
            # KeyError means key is not yet in dictionary,
            # so add key:value pair to dictionary.
```

```
            symbolDict[symbol] = 1

    return symbolDict
```

Figure 10-91 A symbol-counting function

```
In [2]: get_symbol_count('gattaca')
Out[2]: {'g': 1, 'a': 3, 't': 2, 'c': 1}
```

Figure 10-92 Invoking our function, which at this point is just a rough draft

With exception handling, it now runs right.

This function is good and valuable enough to add to my_module, which you should do after taking steps to make it production-ready; that is, add garbage filters and set up automated testing.

10.9   IPython Magics

In this brief lesson, we look at a few IPython magics that we'll use again and again.

```
In [20]: %whos
Variable        Type      Data/Info
-----------------------------------
complDict       dict      n=4
inputStr        str       bye
letter          str       e
nuclStr         str       gattaca
nucleotide      str       a
outputStr       str       tgtaatc
testDict        dict      n=4
```

Figure 10-93 Magic whos

This IPython magic shows us objects that occupy current session memory.

```
In [21]: %hist
testDict = {}
testDict[1] = 3.141
testDict['a'] = 'hello'
testDict['zebra'] = [0, 1, 2]
testDict
testDict['b'] = 'good-bye'
testDict['a'] = 'world'
testDict
testDict['zebra']
'b' in testDict
'world' in testDict
```

Figure 10-94 Magic hist

This IPython magic shows us the history of our current session. Here, we are showing just the first few lines.

```
In [22]: %rerun 1
=== Executing: ===
testDict = {}
=== Output: ===
```

Figure 10-95 Magic rerun

This IPython magic lets us rerun input in our session.

```
In [23]: %hist -f sessionHistory.py
```

Figure 10-96 Saving our current session to a file

If we want to save specific lines in our session, we can use **magic save** to save those lines to a text file.

10.10 Introduction to Programming V: Good Programming Practices

PEP 8 – Style Guide for Python Code

Author: Guido van Rossum <guido at python.org>, Barry Warsaw <barry at python.org>, Nick Coghlan <ncoghlan at gmail.com>
Status: Active
Type: Process
Created: 05-Jul-2001
Post-History: 05-Jul-2001, 01-Aug-2013

Figure 10-97 The Python Style Guide, a.k.a. pep 8. Click the image to go to the online style guide at python.org. https://peps.python.org/pep-0008/

Learning good programming style early on is important:

(1) It shows that you are serious and committed to doing a good job.
(2) It prevents you from having to unlearn bad style habits in order to adopt good ones.

Bad programmers generally don't know—and certainly would never acknowledge—that they're bad programmers. Yet, others know them as bad programmers.
What makes a bad programmer?
There's not a single trait that distinguishes a programmer as a bad programmer; however, bad programmers are known primarily for ignoring good, even best, programming practices when they write code.

Among the traits that earn programmers the anathema of "bad" by users of their code and programmers who have to maintain that code:

- Lack of documentation
- Lack of testing
- Code that breaks easily

Nobody wants to be known as a bad programmer. We believe that a well-rounded education for beginning programmers includes an emphasis on best programming practices, for best programming practices taught early on lead to good coding habits; and good coding habits are what makes a programmer known as a good programmer.

Figure 10-98 Pylint is a linter that finds problems and issues, including matters of style, with Python code. Click or scan the QR code to go to the homepage of pylint. https://www.pylint.org/

Learning from the Machines

Aside from linting your code, you can submit a copy of it to a large language model (LLM) like OpenAI's ChatGPT and ask it to improve your code. Note that this is not the same as asking an AI to write your code. The LLM could very well indeed find parts of your code to improve; this in itself becomes an opportunity to learn.

You should study all the suggestions for improvement and decide which to accept, and which not. You may have very good reasons not to accept a suggestion from an LLM.

For example, an LLM suggested that I insert a garbage filter that ensured that nucleotide strings put into the function I had written were clean by removing non-nucleotide characters from the string—silently, with no warnings to the user.

In my opinion, this is wrong. The user should be alerted about the non-nucleotides in the string (the characters and their positions in the string), and it should be for the user to decide how to handle the situation.

Perhaps she decides to remove the non-nucleotides from the string, then continue processing it, in which case the code the LLM suggested as a garbage filter can be used to clean the string.

But even worse than suggesting a garbage filter that doesn't alert the user of bad data, the LLM suggested rewriting a for-loop so that, instead of iterating over each nucleotide in a nucleotide string as the code requires, it skipped every two nucleotides. In other words, the algorithm works with indices and needs to work with the nucleotides at positions (**0, 1, 2, 3, 4, ..**), but the LLM returned code that works with the nucleotides only at positions whose indices are wholly divisible by 3 (**0, 3, 6, ..**). This is just plain wrong.

So, again, do not blindly incorporate suggestions from anyone—not even LLMs. This is in keeping with OpenAI's own warning to users: "ChatGPT can make mistakes. Check important info."

Understand what the correct, functionally equivalent changes do, and weigh that against the needs and expectations of your users.

And if you do decide to refactor your code, incorporating a suggestion, you should comment the code noting the source and the suggestion.

10.11 Programs = Algorithms + Data Structures

> A person does not really understand something until after teaching it to a computer.
>
> D.E. Knuth

> Before a program can run, it must be loaded into memory.
> Before a dataset can be processed, it must be loaded into memory.

```
In [1]: import this
The Zen of Python, by Tim Peters

Beautiful is better than ugly.
Explicit is better than implicit.
Simple is better than complex.
Complex is better than complicated.
Flat is better than nested.
Sparse is better than dense.
Readability counts.
Special cases aren't special enough to break the rules.
Although practicality beats purity.
Errors should never pass silently.
Unless explicitly silenced.
In the face of ambiguity, refuse the temptation to guess.
There should be one-- and preferably only one --obvious way to do it.
Although that way may not be obvious at first unless you're Dutch.
Now is better than never.
Although never is often better than *right* now.
If the implementation is hard to explain, it's a bad idea.
If the implementation is easy to explain, it may be a good idea.
Namespaces are one honking great idea -- let's do more of those!
```

Figure 10-99 The Zen of Python, PEP 20

> A program is a set of instructions for a computer to execute.
> For our purposes, algorithms are step-by-step procedures for rendering input into desired output.
> A program can contain one or many algorithms, depending on its purpose.
> Algorithms are considered correct when, for all input, they give correct output.
> Two algorithms that return identical output given identical input are "functionally equivalent."
> Algorithms are judged by their effectiveness—how much memory they occupy and how fast they run.

A program is a set of instructions for a machine to execute. The order in which those instructions are executed—sequentially; conditionally, depending on whether at least one condition is true; or repeatedly, in loops, again depending on whether at least one condition is true—is determined by the control flow that programmers write into their code.

For our purposes, we can say that a program is a set of instructions we write to tell a machine step by step how to process a dataset. We may want the machine to get information about the data; we may want the machine to reformat the structure of the data; we may want the machine to transform the data into other data.

For the program to run, it must be loaded into memory. For a dataset to be processed, it must be loaded into memory. Often programs and datasets are saved in mass-storage devices as files. When a program is run, a copy of it is first loaded into memory, then run. When it is no longer needed, the memory manager marks the space it occupies as free for other programs and data to be written into.

Note that the data and instructions in memory are not erased, just overwritten as the space is put to new use.

When we talk about computer programs, we don't just talk about sets of instructions that we give computers to execute. Rather, we talk about algorithms, which, roughly speaking, are sets of instructions arranged in steps to accomplish specific tasks. You may have a book in your kitchen that is full of algorithms—a cookbook.

10.12 Interlude: Ilayda Develops Her Stoichiometry Code

Chemistry student Ilayda Gökkr has written **SymPy** code in an IPython session that uses the linear algebra equation **Ax=b** to balance a chemical equation.

```
In [1]: from sympy import *
   ...: x1, x2, x3 = symbols('x1 x2 x3')

In [2]: A, b, x = Matrix([4, 0, -1, 0, 2, -5, 0, 0, 1]).reshape(3, 3),\
   ...:                  (0, 0, 1), (x1, x2, x3)

In [3]: from sympy.solvers.solveset import linsolve

In [4]: system = A, b

In [5]: [ans] = linsolve(system, x); print(ans)
(1/4, 5/2, 1)
```

Figure 10-100 Her answer was a tuple of rational fractions; she had to calculate their proportional whole numbers by hand

With a little programming experience, she is ready to write the code to render those whole numbers automatically.

Ilayda starts by rerunning her code.

10.12 Interlude: Ilayda Develops Her Stoichiometry Code

```
In [6]: print(ans[0]); type(ans[0])
1/4
Out[6]: sympy.core.numbers.Rational
```

Figure 10-101 Now Ilayda investigates what she has to work with

In the next cell, she prints the first item in the tuple; then in a second statement, she finds out what type of data the item is.

It is a SymPy **Rational** number.

```
In [7]: Rational?
Init signature: Rational(p, q=None, gcd=None)
Docstring:
Represents rational numbers (p/q) of any size.

Examples
========

>>> from sympy import Rational, nsimplify, S, pi
>>> Rational(1, 2)
1/2
```

Figure 10-102 From the built-in documentation, Ilayda sees that the numerator and denominator of a rational number are held as separate integers called "p" and "q," respectively, and that she can invoke either one by these names

Hence, in this case, invoking:
ans[0].p
returns **1**
while invoking:
ans[0].q
returns **4**.

```
In [8]: print(ans[0] + ans[1] + ans[2])
15/4

In [9]: print((ans[0] + ans[1] + ans[2]).q)
4
```

Figure 10-103 From a search engine query, Ilayda realizes that she can get the **lowest common denominator** of the SymPy Rationals simply by adding them together

Perfect.

```
In [10]: sum = 0

In [11]: for item in ans:
    ...:     sum = sum + item
    ...: lcd = sum.q; print(lcd)
4
```

```
In [12]: sol = []

In [13]: for item in ans:
    ...:     sol.append(int(item.p * (lcd / item.q)))
    ...: print(sol)
[1, 10, 4]
```

Figure 10-104 Ilayda writes one for-loop to sum the Rationals in the tuple and get their lowest common denominator; then she writes a second for-loop to reckon the whole-number coefficients that balance the original chemical equation

Brava, Ilayda. You are well on your way to writing a general chemical stoichiometry solver.

Chapter Summary

In this chapter, we learned that (1) finding the right algorithm to solve our problems and (2) implementing that algorithm in our chosen programming language are but two tasks in basic programming. We wish also to write our programs so that they are easily saved and recalled later; we wish to provide users with documentation on the use of our programs (especially what is expected input and output); we wish to document and comment our programs to make their use and maintenance as easy as possible; we wish to ensure that values passed into our programs are expected input before having our programs process them; we want them as well-written as we can make them; and we wish to test our programs for correctness and make sure they pass those tests before we put them into production. All of this we covered in this chapter. To summarize, we covered basic python functions, saving them in modules and importing our modules into our sessions and scripts in order to invoke their functions; we learned about type hints and self-documenting code; we learned about garbage filters; we used already-written unit tests before writing our own. And we walked through algorithms before implementing them into Python and writing them into our functions.

11   Functions

To write code, we have already learned the basics of how to write functions in Python, as well as how to document them. In this chapter, we will expand on what we already know about functions, both to use and write them better.

> **Review: Functions, Modules, and Lambdas**
> To create a function, we use the keyword **def**.
>   To return values from a function, we use the keyword **return**.
>   To save our functions, we can write them into text files that we then use as **modules**. Because modules can be imported into Python scripts and IPython sessions, using them allows us to write our functions once, but run everywhere.
>   In IPython, we can write into a text file using the magic command **%edit**. The default text editor of IPython is **vi** or **vim**.
>   To reload an edited module in IPython, we begin an IPython session with these two lines:
>   **%load_ext autoreload**
>   **autoreload 2**
>   A **lambda** is an anonymous function. It runs in the code where it is created and then forgotten. To create an anonymous function, we use the keyword **lambda**.

11.1   Subroutines: The Genesis of Functions in Programming Languages

Kay Antonelli, née McNulty, was born in County Donegal in Ulster, Northern Ireland. Click or scan the QR code to go to the Wikipedia article on Kay Antonelli. https://en.wikipedia.org/wiki/Kathleen_Antonelli

Kay Antonelli was educated as a mathematician (June 1942) and became one of the six original programmers (all women) of the ENIAC.

She is credited with being the first person to implement subroutines.

A subroutine can be defined as a sequence of instructions packaged as a unit that can be called numerous times within a program, or even by different programs.

At a symposium in January 1947, co-inventor of the ENIAC John Mauchly laid out the concept of subroutines and even libraries (he used the term "list") of subroutines.

A programmer of the ENIAC, the Irish-American mathematician Kathleen "Kay" McNulty Mauchly Antonelli, is credited with being the first to implement subroutines as a way of dealing with limitations of the ENIAC.

11.2 Functions

Leonhard Euler (1707–1783) was one of the greatest mathematicians in history. Click or scan the QR code to go to the Wikipedia article on Leonhard Euler. https://en.wikipedia.org/wiki/Leonhard_Euler

Among his many and varied achievements, Euler wrote the first proof in graph theory, and he introduced the concept of a function, as well as the notation f(x) to mean the function f applied to the argument x.

In Python, a function looks much like a mathematical function in notation first used by Leonard Euler in 1734:

$f(x)$

Like the mathematical function, the Python function has a name, called a symbol, followed immediately by an open parenthesis, followed by the argument or arguments that it takes as input (or even no arguments if the function takes none), followed by a close parenthesis:

f(x)

We say that a Python function encapsulates a task. That is, it combines many lines in its block of code into just one line. First, we define the function and write what it does to the arguments and what it returns in its block of code; then we use the function by calling it by name in our scripts. By defining our function in a module, we can invoke it over and over.

Functions allow us to organize our code into manageable chunks, and they allow us to write our code once and run that same code in all our scripts.

The Python assignment statement in which a function is invoked also strongly resembles its mathematical counterpart:

math function: y = $f(x)$
Python function: y = f(x)

Python makes it easy for us to write and use our own functions. We define a function using the keyword **def** (for *definition*), followed by the name of the argument and the arguments it takes in parentheses, followed by a full colon:

In [1]: def testFunc(someNumber): *# spaces added to emphasize that the open parenthesis must*
...:   *# immediately follow the function name*
...:

Next, we add the function's block of code, in which we write our Python statements telling the machine how to transform the function's input—in this case, *someNumber*—into output:

In [1]: def testFunc(someNumber):
...: return someNumber**(1/2) *# return the square root of someNumber*
...:

Finally, now that the function has been loaded into session memory, we test it by invoking it on the command line and passing it some number as an argument:

In [2]: testFunc(3)
Out[2]: 1.7320508075688772

Finally, it is important to note that the Python interpreter evaluates nested Python functions in the same manner that we evaluate nested mathematical functions: from innermost to outermost. The innermost function is evaluated first, then its return value is passed to the calling function, and it is evaluated, and so on.

nested math functions: $y = f(g(x))$
nested Python functions: y = f(g(x))

As an example, consider this Python statement that is also a nesting of functions:

str(testFunc(3))

The Python parser reads the statement, ensures that it is complete and syntactically correct, then passes it on for evaluation, inner function first, outer function last: get the square root of three, then stringify it:

In [3]: str(testFunc(3))
Out[3]: '1.7320508075688772'

11.3 Modules

Modules are text files in which we can write and save our functions and through which we can import those functions into any of our scripts and interactive sessions. Let's learn how to save our work writing and developing functions before we do any more work on functions.

According to the Python documentation, "A module is a file containing Python definitions and statements." In other words, in Python, we can write our functions into files that we create and maintain, then call them into our scripts and interactive sessions whenever we need them by using the **import** keyword.

As you might expect, Python makes it easy for us to create and use our own modules. This ability allows us to follow the coding philosophy of "Write once, run anywhere."

11.4 Documenting Your Functions, Making Them Robust with Error-Trapping and Exception Handling, and Proofing Them

> We document our code to enhance its readability.
>
> **Self-documenting code** makes use of meaningful variable and function names—that is, meaningful to others who read and maintain the code.
>
> In Python, we can add comments to lines by preceding them with the **hash (#)**.
>
> In Python, we use **docstrings** to provide documentation of our modules and functions to users. Docstrings are enclosed with either three single or three double quotes. The text in docstrings is returned to users when they follow a module or function name immediately with a question mark (?) in an interactive shell.
>
> To document our functions, we follow the **function design recipe** (FDR). If we cannot provide type hints in the function header, then we start our docstring with the type contract, followed with a simple statement of what our function returns when passed good arguments, and we finish our docstring with at least one example.
>
> Python provides us with different ways to trap errors.
>
> An **assert** statement enforces data to be of acceptable type, within acceptable range, or of acceptable value, or it halts execution. **assert** statements can also be used to ensure requisite conditions are met (e.g., that a datafile used as input does exist).
>
> **try...except** allows us to tell the computer how to handle errors that may arise as it executes a statement or a block of code. This allows program execution to continue, even as the computer encounters errors.
>
> To proof our functions and scripts, we can run them through **pylint**.

As a programmer, your job entails more than writing code to solve problems. It includes communicating with two audiences: the users of your programs and the programmers who have to maintain them.

We communicate to other programmers through comments and self-documenting code. We communicate to our users through interactive code and docstrings, whose contents are held in an object's _doc_ (pronounced "dunder doc") attribute and which can be invoked using the built-in help() function.

Drs. Jennifer Campbell and Paul Gries of the University of Toronto have developed a template for documenting Python functions that they have dubbed the "Function Design Recipe," or FDR, that I believe serves us well to follow.

The FDR requires that in a function's docstring, we add a type contract, a simple statement of what output the function returns, given the input, and at least one example of invoking the function with input that shows the output. Expect users to run the examples themselves to gain familiarity with the function.

11.5 Positional vs. Named Arguments

> We pass arguments into a function following the function's defined **argument list**—sometimes also called the **parameter list**. When we pass simply the arguments into a function, the meaning or significance of each argument depends on its position in the argument list, and we refer to them as **positional arguments**.
>
> However, in Python, when we write a function, we can define the arguments using **keyword=value pairs**. The keywords become the variable names in the function's block of code, and the given values are default values for the variables.
>
> In many published functions, if the function must take at least one argument, that argument leads the argument list and is in many cases a positional argument.
>
> When invoking a function, keyword=value pairs do NOT have to be passed in the order that they're defined in the function's argument list.
>
> You can pass a mix of positional and named arguments into a function; however, positional arguments MUST precede named arguments.

```python
def getSample(ID: str, length: float=None, mass: float=None,
 age: float=None) -> tuple:
    return ID, length, mass, age
```

Figure 11-1. To understand positional and named arguments, we can create a simple function whose argument list contains one positional argument and three named arguments to play around with

Here, we're introduced to the **Nonetype** datatype and to the **tuple** collection.

The arguments are listed in order; a function's writer has to decide the order of their importance. The most important argument is listed first, and most of the time it is a positional argument (where its meaning or significance is signaled by its position in the argument list). Positional arguments MUST be passed into a function when it's invoked.

Named arguments are defined in **keyword=value** pairs, where the keyword is the variable name used in the function's block of code, and the value is the default value assigned to the variable.

Because named arguments include default values, a user who invokes a function that has named arguments doesn't have to explicitly provide values for the named arguments.

When the user doesn't pass in a value for a named argument, its default value is used.

Multiple return values are separated by commas in the **return** statement. Functions return multiple values in a tuple.

```python
getSample('1')
('1', None, None, None)
```

Figure 11-2. Only the positional arguments in a function's argument list must be provided by the user, and they must be in the order listed in the function header

By convention, the most important argument is a positional argument first in the argument list.
Multiple return values are returned in a tuple.

```
getSample('1', 15.4)
('1', 15.4, None, None)
```

Figure 11-3. When creating a function, ordering arguments by their importance, or likelihood that users will have to provide their own values, matters

Even when an argument is a named argument, you can pass in just a value for it, but ONLY in the named argument's position in the argument list.

When invoking a function that contains positional and named arguments, you MUST provide positional arguments first, then named arguments.

```
getSample('1', mass=25, age=2, length=15.4)
('1', 15.4, 25, 2)
```

Figure 11-4. When passing in named arguments by *keyword=value pairs*, users are free to put them in any order they want though the rule *first positional arguments, then named arguments* still holds

```
Docstring:
array(object, dtype=None, *, copy=True, order='K', subok=False, ndmin=0,
like=None)

Create an array.

Parameters
----------
object : array_like
    An array, any object exposing the array interface, an object whose
    ``__array__`` method returns an array, or any (nested) sequence.
    If object is a scalar, a 0-dimensional array containing object is
    returned.
dtype : data-type, optional
    The desired data-type for the array. If not given, NumPy will try to use
    a default ``dtype`` that can represent the values (by applying promotion
    rules when necessary.)
copy : bool, optional
    If ``True`` (default), then the array data is copied. If ``None``,
    a copy will only be made if ``__array__`` returns a copy, if obj is
    a nested sequence, or if a copy is needed to satisfy any of the other
    requirements (``dtype``, ``order``, etc.). Note that any copy of
    the data is shallow, i.e., for arrays with object dtype, the new
    array will point to the same objects. See Examples for `ndarray.copy`.
    For ``False`` it raises a ``ValueError`` if a copy cannot be avoided.
    Default: ``True``.
order : {'K', 'A', 'C', 'F'}, optional
```

Figure 11-5. User documentation for the numpy *array()* function

Please note that the first item in the argument list—the array-like object to be converted by the function into a numpy ndarray—is a positional argument, while the remainder is named arguments.

I can imagine lively discussions among programmers who maintain functions regarding the order of arguments in argument lists.

Arguments that users are most likely to modify should go to the front of the argument list while arguments that users are least likely to change from default values should be named arguments at the end of the argument list.

I recommend always requiring a record or sample's unique ID go first if it is an argument to be entered in a function.

11.6 Multiple Return Values from a Python Function

> In a **return** statement, multiple values, separated by commas, are returned in a tuple that preserves their order.
>
> If a return tuple is to be read by the function's users, consider making the return tuple a **named tuple**, which labels the tuple and its items.

```
In [1]: def testFunc():
   ...:     # computation (here, a simple multiple assignment statement)
   ...:     side1, side2, side3, angle1, angle2, angle3 = 3, 4, 5, None, None, None
   ...:
   ...:     # return multiple values, separated by commas
   ...:     return side1, side2, side3, angle1, angle2, angle3
   ...:

In [2]: # invoking the function...
   ...: testVal = testFunc()

In [3]: # ...then invoking the variable that holds the function's return value
   ...: testVal
Out[3]: (3, 4, 5, None, None, None)
```

Figure 11-6. When a function returns multiple items, and the items are written into the **return** statement separated by commas, the items are returned in a tuple that preserves their order

In this example, the **return** statement holds the names of the variables whose values are to be output when the function is invoked, and when the function is invoked, its return tuple holds the values of those variables.

```
In [4]: # we can extract some items from the return tuple,
   ...: # then contain the remaining items in a list
   ...: # by using the prefix star operator
   ...: val1, val2, *testVal = testFunc()

In [5]: print(f"val1: {val1}\nval2: {val2}\ntestVal: {testVal}")
```

```
val1: 3
val2: 4
testVal: [5, None, None, None]
```

Figure 11-7. The order of return values in a return statement matters

We can extract items from the return tuple by using a multiple assignment statement.

When there are more items in the return tuple than what we want to extract individually, we can use the star prefix operator with the name of a variable that will pack the remaining items in a list (Figure 11-7).

```
In [1]: def testFunc():
   ...:     # initialization
   ...:     from collections import namedtuple
   ...:     Triangle = \
   ...:     namedtuple('Triangle', 'side1 side2 side3 angle1 angle2 angle3')
   ...:
   ...:     # computation (here, a simple multiple assignment statement)
   ...:     side1, side2, side3, angle1, angle2, angle3 = 3, 4, 5, \
   ...:     None, None, None
   ...:
   ...:     # we return the values from within the named tuple
   ...:     return Triangle(side1, side2, side3, angle1, angle2, angle3)
   ...:

In [2]: testFunc()
Out[2]: Triangle(side1=3, side2=4, side3=5, angle1=None, angle2=None,
        angle3=None)
```

Figure 11-8. When a function is intended to return its multiple values directly to users, we recommend doing so using a **named tuple**

The **namedtuple()** function creates an object as a subclass of the **tuple**.

As shown in the example, the return named tuple is labeled, and its items are name/value pairs.

Using named tuples makes it easier for the function's users to read and understand the output.

```
In [3]: Triangle = testFunc() # creating and instantiating a
                              # variable with a named tuple

In [4]: Triangle[1] # getting the value in index position 1
Out[4]: 4
```

Figure 11-9. We can use returned named tuples much like we use regular tuples

We can still read an item by index, for example.

```
In [5]: Triangle.side3 # invoking an item in a named tuple by name
Out[5]: 5

In [6]: # using a for loop to get the name/value pairs in the named tuple
   ...: for name in Triangle._fields:
```

```
    ...:         print(f"{name} \t= {getattr(Triangle, name)}")
    ...:
side1           = 3
side2           = 4
side3           = 5
angle1          = None
angle2          = None
angle3          = None

In [7]: # coercing the named tuple into a dictionary,
   ...: # which can be easier to work with
   ...: Triangle._asdict()
Out[7]:
{'side1': 3,
 'side2': 4,
 'side3': 5,
 'angle1': None,
 'angle2': None,
 'angle3': None}
```

Figure 11-10. However, to aid the user, we can invoke the values in the named tuple by name, as in In[5]

Additionally, with named tuples, we can iterate over the named tuple to get the name/value pairs, as in In[6]—please note the underscore in the _fields attribute; or we can coerce the named tuple into a dictionary, as in In[7]—again, there's an underscore prepending the _asdict() method.

11.7 Lambdas

> **lambdas** are anonymous functions.
> They are used for single-statement calculations and are used when the function does not have to persist throughout a session. Think of them as "once-and-done" functions.
> We will put them to use in the calculus primer at the end of this chapter.

```
In [1]: mul = lambda a, b: a * b

In [2]: %whos
Variable     Type         Data/Info
-----------------------------------
mul          function     <function <lambda> at 0x740067d81580>

In [3]: mul(4, 5)
Out[3]: 20
```

Figure 11-11. An example of a lambda

Lambdas are anonymous functions not bound to identifiers.

For examples of how we can put lambdas to use, please refer to the numerical integral and numerical derivative sections in the calculus primer below.

11.8 Matters of Style When Writing Functions

Write short, concise functions.

Use meaningful names. Function names should be meaningful in the context in which you and your colleagues use them. The same goes for the names of their arguments.

11.9 A Calculus Primer: Numeric Integration and Differentiation Using Python

In Python, functions are first-order functions. This means they can take functions as arguments, and they can return functions, as well.

NumPy is a fundamental library of the SciPy software stack. Central to NumPy is the ndarray (n-dimensional array), which allows fast manipulation of large, multidimensional arrays and matrices. NumPy requires that all the elements of an array or matrix be of the same datatype (i.e., int64s, int32s, float64s, etc.). By design, NumPy's functions largely look and behave like MATLAB's.

What You Need to Know

In Python, you can write functions that take functions as arguments.

We will be using this ability to write functions that return the numerical integral and numerical derivative of the math functions we pass into them.

Calculus textbooks traditionally cover differentiation first, then integration. In this short primer, however, we start with integration.

11.9.1 Numerical Integration

Fig. 11.12 Scan or click the image to go to the article on numerical integration in Wikipedia. https://en.wikipedia.org/wiki/Numerical_integration

Numerical integration involves calculating the area of a definite integral. In a definite integral, the upper and lower bounds of x are given, and the area under a general curve bound by these values of x is calculated.

Fig. 11.13 The relationship between area and multiplication

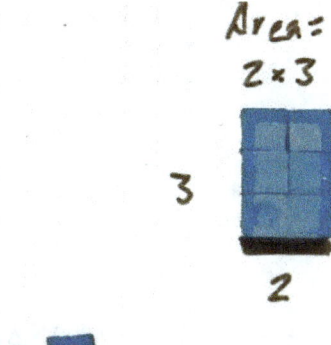

The Ancients of all civilizations had a richly developed plane geometry, and area solutions worked out for the circle and regular polygons. From this basis, many tried to find the area of figures in which two sides were straight lines meeting at a right angle, and the third side was defined by a curve, or in which three sides were straight lines meeting at right angles, and the fourth was defined by a curve.

They had solutions for special cases—for example, when the curve was part of a conic section (circle, ellipse, parabola, hyperbola).

Fig. 11.14 Ancient Babylonian astronomers calculated Jupiter's position from the area under a time-velocity graph. Scan or click the image to go to the article in Science magazine. https://science.sciencemag.org/content/351/6272/482

The Greeks weren't the only Ancients who used the geometric relationship between multiplication and area to do sophisticated calculations. Cuneiform tablets from 350 to 50 BCE show that by determining the area of a trapezium under a time-velocity graph, Babylonian astronomers calculated the position of Jupiter.

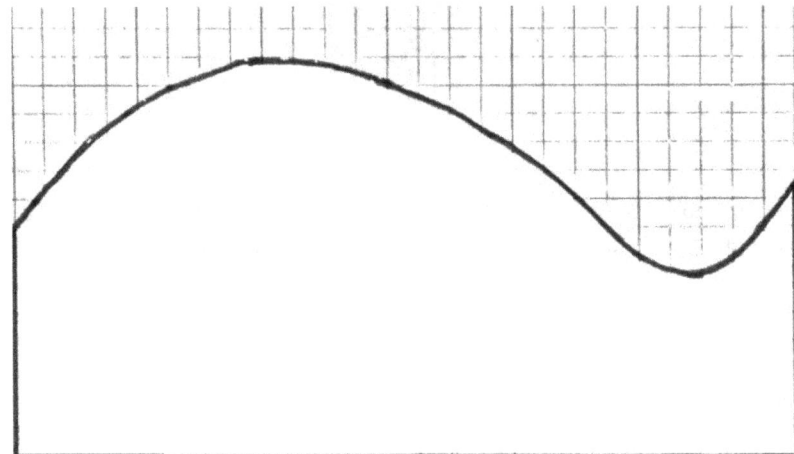

Fig. 11.15 Although the Ancients found area solutions for special cases, solutions for general curves like this one eluded them

11.9.2 The More You Know

Fig. 11.16 Click or scan QR code to go to Wikipedia article on Archimedes' method. https://en.wikipedia.org/wiki/The_Method_of_Mechanical_Theorems

Archimedes, whom some mathematicians believe is the greatest mathematician who ever lived, deserves special mention. In a letter to his colleague Eratosthenes, who was a faculty member/researcher at the Library of Alexandria, Archimedes described **The Method**, a systematic approach to getting the area of any bounded plane surface by filling it with triangles whose areas are known or can be extrapolated from other triangles already added to the fill.

> The mathematician Steven Strogatz gives a good explanation of The Method in his book on the history of calculus, *Infinite Powers*. Strogatz concludes his section on Archimedes' method by noting that computer graphics animators use triangles to fill areas.[a]
>
> ---
> [a]Strogatz, Steven. *Infinite Powers*. Houghton, Miflin, Harcourt, 2016. pp. 42–57.

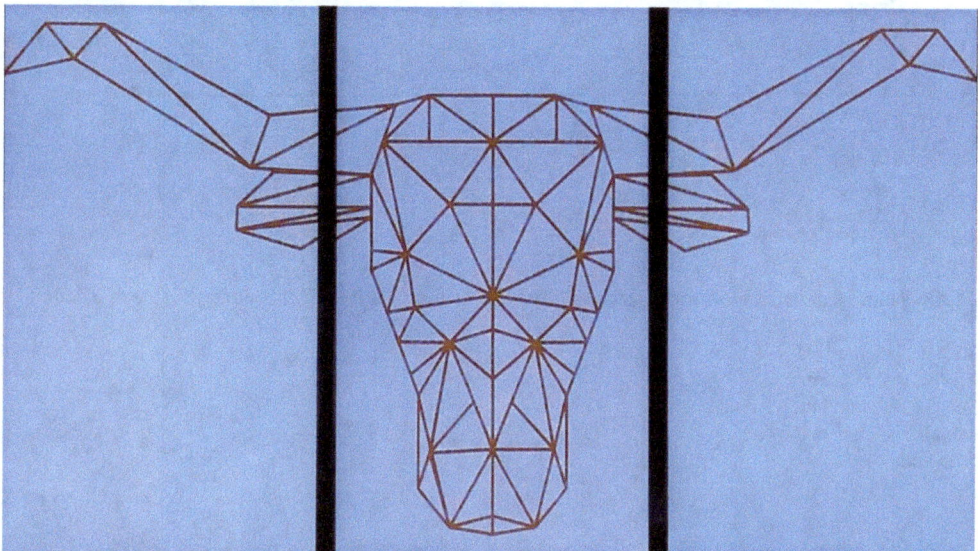

Fig. 11.17 A Bevo made of triangles. On triptych digital displays in the ground floor lobby of the Gates-Dell Complex (GDC), home of the Department of Computer Science at the University of Texas at Austin, Bevo shines in a composite of burnt-orange triangles.

11.9.3 Back to Numerical Integration

In our case, this means the area bounded by:

1) The x-axis
2) Two values of x (the first of which in this primer we'll set at zero and the second of which we'll call x_n
3) A curve like the one described by function f in the figure

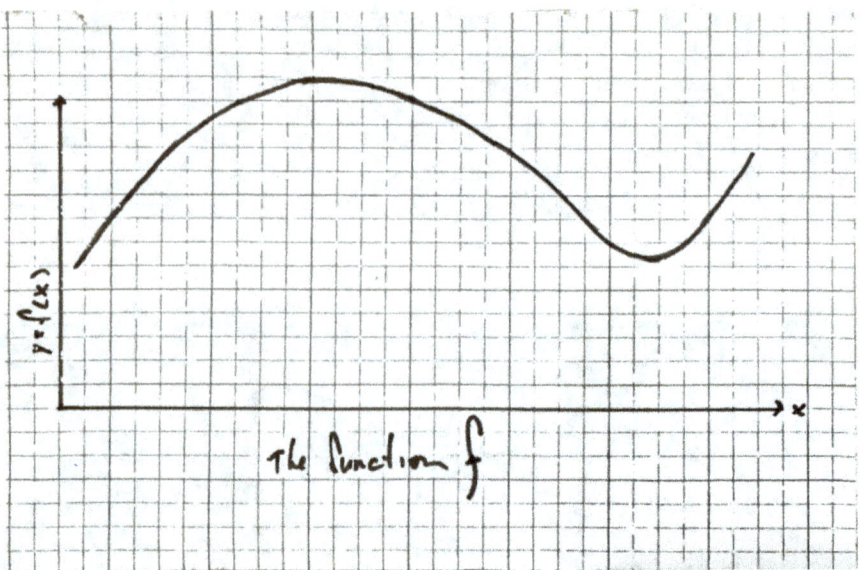

Fig. 11.18 Numerical integration comprises a family of algorithms for finding the numeric value of a definite integral

Fig. 11.19 The method we will use in this primer is called the rectangular method, also known as the Riemann sum

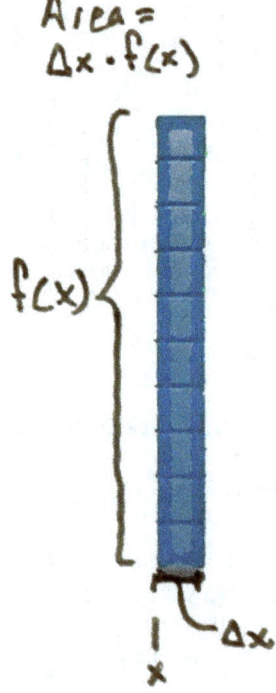

We start by choosing how many evenly spaced values of x in the interval between 0 and x_n we want to use in our calculations.

We designate the distance between these values Δx.

11.9 A Calculus Primer: Numeric Integration & Differentiation Using Python

For each x, we calculate y=f(x), then multiply that by Δx to get an area from that x to the next x. Note that in general, these areas are rectangular; hence, the name of the method.

Finally, we sum all the areas to arrive at an estimate of the area under the curve bounded by 0 and x_n.

This is the numeric value of the definite integral.

In modern notation, we would write this definite integral as $\int_0^{x_n} f(x)dx$.

The elongated "S" means *summa* for "sum."

Fig. 11.20 Riemann sum. Click or scan QR code to go to Wikipedia article on Riemann sum. https://en.wikipedia.org/wiki/Riemann_sum

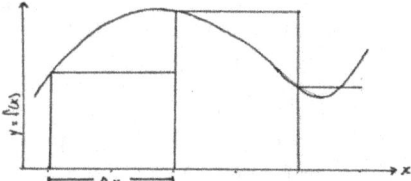

Fig. 11.21 As you can see, the simple rectangular method both leaves out areas under the curve and includes areas above the curve

These lapses affect the accuracy of the result. Nevertheless, this method is much like that used by Newton and Leibniz, except that they asked their audience to imagine that Δx diminishes infinitesimally though nobody was clear whether it reaches zero, or what happens when it does.

Vanishingly small values exist in differentiation, just as they do in integration. Leibniz called his vanishing quantities "infinitesmals"; Newton called his "fluxions." Newton spoke in terms of quotients in which the numerator and denominator vanish simultaneously.

But until any of this was mathematically proved, it was merely hand-waving. Today, we call the missing piece of math needed to save calculus **"The Theory of Limits"**.

Fig. 11.22 Intuitively, when Δx is infinitesimally small, the rectangles include all the area under the curve, and no more

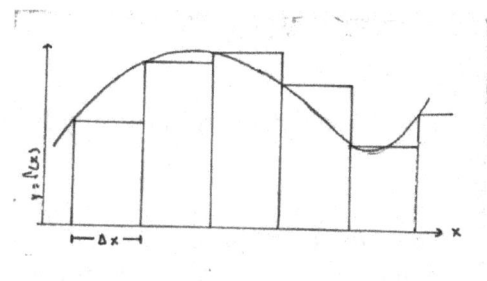

In numerical calculations on computers, there is no setting for Δx called "infinitesimally small." As programmers, we set the value of Δx for ourselves, and we let the users of our functions that depend on it set it (if they wish to override the default value we give it).

Fig. 11.23 The choice of Δx determines the accuracy of the result, as illustrated by these three figures

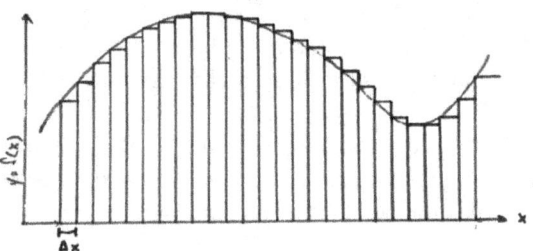

We should choose a value of Δx as small as possible, or at least so small that the error in the result will not adversely impact subsequent calculations that rely on it.

Parenthetically, for almost 200 years, the inventors of and the mathematicians who used and expanded on The Calculus knew they were on shaky ground as long as these "infinitesmals" were not mathematically proved.

A contemporary of Leibniz and Newton's, Bishop Berkeley, would have none of accepting mathematical results on faith alone. His essay title says it all:

> *A Discourse Addressed to an Infidel Mathematician, wherein It Is Examined Whether the Object, Principles, and Inferences of the Modern Analysis Are More Distinctly Conceived, or More Evidently Deduced, than Religious Mysteries and Points of Faith*

In the early 19th century CE, the engineer-turned-mathematician Augustin-Louis Cauchy provided the foundation that The Calculus had heretofore lacked: a rigorous definition of limits; hence, The Theory of Limits.

Fig. 11.24 Click or scan QR code to go to Wikipedia article on the French engineer-turned-mathematician Augustin-Louis Cauchy https://en.wikipedia.org/wiki/Augustin-Louis_Cauchy

In his textbook *Cours d'Analyse*, Cauchy established a theory of limits, putting The Calculus on a firm footing.

The Calculus was saved. Hurray.

11.9.4 Using Python and Numpy for Numerical Integration

> **What You Need to Know**
> **NumPy** is a central library of the SciPy software stack for working with quantitative data.
> From NumPy:
> **linspace**: Return evenly spaced numbers over a specified interval.
> **sum**: Sum of array elements over a given axis.

11.9 A Calculus Primer: Numeric Integration & Differentiation Using Python

```
In [1]: from numpy import linspace, sum as s
   ...: def getNumIntegral(f, end_x, start_x=0, delta_x=1e-8):
   ...:     x = linspace(start_x, end_x, int((end_x - start_x) / delta_x))
   ...:     return s(f(x) * delta_x)

In [2]: # a scipy function that "calls routines
   ...: # from the FORTRAN library QUADPACK";
   ...: # returns more accurate results
   ...: # than our own algorithm
   ...: from scipy.integrate import quad
```

Figure 11-25. Our numerical integration function

The first argument we pass in is the function we wish to integrate; the second argument is the value x at the end of the interval under consideration. By default, the value of x at the start of the interval is set to zero, and the value of Δx is set to .00000001.

Together with our numerical integration function, we will run a numerical integration function from the scipy library to compare results. SciPy offers several functions at **scipy.integrate**. Please refer to the online documentation at the scipy.org website for more info.

At a minimum, we need to pass into the quad function a function, as well as values a, b between which to integrate the function. The return value is a tuple containing a float that is the integral from a to b and an estimate of the absolute error of the result.

```
In [3]: # lambda returns x given x; integrate from x = 0 to 5
   ...: getNumIntegral(lambda x: x, 5)
Out[3]: np.float64(12.499999999999998)

In [4]: # same lambda: returns x given x
   ...: quad(lambda x: x, 0, 5)
Out[4]: (12.5, 1.3877787807814457e-13)

In [5]: # lambda returns x**2 given x; integrate from x = 0 to 5
   ...: getNumIntegral(lambda x: x**2, 5)
Out[5]: np.float64(41.666666708333246)

In [6]: # same lambda: returns x given x
   ...: quad(lambda x: x**2, 0, 5)
Out[6]: (41.66666666666666, 4.625929269271485e-13)

In [7]: # integrate from x = 0 to 5
   ...: getNumIntegral(lambda x: ((1 + x**2) / (1 + x**4))**(1/2), 5)
Out[7]: np.float64(2.7592133568040116)

In [8]: # same lambda: returns x given x
   ...: quad(lambda x: ((1 + x**2) / (1 + x**4))**(1/2), 0, 5)
Out[8]: (2.759213356303459, 4.8206097445563057e-11)
```

Figure 11-26. Some sample functions to pass into our function and the *quad()* function, allowing us to compare the accuracy of our function's results

Fig. 11.27 Numerical integration on Wolfram Alpha. Clicking or scanning the QR code will take you to the page on Wolfram Alpha where you can compare/verify the output of our numerical integration function. https://www.wolframalpha.com/examples/mathematics/calculus-and-analysis

11.9.5 Numerical Differentiation

Fig. 11.28 Click or scan QR code to go to Wikipedia article on numerical differentiation. https://en.wikipedia.org/wiki/Numerical_differentiation

Like the integral, the derivative is based on geometry.

The numerical derivative is the tangent to the curve at (x, f(x)) for any x. It gives us information about the characteristics of the curve at (x, f(x)). The sign of the derivative tells us whether the curve at that point is ascending (positive) or descending (negative), while the value tells us how steeply (and zero tells us that (x, f(x)) is a minimum or maximum value of the curve—though from the derivative alone we cannot know if the minmax is local or global.

```
In [1]: def getNumDerivative(f, x, h=1e-11):
   ...:     return (f(x + h) - f(x)) / h
```

Figure 11-29. This function is a transliteration of Newton's difference quotient, a formula that defines the derivative at the start of every section on derivatives in every calculus textbook I know of

Nothing could be more straightforward.

```
In [2]: from scipy.differentiate import derivative
```

Figure 11-30. This function comes from the scipy library

derivative() takes at a minimum a function f and a value of x. It returns an object containing several attributes, including: **success**, which is true if the algorithm terminates successfully, and **df**, which is a float, the derivative of f at x.

```
In [3]: getNumDerivative(lambda x: x, 5)
Out[3]: 1.000000082740371

In [4]: derivative(lambda x: x, 5)
Out[4]:
success: True
status: 0
df: 1.0
```

11.9 A Calculus Primer: Numeric Integration & Differentiation Using Python

```
error: 1.4210854715202004e-14
nit: 2
nfev: 11
x: 5.0

In [5]: getNumDerivative(lambda x: x**2, 5)
Out[5]: 9.99982319171977

In [6]: derivative(lambda x: x**2, 5)
Out[6]:
success: True
status: 0
df: 10.0
error: 5.684341886080802e-14
nit: 2
nfev: 11
x: 5.0

In [7]: getNumDerivative(lambda x: ((1 + x**2) / (1 + x**4))**(1/2), 5)
Out[7]: -0.042194026050879074

In [8]: derivative(lambda x: ((1 + x**2) / (1 + x**4))**(1/2), 5)
Out[8]:
success: True
status: 0
df: -0.04219701469300041
error: 1.3145040611561853e-13
nit: 2
nfev: 11
x: 5.0
```

Figure 11-31. The numerical derivatives of several anonymous functions

We are reusing the functions that we passed into the numerical integration functions in the last section. Again, we compare our function's results with the **df** value reported in the output of the scipy **derivative()** function.

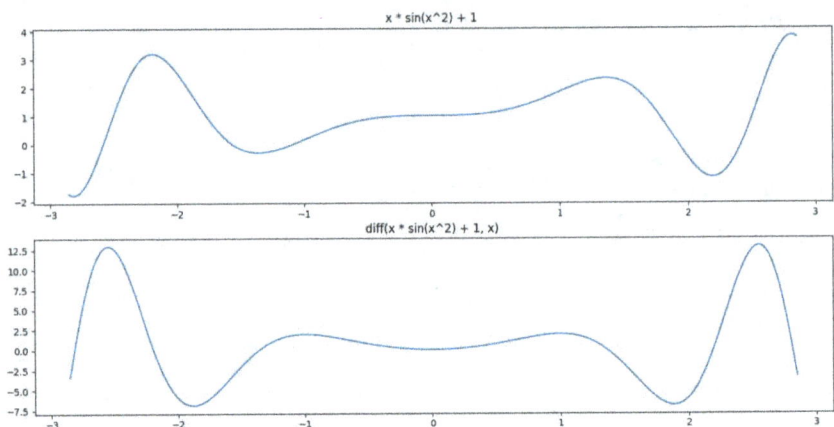

Fig. 11.32 The function **x * sin(x**2) + 1** and its derivative function, **2 * x**2 * cos(x**2) + sin(x**2)**

The x-axes of the plots are aligned. The y-values of the derivative function equal the slopes of the tangent lines for the same x-values of the original function.

In this example, we have the algebraic expression that defines the original curve. We differentiate the expression with respect to x to obtain the algebraic expression that is the derivative.

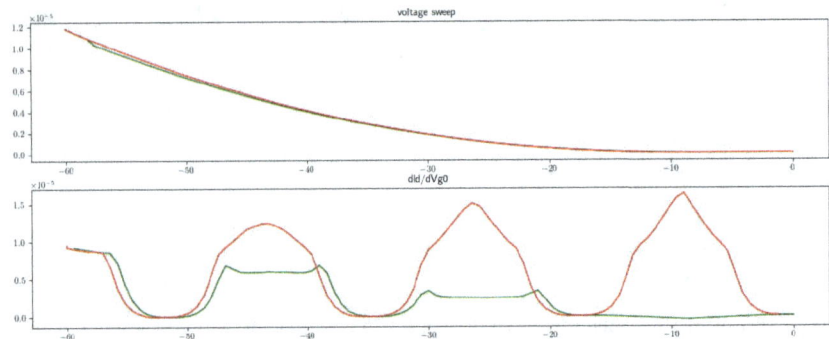

Fig. 11.33 In many experiments, we have discrete sensor readings—sometimes taken over the time domain—that when we string together in order, we interpret as the points on a continuous curve described by a differentiable function

Such is the voltage sweep of the first plot. Green signifies sweep out from origin; red signifies sweep back to origin.

We don't have an algebraic expression to describe the curve. In this case, we recall that the slope of the tangent line at *f(x)* for each *x* equals the derivative at that point. We also recall that the secant line of two closely placed points on a differentiable curve approximates the tangent line of some point between them.

11.9.6 Numerical Calculus with SymPy

We end this chapter by showing how we might perform the same operations with SymPy.

```
# if it doesn't already exist, create a notebook directory in home dir
```

11.9 A Calculus Primer: Numeric Integration & Differentiation Using Python

```
$ mkdir -p ~/notebook && cd ~/notebook
# launch jupyter notebook. once in jupyter, create a new notebook
$ jupyter notebook

# to init sympy
from sympy import init_session
init_session()

IPython console for SymPy 1.13.3 (Python 3.13.2-64-bit) (ground types: python)

These commands were executed:
>>> from sympy import *
>>> x, y, z, t = symbols('x y z t')
>>> k, m, n = symbols('k m n', integer=True)
>>> f, g, h = symbols('f g h', cls=Function)
>>> init_printing()

Documentation can be found at https://docs.sympy.org/1.13.3/

expr = Integral(x**2, (x, 0, n)) # we want to change values of n
expr # show the definite integral
```

$$\int_0^n x^2\,dx$$

```
expr.doit() # evaluate the integral
```

$$\frac{n^3}{3}$$

```
expr.subs(n, 3).doit() # sympy allows us to substitute and solve
```

$$9$$

Figure 11-34. The SymPy library also allows us to work with definite integrals, as well as to return numeric values for symbolically solved expressions

We use Jupyter notebooks for SymPy because of MathJax, which renders math expressions in textbook format.

Notice that the result is exact. This is because the substitution for **n** is an **int**, and the calculations are done with **ints**.

Chapter Summary

Functions are a basic element of Python. Among the topics covered in this chapter are positional vs. named arguments, the use of named tuples to attach labels to return values, and the use of anonymous functions called lambdas. In the next chapter, we learn how to use Python functions as subroutines, to organize our code into independent, interchangeable modules, making it easier to design and maintain large programming projects.

Software Design   12

In this chapter, we learn about the top-down design (TDD) methodology for organizing code in large programming projects. Then we learn how to implement that methodology using Python functions. Implemented thus, they act as subroutines and the main routine of a program. Also implemented thus, we can put our subroutines in one text file (module) and invoke them from the main routine in another text file (module). Organizing our code in this way emphasizes its modularity.

Organizing your code is important. As you write code for your research, a single script can grow into many scripts, each solving a different problem. Furthermore, a script originally conceived as simple can grow in ad hoc complexity as it is modified to meet new requirements, until it is no longer maintainable and must be rewritten from the ground up.

We have already considered how you might write a script that creates project filesystems for organizing the files that make up your code base.

Now we consider a design methodology for organizing a large program called "top-down design," or TDD (yes: unfortunately, its acronym is the same as that of "test-driven development"). In top-down design, the programmer breaks down a specification for a program into subproblems, and these subproblems into even smaller subproblems, and so on until the design is single discrete steps, each of which can be rendered into a statement for a computer to execute.

The top-down design thus becomes the programmer's guide for implementing the function or script that meets the specification.

A top-down design is useful in another way. When the program grows large enough, its subproblems become a guide on how to break the program down into subroutines, where each subroutine contains the code that solves one subproblem.

By organizing large programs into sets of subroutines, we can assign subroutines to different programmers to write; and when maintaining a large program, we can more easily isolate which part of the code is causing problems, as well as swap out one subroutine for another that is functionally equivalent but may, for example, implement an algorithm that runs much faster than the algorithm in the old subroutine.

Let's consider now software design.

12.1 Writing Programs: Top-Down Design Methodology

> Top-down design methodology is an approach to writing programs that moves development from the general to the specific.
>
> It starts with a written specification, usually given by the person requesting the program (its eventual user). The specification should state what the input will be (datasets of a specific or specifically formatted kind), what transformations or operations the programs will do upon the input, whether or not the program will be interactive, what input the user is expected to provide when using the program, and what the output will be (data of a specific or specifically formatted kind).
>
> The programmer breaks the specification into a sequence of discrete problems that must be solved as the input moves through the program.
>
> Each of these problems is broken down into smaller subproblems, each of which must be solved.

In preparing for battle I have always found that plans are useless, but planning is indispensable.
—Dwight D. Eisenhower

The competent programmer is fully aware of the limited size of his own skull. He therefore approaches his task with full humility, and avoids clever tricks like the plague.
—Edsger Dijkstra

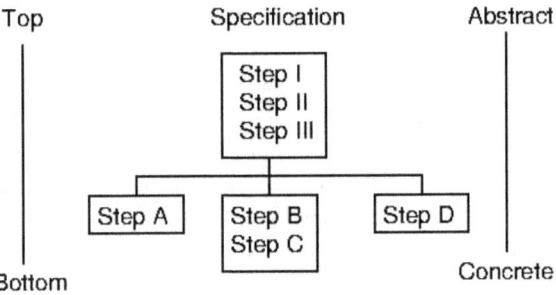

Figure 12-1 Top-down design

In top-down design, the programmer breaks down the specification for a program into subproblems, each of which in turn is broken down to more refined steps, and so on, until the program details have been rendered into pseudocode that can then be translated into whichever programming language serves as the implementation language.

Note that our top-down design also serves as a template for structuring a large program into a main routine and a set of subroutines. In that case, the upper block in this diagram is the main routine, and the blocks below it are the subroutines.

To ensure that the program does what the requestor wants or envisions, the programmer should press for as much specific detail as possible. Both should prepare for intensive testing, feedback, and discussions during development. If you are the programmer, and you are developing code for your lab or group to use, a trusted colleague who's willing to give constructive feedback is your best friend while you're developing and testing your code.

12.2 Writing Programs: Converting a Top-Down Design into a Program of Subroutines

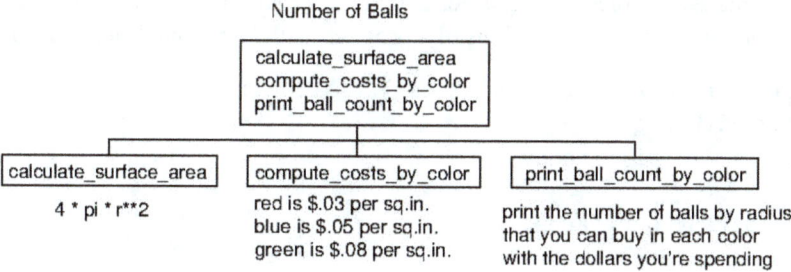

Figure 12-2 The top-down design of a program

The program calculates how many balls of a certain size and color you can buy, given how much you're willing to spend.

The program takes dollars and ball radius as input and prints out how many blue, red, or green balls you can buy with that money. The balls are priced by size and color.

```python
def calculateSurfaceArea(inches: float) -> float:
    from math import pi
    return 4 * pi * inches**2

def computeCostsByColor(area: float) -> dict:
    return {'red': area * .03, 'blue': area * .05, 'green': area * .08}

def printNumBallsByColor(inches: float, dollars: float, costDict: dict):
    print(f"\nThe number of {inches:4.2f}-inch balls "
          f"you can buy with ${dollars:4.2f} dollar(s) by color is:")
    for color, cost in costDict.items():
        numBalls = int(dollars / cost)
        print(f"{color:<6} {numBalls}")

def numBalls(dollars: float, inches: float) -> int:
    ''' Given available dollars desired radius of balls,
        calculate how many red, blue, or green balls
        of that size you can buy.
    '''
    area = calculateSurfaceArea(inches)
    costDict = computeCostsByColor(area)
    printNumBallsByColor(inches, dollars, costDict)
```

Figure 12-3 The code is organized into a main routine (or main module) and subroutines, which in Python we realize as functions

The subroutines will take the names of their modules. They will be executed in the order they're written in the main routine. Often, the output value (or values) of one subroutines becomes the input(s) of the next subroutine.

This approach to programming allows us as programmers to test each section of a program in isolation, which makes troubleshooting faster than if the program were monolithic. It also allows us as programmers to quickly replace sections of a program with improved functional equivalents.

```python
def calculateSurfaceArea(inches: float) -> float:
    from math import pi
    return 4 * pi * inches**2

def computeCostsByColor(area: float) -> dict:
    return {'red': area * .03, 'blue': area * .05, 'green': area * .08}

def printNumBallsByColor(inches: float, dollars: float, costDict: dict):
    print(f"\nThe number of {inches:4.2f}-inch balls "
          f"you can buy with ${dollars:4.2f} dollar(s) by color is:")
    for color, cost in costDict.items():
        numBalls = int(dollars / cost)
        print(f"{color:<6} {numBalls}")
```

The file of subroutines, numBalls_sbr.py

```python
def numBalls(dollars: float, inches: float) -> int:
    ''' Given available dollars desired radius of balls,
        calculate how many red, blue, or green balls
        of that size you can buy.
    '''
    from numBalls_sbr import calculateSurfaceArea, computeCostsByColor, printNumBallsByColor

    area = calculateSurfaceArea(inches)
    costDict = computeCostsByColor(area)
    printNumBallsByColor(inches, dollars, costDict)
```

Figure 12-4 A Python implementation of the top-down design of the program without documentation or garbage filters yet written

Here we put the subroutines into one file that we call numBalls_sbr.py (above) and the main routine into another file that we call numBalls.py (below). In the main routine, we import the subroutines into session memory.

This separation hides the details of the subroutines in the main file. You only need to import the main file; and if you look in the main file, of the subroutines, you see only their names, and it's from their names that we infer what they do.

This structure allows us to encapsulate specific functionality within subroutines. If we realize that a subroutine can be replaced with another that is functionally equivalent yet faster, the maintenance is easy to do.

```
In [1]: from numBalls import numBalls

In [2]: numBalls(2, 1)

The number of 1.00-inch balls you can buy with $2.00 dollar(s) by color is:
```

```
red     5
blue    3
green   1
```

Figure 12-5 *Using our program*

We import it into our IPython session or script, then it's ready to use.

Note the effect of format printing directives on the output. As Python iterates through the **costDict** dictionary, the colors are left-justified in a six-space column, while the costs are aligned along their decimal points.

12.3 Writing Your Code Base As a Set of Files

Having covered top-down design and how we might implement it for a project as a set of Python functions working as subroutines—with one function working as the main routine in which we invoke the subroutines—we will now look at how to carry our top-down design even further, to help us organize our code across multiple files.

Please take a moment to review the Python code at the end of the previous chapter.

Imagine if we had to put all the code we wrote for all of our programs into a single file—in our case, into **myModule.py**. That file would grow very large with subroutines that we wouldn't normally directly access; and every time we opened the file to add or modify a function, we'd risk accidentally changing code already in the module, breaking it.

Fortunately, Python gives us the means to separate our main routines from their subroutines by putting the subroutines into their own files, then invoking them from within the main routine.

Let's take at a quick look at how.

```python
# subroutines
def calculateSurfaceArea(inches: float) -> float:
    from math import pi
    return 4 * pi * inches**2

def computeCostsByColor(area: float) -> dict:
    return {'red': area * .03, 'blue': area * .05, 'green': area * .08}

def printNumBallsByColor(inches: float, dollars: float, costDict: dict):
    print(f"\nThe number of {inches:4.2f}-inch balls "
          f"you can buy with ${dollars:4.2f} dollar(s) by color is:")
    for color, cost in costDict.items():
        numBalls = int(dollars / cost)
        print(f"{color:<6} {numBalls}")

# main routine
def numBalls(dollars: float, inches: float) -> int:
    ''' Given available dollars desired radius of balls,
        calculate how many red, blue, or green balls
        of that size you can buy.
    '''
    area = calculateSurfaceArea(inches)
```

```
costDict = computeCostsByColor(area)
printNumBallsByColor(inches, dollars, costDict)
```

`%hist`

Figure 12-6 Using *%hist* to generate the subroutines so we can copy and paste them

If you are in the same **ipython** session in which you developed the subroutines, you can use **%hist** to have ipython print them out in a format that allows you to directly copy and paste them into text files.

Optionally, if you know the input cell numbers in which you wrote the subroutines, you can use the **%save** command to save the subroutines directly to a text file.

Figure 12-7 Modules invoking modules, on and on, levels deep

By writing our code as subroutines in a large programming task, then having those subroutines called within the routines that use them, we can efficiently divvy up portions of the code among programmers working on the task.

Even when we are working alone, applying the top-down design methodology to the organization of files holding the functions that make up our code base makes maintaining a large code base much easier than if you try to maintain all of your code within a single file.

12.4 Writing Programs: A Practical Perspective

> Premature optimization is the root of all evil.
>
> Donald Knuth

The prescriptive ways to write programs and expository essays have parallels. In each, we should start by sketching out a plan for what we intend to write. We then move to writing out a rough draft. In both cases, we try out expressions of ideas we have, to see if they get us any closer to our goals of either persuasion, explication, or solving a problem and yielding correct output.

In programming, we may consider our rough draft finished when the program runs and gives expected output for test input. For beginners, getting this far is an achievement, and many beginners may believe that with this, they have completed the assignment.

This may be true in an introduction to programming class, but it is a foolhardy assumption to make in the real world when your goal is to put your programs into production.

In practice, you will find that sometimes you code for yourself alone and sometimes you code for others. When you code for yourself alone, sometimes it's ok not to do much with your program once you've got it running. Given that you've sufficiently commented it so that you can dig into it later if you have to in order to modify or maintain it, you may be perfectly satisfied with what you have.

Your task is greater if you are writing code for others to use.

First and foremost, you must remain mindful of the two audiences you are writing for: your users and those who have to maintain your code.

Is your code easy for its intended audience to use? Is the documentation easy for the nonprogrammers in your intended audience to understand and follow?

Now that you intend to release your code for others to use (we say, "put into production"), does it run sufficiently fast?

Our machines, which can execute instructions in millionths and billionths of a second, are in the service of beings whose perception and reaction times are measured in milliseconds.

If your code in its intended and actual use of humans interacting with it runs to completion in tens of milliseconds, it may not need any time optimization.

But if your code in its intended and actual use takes longer to run to completion, even if it's processing large datasets in batch—but especially if it's intended to be used interactively—you may be justified investing the time profiling your code to find and eliminate bottlenecks.

The fix may be as straightforward as replacing one algorithm with another.

> The most basic argument for prototyping first is Kernighan and Plauger's; "90% of the functionality delivered now is better than 100% of it delivered never". Prototyping first may help keep you from investing far too much time for marginal gains.
>
> For slightly different reasons, Donald Knuth (author of *The Art of Computer Programming*, one of the field's few true classics) popularized the observation that "Premature optimization is the root of all evil"[‡‡] And he was right.
>
> Rushing to optimization before the bottlenecks are known may be the only error to have ruined more designs that feature creep. From tortured code to incomprehensible data layouts, the results of obsessing about speed or memory or disk usage at the expense of transparency and simplicity are everywhere. They spawn innumerable bugs and cost millions of man-hours—often, just to get marginal gains in the use of some resource much less expensive than debugging time.
>
> Disturbingly often, premature local optimization actually hinders global optimization (and hence reduces overall performance). A prematurely optimized portion of a design frequently interferes with changes that would have much higher payoffs across the whole design, so you end up with both inferior performance and excessively complex code.
>
> In the Unix world there is a long-established and very explicit tradition (exemplified by Rob Pike's comments in Ken Thompson's maxim about brute force) that says: *Prototype, then polish. Get it working before you optimize it.* Or: Make it work first, then make it work fast. "Extreme programming" guru Kent Beck, operating in a different culture, has usefully amplified this to: "Make it run, then make it right, then make it fast."
>
> The thrust of these quotes is the same: get your design right with an un-optimized, slow, memory-intensive implementation before you try to tune. Then, tune systematically, looking for the places where you can buy big performance wins with the smallest possible increases in local complexity.

—From **Rule of Optimization: Prototype before polishing. Get it working before you optimize it.**[*]

Please note what we are suggesting: your time is precious, and not every program or function you write warrants optimization. However, optimization IS a critical part of a programmer's job when it saves you or your users' time. Their time is precious, too.

For this reason, we profile our code (find out how long it takes to run to completion), we study algorithms; and we develop an appreciation of analyzing algorithms in their time complexities (how much space—or memory—they use is also important when we're writing for machines with memory constraints, like single-board computers and microcontrollers so we may also have to consider an algorithm's time complexity).

We'll discuss these subjects more later.

[‡‡] In full: "We should forget about small efficiencies, say about 97% of the time: premature optimization is the root of all evil". Knuth himself attributes the remark to C.A.R. Hoare.
Hoare himself denies having said it.

[*] Eric Raymond. *The Art of UNIX Programming*. Addison-Wesley. 2003. p.23.

Chapter Summary

The Python function not only allows us to implement—say—mathematical functions, it also allows us to organize our code to make it modular and manageable. As your code base grows, look for repeating patterns that could be distilled into single functions that can be invoked again and again where needed. And as your code base grows, look for opportunities to organize programs into main routines and subroutines, implemented by the Python function.

13 Working with Datasets

Of all aspects of research that can or does benefit from automation, the one common to all STEM research is the processing of datasets, especially large datasets. Our focus will be on the most common type of datasets, tabular datasets, in which each row is a record. When recordsets have one row per record (and the record separator is the newline character (\n)), they are easiest to work with, whether we are working in Bash or Python.

The datasets used in the class I teach are publicly available on GitHub and can be downloaded, along with other class materials, using these Bash commands:

```
$ mkdir -p ~/repo && cd ~/repo
$ git clone https://github.com/jderry/intro_to_programming
```

Once the repo has finished getting cloned into the directory, you can extract the datafile used in this chapter using these Bash commands:

```
$ mkdir -p ~/datafile
$ unzip ~/repo/intro_to_programming/datafile/reformatted_Unigene.fa.zip -d ~/datafile
```

Once you've got the reformatted_Unigene.fa file in ~/datafile, you're good to go.
Make sure you're in your home directory, then follow along in the Python portion in either IPython interactive shell or Jupyter notebook.

13.1 Accessing the Tabular Contents of Datafiles in Python Using a List of Lists (LoL)

We start by familiarizing ourselves with the reformatted_Unigene.fa file in ~/datafile using Bash tools.

First, on the Bash command line, type:

```
$ ls -lh ~/datafile/reformatted_Unigene.fa
-r--r--r-- 1 user user 76M Jan 26  2014 /home/user/datafile/reformatted_Unigene.fa
```

We observe that the datafile is 76 MB in size.

Second, type:

```
$ wc -l !$    # !$ bash variable holding last command argument
wc -l ~/datafile/reformatted_Unigene.fa
148787 /home/user/datafile/reformatted_Unigene.fa
```

We observe that there are 148787 lines in the file. If each record is one line and if there is no label line, then this is the number of records in the datafile.

Finally, type:

```
$ head -n 1 !$
head -n 1 ~/datafile/reformatted_Unigene.fa
Unigene1_All size 535 gap 0 0% ATCATTATTGATAGCAACAACAATCCGGAGCACTTCCTCACCACCAATCCAT
ACTATGATTCTCGCGTTGTGGGTAAATATTGTGAGAAACGTGATCCTACCCTGGCAGTTGTAGCTTACAGGAGAGGACAATGT
GATGATGAACTCATCAATGTTACGAATAAGAACTCTTTGTTCAAACTGCAGGCCAGATATGTAGTTGAAAGGATGGACGGCGA
TCTGTGGGAAAAGGTTCTTACTCCTGATAATGCCTTTAGAAGACAGCTCATTGATCAAGTTGTGTCAACAGCTTTGCCTGAGA
GTAAAAGCCCAGAGCAAGTTTCTGCTGCTGTTAAGGCTTTCATGACTGCTGATCTTCCCCATGAATTAATTGAGCTTCTTGAA
AAGATAGTATTGCAGAATTCAGCATTCAGTGGGAACTTTAATCTGCAAAACCTGCTTATCTTAACAGCCATTAAAGCAGATCC
AACTCGAGTTATGGATTACATTAATAGATTGGATAACTTTGATGGACCAGCTGTTGGTGAAGTGGCTA
```

We observe that the first line is a record, that the first field holds the unique ID for the record, and that the last field holds the record data, which is a nucleotide string.

We are ready to work with the file and its contents in Python.

content...

```
In [1]: with open('datafile/reformatted_Unigene.fa') as inFile:
   ...:     LoS = inFile.read().splitlines() # method chaining
```

Figure 13-1 The unique ID and the record data, which is a nucleotide string

We start by noting that we open our text datafiles using a *with* clause because when we do, the machine will automatically close the file once the block of code associated with the with clause has been executed.

Second, we note that there are three ways using the Python **open**() function to open a text file: for reading, for writing, and for appending. The default is to open a file read-only, which is what we're doing.

The first line of the with clause's block of code is an assignment statement. We are telling the machine to create a variable named **LoS**, while on the RHS, we have a statement that is instructing the machine to do two things: (1) read the contents of the file into a string and (2) split the string along the newline characters into substrings and put the substrings into a list.

In many programming languages, **split** and **join** are inverse commands or functions: **split** splits a string into substrings and puts the substrings into a list, while **join** joins the strings in a list into a single string.

In Python, **split**() and **join**() are both string methods; and because splitting along newline characters is a common task, Python strings also have a **splitlines**() method.

The name of the variable, **LoS**, means "list of strings."

A final observation. Python allows for **method chaining**. The RHS of the assignment statement is an example of method chaining. The first method, .read(), reads the contents of the file into a string. Now that the contents are a string, we can invoke string methods on them, which is why the .splitlines() method immediately follows.

Method chaining makes it easy to read how the data is being transformed—in this case, as it's being read from the file into a string, then, as a string, split along newline characters, with the substring put into a list called "LoS."

13.1 Reading Tabular Data in LoLs

```
In [2]: %whos
Variable   Type           Data/Info
-----------------------------------
LoS        list           n=148787
inFile     TextIOWrapper  <_io.TextIOWrapper name='<...>ode='r' encoding='UTF-8'>

In [3]: LoS[0]
Out[3]: 'Unigene1_All size 535 gap 0 0% ATCATTATTGATAGCAACAACAATCCGGAGCACTTCCTCACCA
CCAATCCATACTATGATTCTCGCGTTGTGGGTAAATATTGTGAGAAACGTGATCCTACCCTGGCAGTTGTAGCTTACAGGAGA
GGACAATGTGATGATGAACTCATCAATGTTACGAATAAGAACTCTTTGTTCAAACTGCAGGCCAGATATGTAGTTGAAAGGAT
GGACGGCGATCTGTGGGAAAAGGTTCTTACTCCTGATAATGCCTTTAGAAGACAGCTCATTGATCAAGTTGTGTCAACAGCTT
TGCCTGAGAGTAAAAGCCCAGAGCAAGTTTCTGCTGCTGTTAAGGCTTTCATGACTGCTGATCTTCCCCATGAATTAATTGAG
CTTCTTGAAAAGATAGTATTGCAGAATTCAGCATTCAGTGGGAACTTTAATCTGCAAAACCTGCTTATCTTAACAGCCATTAA
AGCAGATCCAACTCGAGTTATGGATTACATTAATAGATTGGATAACTTTGATGGACCAGCTGTTGGTGAAGTGGCTA'
```

Figure 13-2 Objects in session memory and the first string in the LoS

%whos shows us the objects in our session memory. Note that LoS is a list containing 148787 items, which is the number of records in the recordset.

We can invoke each item by index in the LoS. The first item is indeed a string. It is the first record in the recordset.

We *could* work with the records as strings, but it would not be straightforward working with individual items in each record.

Fortunately, we can split each record along a separator—in this case, spaces—and put the substrings of each record into its own list. Then we can access each individual item in the recordset by two indices: a row index and a column index.

```
In [4]: with open('datafile/reformatted_Unigene.fa') as inFile:
   ...:     LoS = inFile.read().splitlines() # method chaining
   ...:     LoL = [] # initialization
   ...:     for record in LoS:
   ...:         LoL.append(record.split())
   ...:

In [5]: %whos
Variable   Type           Data/Info
-----------------------------------
LoL        list           n=148787
LoS        list           n=148787
inFile     TextIOWrapper  <_io.TextIOWrapper name='<...>ode='r' encoding='UTF-8'>
record     str            Unigene148787_All size 43<...>ACATCAAACGAAACCTGCGAACTTT

In [6]: LoL[0][6]
Out[6]: 'ATCATTATTGATAGCAACAACAATCCGGAGCACTTCCTCACCACCAATCCATACTATGATTCTCGCGTTGTGGG
TAAATATTGTGAGAAACGTGATCCTACCCTGGCAGTTGTAGCTTACAGGAGAGGACAATGTGATGATGAACTCATCAATGTTA
CGAATAAGAACTCTTTGTTCAAACTGCAGGCCAGATATGTAGTTGAAAGGATGGACGGCGATCTGTGGGAAAAGGTTCTTACT
CCTGATAATGCCTTTAGAAGACAGCTCATTGATCAAGTTGTGTCAACAGCTTTGCCTGAGAGTAAAAGCCCAGAGCAAGTTTC
TGCTGCTGTTAAGGCTTTCATGACTGCTGATCTTCCCCATGAATTAATTGAGCTTCTTGAAAAGATAGTATTGCAGAATTCAG
CATTCAGTGGGAACTTTAATCTGCAAAACCTGCTTATCTTAACAGCCATTAAAGCAGATCCAACTCGAGTTATGGATTACATT
AATAGATTGGATAACTTTGATGGACCAGCTGTTGGTGAAGTGGCTA'
```

Figure 13-3 And now we have our LoL

We can access any element in the dataset by row and column indices.

For example, **LoL[0][6]** returns the data column (the nucleotide string) in the first record of the recordset.

Now that we can access each element of the dataset, we can ask questions of the data.

13.2 Nested Collections

LoL[0][6][10]

Nesting collections inside one another.

LoL: Name of outermost collection

[0]: Row index of outermost collection

[6]: Item index in row of outermost collection

In this case, it is a string, which is another collection.

[10]: Item index of innermost collection

Note that the indices, ordered left to right, allow us to refer to collections nested deeper and deeper in the outermost collection, named **LoL** for **list-of-lists**.

In this case, we have a string inside a list, which itself is inside a list, and we are getting the letter in index position 10 in the string.

If we invoke the outermost collection by its name alone, the Python interpreter returns the entire list, from opening square bracket to closing square bracket.

This is **Level 0** of the nested collection.

Let's go into this nested collection one level at a time.

```
In [2]: LoL[0]
Out[2]:
['Unigene1_All',
 'size',
 '535',
 'gap',
 '0',
 '0%',
 'ATCATTATTGATAGCAACAACAATCCGGAGCACTTCCTCACCACCAATCCATACTATGATTCTCGCGTTGTGGGTAAATATT
GTGAGAAACGTGATCCTACCCTGGCAGTTGTAGCTTACAGGAGAGGACAATGTGATGATGAACTCATCAATGTTACGAATAAG
AACTCTTTGTTCAAACTGCAGGCCAGATATGTAGTTGAAAGGATGGACGGCGATCTGTGGGAAAAGGTTCTTACTCCTGATAA
TGCCTTTAGAAGACAGCTCATTGATCAAGTTGTGTCAACAGCTTTGCCTGAGAGTAAAAGCCCAGAGCAAGTTTCTGCTGCTG
TTAAGGCTTTCATGACTGCTGATCTTCCCCATGAATTAATTGAGCTTCTTGAAAAGATAGTATTGCAGAATTCAGCATTCAGT
GGGAACTTTAATCTGCAAAACCTGCTTATCTTAACAGCCATTAAAGCAGATCCAACTCGAGTTATGGATTACATTAATAGATT
GGATAACTTTGATGGACCAGCTGTTGGTGAAGTGGCTA']
```

Level 1

Here, the index refers to the first list in the outermost container, which is itself a list.

Note that this is a **list-of-strings** and that the strings all together make up the first record in the dataset.

```
In [3]: LoL[0][6]
Out[3]: 'ATCATTATTGATAGCAACAACAATCCGGAGCACTTCCTCACCACCAATCCATACTATGATTCTCGCGTTGTGGG
TAAATATTGTGAGAAACGTGATCCTACCCTGGCAGTTGTAGCTTACAGGAGAGGACAATGTGATGATGAACTCATCAATGTTA
CGAATAAGAACTCTTTGTTCAAACTGCAGGCCAGATATGTAGTTGAAAGGATGGACGGCGATCTGTGGGAAAAGGTTCTTACT
CCTGATAATGCCTTTAGAAGACAGCTCATTGATCAAGTTGTGTCAACAGCTTTGCCTGAGAGTAAAAGCCCAGAGCAAGTTTC
TGCTGCTGTTAAGGCTTTCATGACTGCTGATCTTCCCCATGAATTAATTGAGCTTCTTGAAAAGATAGTATTGCAGAATTCAG
CATTCAGTGGGAACTTTAATCTGCAAAACCTGCTTATCTTAACAGCCATTAAAGCAGATCCAACTCGAGTTATGGATTACATT
AATAGATTGGATAACTTTGATGGACCAGCTGTTGGTGAAGTGGCTA'
```

Level 2

The second index refers to the data string in the list that is the first record in the dataset.

The two indices are in the order of **[row][column], the same order we use to refer to items in a matrix**.

```
In [4]: LoL[0][6][10]
Out[4]: 'A'
```

Level 3

Finally, we use a third index to extract a letter from the data string.

13.3 Finding the Minimum and Maximum Values in an Unsorted Collection

```python
# pseudo-code
''' The floating-point implementation used today
for handling floating-point storage and computation
is the IEEE754, one of whose chief authors was
the Canadian mathematician William Kahan.
The IEEE754 provides definitions of positive
and negative infinity, which we will put to use
in this algorithm.
'''
# create minLen and maxLen variables.
# initialize the value of minLen to infinity.
# initialize the value of maxLen to negative infinity.
# this forces both variables to get updated
# the first time they're compared to a value
# in the collection.
minLen, maxLen = float('inf'), float('-inf')
for value in collection:
    if value > maxLen:
        maxLen = value
    if value < minLen:
        minLen = value
```

Figure 13-4 A pseudocode rendering of the algorithm to find the largest and smallest numeric values in an unsorted collection

(Yes, it's Python code, but the intent is to generalize the algorithm to stress that it can be used in different situations.)

```python
minLen, maxLen = float('inf'), float('-inf')
for record in LoL:
    if len(record[6]) > maxLen:
        maxLen = len(record[6])
    if len(record[6]) < minLen:
        minLen = len(record[6])
```

Figure 13-5 Here, we implement the algorithm to find the smallest and largest nucleotide string lengths in our LoL dataset

13.4 Parsers

> **"Parsing"** refers to machine processing of text. Because the processing of text is fundamental to IT (information technology), the word "parser" has different meanings in IT, based on context. Here, the term means separating elements of recordsets (records and fields), either to put them into data structures to make operations on their data (read, modify, create, or delete) more efficient or to reformat records of the recordset to make them conformable for further processing.
> As an example, please recall the Bash script in the section **Reformatting Records in a Dataset** that reformats fasta records using at least two lines to each record occupying only one line, with the record separator being the newline character (\n).

Researchers many times face having datafiles that are output from one machine in a format that another machine cannot accept as input. Or the records generated by one program cannot be read by another. In yet another scenario, researchers may need to prepare data to feed it into their data pipelines.

When this happens, researchers must find a way to efficiently transform the output into input suitable for further processing. Such researchers are in need of parsers.

In this chapter, we will look at the writing of several parsers and discover if we can some do's and don'ts to apply when it comes to parsers. The first rule I hope is obvious:

Rule 1: Do not reinvent the wheel. If you are in need of a parser, try to find a suitable one that already exists.

Rule 2: If you must write a parser, clearly state why one is needed, what the parser should accept as input, and what it should yield as output. *Even as you are articulating what your code should do, your mind is likely dwelling on what code you will write to instruct the machine to do the parsing.*

Rule 3: Make sure you are familiar with the structure of the input records and recordset. *Remember, "parsing" as we're using the term means separating the elements of the records and recordsets, and you can't do that if you don't understand their structure.*

13.4.1 Revisiting fasta Parsers

Figure 13-6 Scan or click QR code to go to the Wikipedia article on FASTA format. https://en.wikipedia.org/wiki/FASTA_format

```
$ unzip ~/repo/intro_to_programming/datafile/All-Unigene.fa.zip -d ~/datafile
Archive:  /home/user/repo/intro_to_programming/datafile/All-Unigene.fa.zip
  inflating: /home/user/datafile/All-Unigene.fa
$ head -32 ~/datafile/All-Unigene.fa
```

13.4 Parsers

```
>Unigene1_All    size   535     gap  0  0%
ATCATTATTGATAGCAACAACAATCCGGAGCACTTCCTCACCACCAATCC
ATACTATGATTCTCGCGTTGTGGGTAAATATTGTGAGAAACGTGATCCTA
CCCTGGCAGTTGTAGCTTACAGGAGAGGACAATGTGATGATGAACTCATC
AATGTTACGAATAAGAACTCTTTGTTCAAACTGCAGGCCAGATATGTAGT
TGAAAGGATGGACGGCGATCTGTGGGAAAAGGTTCTTACTCCTGATAATG
CCTTTAGAAGACAGCTCATTGATCAAGTTGTGTCAACAGCTTTGCCTGAG
AGTAAAAGCCCAGAGCAAGTTTCTGCTGCTGTTAAGGCTTTCATGACTGC
TGATCTTCCCCATGAATTAATTGAGCTTCTTGAAAAGATAGTATTGCAGA
ATTCAGCATTCAGTGGGAACTTTAATCTGCAAAACCTGCTTATCTTAACA
GCCATTAAAGCAGATCCAACTCGAGTTATGGATTACATTAATAGATTGGA
TAACTTTGATGGACCAGCTGTTGGTGAAGTGGCTA
>Unigene2_All    size   3942    gap  0  0%
CCCATTCCCGGCATAGGTGGTGCAGGTAAAGCAAGAGGCAAAAGCTGAGC
ATACATATTCTGCTGTGCAAGTACTTCTTTCTCTTCATGCTCCTTGGCTT
TGACTTCCTTTTGAGCTTCAATTTTGTCCTTCACAAGCTCGTCGACTTTT
CCGGTATACTCGCGCATAAACTGTAACAAGTATGGGAAGGCAAAGTCGAT
CATATTGTTTACCCAGGCAAGTTCAAGAGCCACATCAGGCCGAACTAAAT
CGTAACAAACGAAGAGGCATGAGGCAAAGCATTCTTTCTTTCCCTTTTCG
ATGAAGTAAACAAGCAACTCCTCTGCAAGTTCACGGTCACCAGATTGTGA
GGCCGTCTCCATGGCATCTTTGTAAAGGTTGTCTTTCTTAGACAGCGCAA
TTGACTGTCTCCATCTGCCTGCTTTCTTATAAATGTAAGCAGCCACACGT
CTCATTTCAAGAAGCTCGTGTTTCTCAATCTTCTGTGCGAGGCCAATCTG
GTCAAAGTTATCATGCAAATCTATTGATTCATGAAGCCTGTCATAGTCTT
CGTCCTCAACATAAATCTCATTTAAAGCCTCGTTCACAGCAGACACGTTA
TTACTCTGAACTGCAACCATGTATGGCTTCACAAGACGCAAATGACCAGC
CTTCCGCATAATGTCAACAACACGTGTATGATCCACACGGAGTGCAAGCA
CATTGAGCATATCATTGATAAGATCAGGATGTTCTTGCAAGTAAAAATGA
ACGGCCTTATAATATAGCTCCACATTTGCAACTTTAACAGCAACATCCTT
GAACTGCATGTGATCCCATGCTTCAGGAGAATGGTTCATAATGGTGGTTG
CAGCATTATCAAACTCATCATACTGGATGTACAAATAAGTAAGTTCCTTC
CAATGCTGTTGTTCATCGCAAGCTCGTATAAGCTTGGGAATATTGAGACG
```

Figure 13-7 Unzipping the fasta recordset and printing its first 32 lines

For fasta records, each record starts with '>'. Hence, '>' is the record separator.

The first line of each record is metadata.

The data sequence follows on subsequent lines, which are of a fixed max width.

Piping these lines through **cat -vet** reveals newline characters as dollar signs ($).

Key to writing a parser for this recordset is keeping in mind that the '>' is the record separator and that if we read the contents of the fasta file into a list of strings (LoS), we can write the parser to tell the machine to concatenate all the strings of each record into a single string, which we'll then tell the machine to write out as a single line.

In general, the datafile contains only two types of lines: metadata lines (all of which begin with '>') and data sequence lines.

```python
def reformatFastaRecordset(fastaFile: str):
    ''' Given a fasta recordset in a text file,
        write out a text file of reformatted
```

```python
        fasta records, one record per line.
    '''
    # read the fasta recordset into a list of strings
    with open(fastaFile, 'r') as inFile:
        LoS = inFile.read().splitlines()
    with open('reformattedFastaFile', 'w') as outFile:
        # initialization
        head, data, record = '', '', ''
        for line in LoS:
            # the machine iterates
            # down the LoS
            # one string at a time
            if line.startswith('>'):
                # if line is first line
                # of new record,
                # write out the old record &
                # prepare for the new record
                pass # placeholder statement
            else:
                # if the line is a data line,
                # concatenate line to data string
                # & update data variable
                data = data + line
```

Figure 13-8 Starting writing the parser

Our parser should of course read in the contents of a fasta file and write out the reformatted records to a new file.

Given the structure of the fasta records, we have only two cases for type of line: the first line, which contains the record separator AND metadata, and all the other lines of a record, which are the data lines.

The **for** loop means the machine iterates through the lines in the same sequence of the original datafile.

First, it reads the metadata line of the first record, then each of the data lines of the first record; then it reads the metadata line of the second record, and so on.

The block of code associated with the **else** clause handles all the data lines, but although the data lines are far more numerous than the metadata lines, we need to instruct the machine to do just one thing: concatenate the string that is the current line to the string that is the value of the data variable; then update the data variable.

The block of code associated with the **if** clause is much more interesting.

```python
def reformatFastaRecordset(fastaFile: str):
    ''' Given a fasta recordset in a text file,
        write out a text file of reformatted
        fasta records, one record per line.
    '''
    # read the fasta recordset into a list of strings
    with open(fastaFile, 'r') as inFile:
        LoS = inFile.read().splitlines()
```

13.4 Parsers

```python
    with open('reformattedFastaFile', 'w') as outFile:
        # initialization
        head, data, record = '', '', ''
        for line in LoS:
            # the machine iterates
            # down the LoS
            # one string at a time
            if line.startswith('>'):
                # if line is first line
                # of new record,
                # write out the old record
                record = f"{head[1:]} {data}"
                # head[1:] is a slice
                # EXCLUDING the 1st char
                outFile.write(f"{record}\n")
                # ^^^ don't forget \n !
            else:
                # if the line is a data line,
                # concatenate line to data string
                # & update data variable
                data = data + line
```

Figure 13-9 Developing the *if* clause

At the top of the **if** clause, we instruct the machine to write out the contents of the old record.

"But there is no record before the first record in the recordset!"—true. The values of the string variable **head**, **data**, and **record** are all empty strings. As a result, the write statement at this point writes out an empty line.

We'll deal with that later.

For now, let's think about how to prepare or reinitialize for the contents of the new record.

Still in development, we might tell the machine simply:

head, data = line, ''

And in many cases, this would work. However, because spaces are used as value separators, we want to remove the extra spaces from the metadata lines in this dataset.

There is a Pythonic way to do this using the string methods **str.split**() and **str.join**():

head, data = ' '.join(line.split()), ''

Now, let's return to considering how we might prevent an empty line from being written when the machine encounters the first metadata line. We could instruct the machine to execute a block of code only if the value of **record** is not an empty string with this:

if record: # if record not empty

Now let's put it all together...

```python
def reformatFastaRecordset(fastaFile: str):
    ''' Given a fasta recordset in a text file,
    write out a text file of reformatted
    fasta records, one record per line.
    '''
    # read the fasta recordset into a list of strings
    with open(fastaFile, 'r') as inFile:
```

```python
        LoS = inFile.read().splitlines()
    with open('reformattedFastaFile', 'w') as outFile:
        # initialization
        head, data, record = '', '', ''
        for line in LoS:
            # the machine iterates
            # down the LoS
            # one string at a time
            if line.startswith('>'):
                # if line is first line
                # of new record,
                # write out the old record
                record = f"{head[1:]} {data}"
                # head[1:] is a slice
                # EXCLUDING the 1st char
                if record:
                    outFile.write(f"{record}\n")
                    # ^^^ don't forget \n !
                head, data = ' '.join(line.split()), ''
                # ^^^ re-initialize and re-instantiate
            else:
                # if the line is a data line,
                # concatenate line to data string
                # & update data variable
                data = data + line
```

Figure 13-10 A functioning fasta parser

We are still in development! We need garbage filters that test that the argument is a string and that a file exists in the path defined by the string.

We should add a second argument for the user to pass in a path to the output file, perhaps as a named argument that writes one out called 'reformattedFastaFile' to the working directory.

But now we have a function that, when invoked, returns a reformatted fasta dataset.

And now that we have a recordset with one record per row, we can treat our recordset as we would any other tabular recordset.

```
!ls -lh reformattedFastaFile
-rw-rw-r-- 1 user user 76M Mar 22 15:03 reformattedFastaFile
!wc -l reformattedFastaFile
148786 reformattedFastaFile
!head -n 1 reformattedFastaFile
Unigene1_All size 535 gap 0 0% ATCATTATTGATAGCAACAACAATCCGGAGCACTTCCTCACCACCAATCCAT
ACTATGATTCTCGCGTTGTGGGTAAATATTGTGAGAAACGTGATCCTACCCTGGCAGTTGTAGCTTACAGGAGAGGACAATGT
GATGATGAACTCATCAATGTTACGAATAAGAACTCTTTGTTCAAACTGCAGGCCAGATATGTAGTTGAAAGGATGGACGGCGA
TCTGTGGGAAAAGGTTCTTACTCCTGATAATGCCTTTAGAAGACAGCTCATTGATCAAGTTGTGTCAACAGCTTTGCCTGAGA
GTAAAAGCCCAGAGCAAGTTTCTGCTGCTGTTAAGGCTTTCATGACTGCTGATCTTCCCCATGAATTAATTGAGCTTCTTGAA
AAGATAGTATTGCAGAATTCAGCATTCAGTGGGAACTTTAATCTGCAAAACCTGCTTATCTTAACAGCCATTAAAGCAGATCC
AACTCGAGTTATGGATTACATTAATAGATTGGATAACTTTGATGGACCAGCTGTTGGTGAAGTGGCTA
```

Figure 13-11 Verifying the output

We can execute Bash commands within the IPython interactive shell by preceding each Bash statement with an exclamation point.

13.5 Too Big to Handle: Preprocessing Large Datasets, Extracting Only Needed Dimensions

As we know, datasets can get very, very big. At some point, dataset sizes can tax even the fastest machines processing the data with compiled programs like C or Fortran. When we find that the runtimes of our data analytic programs are painfully long because the datasets that are their input are so large, we may elect instead to sample our datasets, or find other ways to make the input data of manageable size.

The dataset we're considering now was part of a graduate student's research project. The problem she encountered is that over time her dataset grew substantially; and by the time she contacted me, it had grown so large that the time it was taking just to feed it into her session memory had grown to tens of minutes.

Here is the byte size and record count of the original datafile:

```
$ ls -lh orig_data_03-02.txt
-rwxrwx— 1 user user 2.5G Mar 17 10:48 orig_data_03-02.txt
$ wc orig_data_03-02.txt
1554177 43485755 2606365878 orig_data_03-02.txt
```

So the dataset has ~2.5 GB of data in ~1.6 million lines.

The researcher confirmed that each line is a record and that they're in JSON format.

According to Wikipedia, JSON "is an open-standard format that uses human-readable text to transmit data objects consisting of attribute-value pairs."

The researcher was using Python's built-in **json** library to read the recordset into session memory for further processing, but as has already been noted, the read operation was taking a very long time, and each week it was taking even longer.

The researcher assumed, reasonably, that the performance drag might lie in her code, so she contacted me for help.

After getting access to her code and dataset, I wrote a **driver**.* All my driver did was import the built-in json library, then read in the recordset using the same library function the researcher used.

My plan was to find the bottleneck in the researcher's code by profiling the execution of her program statements, starting at the top.

Just loading the records through the json library's function took forever. I'd found the bottleneck.

The problem wasn't with the researcher's code.

Not having any experience working with json datasets and not sure what the researcher's options might be, I turned to a colleague, Dr. Dennis Wylie. I explained to him the situation as I understood it and asked if he was willing to take a look.

Long story short, he and the researcher got in contact, and Dr. Wylie found out that the researcher didn't need **all** the data in the records. For her project, she needed just a subset of the data included in the records.

Dr. Wylie then wrote her a small Bash script that used **grep**, a command-line JSON processor called **jq** that can be **apt**-installed on Ubuntu machines, and **perl**. The script can be found in the **script** directory of the repo. It is named "parsing_json.sh."

---

* **driver**: a small main script written to test a lower-level interface.

Run against the 2.5 GB dataset, the script returned a recordset, each of whose records held only the data the researcher needed. It was much smaller in bytes than the original dataset; and when the researcher fed this recordset into her code, it loaded very quickly.

From this experience, I would like to derive one more rule and one piece of advice. The advice is: **If you need help, ask.** Dr. Wylie resolved the issue, but only because the researcher was willing to ask me for help, and I was willing to ask Dr. Wylie for help.

Rule 5: Preprocessing your data, or preparing it before having your main program process it, might solve whatever problems or issues you're facing in working efficiently with the dataset in your main program. *In the war story above, the solution was to generate a reduced dataset—same number of records, but less data in each record. But sometimes even just sorting the recordset by one column or two (a major and minor sort) will do the trick.*

13.6 One Record per Text File

Sometimes the machines collecting data during experimental runs output the data in one text file for each sample. Our next example comes from the top portions of voltage-sweep records, in which the data is formatted in label/value pairs, one pair per line.

```
$ cp -r ~/repo/intro_to_programming/datafile/key_value_samples/ ~/datafile/
$ head ~/datafile/key_value_samples/record1
Setup title "IDVD p-type PDPP2T-TT-OD"
Classic test name "I/V Sweep"
Test date 11/3/2018
Test time 21:22:11
Device ID "CMM III.50 dpp-dtt s1 control 300K 11_3_18 dev3 Vg0,-50 Vd0,-50"
Count 1
Flags
Remarks
Context.MainFrame 4155C
Channel.UnitType SMU SMU SMU
```

Figure 13-12 We start by copying the samples directory from our repo into datafile directory in our home directory; then we inspect the first ten lines of *record1*

The filename is the sample name, and the lines are label/value pairs.

```
$ head !$ | cat -vet
head ~/datafile/key_value_samples/record1 | cat -vet
Setup title^I"IDVD p-type PDPP2T-TT-OD"$
Classic test name^I"I/V Sweep"$
Test date^I11/3/2018$
Test time^I21:22:11$
Device ID^I"CMM III.50 dpp-dtt s1 control 300K 11_3_18 dev3 Vg0,-50 Vd0,-50"$
Count^I1$
Flags^I$
Remarks^I$
Context.MainFrame^I4155C$
Channel.UnitType^ISMU^ISMU^ISMU$
```

Figure 13-13 The first ten lines of *record1* piped into *cat -vet*

13.6 One Record per Text File

Friendly reminder: The Bash variable !$ holds the argument of the last Bash command.

Using cat -vet, the caret-capital I combination (^I) signifies a tab.

From this, we see that the first tab on each line separates a label from its value.

```
$ wc -l ~/datafile/key_value_samples/*
 109 /home/user/datafile/key_value_samples/record0
 109 /home/user/datafile/key_value_samples/record1
 109 /home/user/datafile/key_value_samples/record10
 109 /home/user/datafile/key_value_samples/record11
 109 /home/user/datafile/key_value_samples/record12
 109 /home/user/datafile/key_value_samples/record13
 109 /home/user/datafile/key_value_samples/record14
 109 /home/user/datafile/key_value_samples/record15
 109 /home/user/datafile/key_value_samples/record16
 109 /home/user/datafile/key_value_samples/record17
 109 /home/user/datafile/key_value_samples/record18
 109 /home/user/datafile/key_value_samples/record19
 109 /home/user/datafile/key_value_samples/record2
 109 /home/user/datafile/key_value_samples/record3
 109 /home/user/datafile/key_value_samples/record4
 109 /home/user/datafile/key_value_samples/record5
 109 /home/user/datafile/key_value_samples/record6
 109 /home/user/datafile/key_value_samples/record7
 109 /home/user/datafile/key_value_samples/record8
 109 /home/user/datafile/key_value_samples/record9
2180 total
```

Figure 13-14 Line count of these sample records

```
In [1]: def make_dict_from_record_files(folder: str) -> dict:
   ...:     ''' Given the path to folder holding 1 record/file
   ...:         files, and files holding 1 key:value pair per line,
   ...:         make a DoD from the files' contents.
   ...:     '''
   ...:     import os
   ...:     filelist = os.listdir(folder)
   ...:     return filelist
   ...:

In [2]: make_dict_from_record_files('datafile/key_value_samples/')
Out[2]:
['record6',
 'record16',
 ...]
```

Figure 13-15 Developing a solution is very often an act of brainstorming

In this case, we want to be able to instruct the machine to iterate over the files holding the sample records. The **listdir**() function in Python's built-in **os** library, which we learn about from googling, is key. With it, we can **open**() each file in the directory holding the sample records.

Note that for development use only, we return the fileList from our function. This is because the variable **fileList** is local to the function. To inspect its value, we could print the value from within the body of the function, or we could make it a return value of the function.

```python
def make_dict_from_record_files(folder: str) -> dict:
    ''' Given the path to folder holding 1 record/file
        files, and files holding 1 key:value pair per line,
        make a DoD from the files' contents.
    '''
    import os
    filelist = os.listdir(folder)
    # outer dictionary of DoD
    resultsDict = {} # initialization
    for file in filelist:
        # full file path
        filepath = folder + file
        # inner dictionary of DoD
        contentsDict = {}
        with open(filepath) as inFile:
            LoS = inFile.read().splitlines()
            for line in LoS:
                # handle label with no value
                try:
                    # split along only 1st tab in line
                    label, value = line.split("\t", 1)
                except ValueError:
                    continue
                contentsDict[label]= value
        # add the inner dict to the outer dict
        resultsDict[file] = contentsDict
    return resultsDict
```

Figure 13-16 Working function, still in development

Note that we've seen much of this code before: the **with** clause, the making of the **LoS**, and the splitting of each line.

We tell the machine to add each label/value pair to the inner dictionary; and once the machine has iterated through the LoS, we tell it to add the inner dictionary to the outer dictionary.

```
In [2]: resultsDict = make_dict_from_record_files('datafile/key_value_samples/')

In [3]: len(resultsDict)
Out[3]: 20

In [4]: resultsDict['record1']['Test date']
Out[4]: '11/3/2018'
```

Figure 13-17 Invoking our working function and testing

As we expect, the outer dictionary contains 20 items.

13.6 One Record per Text File

The outer keys are the sample names, while the inner keys are the dimensions of the samples.

We can read a value by invoking a key of the outer dictionary, followed by a key of the inner dictionary.

We can add new items to this dictionary by modifying our function to use the outer dictionary if it already exists and bypassing the line to create a new, empty dictionary. We can also have the machine ensure that the names of the files being passed in do not already exist as keys in the outer dictionary, and if they do, to verify that the user wants to update those entries.

I hope that at this point, you are starting to think about how you might code such functionality into your parser to make it more robust.

But for now, let's assume that we want to keep the DoD and focus on saving it by pickling it to a file.

If you don't already have a **pickle** directory in your home directory, go ahead and create one:

```
In [6]: !mkdir -p ~/pickle

In [7]: import pickle

In [8]: with open('pickle/resultsDict.bin', 'wb') as outFile:
   ...:     pickle.dump(resultsDict, outFile)
```

Figure 13-18 Pickling our collection to preserve it

We pickle collections that we create while processing our datasets, especially if we intend them not to be read-only but mutable, capturing the state of our data at the moment we pickle the collection. Our ability to pickle the collections we use in our research allows us to do our work over multiple sessions:
When we have to end our current session, we pickle those collections whose current state we wish to preserve. Once they're pickled, we can quit our session, close the clamshells of our laptops, and move on to our next task.

```
In [1]: import pickle
   ...: with open('pickle/resultsDict.bin', 'rb') as inFile:
   ...:     resultsDict = pickle.load(inFile)
```

Figure 13-19 Unpickling our collection to continue working with it

Once we're ready to pick up where we left off on working with our datasets, we start up a new **ipython** session, unpickle the collections we need, which reads them into session memory in the state we preserved them, and carry on.

```
In [2]: import pandas as pd
   ...: df = pd.DataFrame(resultsDict)
   ...: df = df.T # transpose
   ...: df.to_csv('results.csv')
```

Figure 13-20 Transforming our DoD to a tabular dataset

If our intent is to transform our original dataset into a tabular dataset, we can use **pandas** to simplify the task.

```
In [3]: !tail -n +2 results.csv | head -n 1
record6,"""IDVD p-type PDPP2T-TT-OD""","""I/V Sweep""",11/3/2018,23:20:09,
"""CMM III.50 dpp-dtt s1 control 300K 11_3_18 dev1 Vg0,-50 Vd0,-50
reprobe""",1,,,4155C,SMU SMU SMU,SMU1:MP SMU2:MP SMU3:MP,Id Is Ig,
Vd Vs Vg,V V V,VAR1 CONST VAR2,,,SMU1:MP SMU2:MP SMU3:MP,NONE  NONE NONE,
ON ON ON,Double,LINEAR,0,-50,-0.5,0.0001,0,"""CONTINUE AT ANY""",START,OFF,
0,6,-10,0.0001,0,0 0 0,0.0001 0.0001 0.0001,SMU1:MPSMU2:MP SMU3:MP,
"""HR ADC"" ""HR ADC"" ""HR ADC""",LIMITED LIMITED LIMITED,1nA 1nA  1nA,
"""BY FULL RANGE"" ""BY FULL RANGE"" ""BY FULL RANGE""",50 50  50,0,0,OFF,
AUTO,1,DEFAULT,DEFAULT,true,Vd,Linear,-1,0,Id Ig,Linear Linear,
-1E-05 -1E-05,1E-05 1E-05,,false,false,1,True,0,0,,,,,false,,,0,,,,,false
,,,0,false,1,True,0,0,,,,,false,,,0,,,,,false,,,0,false,,,false,,
...
```

Figure 13-21 The resultsDict csv file, without the label line

tail +2 sends to STDOUT the contents of the file starting with line 2.

Note that the records are in no particular order. The items in dictionaries are unsorted.

Chapter Summary

One feature STEM professions share is the generation and processing of datasets. Especially when datasets are large, or they are continuous, being generated over the span of a long-term experimental run, processing the datasets with automation vastly improves the accuracy and efficiency of researchers working on those datasets. In the next chapter, we consider the efficiency of the algorithms themselves.

Programming Efficiency 14

We humans are creatures of perception and reaction times measured in milliseconds. Our modern computers execute instructions in billionths of a second. If a calculation taking millions of instructions completes in a millisecond, it still seems instantaneous to us. But if we have to run that calculation against the million records in our recordset—and it runs in linear time—then it takes ~17 minutes to run to completion. When processing even moderately sized datasets, programming efficiency matters. In this chapter, we will consider the time complexities of algorithms, and we will profile our code to compare the runtimes of functionally equivalent programs on our hardware.

14.1 The Analysis of Algorithms

> The analysis of algorithms finds the cost in resources (time and memory space) to execute algorithms. The cost in time is called an algorithm's time complexity; the cost in memory is called an algorithm's space complexity. We will focus mostly on the cost in time.
> Donald Knuth came up with this way of analyzing algorithms.
> It is independent of hardware.
> It lets us measure an algorithm's efficiency, given the size of input.
> An algorithm's runtime efficiency can have three measures: its best time, its average time, and its worst time. Of the three, we are most concerned with our algorithms' worst times.

Many algorithms run in linear time—that is, if one record gets processed in one unit of time, then two records get processed in two units of time, and so on.

This is what Donald Knuth discovered. We say that if two algorithms are functionally equivalent, but one has a better time complexity than the other, then the one with the better time complexity is more efficient. An active area of computer science research lies in finding algorithms that are more efficient in time or space than algorithms currently in production software.

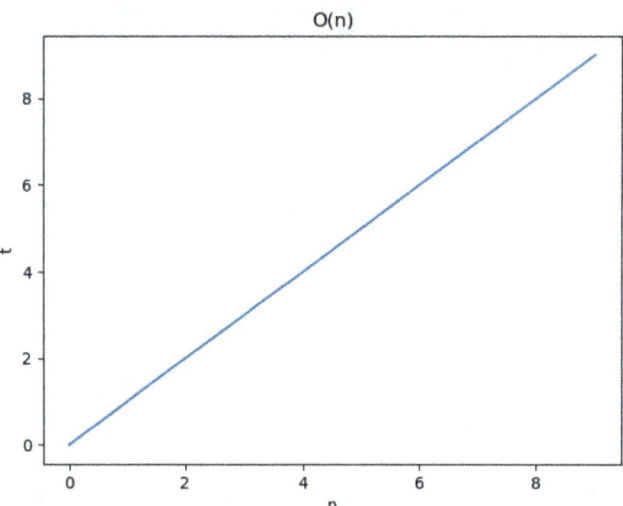

Figure 14-1 Linear time complexity

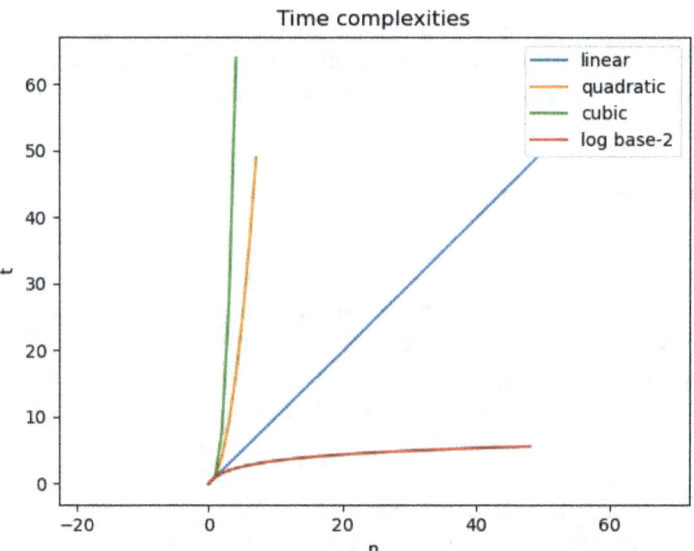

Figure 14-2 But other algorithms run in other time complexities

Al Aho, co-developer of AWK (first version implemented in 1977) while at Bell Labs:*

> I would say AWK is an easy-to-learn and easy-to-use scripting language that excels at routine data-processing applications...Whenever possible, we implemented algorithms that were linear in time, in either the worst case or the average case...When we designed AWK, I thought a megabyte dataset was huge. If we consider the exabytes of data now available on the Internet, we were many orders of magnitude off in what's now considered a large dataset. Of course, even a linear-time scan of a terabyte of data is far too slow, so a whole new approach is necessary to process relevant data on the Internet.

---

* Federico Biancuzzi and Shane Warden, Editors. "AWK," *Masterminds of Programming: Conversations with the Creators of Major Programming Languages*. O'Reilly. 2009. pg.109.

14.2 Finding a Value in an Unsorted Collection

In the following three sections, we will consider example algorithms with linear, cubic, and logarithmic time complexities, respectively.

Figure 14-3 Scan or click the QR code to go to the Wikipedia article on the analysis of algorithms.https://en.wikipedia.org/wiki/Analysis_of_algorithms

Figure 14-4 Scan or click the QR code to go to the Wikipedia article on the bubblesort algorithm.https://en.wikipedia.org/wiki/Bubble_sort

Articles in Wikipedia of well-known and well-studied algorithms in the algorithms' time and space efficiencies, which generally you can find at the top of the articles.

In the following sections, we will consider examples of algorithms that run in a few different time complexities, then we will consider examples of functionally equivalent algorithms that have different time complexities.

14.2   O(n): Finding a Value in an Unsorted Collection of Index/Value Pairs

Our algorithm to find a specific value in an unsorted collection whose items are index/value pairs, implemented in Python, may look like this:

```python
for index, value in enumerate(someCollection):
    if value == someValue:
        print(f"found {value} at index position {index}!")
        break
```

Figure 14-5 Searching through a collection whose items are index/value pairs

The collection may be, for example, a string, a list, or a tuple.

Figure 14-6 An unsorted collection of index/value pairs

We cannot know any of the value in any position in the collection until we read it, which can be done in Python with the statement **print(someCollection[*index*])**, where *index* is position in the collection whose value we want to get.

Figure 14-7 The most straightforward way to find the value we're looking for is to use a *for-loop*, which iterates through the collection sequentially item by item, starting with the first item and ending with the last

Using a **for-loop**, the fastest search ends if the value we're looking for is in the first position we read.

Figure 14-8 Otherwise, we go position by position through the collection, reading the value in each, checking whether it is the value we're looking for

Figure 14-9 The longest search ends if the value we're looking for is in the last position we read, or if it isn't in the collection at all

14.3 Nested Loops

Because we are interested mostly in the worst time performance of the algorithms we use, we say that the algorithm to find a value in an unsorted collection of index/value pairs runs in linear time, or **O(n)**.

14.3 O(n^m): Nested Loops and Their Time Complexity

Our nested loop example looks like this:

```python
n = 3
for i in range(n):
    for j in range(n):
        for k in range(n):
            print(f"i: {i}\tj: {j}\tk: {k}\n")
```

Figure 14-10 Example with-loops nested three deep

The time complexity of nested loops is O(n^m), where *m* is the number of loops. In our example, that's O(n^3).

14.3.1 Illustrating Executing Nested Loops with Nested Dolls

Figure 14-11 In this example, we use matryoshka dolls to demonstrate the execution of nested loops

The biggest doll represents the counter of the outermost loop, the middle one represents the counter of the first nested loop, and the littlest represents the counter of the innermost loop. The counters start in this example as uncreated.
i = u, j = u, k = u

Figure 14-12 The program counter reaches the statement for the first for-loop

The statement is executed. The range function creates an iterable range object, **(0, 1, 2)**. **i** is created and instantiated with the first value in the range object, **0**.
i = 0, j = u, k = u
At this point, the program counter has entered the block of code for the outermost loop...

Figure 14-13 Having entered the block of code for the outermost loop, the program counter comes to the statement to create and instantiate the middle for-loop, its local variable **j**, and its range object to iterate through

i = 0, j = 0, k = u
At this point, the program counter has entered the block of code for the middle loop.

14.3 Nested Loops

Figure 14-14 And the program counter comes to the statement to create and instantiate the innermost for-loop

i = 0, j = 0, k = 0

At this point, the program counter has entered the block of code for the innermost loop. Statements here are interpreted and executed the first time.

Figure 14-15 We are still in the innermost loop

Statements are again executed.
i = 0, j = 0, k = 1

Figure 14-16 Statements in the innermost loop are executed a final time

The program counter leaves the innermost loop...
i = 0, j = 0, k = 2

Figure 14-17 The middle loop counter **k** takes the value of the next item in its range object

14.3 Nested Loops

The program counter is not yet at the end of that range object so it enters the block of code of the middle loop again.

The iterator of innermost loop is reinstantiated and initialized, and the block of code for the innermost loop is executed.

i = 0, j = 1, k = 0

Figure 14-18 i = 0, j = 1, k = 1

Figure 14-19 i = 0, j = 1, k = 2

Figure 14-20 i = 0, j = 2, k = 0

Figure 14-21 i = 0, j = 2, k = 1

Figure 14-22 i = 0, j = 2, k = 2

14.3.2 The Output from Running Our Example Nested Loop

```
i: 0    j: 0    k: 0
i: 0    j: 0    k: 1
i: 0    j: 0    k: 2
i: 0    j: 1    k: 0
i: 0    j: 1    k: 1
i: 0    j: 1    k: 2
i: 0    j: 2    k: 0
i: 0    j: 2    k: 1
i: 0    j: 2    k: 2
i: 1    j: 0    k: 0
i: 1    j: 0    k: 1
i: 1    j: 0    k: 2
i: 1    j: 1    k: 0
i: 1    j: 1    k: 1
i: 1    j: 1    k: 2
i: 1    j: 2    k: 0
i: 1    j: 2    k: 1
i: 1    j: 2    k: 2
i: 2    j: 0    k: 0
i: 2    j: 0    k: 1
i: 2    j: 0    k: 2
i: 2    j: 1    k: 0
i: 2    j: 1    k: 1
i: 2    j: 1    k: 2
i: 2    j: 2    k: 0
i: 2    j: 2    k: 1
i: 2    j: 2    k: 2
```

Figure 14-23 Output from our nested loop example

14.3.3 Can We Do Better? Algebra to the Rescue!

Our example nested loop runs in $O(n^3)$, or cubic time complexity. If we must use all three variables in our calculation at one time, then this is the solution, and we are stuck with this time complexity.

However, if we must use all three variables in our calculation two at a time, or *pairwise*, like this: (i, j), (i, k), and (j, k), then we may be able to reorganize our code like this:

```python
n = 3
for i in range(n):
    for j in range(n):
        print(f"i: {i}\tj: {j}\n")
for i in range(n):
    for k in range(n):
        print(f"i: {i}\tk: {k}\n")
for j in range(n):
```

```
    for k in range(n):
        print(f"j: {j}\tk: {k}\n")
```

Figure 14-24 Reorganizing our nested loops if we are doing calculations using only pairwise input

In this case, each nested loop runs in O(n^2), or quadratic time complexity, which we add together, giving us O($3 \cdot n^2$).
When *n* is large, O(n^3) is greater than O($3 \cdot n^2$), even quite significantly so.

Section Summary
This section comes with a couple of lessons learned:

(1) Cubic time complexity separates good time complexities from bad ones. If the algorithm you are developing includes nested loops more than three deep, you might want to reevaluate your algorithm.
(2) Reorganizing your nested loops, if possible, can greatly improve the overall time complexity of your code. It's worth reevaluating your nested loops to see if they can be rewritten to run in better time complexities.

14.4   O(ln_2 n): Binary Trees

Some algorithms run in better time complexities than linear time O(n). The search algorithm to find an item in a sorted collection organized as a binary tree is such an algorithm. It runs in O(ln_2n), or base-2 logarithmic time complexity.

Figure 14-25   A binary tree

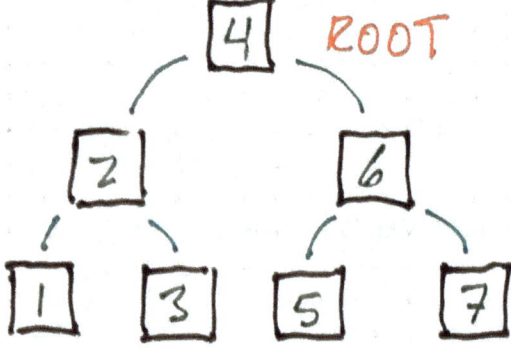

Binary trees are a special kind of graph, or network. The topmost node of all trees is called *the root*. Binary trees have many interesting properties. In a fully balanced binary tree, half of the nodes are to the left of the root, and half are to the right.

14.4 O(ln₂ n): Binary Trees

Figure 14-26 Any node in a binary tree can have descendants, and any node can have 0, 1, or at most two child nodes

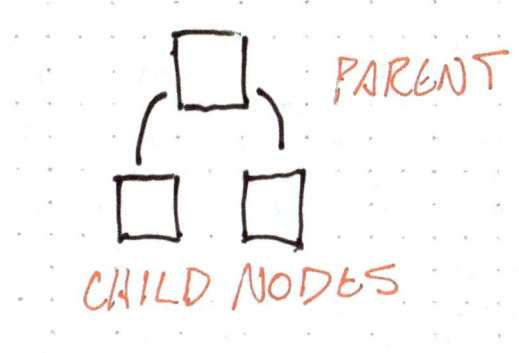

Binary trees have useful properties, too. When information can be sorted into a binary tree, finding information in a binary tree takes logarithmic time.

Botany field guides based on *dichotomous keys* take advantage of this property.

Dichotomous ("to cut in two") keys used to make an identification work by offering two choices at each step in the identification.

For example, a botany field guide may start by asking the user if the plant under consideration has needles or leaves. The answer decides which page to turn to, where another dichotomous key further refines the identification. Each turn to another dichotomous key is called a "hop."

A field guide organized in this manner is organized as a binary tree.

Organized as such, using it makes it possible to uniquely identify one species of plant out of a million listed species in just 20 hops.

We say the search algorithm for elements organized into a binary tree runs in base-2 logarithmic time, $O(ln_2 n)$.

Max number of hops =

$$ceiling(log_c n / log_c b) \tag{14-1}$$

where:
ceiling rounds result up to next integer.
c is the common base.
n is the size of input.
b is the base to convert to.

Figure 14-27 It is possible to calculate the maximum number of hops that it would take to search for an item in any binary tree.

Figure 14-28 The natural numbers in a number line

Another example of the advantage of organizing information in a binary tree is in playing a children's two-player game called "high or low".

In this game, one player announces, for example, "I'm thinking of a (natural) number between 1 and 15."

The naïve player might play along using an algorithm that runs in linear time (new guess = old guess + 1): "Is it 1?" "Higher." "Is it two?" "Higher." "Is it three?" "Higher."

Algorithms that run in linear time are considered good algorithms.

But if you've played this game before, you are probably aware of an algorithm that lets you get to the answer in logarithmic time.

And it requires organizing the natural numbers not in a line, but in a binary tree.

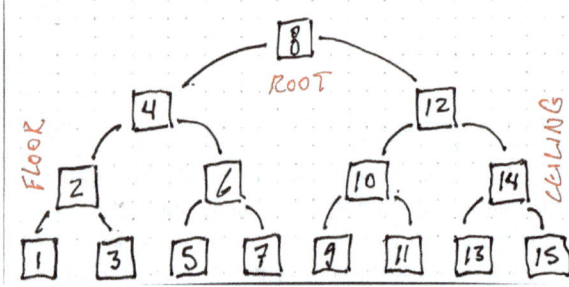

Figure 14-29 The natural numbers structured in a well-balanced binary tree

The algorithm for searching the number requires setting an adjustable floor and an adjustable ceiling, which we set at the start as the endpoints of the interval under consideration—in this case, that's 1 (floor) and 15 (ceiling).

Our guess is (floor + ceiling)/2. If we get a fractional number, we round up or down (it doesn't matter which—but we must stay consistent throughout the game).

If we are told "higher," we set the floor to be the number we guessed and recalculate. Likewise, if we are told "lower," we set the ceiling to the number we guessed and recalculate.

By using this algorithm, if the other player chooses a number between 1 and one million, we should guess it in more than 20 turns.

```python
from math import ceil, log

# in this interactive while loop, the script explains the game,
# gets highest integer of range from user;
# and initializes floor and ceiling variables
while True:
    rules_of_game = \
    ("\nin this game you give me a range of integers from 1 to some number you choose.\n"
    "then you will pick a number within this range for me to guess.\n"
    "i will try to guess your number in the fewest number of tries.\n"
    "for each guess, you will tell me if your number is higher than (h),\n"
    "lower than (l), or equal to (=) your number. ready?\n")
    print(rules_of_game)
    floor = 1
    ceiling = input(f"please enter the highest number of your range: ")
    ceiling = int(ceiling)
    
    # 'continue' is related to 'break' ---
    # it returns the program counter to the top of the while loop.
    if not isinstance(ceiling, int) and\
       not ceiling > 1:
        bad_answer = (f"that's not a legitimate value."
                      f"please enter a counting number greater than 1.")
```

14.4 O(ln₂ n): Binary Trees

```python
            print(bad_answer)
            continue

    else:
        break

# print the challenge of fewest guesses using this algorithm
# use the math module's ceil() and log() functions
nguesses = ceil(log(ceiling)/log(2))
print("\n")
print(f"i can guess your number in at most {nguesses} guesses!\n")

# initalize the guess counter
guessCnt = 0
while True:
    guessCnt = guessCnt + 1
    guess = (floor + ceiling)//2

    answer = input(f"i guess {guess}! Is your number higher (h), lower (l), or equal (=)? ")

    # several if-statements, each processing different user input
    if answer == 'h':
        floor = guess
    elif answer == 'l':
        ceiling = guess
    else:
        print(f"\nyee-haw! i guessed your number is {guess} in {guessCnt} guesses!\n")
        break
```

Figure 14-30 The hi-lo game

The machine uses an algorithm in which the number line is treated as a binary tree.

```
$ python hi-lo_game.py

in this game you give me a range of integers from 1 to some number you choose.
then you will pick a number within this range for me to guess.
i will try to guess your number in the fewest number of tries.
for each guess, you will tell me if your number is higher than (h),
lower than (l), or equal to (=) your number. ready?

please enter the highest number of your range: 1000000


i can guess your number in at most 20 guesses!

i guess 500000! Is your number higher (h), lower (l), or equal (=)? l
i guess 250000! Is your number higher (h), lower (l), or equal (=)? l
i guess 125000! Is your number higher (h), lower (l), or equal (=)? l
i guess 62500! Is your number higher (h), lower (l), or equal (=)? h
i guess 93750! Is your number higher (h), lower (l), or equal (=)? =

yee-haw! i guessed your number is 93750 in 5 guesses!
```

Figure 14-31 Playing the hi-lo game

14.5 Functional Equivalence and Profiling Code

We call two algorithms **functionally equivalent** if for all input they generate the same output. All things being equal, we prefer the algorithm with the better time complexity though in practice (e.g., in microcontrollers, where memory is quite limited) we may have to go with the algorithm with the better space complexity.

14.5.1 Dictionary As Lookup Table vs. Conditional Testing

```python
def getComplement(nucleotide):
    if nucleotide == 'a':
        complement = 't'
    if nucleotide == 'c':
        complement = 'g'
    if nucleotide == 'g':
        complement = 'c'
    if nucleotide == 't':
        complement = 'a'
    return complement

def revCompl_if(nuclStr):
    outputStr = ''
    for nucleotide in nuclStr:
        outputStr = getComplement(nucleotide) + outputStr
    return outputStr
```

Figure 14-32 Example to illustrate functional equivalence

```python
complDict = {'a':'t', 'c':'g', 'g':'c', 't':'a'}

def revCompl_dict(nuclStr):
    outputStr = ''
    for nucleotide in nuclStr:
        outputStr = complDict[nucleotide] + outputStr
    return outputStr
```

Figure 14-33 Example to illustrate functional equivalence (cont.)

revCompl_elif() uses a function of logical comparison operations to get the complement of a nucleotide, while **revCompl_dict**() uses a dictionary as a lookup table in memory to do the same.

(Note that **revCompl_dict**() uses one positional argument and one named argument. We set the named argument's value to **None**, and if a complement dictionary is not passed into the function, code within the function creates and instantiates the **complDict**.)

In general, we say that two pieces of code are functionally equivalent if, for all input, they generate the same state (or output).

So the question becomes, for any two functionally equivalent pieces of code, which should we prefer to use in our own code?

```
In [3]: %timeit revCompl_if('gattaca')
525 ns ± 5.31 ns per loop (mean ± std. dev. of 7 runs, 1,000,000 loops each)

In [4]: %timeit revCompl_dict('gattaca')
250 ns ± 1.19 ns per loop (mean ± std. dev. of 7 runs, 1,000,000 loops each)
```

Figure 14-34 Here we profile the code to see which is faster

Reminder: μs is a millionth of a second, and ns is a billionth of a second.

The code that uses the dictionary as a lookup table in memory runs more than twice as fast as the code that uses conditional branching.

14.6 Finding Min and Max Values in an Unsorted Collection II

```python
!cp ~/repo/intro_to_programming/datafile/reformatted_Unigene.fa ~/datafile
import os; home = os.path.expanduser('~')
with open(home + '/datafile/reformatted_Unigene.fa') as inFile:
    LoS = inFile.read().splitlines() # method chaining
    LoL = [] # initialization
    for record in LoS:
        LoL.append(record.split())

def min_max_cond(LoL):
    minLen, maxLen = float('inf'), float('-inf')
    for record in LoL:
        if len(record[6]) > maxLen:
            maxLen = len(record[6])
        if len(record[6]) < minLen:
            minLen = len(record[6])
    return minLen, maxLen

def min_max_builtins(LoL):
    minLen, maxLen = float('inf'), float('-inf')
    for record in LoL:
        minLen = min(minLen, len(record[6]))
        maxLen = max(maxLen, len(record[6]))
    return minLen, maxLen
```

Figure 14-35 Here we revisit finding the minimum and maximum values in an unsorted collection, using as we did before our reformatted fasta recordset, which we read into session memory as a list of lists

Our first algorithm is the one we used in Chapter 10. It uses conditional branches to get both the min and max lengths of nucleotide strings in our dataset, as well as how many records have nucleotide strings of those lengths.

Our second algorithm uses the built-in functions **min()** and **max()** to find the min and max string lengths.

```
In [3]: %timeit min_max_cond(LoL)
6.53 ms ± 95.9 microseconds per loop (mean ± std. dev. of 7 runs, 100 loops each)

In [4]: %timeit min_max_builtins(LoL)
25.6 ms ± 196 microseconds per loop (mean ± std. dev. of 7 runs, 10 loops each)
```

Figure 14-36 Here we profile the code to see which is faster

The code that uses conditional branching runs more than four times as fast as the code that uses built-ins. Without testing, I would have assumed otherwise.
Lesson learned: Never assume. It pays to profile your code.

14.7 Multiple Passes Through Dataset vs. Single Pass

SPECIFICATION: A researcher has merged two datasets of galaxies, only to find some galaxies do not match up in their coordinates in the two datasets. As a result, these galaxies appear as separate objects, though very close together, in the merged dataset. Write a program that finds candidate pairs in the merged dataset for further processing. (The researcher will apply tests to the pairs to decide which of each pair to keep and which to discard.)

14.7.1 An Outline of the Problem and a Solution

```
In [1]: !cp ~/repo/intro_to_programming/datafile/galaxy_coordinates.txt ~/datafile/

In [2]: !head ~/datafile/galaxy_coordinates.txt
id          RA_MODELING          DEC_MODELING
75930        269.08597400518556    66.87087896446573
75937        269.16871355832023    67.01271788239829
75938        269.1679988225846     67.01314308897464
75939        269.1178623463331     67.01379619992419
75940        269.0686060799391     67.01425463939361
75941        269.0886741850958     66.87097504287637
75942        269.3775938349732     67.0107140524922
75943        269.36177574327894    67.00949030247915
75944        269.3625209643527     67.01048889824702
```

Figure 14-37 The dataset of *galaxy_coordinates.txt*

It contains 1 label line and 1078 records. In the dataset, right ascension (RA) and declination (dec) are given in decimal degrees.
Note that the dataset is sorted by record IDs.

```python
import os; home = os.path.expanduser('~')
with open(home + '/datafile/galaxy_coordinates.txt') as inFile:
    LoS = inFile.read().splitlines()
    LoS.pop(0) # remove the label line
    LoL = []
    for record in LoS:
```

14.7 Multiple Passes Through Dataset vs. Single Pass

```
        LoL.append(record.split())
    for record in LoL:
        # coerce the coordinates from strings into floats
        record[1], record[2] = float(record[1]), float(record[2])
```

Figure 14-38 While reading the dataset into a list of lists (LoL) in session memory, we remove the label line and coerce the coordinates, which Python reads in as strings, into floats so that we can use them in arithmetic calculations

This is much more efficient than if we coerce them into floats repeatedly within the loops of the algorithms we're studying below.

We consider any two objects in the dataset a candidate pair (possible duplicates of the same galaxy) if they are at or within a distance of 1.5 arcseconds of each other. To determine this, we apply the formula:

$$\sqrt{(RA_a - RA_b)^2 + (dec_a - dec_b)^2} \leq r,$$

where RA and dec are the right ascension and declination of objects a and b.

Note that this requires arithmetically combining the RA and dec of each object in the dataset with the RA and dec of all the other objects in the dataset. How we do this is the subject of this section.

Note also that in our dataset, RA and dec are given in decimal degrees, and 1.5 arcseconds equals **0.000416667** decimal degrees.

```
In [4]: %%timeit
   ...: r = 0.000416667 # define r
   ...: candidate_pairs_n = set()
   ...: for i in range(len(LoL)):
   ...:     for j in range(len(LoL)):
   ...:         # do not process the same record
   ...:         if LoL[i][0] != LoL[j][0] and \
   ...:         ((LoL[i][1] - LoL[j][1])**2 \
   ...:         + (LoL[i][2] - LoL[j][2])**2)**(1/2) <= r:
   ...:             candidate_pairs_n.add(frozenset([LoL[i][0], LoL[j][0]]))
   ...:
```

```
209 ms ± 2.61 ms per loop (mean ± std. dev. of 7 runs, 1 loop each)
```

Figure 14-39 Profiling functionally equivalent code in IPython

We start with an algorithm that may be the easiest to come up with and that gets the job done. It instructs the computer to go through the dataset $n x n$ times, getting the distance from each object to all the others; if the distance from an object to another falls within a specified distance **r**, the records of each are added to a set of candidate pairs for further inspection. The time complexity of this algorithm is $O(n^2)$.

We can improve our time complexity by modifying this algorithm. Let me show you how.

```
In [5]: %%timeit
   ...: r = 0.000416667 # define r
   ...: candidate_pairs_n_half = set()
   ...: for i in range(len(LoL)-1):
   ...:     for j in range(i+1, len(LoL)):
   ...:         if ((LoL[i][1] - LoL[j][1])**2 \
   ...:             + (LoL[i][2] - LoL[j][2])**2)**(1/2) <= r:
   ...:             candidate_pairs_n_half.add(frozenset([LoL[i][0], LoL[j][0]]))
   ...:
92.6 ms ± 624 microseconds per loop (mean ± std. dev. of 7 runs, 10 loops each)
```

Figure 14-40 This second algorithm is a modification of the first

The inner loop starts one record below the current record of the outer loop. As you might expect, this cuts in half the runtime of the code. The time complexity is still quadratic time, or $O(n^2)$.

But we can do better. In these instances, the dataset is sorted by record ID, and not by the angular dimension distances, right ascension and declination used to reckon **r**.

```
In [8]: candidate_pairs_n == candidate_pairs_n_half
Out[8]: True
```

Figure 14-41 We run both algorithms without profiling them (remove the %%timeit lines), then test if the two sets populated by the algorithms are equivalent (contain the same members)

```
In [9]: !sort -k3 ~/datafile/galaxy_coordinates.txt >
~/datafile/dec_galaxy_coordinates.txt

In [10]: !head ~/datafile/dec_galaxy_coordinates.txt
76284         269.44148921992644      66.86724166571999
75983         269.39815152799156      66.86738552114454
75963         269.40034629768326      66.86738799360327
76014         269.37210885338027      66.86776855013143
76003         269.28764408880585      66.86778537296743
75994         269.2847853775924       66.8683220022235
76025         269.3316934607369       66.86845742526116
76350         269.3534472137342       66.86867774608862
76109         269.3093670552318       66.86883590760532
75952         269.26434341609945      66.86885817395644
```

Figure 14-42 The same dataset, now sorted by declination

We have to create a new LoL in session memory from this dataset before we run the next algorithm against it.

```
In [12]: %%timeit
   ...: r = 0.000416667 # define r
   ...: candidate_pairs_lin = set()
   ...: for i in range(len(LoL)-5):
   ...:     # unrolling the loop
```

14.7 Multiple Passes Through Dataset vs. Single Pass

```
   ...:         if ((LoL[i][1] - LoL[i+1][1])**2\
   ...:            + (LoL[i][2] - LoL[i+1][2])**2)**(1/2) <= r:
   ...:               candidate_pairs_lin.add(frozenset([LoL[i][0], LoL[i+1][0]]))
   ...:         if ((LoL[i][1] - LoL[i+2][1])**2\
   ...:            + (LoL[i][2] - LoL[i+2][2])**2)**(1/2) <= r:
   ...:               candidate_pairs_lin.add(frozenset([LoL[i][0], LoL[i+2][0]]))
   ...:         if ((LoL[i][1] - LoL[i+3][1])**2\
   ...:            + (LoL[i][2] - LoL[i+3][2])**2)**(1/2) <= r:
   ...:               candidate_pairs_lin.add(frozenset([LoL[i][0], LoL[i+3][0]]))
   ...:         if ((LoL[i][1] - LoL[i+4][1])**2\
   ...:            + (LoL[i][2] - LoL[i+4][2])**2)**(1/2) <= r:
   ...:               candidate_pairs_lin.add(frozenset([LoL[i][0], LoL[i+4][0]]))
   ...:         if ((LoL[i][1] - LoL[i+5][1])**2\
   ...:            + (LoL[i][2] - LoL[i+5][2])**2)**(1/2) <= r:
   ...:               candidate_pairs_lin.add(frozenset([LoL[i][0], LoL[i+5][0]]))

1.01 ms ± 6.64 microseconds per loop (mean ± std. dev. of 7 runs, 1,000 loops each)
```

Figure 14-43 Profiling functionally equivalent code in IPython

The plan is to get the same resultset as we got from comparing each record to all other records in the algorithms that run in quadratic time, but to do so in linear time, or $O(n)$. We start by numerically sorting the dataset by declination. Then we go through the dataset in a single pass.

Note the complication—candidate pairs lie nearby in the sorted dataset, but they aren't necessarily all contiguous. It turns out that the records of a candidate pair can be five records apart.

I've opted to use 15 conditional clauses in sequence to ensure that records are tested out to five from the current record and that the last records in the dataset are tested. Writing out code sequentially that could be run in a loop is called "unrolling the loop," and in general, it runs much faster than the loop it replaces.

PLEASE NOTE: Only the top lines of the solution are printed here. The solution is 54 lines long.

With a single pass through the dataset, we get the same resultset as we did with multiple passes, but in 1.01 milliseconds. Profiling shows that this algorithm runs significantly faster on this dataset in these timing runs: 207× faster than the original algorithm and 92× faster than the original algorithm modified.

```
In [14]: candidate_pairs_lin == candidate_pairs_n
Out[14]: True
```

Figure 14-44 Here we test the resultsets generated by the linear-runtime algorithm and the original algorithm for equivalence

They are the same.
The takeaway lessons are as follows:

(1) Search algorithms running on sorted data tend to be significantly faster than those dealing with unsorted data.
(2) Unrolling loops into sequential code can significantly increase execution speed.

(3) If you are automating the processing of datasets that will be generated many times, or even of a single very large dataset that will be generated only once, working on how to meet a specification with an algorithm that has a better time complexity than the first one you come up with could easily be time well spent.

14.7.2 Extending the Solution

Rule of Generation: Avoid hand-hacking; write programs to write programs when you can.[*]

The astute reader may have noticed that this solution has its own problems. First, the defined interval of five records checked is arbitrary. Sure, it captures all the candidate pairs in this sample dataset, but how do we know it is sufficient to capture all such pairs in the complete dataset? And this leads to the second problem: writing the code by hand to unroll the loop is tedious, highly repetitive, and prone to error.

If we can solve the second problem, we might get a handle on the first. To solve the second, we can write a Python function that writes the Python script to unroll the loop.

```python
def unroll_loop(inputFile, outputFile, num):
    '''unroll_loop(inputFile of dataset, outputFile of script,
                number of records to compare to 1 record)
    '''
    with open(inputFile) as inFile:
        LoS = inFile.read().splitlines()
    LoL = []
    for record in LoS:
        LoL.append(record.split())
    LoL.pop(0) # pop off the label line

    with open(outputFile, 'a') as outFile:
        # outFile.write("#!/usr/bin/python\n")
        outFile.write("with open(" + "'" + inputFile + "'" + ") as inFile:\n")
        outFile.write("    LoS = inFile.read().splitlines()\n")
        outFile.write("    LoL = []\n")
        outFile.write("    for record in LoS:\n")
        outFile.write("        LoL.append(record.split())\n")
        outFile.write("    LoL.pop(0)\n")

        outFile.write("num = " + str(num) + "\n")
        outFile.write("r = float(0.000416667) # define r\n")
        outFile.write("candidate_pairs_lin = set()\n")

        outFile.write("for i in range(len(LoL) - num):\n")
        for j in range(1, num):
            outFile.write("    if ((float(LoL[i][1]) - float(LoL[i+" + str(int(j))
                + "][1]))**2 + (float(LoL[i][2]) - float(LoL[i+" + str(int(j)) +
                "][2]))**2)**(1/2) <= r: \n")
            outFile.write("        candidate_pairs_lin.add(frozenset([LoL[i][0],
                LoL[i+" + str(int(j)) + "][0]]))\n")
```

---

[*] Eric S. Raymond. *The Art of UNIX Programming*. Addison-Wesley. 2004. p22.

14.7 Multiple Passes Through Dataset vs. Single Pass

```
outFile.write("for i in range(len(LoL) - num, len(LoL)-1):\n")
outFile.write("    for j in range(i+1, len(LoL)):\n")
outFile.write("        if ((float(LoL[i][1]) - float(LoL[j][1]))**2 +
            (float(LoL[i][2]) - float(LoL[j][2]))**2)**(1/2) <= r: \n")
outFile.write("            candidate_pairs_lin.add(frozenset([LoL[i][0],
            LoL[j][0]]))\n")
```

Figure 14-45 Python function to unroll the loop

Chapter Summary

Because we process data in bulk—as in STEM datasets that can be quite large—we concern ourselves with the efficiency in time and space of the algorithms we use. The analysis of algorithms lets us compare the time complexities of the algorithms we use while profiling code lets us see just how fast implementations of those algorithms run on our machines. As we have seen, taking time to write a program that is functionally equivalent to one we find useful but that has a better time complexity can make all the difference in whether our processing completes in a month or a single long weekend.

Other Subjects

15

In previous chapters on programming, we considered what it takes to automate a hand algorithm and make it ready for production, how to design and implement a large program as a main routine and set of subroutines; and how to assess the efficiency, especially in runtime, of our programs. In this chapter, our general approach will be less theory and more Python, more algorithms, and more applications.

15.1 An Introduction to Graph Theory

Table 15-1 Brief lexicon of graph theory

graph	G(v,e), also known as a network	a math structure made of vertices and edges
vertex	v, fundamental unit of a graph	also known as nodes
edge	e, relationship between vertices	represented by a line connecting 2 vertices
weight	value assigned to an edge	examples include simple labels and distances between edges
degree	number of edges connected to a vertex	directed edges result in in-degrees and out-degrees

A graph is defined as a set of nodes and the connections between them (called *edges*). To many people, a computer network, with its computers and network hardware as nodes and cables and wireless connections as edges, is the archetype of graphs.

However, social networks, with people as nodes, are also graphs. In fact, graph theory took off in the 1950s and 1960s sociologists and social scientists, in their research on group dynamics, wished to make strong statements on their findings; and nothing can make your statements stronger than being able to show that mathematical proofs underlie them. Mathematicians collaborating with these scientists worked on graph theory and extended it in part to help those scientists buttress their claims.

Figure 15-1 The seven bridges of Königsberg in Euler's time.—Bogdan Giusca. *The problem of the Seven Bridges of Königsberg*. Public domain

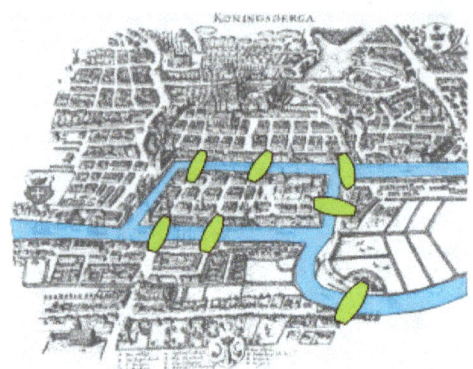

Leonhard Euler's solution to a popular puzzle regarding traversing the seven bridges over the Pregel river, published in 1736 CE, is today considered the seminal paper in graph theory.

In this chapter, we will work with a datafile called "hewitsoni_males.txt." Please copy the file into the datafile directory in your home directory, and make your home directory your working directory.

```
$ cp ~/repo/intro_to_programming/datafile/hewitsoni_males.txt ~/datafile/
$ head -n 21 ~/datafile/hewitsoni_males.txt
spec #         station         day #          time
1              396             699            1412
1              408             701            859
1              408             702            912
1              109             703            915
1              409             703            1407
1              109             704            819
1              408             704            946
1              408             705            837
1              401             707            825
2              690             710            934
2              690             711            1022
3              442             1071           1105
4              408             699            1435
4              372             700            1005
4              440             707            1120
4              114             709            1302
4              362             716            1116
4              409             730            1020
4              409             732            1002
4              409             735            1101
```

Figure 15-2 Copying the hewitsoni_males.txt file into the datafile directory in our home directory, then viewing the first 20 records in the file

Note that the researcher has already sorted this dataset. The major sort is by specimen number. The minor sort is by day/time.

These records describe when a butterfly by specimen number was observed at a nectar-feeding station.

15.1 Graph Theory

In the graph we're to describe, each station is a node, and the observed path of a butterfly from station-to-station describes an edge.

Put another way, in the recordset, each two consecutive records for a specimen by number describes an edge.

So, for example, Speciment #1 was first observed at Station #396; next, he was observed at Station #408. His path describes an edge from node 396 to node 408.

In our edge list, we would write for our first record:

```
1          396          408
```

We call the specimen number the "weight" of the edge.
The complete edge list fully describes the graph.

```python
import os; home = os.path.expanduser('~')
# first, we read the contents
# of the hewitsoni_males datafile
# into an LoL in session memory
with open(home + '/datafile/hewitsoni_males.txt') as inFile:
    LoS = inFile.read().splitlines()
    LoL = [] # initialization
    for record in LoS:
        LoL.append(record.split())

# then we write out an edge list from the LoL
with open(home + '/datafile/edge_list', 'w') as outFile:
    # we shorten the range object by 1
    # to prevent an IndexError
    for index in range(len(LoL)-1):
        if LoL[index][0] == LoL[index+1][0]:
            edge_record = (f"{LoL[index][0]}\t"
                           f"{LoL[index][1]}\t"
                           f"{LoL[index+1][1]}\n")
            outFile.write(edge_record)
```

Figure 15-3 The Python code to make an edge list file out of the hewitsoni_males.txt file

```
$ head -n 20 ~/datafile/edge_list
1          396          408
1          408          408
1          408          109
1          109          409
1          409          109
1          109          408
1          408          408
1          408          401
2          690          690
4          408          372
4          372          440
4          440          114
4          114          362
```

4	362	409
4	409	409
4	409	409
4	409	409
10	408	408
10	408	315
15	114	119

Figure 15-4 The first 20 records in the edge list file

With these two datafiles—hewitsoni_males.txt and edge_list—we can use Bash pipelines to answer many questions about the graph composed of nectar-feeding stations and butterflies flying between them:

```
tail -n +2 "$HOME"/datafile/hewitsoni_males.txt |# read into pipeline only records
gawk -F"\t" '{print $1}' |# extract column 1
uniq |# return single instance of each contiguous identical group of specimen
wc -l # return the number of unique specimen labels
```

Figure 15-5 Returns the number of specimens in hewitsoni_males file

```
tail -n +2 "$HOME"/datafile/hewitsoni_males.txt |# read into pipeline only records
gawk -F"\t" '{print $2}' |# extract column 1
uniq |# return single instance of each contiguous identical group of specimen
wc -l # return the number of unique specimen labels
```

Figure 15-6 Returns the number of nodes in hewitsoni_males file

```
gawk -F"\t" '{print $1}' ~/datafile/edge_list |# extract column 1
uniq |# return a single instance of each contiguous identical group of specimens
wc -l # return the number of specimens
```

Figure 15-7 Returns the number of specimens in hewitsoni_males file that made it into the edge list

```
gawk -F"\t" '{print $2}' ~/datafile/edge_list > ~/all_stations
gawk -F"\t" '{print $3}' ~/datafile/edge_list >> ~/all_stations

cat ~/all_stations |# read all stations into pipeline
sort |# sort station labels
uniq |# return a single instance of each contiguous identical group
wc -l # return the number of feeding stations in edge_list
```

Figure 15-8 The number of stations in hewitsoni_males file that made it into the edge list

```
$ gawk -F"\t" '{print $1}' ~/datafile/hewitsoni_males.txt | uniq -c | sort -n | tail
10 7532
10 862
11 308
12 373
12 906
13 892
14 34
15 1737
17 312
```

15.1 Graph Theory

```
17 354

$ gawk -F"\t" '{print $2}' ~/datafile/hewitsoni_males.txt | uniq -c | sort -n | tail
   4 971
   4 975
   5 688
   5 971
   5 971
   5 975
   6 971
   6 971
   7 123
   7 690
```

Figure 15-9 Specimens that appear the most frequently in hewitsoni_males.txt (top) and nectar-feeding stations that appear most frequently (bottom)

```
$ gawk -F"\t" '{print $2}' ~/datafile/edge_list | sort | uniq -c | sort -n | tail
  32 395
  32 975
  33 971
  47 689
  57 119
  62 688
  66 408
  69 123
 100 409
 145 690

$ gawk -F"\t" '{print $3}' ~/datafile/edge_list | sort | uniq -c | sort -n | tail
  32 395
  35 975
  39 442
  48 689
  56 119
  56 408
  63 123
  73 688
 103 409
 165 690
```

Figure 15-10 Nodes with the highest out-degree (top) and nodes with the highest in-degree (bottom)

Nectar-feeding station 690 has the highest degree (both in and out) of all the stations.

There are several ways to measure or define centrality in a network. One is "edge centrality," which simply means that the node with the highest edge count is considered the central node of the network. In this network, station 690 would be that node.

15.1.1 Saving Our Python Collections by Pickling Them

> **pickling** lets us write our collections from session memory directly to binary files on our mass-storage device.
> It also allows us to read collections saved to binary files directly into session memory.
> Over long-term research projects, **pickling** allows us to preserve our data in the state where we leave off in one session, then restore it at the start of our next session.
> If we wish, we can also "snapshot" the state of our data at any time using **pickling**, where we include the time and date in the filename of the binary file holding the snapshot.

```python
import os; home = os.path.expanduser('~')

with open(home + '/datafile/hewitsoni_males.txt') as inFile:
    LoS = inFile.read().splitlines()
    LoL = [] # initialization
    for record in LoS:
        LoL.append(record.split())

# then create an edge list from the LoL
edge_list = []
for index, record in enumerate(LoL[:-1]):
    if LoL[index][0] == LoL[index+1][0]:
        edge = [LoL[index][0], LoL[index][1], LoL[index+1][1]]
        edge_list.append(edge)
```

Figure 15-11 Making the edge list an LoL

We're doing this with the intention of pickling the collection to a binary file.

```python
# if directory does not exist, create it
from pathlib import Path
Path(home + '/pickle').mkdir(parents=True, exist_ok=True)

# write pickle file into pickle directory
from pickle import dump
with open(home + '/pickle/edge_list.pickle.bin', 'wb') as outFile:
    dump(edge_list, outFile)
```

Figure 15-12 Pickling our edge_list LoL to a binary file

The function to do so is **dump** from the built-in pickle library.

We make the name of the binary file match the name of the collection to make it easier for us later to know what its contents are. We save all our pickle files in a pickle directory to make it easier to locate them.

Note the second argument in the **open**() function, 'wb'. It means "write binary."

```python
from pickle import load
with open(home + '/pickle/edge_list.pickle.bin', 'rb') as inFile:
    edge_list = load(inFile)
```

Figure 15-13 Unpickling our edge_list LoL in a new session

We're also giving the same name as we have been using. Again, this consistency in naming reduces confusion.

The state of the data as it was when we pickled the collection has been preserved.

Once our LoL is restored to session memory, we're ready to pick up where we left off working with the data it contains.

15.2 Writing Python Scripts That Write Scripts

Rule of Generation: Avoid hand-hacking; write programs to write programs when you can.[*]

> Abstractly, a script is a collection of strings in a text file.
> Lines in the file are instructions in a regular language whose patterns are easy for an interpreter to read.
> These lines are also easy for an interpreter to write.
> Through Python, we can instruct a machine to write a script that either that machine or another machine can then run.
> The output script can be in Python, but it doesn't have to be.

This GUI is the standard interface used for configuring the windows firewall.

Shown is the Properties tab showing IP addresses or address ranges of devices that will get a reply when it pings this machine. The radio buttons chosen say, "Any IP address."

Using this GUI to modify the firewall to restrict which IP addresses the firewall will allow ping requests through is convenient if the number of IP addresses is small.

When the number of rules to be modified is large, or the number of IP addresses that have to be added is large, doing so through this GUI is impractical.

---

[*] Eric S. Raymond. *The Art of UNIX Programming*. Addison-Wesley. 2004. p22.

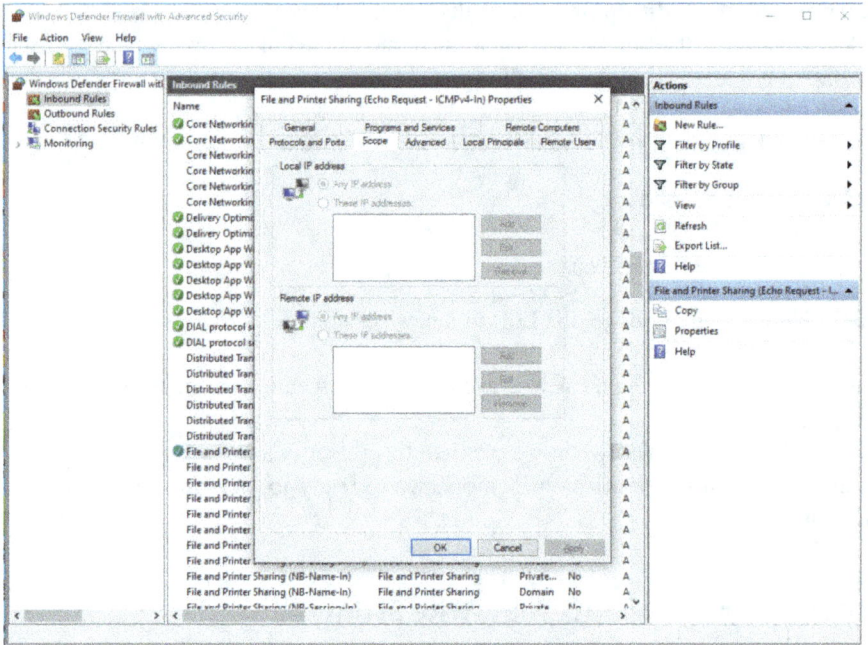

Figure 15-14 Windows Defender Firewall with Advanced Security

Figure 15-15 Network shell (netsh) Scan or click the QR code to go to Microsoft's online reference on **netsh**. https://learn.microsoft.com/en-us/windows-server/networking/technologies/netsh/netsh

We can use **netsh** to more easily configure the Windows firewall.

Please note: Although **netsh** is available for use, Microsoft recommends that users use the newer PowerShell and its set of commands, instead.

```
# on the windows machine, run:
c:\>netsh advfirewall export c:\firewallpolicy.wfw
# this creates a file of all the firewall rules as they exist when the file is made

# if you need to roll back your firewall rules to the earlier state, run:
c:\>netsh advfirewall firewall import c:\firewallpolicy.wfw
```

Figure 15-16 We can use the **netsh** command to export and import the firewall ruleset

We want to export a copy of the ruleset before we run our script to modify the firewall in case we muck up the firewall so we can roll back our changes, which we would do by importing the firewallpolicy.wfw file.

15.2 Scripts That Write Scripts

```
# on the windows machine, run:
c:\>netsh advfirewall firewall show rule all > c:\fwrules.txt
# this outputs a text file with all the firewall rules.
```

Figure 15-17 This **netsh** command outputs a text file of the firewall's rules

This is the file that we will direct the machine to parse with our Python script.

```
Rule Name:                            Inbound Rule for Remote Shutdown (TCP-In)
----------------------------------------------------------------------
Enabled:                              No
Direction:                            In
Profiles:                             Domain,Private,Public
Grouping:                             Remote Shutdown
LocalIP:                              Any
RemoteIP:                             Any
Protocol:                             TCP
LocalPort:                            RPC
RemotePort:                           Any
Edge traversal:                       No
Action:                               Allow
```

Figure 15-18 An example of the text output from the last **netsh** command

Note that for each firewall rule, the output includes the rule's name, direction, and remote IP addresses that the rule applies to.

This pattern of rule names and rule attributes is regular within the file, which guides our consideration of which Python collection would be best for holding the firewall ruleset in memory.

We will use a dictionary of dictionaries, or DoD, in which the keys of the outer dictionary are rule names, and the value of each key/value pair is a dictionary of the rule's attributes.

The specification of exactly how we want to modify the machine's Windows firewall informs the crafting of our code:

For this exercise, we want to allow only unsolicited inbound traffic coming from private networks. Any unsolicited inbound traffic coming from anywhere else (i.e., the Internet) is rejected.

For later configurations, we will want to modify rules that pertain to specific ports, protocols, or other attributes.

Figure 15-19 **Private networks.** Scan or click the QR code to go to the Wikipedia article on private networks. https://en.wikipedia.org/wiki/Private_network

```
##### STEP 1 #####
import os

fwRulesFile = os.environ['HOME'] + '/datafile/fwrules.txt'
# the file generated by:
# netsh advfirewall firewall show rule all
```

```
##### the next statements hold the start and end
##### of the netsh command to modify firewall rules
netshLineStart = 'netsh advfirewall firewall set rule name='
netshLineEnd = (' new '
                'remoteip=10.0.0.0/255.0.0.0,'
                    '172.16.0.0/255.240.0.0,'
                    '192.168.0.0/255.255.0.0')
#####                   ^^^ private networks ^^^
```

Figure 15-20 Our first step is initialization

We will create a string that is the absolute filepath to the file whose contents the machine will read into a dictionary of dictionaries.

Then we will create strings that will be the start and end of each **netsh** command in our output file.

```
##### STEP 2 #####
# build the fwRuleDictionary
with open(fwRulesFile, 'r') as inFile:
    LoS = inFile.read().splitlines()
    fwRuleDict = dict()
    for line in LoS:
        if 'Rule Name' in line:
            ruleName = line.split(':')[-1].strip()
            attrDict = dict()
        if line:
            if 'Rule Name' not in line and '---------' not in line:
                if ':' in line:
                    attr, colon, value = line.partition(':')
                    attr, value = attr.strip(), value.strip()
                else:
                    continue
                attrDict[attr] = value
        if not line: # empty string/empty line
            fwRuleDict[ruleName] = attrDict
# build the fwRuleDictionary
```

Figure 15-21 Building the Dictionary of Dictionaries

The dictionary of dictionaries is key to solving the specification efficiently.

We write the code that parses the lines in the file in the same order that the machine encounters the lines: Rule Name, dashed line, attributes.

Note the use of string literals to ensure we have a match—"Rule Name" and ":".

Rule Names are the keys of the fwRuleDict.

Once we get an attribute:value pair (each stripped of whitespace characters), we add them as key:value pairs into the attribute dictionary mapped to the Rule Name key.

```
##### STEP 3 #####
# sample queries that generate a windows scripts which, when run,
# modify the rules that match.
# in this example, we restrict access to all fw rules whose direction is
```

15.3 Making Executable Python Scripts II

```python
# 'In' (inbound)
# to ut-network
with open('netsh.cmd', 'w') as outFile:
    for key, value in fwRuleDict.items():
        if value['Direction'] == 'In':
            outFile.write(netshLineStart + '"' + key + '"' + netshLineEnd + "\n")

# in this example, we restrict access to all fw rules with 'RPC'
# in the key (Rule Name)
with open('netsh.cmd', 'w') as outFile:
    for key, value in fwRuleDict.items():
        if 'RPC' in key:
            outFile.write(netshLineStart + '"' + key + '"' + netshLineEnd + "\n")
```

Figure 15-22 Finding matches in the DoD

And now that we have all the info on the firewall rules in memory, we can write our queries.

Two examples are provided on how we can write a script of sequential netsh commands when a match is found.

In the first example, we want to restrict ALL unsolicited inbound traffic to devices only in our private networks.

In the second example, we want to restrict only traffic to or from RPC ports to devices only in our private networks.

After the machine writes the script, we can run it on the machine with the Windows firewall, thus modifying the firewall quickly and efficiently, exactly the way we want it.

```
netsh advfirewall firewall set rule name="Active Directory Domain Controller (RPC-EPMAP)" new remoteip=10.0.0.0/255.0.0.0,172.16.0.0/255.240.0.0,192.16
netsh advfirewall firewall set rule name="Active Directory Domain Controller (RPC)" new remoteip=10.0.0.0/255.0.0.0,172.16.0.0/255.240.0.0,192.168.0.0/
netsh advfirewall firewall set rule name="File Replication (RPC-EPMAP)" new remoteip=10.0.0.0/255.0.0.0,172.16.0.0/255.240.0.0,192.168.0.0/255.255.0.0
netsh advfirewall firewall set rule name="File Replication (RPC)" new remoteip=10.0.0.0/255.0.0.0,172.16.0.0/255.240.0.0,192.168.0.0/255.255.0.0
netsh advfirewall firewall set rule name="DFS Replication (RPC-EPMAP)" new remoteip=10.0.0.0/255.0.0.0,172.16.0.0/255.240.0.0,192.168.0.0/255.255.0.0
netsh advfirewall firewall set rule name="DFS Replication (RPC-In)" new remoteip=10.0.0.0/255.0.0.0,172.16.0.0/255.240.0.0,192.168.0.0/255.255.0.0
netsh advfirewall firewall set rule name="RPC (TCP, Incoming)" new remoteip=10.0.0.0/255.0.0.0,172.16.0.0/255.240.0.0,192.168.0.0/255.255.0.0
```

Figure 15-23 The first lines of the script written by our script

In this example, we've run the query that gets the Rule Names for all the rules that have the string 'RPC' in either the keys or values.

When we run the script on our Windows machine, all the rules concerning RPC will have their remote IPs set to the private networks. Inbound unsolicited traffic from anywhere else will be dropped.

NB: The right side of this image has been cropped. Some of these lines are rather long.

15.3 Interactive Scripts That Prompt Users for Input

```python
#!/usr/bin/python3

import os

while True:
    proj = input('please give project name: ')
```

```
    if proj == '':
        break

    os.makedirs(proj)

print("and now we're out of the loop!")
```

Figure 15-24 An interactive Python script

This script uses an infinite while loop to keep prompting users for input, just like the interactive Bash script we encountered in our introduction to Bash. And like that script, this one instructs the machine to act on user input to create directories with names made from string input. Once the users have no more input, they hit RETURN at the prompt (inputting an empty string). The Bash interpreter tests for empty strings. Once user input is the empty string, the interpreter executes a "break" to break out of the loop.

15.4 The Python Half-Open Interval, Range Objects, and Slicing

> List comprehension lets us output a list, given an ordered input collection.
> In math, an interval is the set of numbers between two numbers.
> An open interval includes the endpoint numbers in the set:
> for $1 \leq x \leq 5$, x = {1, 2, 3, 4, 5}
> the enclosure for an open interval is square brackets; for example, for [1..5], the set contains 1, 2, 3, 4, and 5.
> A closed interval excludes the endpoint numbers in the set:
> for $1 < x < 5$, x = {2, 3, 4}
> the enclosure for a closed interval is parentheses; for example, for (1..5), the set contains 2, 3, and 4.
> Python makes use of a half-open interval that includes the smaller endpoint and excludes the greater endpoint (e.g., $1 \leq x < 5$) for the range() function and slices.
> A Python slice is a subsequence of an ordered collection, for example, strings, lists, and tuples.

15.4.1 The Python Half-Open Interval

> As in most other programming languages, all indexing in Go uses *half-open* intervals that include the first index but exclude the last, because it simplifies logic.
>
> Alan Donovan & Brian Kernighan *The Go Programming Language*

Alan Donovan & Brian Kernighan. *The Go Programming Language*. Addison-Wesley. 2015. p.22.

15.5 Finding Intervals with Overlap

$$
\begin{aligned}
&a) && 2 \leq i < 13 \\
&b) && 1 < i \leq 12 \\
&c) && 2 \leq i \leq 12 \\
&d) && 1 < i < 13
\end{aligned}
$$

Figure 15-25 Four ways to define an interval, from Edsger Dijkstra's "Why Numbering Should Start from Zero." Click the image to view or download a pdf of Dijkstra's article online. https://www.cs.utexas.edu/users/EWD/ewd08xx/EWD831.PDF

In Figure 15-25, a and b are half-open intervals, c is an open interval (the interval includes its endpoints), and d is a closed interval (it excludes its endpoints). As Dijkstra points out, when programmers were allowed to choose how to define intervals to work with, those who defined their intervals like the half-open interval a, they made fewer mistakes than when using the other three.

Python uses this half-open interval for range() and slicing operations.

(The language that allowed programmers to pick their preferred intervals was *Mesa*, developed by Xerox PARC.)

The Python half-open interval, [a...b), includes the smaller endpoint and excludes the larger endpoint. This half-open interval is used in range objects and slices.

15.4.2 The Range Object Revisited

```
range(stop) -> range object
range(start, stop[, step]) -> range object

Return an object that produces a sequence of integers from start (inclusive)
to stop (exclusive) by step.  range(i, j) produces i, i+1, i+2, ..., j-1.
start defaults to 0, and stop is omitted!  range(4) produces 0, 1, 2, 3.
These are exactly the valid indices for a list of 4 elements.
When step is given, it specifies the increment (or decrement).
```

Figure 15-26 Docstring for the **range()** function

The function is often used passing into it just one argument; however, it can take as many as three.

15.5 Finding Intervals with Overlap

Biologists working with genome sequences might need to find if two sequences overlap. Out-of-the-box Python offers at least two ways to find intervals with overlap. One involves finding the intersection of two sets of natural numbers. The other involves determining if the range of an overlap exists, given the endpoints of the two sequences.

In this section, we will consider each.

Dijkstra, Edsger. "Why Numbering Should Start at Zero" https://www.cs.utexas.edu/users/EWD/ewd08xx/EWD831.PDF

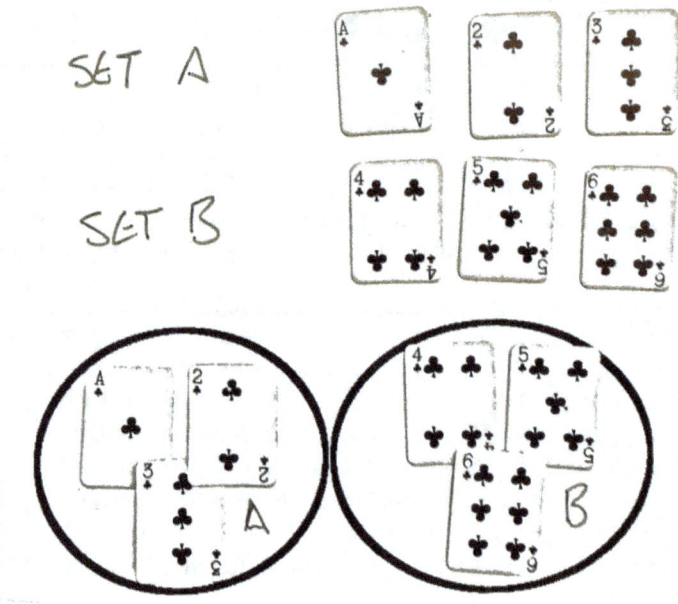

Figure 15-27 Two natural number intervals {1, 2, 3} and {4, 5, 6}

Rendered as sets, their intersection, A and B, yields the empty set { }.

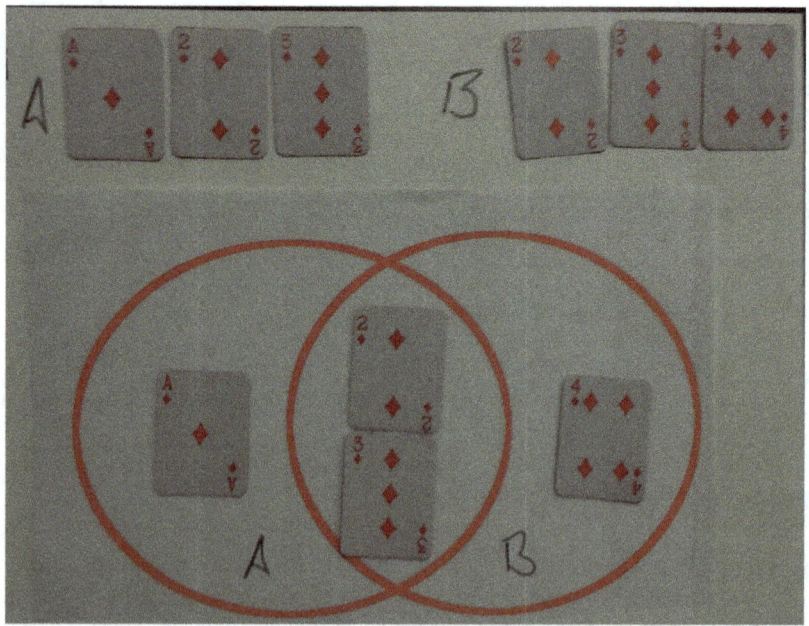

Figure 15-28 Two natural number intervals {1, 2, 3} and {2, 3, 4}

Rendered as sets, their intersection, A and B, yields {2, 3}.

15.5 Finding Intervals with Overlap

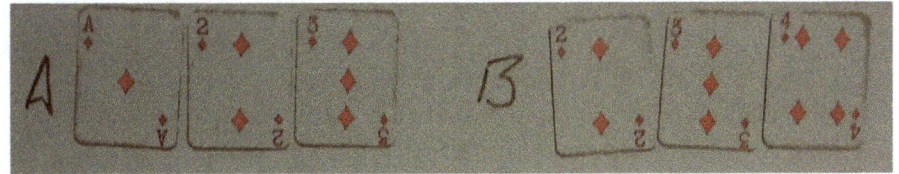

```
In [1]: A, B = range(1, 3+1), range(2, 4+1)
   ...: # return overlap interval endpoints
   ...: max(A[0], B[0]), min(A[-1], B[-1])
Out[1]: (2, 3)
```

Figure 15-29 Finding the overlap interval of two natural number ranges using their endpoints

Index 0 means the first number in the interval, and index -1 means the last number in the interval. We can generate the overlap interval using the range() function; however, because range() uses a half-open interval, to capture the upper endpoint, we would have to add 1 to the end number, that is, range(2, 3+1).

By separating our invocations of the max() and min() functions in the last line with a comma, we instruct the Python interpreter to return their values in a tuple.

```
range(max(interval1[small_endpoint], interval2[small_endpoint]),\
      min(interval1[big___endpoint], interval2[big___endpoint]) + 1)
```

Figure 15-30 Finding the overlap interval of two natural number ranges passing in their endpoints to Python's *max()* and *min()* functions; then passing in the values they return to Python's *range()* function

```
In [1]: small_ep_1, big_ep_1, small_ep_2, big_ep_2 = 0, 10, 10, 15
   ...: print(range(max(small_ep_1, small_ep_2),\
   ...:             min(big_ep_1, big_ep_2) + 1))
   ...: print(list(range(max(small_ep_1, small_ep_2),\
   ...:                  min(big_ep_1, big_ep_2) + 1)))
   ...: print(bool(range(max(small_ep_1, small_ep_2),\
   ...:                  min(big_ep_1, big_ep_2) + 1)))
range(10, 11)
[10]
True

In [2]: small_ep_1, big_ep_1, small_ep_2, big_ep_2 = 0, 9, 10, 15
   ...: print(range(max(small_ep_1, small_ep_2),\
   ...:             min(big_ep_1, big_ep_2) + 1))
   ...: print(list(range(max(small_ep_1, small_ep_2),\
   ...:                  min(big_ep_1, big_ep_2) + 1)))
   ...: print(bool(range(max(small_ep_1, small_ep_2),\
   ...:                  min(big_ep_1, big_ep_2) + 1)))
range(10, 10)
[]
```

```
False

In [3]: small_ep_1, big_ep_1, small_ep_2, big_ep_2 = 0, 10, 5, 15
   ...: print(range(max(small_ep_1, small_ep_2),\
   ...:              min(big_ep_1, big_ep_2) + 1))
   ...: print(list(range(max(small_ep_1, small_ep_2),\
   ...:              min(big_ep_1, big_ep_2) + 1)))
   ...: print(bool(range(max(small_ep_1, small_ep_2),\
   ...:              min(big_ep_1, big_ep_2) + 1)))
range(5, 11)
[5, 6, 7, 8, 9, 10]
True

In [4]: small_ep_1, big_ep_1, small_ep_2, big_ep_2 = 0, 10, 15, 20
   ...: print(range(max(small_ep_1, small_ep_2),\
   ...:              min(big_ep_1, big_ep_2) + 1))
   ...: print(list(range(max(small_ep_1, small_ep_2),\
   ...:              min(big_ep_1, big_ep_2) + 1)))
   ...: print(bool(range(max(small_ep_1, small_ep_2),\
   ...:              min(big_ep_1, big_ep_2) + 1)))
range(15, 11)
[]
False
```

Figure 15-31 range(max(small_endpoint$_1$, small_endpoint$_2$), min(big_endpoint$_1$, big_endpoint$_2$)) tested

To verify that this algorithm works, we instantiate variables representing the endpoints of **interval 1 & 2**, then print the range object, the range object coerced into a list, and the range object coerced into a bool.

Don't forget to recall that the range object uses the half-open interval—the large endpoint is excluded.

Note that if there is even one item in the overlap, the range object tests true when coerced.

15.6 Finding Interval Overlap in Genomic Sequences

The datafiles used in this chapter are in the directory "finding_interval_overlaps" in the repo. Please copy this directory into the datafile directory in your home directory and make your home directory the working directory to follow along.

Figure 15-32 BED files are used to store genomic regions as coordinates, with associated annotations. Scan or click the QR code to go to the Wikipedia article on the BED file format.https://en.wikipedia.org/wiki/BED_(file_format)

15.6 Finding Overlaps

For each record, the first three columns are obligatory:

(1) The chromosome number
(2) Start coordinate on the chromosome
(3) End coordinate

Numbering system indexes on zero.

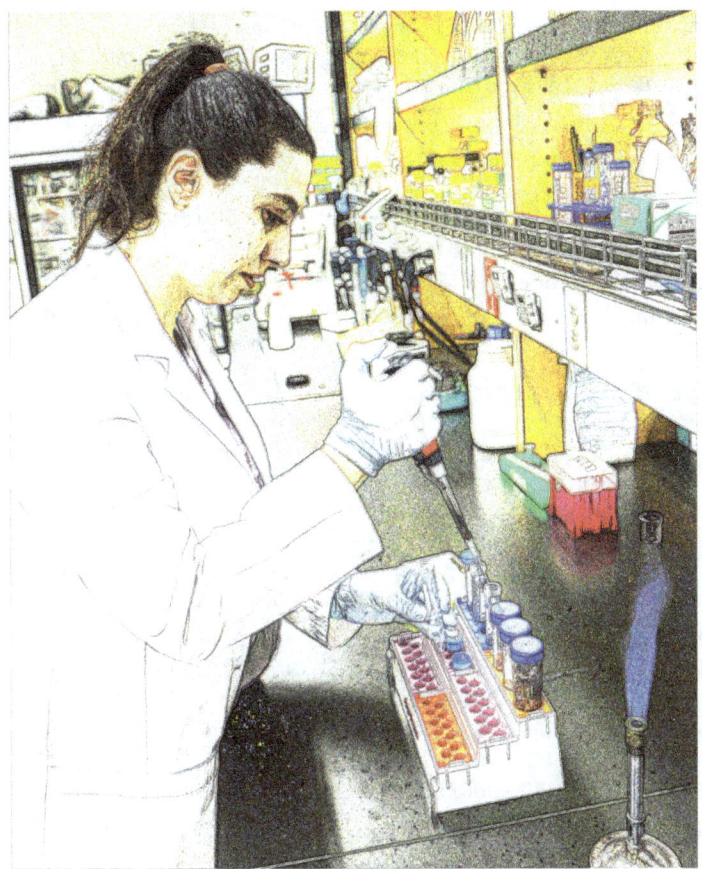

Figure 15-33 Biologist Kubra Velioglu has generated a recordset of genomic sequences.—Credit: Selfinaz K Velioglu and Ryan Kirkbride, photographer

Now she wants to determine which of them share overlaps, if any, with genomic sequences in a reference recordset.

Each recordset is in a BED file. For our use, they are in a folder in our repo's datafile directory called "finding_interval_overlaps."

Let's look at how Kubra might develop the code in Python that finds overlaps between her sequences and the reference sequences and, for each overlap found, writes out a record containing the overlap, as well as identifying info for each sequence.

We start, as we always do, by first familiarizing ourselves with the datasets that we'll be working with.

```
$ cp -r ~/repo/intro_to_programming/datafile/finding_interval_overlaps/ ~/datafile/

$ ls -lh ~/datafile/finding_interval_overlaps
total 9.1M
-rw-rw-r-- 1 user user  9.0M Mar 29 14:55 exon.bed
-rw-rw-r-- 1 user user   98K Mar 29 14:55 test.sort.bed

$ wc -l ~/datafile/finding_interval_overlaps/*.bed
 217118 /home/user/datafile/finding_interval_overlaps/exon.bed
   1522 /home/user/datafile/finding_interval_overlaps/test.sort.bed
 218640 total
```

Figure 15-34 Getting stats on the BED files

We start by copying the files from our repo to the datafile directory in our home directory.
Next, we get the size in bytes of the BED files.
Finally, we get the line count for each file.

We observe that the line count of **exon.bed** is ~140 times greater than the line count of **test.sort.bed**.

```
$ head -n 5 ~/datafile/finding_interval_overlaps/*.bed
==> /home/james/datafile/finding_interval_overlaps/exon.bed <==
1    3630    3913      AT1G01010.1|exon-1    42        +
1    3995    4276      AT1G01010.1|exon-2    42        +
1    4485    4605      AT1G01010.1|exon-3    42        +
1    4705    5095      AT1G01010.1|exon-4    42        +
1    5173    5326      AT1G01010.1|exon-5    42        +

==> /home/james/datafile/finding_interval_overlaps/test.sort.bed <==
1    78931    78952      HWI-D00289:153:C5UPNANXX:6:1101:14618:2103    39    -
1    78931    78952      HWI-D00289:153:C5UPNANXX:6:1101:16625:2748    39    -
1    78932    78952      HWI-D00289:153:C5UPNANXX:6:1101:15423:2096    39    -
1   500411   500432      HWI-D00289:153:C5UPNANXX:6:1101:10621:2717    42    -
1   889458   889482      HWI-D00289:153:C5UPNANXX:6:1101:13943:2521    39    +
```

Figure 15-35 Getting the structure of the BED records and recordsets

Note that there is no label line in either file, and values are tab-delimited.
As a reminder, for each record, the first three columns are obligatory:

(1) The chromosome number
(2) Start coordinate on the chromosome
(3) End coordinate

The comparison of records must be all-to-all; that is, we want the computer to compare the first record of the first recordset to all records in the second recordset, then compare the second record of the first recordset to all records in the second recordset, and so on.

The comparison is to determine if the two records being compared share an overlap. To do this, we will use the algorithm developed in the previous section:

range(max(small_endpoint$_1$, small_endpoint$_2$), min(big_endpoint$_1$, big_endpoint$_2$))

15.6 Finding Overlaps

```python
import os; home = os.path.expanduser('~')

with open(home + '/datafile/finding_interval_overlaps/exon.bed', 'r') as exonFile,\
     open(home + '/datafile/finding_interval_overlaps/test.sort.bed', 'r') as testFile:
    exonLoS, testLoS = exonFile.read().splitlines(),\
                       testFile.read().splitlines()
    exonLoL, testLoL = [], []
    for exonRec in exonLoS:
        exonLoL.append(exonRec.split('\t'))
    for testRec in testLoS:
        testLoL.append(testRec.split('\t'))
```

Figure 15-36 Making LoLs from the BED recordsets

```
%whos
Variable    Type           Data/Info
------------------------------------
exonFile    TextIOWrapper  <_io.TextIOWrapper name='<...>ode='r' encoding='UTF-8'>
exonLoL     list           n=217118
exonLoS     list           n=217118
exonRec     str            Mt        366085       366700        ATMG01410.1|exon-1
home        str            /home/james
os          module         <module 'os' (frozen)>
testFile    TextIOWrapper  <_io.TextIOWrapper name='<...>ode='r' encoding='UTF-8'>
testLoL     list           n=1522
testLoS     list           n=1522
testRec     str            Pt        145060       145080        HWI-D002<...>
```

Figure 15-37 Inspecting the objects in session memory

```
In [3]: exonLoL[:3]
Out[3]:
[['1', '3630', '3913', 'AT1G01010.1|exon-1', '42', '+'],
 ['1', '3995', '4276', 'AT1G01010.1|exon-2', '42', '+'],
 ['1', '4485', '4605', 'AT1G01010.1|exon-3', '42', '+']]

In [4]: testLoL[:3]
Out[4]:
[['1',
  '78931',
  '78952',
  'HWI-D00289:153:C5UPNANXX:6:1101:14618:2103',
  '39',
  '-'],
 ['1',
  '78931',
  '78952',
  'HWI-D00289:153:C5UPNANXX:6:1101:16625:2748',
  '39',
  '-'],
 ['1',
  '78932',
  '78952',
```

```
'HWI-D00289:153:C5UPNANXX:6:1101:15423:2096',
'39',
'-']]
```

Figure 15-38 Inspecting the first three records in each LoL

An approach to getting a file of overlap records is beginning to suggest itself:

if sequences are on the same chromosome **and** bool of the overlap is true, **then** write a record with chromosome number, overlap, and record[3] (the fourth item) in each record.

```
with open(home + '/datafile/overlaps', 'w') as outFile:
    for testRec in testLoL:
        for exonRec in exonLoL:
            overlap = range(max(int(testRec[1]), int(exonRec[1])),\
                            min(int(testRec[2]), int(exonRec[2]))+1)
            if (testRec[0] == exonRec[0]) and bool(overlap):
                pass
                # ready to write out
```

Figure 15-39 Basic structure of the solution

```
import os; home = os.path.expanduser('~')

with open(home + '/datafile/finding_interval_overlaps/exon.bed', 'r') as exonFile,\
     open(home + '/datafile/finding_interval_overlaps/test.sort.bed', 'r') as testFile:
    exonLoS, testLoS = exonFile.read().splitlines(),\
                       testFile.read().splitlines()
    exonLoL, testLoL = [], []
    for exonRec in exonLoS:
        exonLoL.append(exonRec.split('\t'))
    for testRec in testLoS:
        testLoL.append(testRec.split('\t'))

with open(home + '/datafile/overlaps', 'w') as outFile:
    for testRec in testLoL:
        for exonRec in exonLoL:
            if testRec[0] == exonRec[0]\
               and len(testRec) > 3\
               and range(max(int(testRec[1]), int(exonRec[1])),\
                         min(int(testRec[2]), int(exonRec[2]))+1):
                overlap = range(max(int(testRec[1]), int(exonRec[1])),\
                                min(int(testRec[2]), int(exonRec[2]))+1)
                record = (f"{exonRec[0]}\t{overlap[0]}\t"
                          f"{overlap[-1]}\t{exonRec[3]}\t"
                          f"{testRec[3]}\n")
                outFile.write(record)
```

Figure 15-40 Working code, still in development

testLoL has at least one malformed record (fewer than three fields).
if *(len(testRec) > 3) and (len(exonRec) > 3)* handles this.
Note that the machine can extract the endpoints of the overlap referencing them by index—
overlap[0] and **overlap[-1]**.

15.6 Finding Overlaps

The time it takes for this code to run to completion is significant. Profiling the code with the ipython magic **%%timeit** returns: **4min 43s ± 7.04 s**

Because of the nested **for**-loop, the time complexity is **O(mn)**, where **m** is the number of records in exonLoL and **n** is the number of records in testLoL.

Finally, note the use of backslashes to write single statements over multiple lines (the topmost **with** clause, the multiple assignment statement below it, the assignment statement creating and instantiating the **overlap** variable, and the multiline f-string statements, enclosed in parentheses to ensure that extra white space characters are not added to each record).

Writing Python statements over multiple lines not only ensure that long statements don't scroll of to the right-hand side of the terminal windows, but also allow us to align parts of the statements to enhance readability and comprehension—hence, the two **open** functions are aligned, the **file.read().splitlines**() statements are aligned, and so on.

Readability of code is important. Readable code goes a long way to making code maintainable. Code readability can differentiate the good programmer from the bad. Good style deserves study and application. **PEP 8 Style Guide for Python Code** is a worthy style guide.

(Click the hyperlinked text to go to the online style guide.)

```
$ ls -lh ~/datafile/overlaps
-rw-rw-r-- 1 user user 65K Mar 29 17:11 /home/user/datafile/overlaps
$ wc -l ~/datafile/overlaps
822 /home/user/datafile/overlaps
$ head ~/datafile/overlaps
1    78931    78952    AT1G01183.1|exon-1    HWI-D00289:153:C5UPNANXX:6:1101:14618:2103
1    78931    78952    AT1G01183.1|exon-1    HWI-D00289:153:C5UPNANXX:6:1101:16625:2748
1    78932    78952    AT1G01183.1|exon-1    HWI-D00289:153:C5UPNANXX:6:1101:15423:2096
1    935659   935674   AT1G03740.1|exon-4    HWI-D00289:153:C5UPNANXX:6:1101:19338:2188
1    935659   935674   AT1G03740.2|exon-4    HWI-D00289:153:C5UPNANXX:6:1101:19338:2188
1    2410347  2410368  AT1G07780.1|exon-7    HWI-D00289:153:C5UPNANXX:6:1101:12444:2548
1    2410347  2410368  AT1G07780.2|exon-6    HWI-D00289:153:C5UPNANXX:6:1101:12444:2548
1    2410347  2410368  AT1G07780.3|exon-6    HWI-D00289:153:C5UPNANXX:6:1101:12444:2548
1    2410347  2410368  AT1G07780.4|exon-6    HWI-D00289:153:C5UPNANXX:6:1101:12444:2548
1    2410347  2410368  AT1G07780.5|exon-7    HWI-D00289:153:C5UPNANXX:6:1101:12444:2548
```

Figure 15-41 Checking the output

There are 822 overlaps between the sequences in the two recordsets.

Note that even though the code meets the specification of finding the overlaps in these two recordsets, unless Kubra never needs to repeat this task (unlikely!), then her work on the code isn't finished.

She should render it as a function in her Python code module. That includes adding type hints, a docstring, and garbage filters. The function could take as arguments the .bed files whose records are to be searched for overlaps and a path to the output file. The garbage filters would at a minimum assert that the inputs are strings and that the .bed files exist.

Good luck, Kubra!

15.7 Slicing Lists and Strings

> Slicing uses the Python half-open interval.
> Slices take two integers as indices to define the slice interval + an optional stride, which is also an integer, for example, someList[1:5:2]. The arguments defining the slice are enclosed in square brackets and separated by colons.

In Python, slicing allow us efficiently to take a subsequence from a sequential collection—we can easily take a substring from a string, or a sublist from a list.

```
list_primes # in (index, value) pairs
[(0, 2), (1, 3), (2, 5), (3, 7), (4, 11), (5, 13), (6, 17), (7, 19)]
```

Figure 15-42 How we normally first learn index-value pairs in Python sequential collections

Indices are first taught as natural numbers...

```
list_primes # in (negative index, value) pairs
[(-8, 2), (-7, 3), (-6, 5), (-5, 7), (-4, 11), (-3, 13), (-2, 17), (-1, 19)]
```

Figure 15-43 But indices in Python extend into the integers

Note that for all Python sequential collections, the first value has index 0 and the last value has index -1.

```
0|2, 1|3, 2|5, 3|7, 4|11, 5|13, 6|17, 7|19
```

Figure 15-44 In slicing, it may help to visualize indices as shifted half a position to the left of their values

The values between the first and last indices are the values returned in the slice.

```
primes # a list of the first 8 primes
[2, 3, 5, 7, 11, 13, 17, 19]
primes[:3]
[2, 3, 5]
```

Figure 15-45 Slices use two indices, separated by a colon, enclosed in square brackets

The default value of the first index is 0. If the first index of your slice is 0, just leave the first index blank. Also, when the first index is 0, the second index equals the number of values returned in the slice.

Slices use Python's half-open interval.

```
primes[3:]
[7, 11, 13, 17, 19]
```

Figure 15-46 When the second index of the slice is left blank, the slice contains the last value of the Python collection being sliced

```
primes[3:-1]
[7, 11, 13, 17]
```

Figure 15-47 Please note that this slice is NOT the same as the one above

This slice does not return the last value of the collection being sliced.

```
primes[:]
[2, 3, 5, 7, 11, 13, 17, 19]
```

Figure 15-48 A slice that uses default values for both indices returns a copy of the collection being sliced

```
primes[::2]
[2, 5, 11, 17]
```

Figure 15-49 Slices can take a third argument, called a "stride"

The stride specifies which values within an interval to return in the slice. The default value of a stride is 1.

In this example, the slice includes the first value of the collection, then every second value.

```
primes[1::2]
[3, 7, 13, 19]
```

Figure 15-50 To get the alternate values of this collection, start the new slice at index 1

```
primes[::-1]
[19, 17, 13, 11, 7, 5, 3, 2]
```

Figure 15-51 Finally, strides are integers

A slice that uses default values for both indices and a stride of -1 returns a reverse copy of the collection.

15.8 From Nucleotide String to Amino Acid Strings

For this chapter, you will need the file "codon_amino_tabs.txt" in the repo. Please move it into datafile directory in your home directory, and make your home directory your working directory.

In this chapter, we see that the biological processes that convert nucleotides into amino acid strings can be modeled mathematically and distilled to an algorithm that we can implement in Python.

The Central Dogma of Molecular Biology

We should first look at the evidence that DNA itself is not the direct template that orders amino acid sequences. Instead, the genetic information of DNA is transferred to another class of molecules, which then serve as the protein templates. These intermediate templates are molecules of ribonucleic acid (RNA), large polymeric molecules chemically very similar to DNA. Their relation to DNA and protein is usually summarized by the *central dogma*, a flow scheme for genetic information...

DNA...is the template for its self-replication; [and] all cellular RNA molecules are made on DNA templates. Correspondingly, all protein sequences are determined by RNA templates. Most importantly,...RNA sequences are never copied on protein templates; likewise, RNA never acts as a template for DNA.*

—James D. Watson
Molecular Biology of the Gene

Figure 15-52 Genetic code. Scan or click the QR code to go to the Wikipedia article on the genetic code. https://en.wikipedia.org/wiki/Genetic_code

The rules that translate codons into amino acids (which are stringed together to form proteins) can be transformed into an algorithm that general-purpose computers can execute for text-string nucleotide and protein sequences. We will cover an algorithm to do just that in this section.

```
nucleotide string:  G  A  T  T  A  C  A  G  A  T  T  A  C  A
           index:   0  1  2  3  4  5  6  7  8  9 10 11 12 13
       index % 3:   0  1  2  0  1  2  0  1  2  0  1  2  0  1

   reading frame 0: [G  A  T][T  A  C][A  G  A][T  T  A][C  A
   reading frame 1:  G][A  T  T][A  C  A][G  A  T][T  A  C][A
   reading frame 2:  G  A [T  T  A][C  A  G][A  T  T][A  C  A]
```

```
codons in rf0: 'GAT' + 'TAC' + 'AGA' + 'TTA'
codons in rf1: 'ATT' + 'ACA' + 'GAT' + 'TAC'
codons in rf2: 'TTA' + 'CAG' + 'ATT' + 'ACA'

amino acids in rf0: 'Asp' + 'Tyr' + 'Arg' + 'Leu'
amino acids in rf1: 'Ile' + 'Thr' + 'Asp' + 'Tyr'
amino acids in rf2: 'Leu' + 'Gln' + 'Ile' + 'Thr'

return tuple:
('Asp-Tyr-Arg-Leu', 'Ile-Thr-Asp-Tyr', 'Leu-Gln-Ile-Thr')
```

Figure 15-53 We start by noting that although the media conveying the information to create amino acid sequences change as it passes from DNA to ribosomes, the information itself is preserved

This means that if we know which codon sequence in a nucleotide string codes for amino acids, we can translate that sequence directly by algorithm using a codon/amino-acid dictionary into the amino acid sequence. However, for any arbitrary nucleotide string—which may not code at all—we must consider that if it does, the sequence of codons that do code can be in any one of three *reading frames*. Our algorithm must account for that by generating all three of the possible amino acid sequences.

---

* James D. Watson, *Molecular Biology of the Gene*, Third Edition. W.A. Benjamin, Inc. 1976. pp. 281–282.

15.8 From Nucleotide String to Amino Acid Strings

```
cp ~/repo/intro_to_programming/datafile/codon_amino_tabs.txt ~/datafile
```

```python
import os; home = os.path.expanduser('~')
# if directory does not exist, create it
from pathlib import Path
Path(home + '/pickle').mkdir(parents=True, exist_ok=True)

from pickle import dump

with open(home + '/datafile/codon_amino_tabs.txt') as inFile:
    LoS = inFile.read().splitlines()
    codon2amino = {}
    for line in LoS:
        codon, amino = line.split()
        codon, amino = codon.strip(), amino.strip()
        codon2amino[codon] = amino

with open(home + '/pickle/codon_amino_dict.bin', 'wb') as outFile:
    dump(codon2amino, outFile)
```

Figure 15-54 Key to the algorithm is a dictionary of *codon:amino-acid* pairs

The dictionary itself has intrinsic value as a bioinformatics collection, and so we may elect to preserve it across sessions by **pickling** it and unpickling it when we need it.

```python
import pickle
import os
def get_amino_acid(nuclStr: str, codon2amino: dict=None, path_to_pickled_dict: str=''):
    ''' Requires either codon2amino dict passed into function,
        or path to pickled codon2amino dict file passed into it.
        Returns tuple of amino-acid strings for three reading frames.
        >>>get_amino_acid('GATTACAGATTACA', codon2amino)
        ('AspTyrArgLeu', 'IleThrAspTyr', 'LeuGlnIleThr')
    '''
    # garbage filters
    # to do: garbage filter to ensure nuclStr is clean
    assert codon2amino or os.path.isfile(path_to_pickled_dict),\
        "function must have dict passed into it, or dict must exist to pickle dir"
    if not codon2amino and os.path.isfile(path_to_pickled_dict):
        with open(path_to_pickled_dict, 'rb') as inFile:
            codon2amino = pickle.load(inFile)
        # implementation of algorithm
        # assuming nuclStr is clean AND
        # dict may be incomplete or have bad items
        # initialization
        nuclStr = nuclStr.upper()
        rf0, rf1, rf2 = '', '', ''
        for index, value in enumerate(nuclStr[:-2]):
            remainder = index % 3
            codon = nuclStr[index:index+3]
            try:
```

```
        amino = codon2amino[codon]
    except KeyError as e:
        raise Exception(f"Codon {codon} not found in codon2amino dict.\n" \
        f"\tPlease check dictionary for item and codon used as key.") \
        from e
    if remainder == 0:
        rf0 = rf0 + amino
    elif remainder == 1:
        rf1 = rf1 + amino
    else:
        rf2 = rf2 + amino
    return rf0, rf1, rf2
```

Figure 15-55 Function to convert arbitrary nucleotide string to its associated three amino acid strings

This function requires at least two arguments: the nucleotide string AND either (1) the codon2amino dictionary or (2) the path to a pickled copy of the codon2amino dictionary.

Note that if a codon2amino dictionary exists with a global scope in the session, then it can be invoked in the body of the function without passing it in as an argument; however, that is like adding a secret ingredient to a recipe.

By listing all the objects that go into a function into its argument list, we are making the function's input explicit; and in doing so, we make it easier to read and easier to maintain.

The garbage filter for the codon2amino dictionary first asserts that either a copy of the dictionary has been passed in OR a path to a pickled copy of the dictionary has been passed in AND the pickled copy exists. Then, if the path to a pickled copy has been passed in, then that copy is unpickled into the session for use.

15.9 Comprehension

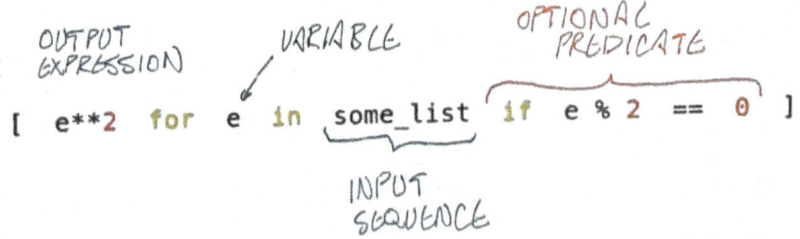

Figure 15-56 List comprehension

Note that a list comprehension is a statement of expressions enclosed in square brackets. An input sequence goes in, its values are evaluated in the output expression, and the output values become the values in the order that they're generated of a new list.

15.9.1 Slicing LoL, Extracting Columns with Comprehension

```
In [1]: import os; home = os.path.expanduser('~')
   ...: with open(home + '/datafile/reformatted_Unigene.fa') as inFile:
   ...:     LoS = inFile.read().splitlines()
   ...:     LoL = []
   ...:     for record in LoS:
   ...:         LoL.append(record.split())

In [2]: [record[0] for record in LoL[:5]]
Out[2]:
['Unigene1_All',
 'Unigene2_All',
 'Unigene3_All',
 'Unigene4_All',
 'Unigene5_All']
```

Figure 15-57 Extracting columns of specific rows using slicing and comprehension

In this example, we slice specific rows from our list of lists and make this the **input sequence** for a list comprehension whose **output expression** is the values in column 0, which are the records' unique IDs.

The output expression can also be a slice.

```
In [5]: [record[::6] for record in LoL[3:5]]
Out[5]:
[['Unigene4_All',
  'CAACACCTGTTTCCATTAACTCCTCTCGATATAAAATTAAATTTCGATTTCAGATTCACAATTCCTACGTAATCGGCCCCTT
GTACATCAAGCCCTCCCTATCCTCTCCCCAATCCCATCCGGCGACGATCTCAATCTCCGCTCCGACTCTCGCCGGAAACACCC
CCATCTCACGCCGGTAATTCGATCGATCACTACCATACACGGCCATGAATCCCGAATACGATTACTTGTTTAAGCTCTTGCTC
ATTGGTGATTCTGGTGTTGGCAAATCATGTCTTCTCCTGAGGTTTGCTGATGATTCATATCTGGATAGTTACATCAGCACCAT
TGGAGTGGACTTTAAAATACGCACCGTGGAGCAGGACGGGAAAACCATTAAGCTCCAAATTTGGGACACTGCTGGTCAAGAAC
GTTTCAGAACAATCACTAGCAGCTACTACCGAGGGGCTCATGGCATTATTGTTGTTTATGATGTCACGGACCAAGAGAGCTTC
AACAATGTTAAGCAATGGTTGAGTGAAATTGACCGTTATGCCAGTGAAAATGTGAACAAGCTTCTAGTTGGAAACAAGTGTGA
TCTCACGACGAACAGGGCTGTGATGTATGACACTGCCAAGGCTTTTGCCGATGAAATTGGAATCCCTTTCATGGAAACTAGTG
CCAAAAATGCTACAAATGTGGAACATGCATTCATGGCTATGTGTTCTGACATCAAGAACAGGATGGCAAGCCAACCGGCTGCA
AACAATGCCCGGCCACCAACAGTACAGATTCGAGGACAGCCAGTCAACCAGAAGTCTGGATGCTGCTCATCTTAATTCTAACC
AGCGTGACGGATGTGTAAAACTGGTCTCTTCTCTTTTCGTATCGACAAAACAGTTGTGTCTTCATTTGAATTTATCATCAGGT
ATTCAGC'],
 ['Unigene5_All',
  'CTCCAAATTCTGCAATCTTGACTGTTTCAGTCTTGGTGTCTACCAGGATATATTTAGGTTCCAAATGGCGATGTAAAACACC
CTTGGAATGACAATGTGCGATGCCAGAGAGAATTTGGCGCAGATATTCTTTTCTTACGGTGGGTAAAATTGGACTAGAAGGGT
CCTTGGTGAGCTCCCCAAAATTATTGTCCACATAATCAAAGTATAAATGAAGAGTGTCGTCTAATTTCCAGGAACCCTGAAAC
CCGACAATATTGGGATGAACA']]
```

Figure 15-58 Let's say we want the unique IDs and data strings of the records index 3 through 4 in our LoL

This is an entirely reasonable pair of columns to extract from our dataset.

The unique IDs are in the first column, and the last column holds the data strings, so now we'll use a skip that spans each record, returning only column index 0 and column index 6.

Figure 15-59 Eratosthenes. Click or scan QR code to go to article in Wikipedia. https://en.wikipedia.org/wiki/Eratosthenes

15.10 The Sieve of Eratosthenes

Referring to the primer on calculus (A Calculus Primer: Numeric Integration and Differentiation Using Python), you may remember that Eratosthenes was the faculty member of the Library of Alexandria to whom Archimedes wrote explaining The Method for finding the area of a surface by filling it with triangles, each of whose area is known or calculated.

Eratosthenes himself was an accomplished mathematician and astronomer.

Eratosthenes (c. 276 BCE - c. 195 BCE) was a faculty member of the Library of Alexandria. He rose to the position of Chief Librarian. A polymath, he is known today, among other things, as a mathematician, a geographer, and an astronomer. Today he is best known for his effort to calculate the circumference of the Earth.

Figure 15-60 The sieve of Eratosthenes. Click or scan QR code to go to article in Wikipedia. https://en.wikipedia.org/wiki/Sieve_of_Eratosthenes

A hand algorithm, the sieve is a way to find all prime numbers in the interval between 2 and *n*, where n is the upper endpoint of the interval.

```
not_primes = [j for i in range(2, 11) for j in range(i*2, 101, i)]
primes = [x for x in range(2, 101) if x not in not_primes]
```

Figure 15-61 One implementation of the sieve of Eratosthenes using list comprehension. Credit: https://stackoverflow.com/questions/23802352/python-lists-comprehension

As written, this solution returns the primes up to 100.

Figure 15-62 Carl Sagan holds forth on Eratosthenes' best-known achievement in Cosmos (1981): proving that the Earth is round and providing an estimate of its circumference. Click or scan the QR code to open the video segment on youtube. https://www.youtube.com/watch?v=G8cbIWMv0rI

15.11 Transposing a Matrix

In linear algebra, the transpose of a matrix is an operator that flips a matrix such that row 1 of matrix M is column 1 of M^T, row 2 of M is column 2 of M^T, and so on.

$$M = \begin{bmatrix} 2 & 3 & 5 \\ 7 & 11 & 13 \\ 17 & 19 & 23 \end{bmatrix} \qquad M^T = \begin{bmatrix} 2 & 7 & 17 \\ 3 & 11 & 19 \\ 5 & 13 & 23 \end{bmatrix}$$

Figure 15-63 The matrix M and its transpose, M^T

Note that for square matrix M, its diagonal stays unchanged in M^T.

Another way to think of the transpose of a matrix is by imagining that the row and column indices of each element in matrix M are swapped to form M^T:

$$[M]_{i,j} = [M^T]_{j,i}$$

```
In [1]: # initialization
   ...: matrix =\
   ...:     [[1, 2, 3],\
   ...:      [4, 5, 6],\
   ...:      [7, 8, 9]]
   ...:
   ...: transpose =\
   ...:     [[0, 0, 0],\
   ...:      [0, 0, 0],\
   ...:      [0, 0, 0]]
   ...:
   ...: # implementation of the algorithm
   ...: # this returns the row indices and rows
   ...: for i, row in enumerate(matrix):
   ...:     # this returns the column indices and scalars
   ...:     # in each row
   ...:     for j, scalar in enumerate(row):
   ...:         # now we swap the order of the indices
   ...:         # to place the scalar in its correct
   ...:         # position in the transpose
   ...:         transpose[j][i] = scalar
   ...:
In [2]: transpose
Out[2]: [[1, 4, 7], [2, 5, 8], [3, 6, 9]]
```

Figure 15-64 Our first algorithm to transpose a matrix using nested loops

The operational statement is the assignment statement that places the scalar in its position in the transpose. For this reason, we initialize the transpose with dummy scalars that get replaced as the algorithm runs.

```
In [1]: # initialization
   ...: matrix =\
   ...:  [[1, 2, 3],\
   ...:   [4, 5, 6],\
   ...:   [7, 8, 9]]
   ...:
   ...: transpose =\
   ...:  [[],\
   ...:   [],\
   ...:   []]
   ...:
   ...: # implementation of the algorithm
   ...: # this returns the row indices and rows
   ...: for i, row in enumerate(matrix):
   ...:     # this returns the column indices and scalars
   ...:     # in each row
   ...:     for j, scalar in enumerate(row):
   ...:         transpose[j].append(scalar)
   ...:

In [2]: transpose
Out[2]: [[1, 4, 7], [2, 5, 8], [3, 6, 9]]
```

Our algorithm to transpose a matrix using nested loops, modified so the transpose is initialized as an empty matrix.

Here, because the operational statement uses the **list.append()** method to add scalars to the transpose, we can initialize the transpose as an empty matrix.

Our two algorithms for creating the transpose of a matrix work as hand algorithms, too. Walking through an algorithm by hand helps better understand how the algorithm works. We can use a packet of playing cards to execute the algorithms by hand.

```
In [1]: # initialization
   ...: matrix =\
   ...:  [[1, 2, 3],\
   ...:   [4, 5, 6],\
   ...:   [7, 8, 9]]
   ...:
   ...: transpose =\
   ...: [[row[i] for row in matrix] for i in range(len(matrix[0]))]

In [2]: transpose
Out[2]: [[1, 4, 7], [2, 5, 8], [3, 6, 9]]
```

Figure 15-65 Using list comprehension to get the transpose of a matrix.
From: docs.python.org/3/tutorial/datastructures.html?highlight=list%20comprehension

15.11.1 Transposing Tabular Datasets in Python

Sometimes, it is useful to treat a tabular dataset as a 2D matrix made up of row and column vectors.

In this exercise, we will determine if a datafile we've been given might be a tabular dataset, whether it might be transposed; then we will use three different ways to transpose it and profile—find out how much time it takes—each.

The researcher who gave us this datafile said it didn't look right. The data looked complete, but somehow the file didn't open right. Could we help straighten it out?

Our datafile is **RSEM.iso_res**, a zipped file in our repo datafile directory. We start by unzipping the file into the datafile directory in our home directory:

```
$ unzip ~/repo/intro_to_programming/datafile/RSEM.iso_res.zip -d ~/datafile/
Archive:  /home/user/repo/intro_to_programming/datafile/RSEM.iso_res.zip
  inflating: /home/user/datafile/RSEM.iso_res
```

Figure 15-66 Unizipping RSEM.iso_res to datafile directory in our home directory

```
$ wc ~/datafile/RSEM.iso_res
8    3969896 33301489 /home/user/datafile/RSEM.iso_res
```

Figure 15-67 line, word, and byte count of the RSEM.iso_res file

Note that the file has 8 lines and 3,969,896 words. A word is defined as a collection of contiguous printable chars bound by space chars. The four million words across eight lines are unusual dimensions for a datafile (though not impossible!).

```
$ factor 3969896
3969896: 2 2 2 7 70891
```

Figure 15-68 The number of words in the file has 8 as a factor

Ah-hah! The data in the datafile does indeed look as if it's structured as a table, with no missing data.

(If it is transposed, then the data is structured as a table with 8 columns and 7*70891, or 496,237, rows.)

Here, we recall that the transpose of a transposed matrix returns the original matrix, or

$$M = (M^T)^T$$

This means that if we are working with a transposed tabular dataset, transposing it will restore it to its original structure.

```
In [1]: import os; home = os.path.expanduser('~')
   ...: with open(home + '/datafile/RSEM.iso_res') as inFile:
   ...:     LoS = inFile.read().splitlines()
   ...:     LoL = []
   ...:     for row in LoS:
   ...:         LoL.append(row.split())
   ...:

In [2]: %timeit transpose = [[row[i] for row in LoL] for i in range(len(LoL[0]))]
94.8 ms ± 1.32 ms per loop (mean ± std. dev. of 7 runs, 10 loops each)

In [3]: %timeit transpose = list(zip(*LoL, strict=True))
```

```
39 ms ± 103 micros per loop (mean ± std. dev. of 7 runs, 10 loops each)

In [4]: from numpy import array
   ...: LoL = array(LoL)
   ...: %timeit transpose = LoL.T
55.9 ns ± 0.539 ns per loop (mean ± std. dev. of 7 runs, 10,000,000 loops each)
```

Figure 15-69 Three different ways to transpose a matrix, profiled for speed

Please note that using list comprehension is the slowest.

The built-in zip() function is mentioned in the Python.org docs at: https://docs.python.org/3/library/itertools.html

The third and fastest way is to first transform the LoL into a NumPy ndarray, then transpose it. For speed, this is the preferred way.

15.12 Stacks and Queues

> Stacks and queues are fundamental abstract datatypes that can be made by modifying permitted add and remove operations to arrays.
> When you permit elements to be added or removed from just one end of an array, you have converted the array into a stack.
> When you permit elements to be added to one end of an array and removed from the other end, you have converted the array into a queue.

15.12.1 Stacks

When you permit elements to be added or removed from just one end of an array, you have converted the array into a stack.

Figure 15-70 The stack

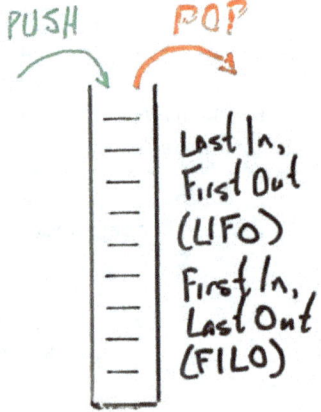

Elements in a stack are added and removed from just one end. The operation to add an element to the stack is "push," and the operation to remove one from the stack is "pop."

15.12 Stacks and Queues

Arrays that serve as stacks are sometimes called LIFO (Last-In First-Out) or FILO (First-In Last-Out) arrays.

Figure 15-71 A Mickey Mouse PEZ candy dispenser

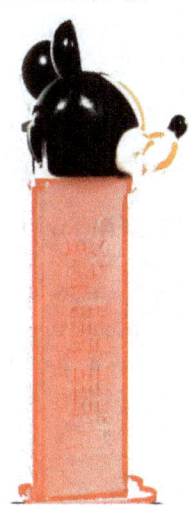

The PEZ dispenser is an example of a real-world object that's a stack. Children push candies into the dispenser from the same end that they pop the candies off.

```
list.
    append()    copy()      extend()    insert()    pop()       reverse()
    clear()     count()     index()     mro()       remove()    sort()
```

Figure 15-72 The Python list and methods

Items can be added and removed from a Python list using different methods, including **list.insert**() and **list.remove**(). When using the Python list as a stack, we restrict ourselves to using only **list.append**() and **list.pop**().

15.12.2 Queues

When you permit elements to be added to one end of an array and removed from the other end, you have converted the array into a queue.

Figure 15-73 The queue

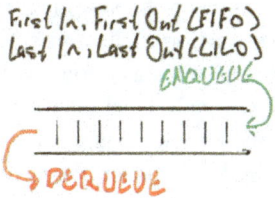

Elements are added at one end and removed from the other end. The operation to add an element to the queue is "enqueue," and the operation to remove one from the queue is "dequeue."

Arrays that serve as queues are sometimes called FIFO (First-In First-Out) or LILO (Last-In Last-Out) arrays.

When using the Python list as a queue, we restrict ourselves to using only list.append() and list.pop(0).

Note: Because the operation of removing an element from the beginning of a list is slow, Python offers an abstract datatype in **collections** called "deque" (pronounced "deck") to use as a queue.

15.12.3 Algorithm: The Josephus Problem

The Josephus Problem is a counting problem that involves a collection in which numbered items are removed according to a rule. The problem as originally posed involves 41 ordered men; if every 3d is removed, which of the men are the last two, numbered by their original positions in the collection?

Figure 15-74 The Josephus Problem. Scan or click QR code to go to the Wikipedia article. https://en.wikipedia.org/wiki/Josephus_problem

In Figure 15-75, we reduce the number of warriors in the circle to 12 and place them in the hour positions on the face of a clock. Warrior 1 stands at hour 1, warrior 2 stands at hour 2, and so on.

The skip, 3, remains the same as in the original problem.

In the first row, the sword, marked by the minute hand, is passed from warrior to warrior.

We follow the skip by calling out "true-true-false," one bool for each warrior. "True" means the warrior stays in the circle; "false" means the warrior is removed from the circle.

When we remove a warrior, we mask his number on the clock, and we write his number into a list. The sword continues to be passed around by the skip "true-true-false," passing over masked out positions.

The final list here is **[3, 6, 9, 12, 4, 8, 1, 7, 2, 11, 5, 10]**.

The original problem asks us to find the last two warriors standing. In this implementation, the answer is 5 and 10.

In Figures 15-76 to 15-79, we reconceive the problem using queues. The live-warrior queue (top) holds the warriors in order while the dead-warrior queue (bottom) is empty and therefore not shown.

In this reconception, the fronts of the queues are to the left and the backs are to the right. The warrior at the front of the live-warrior queue holds the sword. The warrior at the front also is tapped true-true-or-false.

We keep the skip in the original problem. If he is tapped "true," the warrior dequeues from the live-warrior queue and enqueues to the back of the live-warrior queue. If he is tapped "false," the warrior dequeues from the live-warrior queue and enqueues to the back of the dead-warrior queue.

We could label them "true," "true," and "false." The warriors at the front of the live-warrior queue in the first two figures hand the sword to the warrior behind him, dequeues, and enqueues to the back of the live-warrior queue.

15.12 Stacks and Queues

Figure 15-75 A simplification of the original Josephus Problem

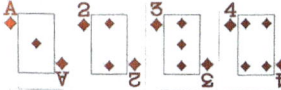

Figure 15-76 The initial state of the data structures in our solution of the Josephus Problem using queues

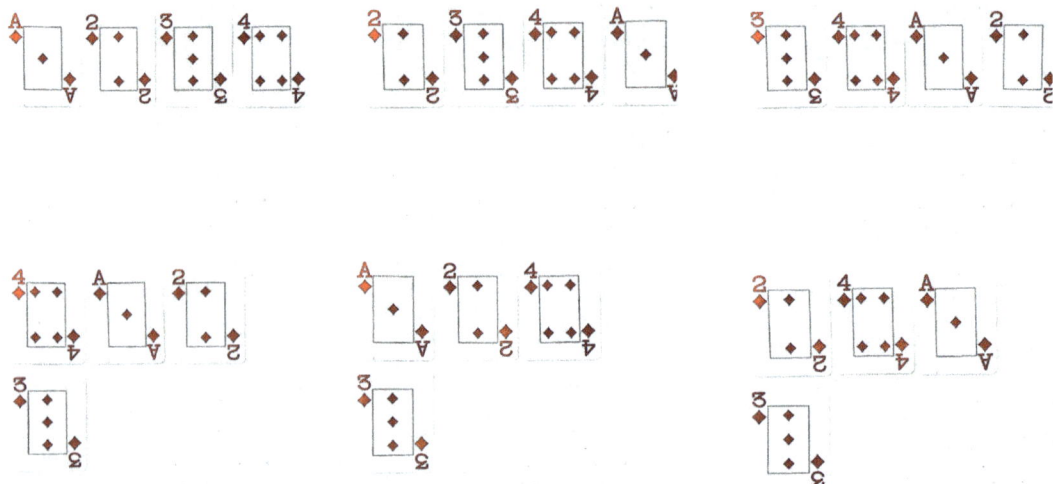

Figure 15-77 The first row shows the first three moves of our algorithm

Warrior 3—"false"—dequeues from the live-warrior queue and enqueues into the dead-warrior queue, as shown in the first figure in the second row.

The second row shows the next three moves. Again, we could label the figures "true," "true," and "false" to describe each warrior at the front of the live-warrior queue. Warrior 2 goes to the back of the dead-warrior queue.

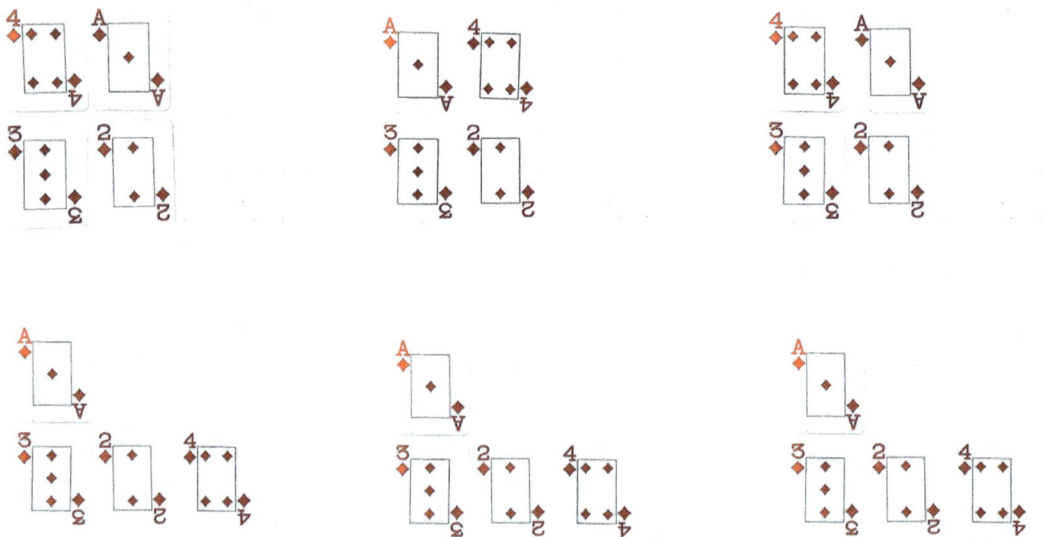

Figure 15-78 Rows 3 and 4 show the results of the next six moves

Row 3: With two warriors left and a skip of 3, the remaining live warriors simply swap places three times. Warrior 4 goes to the back of the dead-warrior queue.

15.12 Stacks and Queues

Row 4: With one warrior left and executing each step of our algorithm, that warrior becomes "true," "true," then "false" before dequeuing from the live-warrior queue and enqueuing to the back of the dead-warrior queue.

Figure 15-79 The final state of the data structures in our solution of the Josephus Problem that uses queues

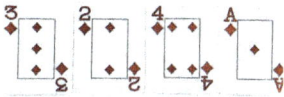

The final list here is **[3, 2, 4, 1]**.

```
# pseudo-code

# create three lists, one for circle_of_objects, one for removed_objects, and one for the skip
circle_of_objects, removed_objects, skip = range(1,42), [], range(3)

# while circle_of_objects == True
while circle_of_objects:

    # for i <- skip-list reversed
    for i in skip[::-1]:

        # dequeue the next object

        # the logical structure of the following
        # if-else clause is not pythonic.
        # in python, we prefer: if someCollection:
        # meaning "True as long as someCollection
        # contains an item"
        # let's refactor to clause.

        # if i == 0

            # append next object to removed_objects list

        # else

            # append next object to circle_of_objects list

# print removed_objects list
removed_objects
```

Figure 15-80 Pseudocode algorithm for solving the Josephus Problem. Click the image to go to the repo on GitHub. The pseudocode is in a Jupyter notebook in the **notebook** directory. https://github.com/jderry/intro_to_programming/

Implementing the algorithm in Python is left as a challenge for the reader.

Please be aware that part of the challenge includes fixing issues as they come up.

15.13 Recursion

Figure 15-81 Recursion Scan or click the QR code to go to the article on recursion on Wikipedia. https://en.wikipedia.org/wiki/Recursion

> A recursive function is a function that calls a copy of itself.
>   The called recursive function can then call a copy of itself, and so on, and so on.
>   Each copy is pushed onto a call stack. The default recursion depth in Python is 1000.
>   Each copy has with it on the stack frame a copy of its own local variables.
>   A copy belongs to one of two cases: (a) the general case or (b) the base case.
>   Each copy of the general case calls a new copy.
>   A copy of the base case brings the recursion to an end.
>   As each copy returns, passing its value to the copy that called it, it is popped off the stack.

Figure 15-82 In introductory CS textbooks, matryoshka dolls, also called nested dolls, are often used to represent recursive functions

We can think of the outermost doll as the copy of the recursive function we call on the command line.

As our introduction focuses on recursive functions that take natural numbers as arguments, when we invoke our recursive function, we pass in some natural number as the argument.

And as we are working writing recursive functions that take natural numbers as arguments, we will define either zero or one (or both) as the base case in the body of our function and all other natural numbers as instances of the general case.

In the body of our recursive function, we use conditional branching to distinguish between whether the argument passed into the copy of the function belongs to the base case or the general case:

15.13 Recursion

if n == 0: *# base case*
    return 1 *# value to return*
else: *# general case*
    # for instances of the general case, the function invokes a copy of itself,
    # passing in a value one less than the value passed into the calling function
    testRecursFunction(n - 1)

A Step-by-Step Illustration of Recursion

Figure 15-83 1. We invoke the recursive function on the command line, passing in 2 as an argument

The function's base case is 0.

Figure 15-84 2. Because 0 is the base case, the copy we invoked holds a value that is an instance of the general case

Therefore, a new copy is created, and a value 1 less than 2 (which of course is 1) is passed into it.
NOTE: The program counter hasn't yet finished executing the code in the body of the function we invoked. That copy of the function is waiting for the copy of the function it has just created to pass up its return value.

Figure 15-85 3. That new copy of the recursive function now creates a third copy of the function, passing into it a value 1 less than 1, which is 0, and zero is the base case for this function

This is the end of making copies of the function.

Figure 15-86 4. Following the instructions in the conditional branch for the base case, this copy returns a value of 1 to the function that called it, then is removed from memory

The copy of the function that called the base case copy can now process that value and finish executing its code.

Figure 15-87 5. This instance of the general case now passes up its value to the copy of the function that called it and be removed from memory

Figure 15-88 6. That copy is the copy we created when we invoked the recursive function on the command line

Now that it has the return value from the copy of the function it created, it can finish executing its code, and once it does, it too is removed from memory.

Figure 15-89 Pythontutor visualizer. Scan or click the QR code to go to the website. https://pythontutor.com/visualize.html

It helps to understand how recursion works by running recursive functions in Phillip Guo's pythontutor visualizer, then clicking through the visualized animation step by step.

15.13.1 A Few Recursive Functions

```python
def recursFactorial(n):
    productValue = 1
    if n > 1: # general case
        productValue = n * recursFactorial(n - 1)
    return productValue
```

Figure 15-90 Example of a recursive factorial function

```python
def recursEuclidGCD(a, b):
    if a % b: # general case
        return recursEuclidGCD(b, a % b)
    else: # base case
        return b
```

Figure 15-91 Example of a recursive fibonacci function

15.13 Recursion

```
def recursFibonacci(index):
    if index < 2: # base case
        return index
    else: # general case
        return recursFibonacci(index - 1) + recursFibonacci(index - 2)
```

Figure 15-92 recursFibonacci is remarkable among our examples in how much memory it consumes

Each call of the general case creates two copies of the recursive function. The consumption of memory, in fact, is exponential.

In the next example, we will look at how we can use a dynamic programming method called memoization to limit this growth through use of a dictionary we'll call the MemoTable to keep track of Fibonacci sequence index/value pairs.

In memoization, this dictionary serves as the lookup table.

> Leonardo Pisano, known today to mathematicians and scientists over the world by the name Fibonacci, was a citizen of the maritime city-state of Pisa from 1170 until after 1240...
> Leonardo was instructed in mathematics as a youth in Bugia, a trading enclave established by the city of Pisa and located on the Barbary Coast of Africa in the Western Muslim Empire. He continued to develop as a mathematician by traveling on business and studying in such places as Egypt, Syria, Provence, and Byzantium. He developed contacts with scientists throughout the Mediterranean world. He became proficient in Euclid's *Elements*, and the Greek mathematical method of definition, theorem, and proof. He learned from the Arabic scientists the Hindu numbers and their place system, and the algorithms for arithmetic operations. He also learned the method of algebra principally found in the work of al-Khwarismi [K]. Through his study and travel and learned disputations with world scientists, he became a very superior creative mathematician. He participated in the academic court of Frederick II, who sought out and recognized great scholars of the thirteenth century. Leonardo with his scientific knowledge saw clearly the advantages of the useful mathematics known to the Muslim scientists, principally their Hindu numerals and decimal place system, their calculating algorithms, and their algebra. Knowledge of the Hindu numerals began to reach Europe in the second half of the tenth century through the Arabs by way of Spain; however, their usage was still not a general practice at Leonardo's time. Leonardo resolved to write his encyclopedic work, *Liber abaci*, to bring to the Italian people the world's best mathematics in a usable form.*

A few words for Fibonacci (c.1170CE - c.1240-50CE), who is commonly remembered for the Fibonacci sequence. Perhaps even more important than that, though, is his importance in bringing to Europe the base-10 system, including the concept of zero, invented and developed by Hindu mathematicians, codified by 700CE, and later adopted by Muslims.

It was through his tutelage under Muslims, and his frequent contacts with Muslims, that Fibonacci learned of the base-10 system and came to appreciate its superiority over other number systems in use at that time in Europe—the commonest being Roman numerals.

Figure 15-93 Memoization. Scan or click the QR code to go to the Wikipedia article on memoization. https://en.wikipedia.org/wiki/Memoization

---

* L.E. Sigler, translator. *Fibonacci's Liber Abaci*. Springer Verlag. 2003. p.3.

Memoization speeds up the execution of many calls of the same function by storing the results of the first calls in memory, then using these results in later calls, instead of rerunning the calculations.

```python
# memorized recursive fibonacci

# dictionary of index/value pairs in fibonacci sequence
# this dict will hold already-computed values for later re-use
memoDict = {} # in memoization, referred to as a lookup table

def memoizedFib(n):
    if n <= 2: # base case
        return 1
    # begin general case #
    if n in memoDict:
        return memoDict[n]
    memoDict[n] = memoizedFib(n - 1) + memoizedFib(n - 2)
    return memoDict[n]
    # end general case #
```

Figure 15-94 Memoized recursive Fibonacci

Memoization is a technique used to speed up computations by storing already-calculated values for reuse later, instead of recomputing them.

We end with an example of a recursive sorting algorithm.

```python
def quick_sort(arry):
    if len(arry) <= 1:
        return arry
    else:
        return quick_sort([item for item in arry[1:] if item <= arry[0]])\
            + [arry[0]] \
            + quick_sort([item for item in arry[1:] if item > arry[0]])
```

Figure 15-95 Quicksort. Source: https://stackoverflow.com/questions/26858358/a-recursive-function-to-sort-a-list-of-ints

Sorting algorithms based on recursion can have a better time complexity than sorting algorithms that work by doing multiple passes through unsorted arrays. Above is an example of the quick sort recursive algorithm implemented in Python using list comprehension.

Chapter Summary

In this chapter, we covered more Python, more algorithms, and more applications, including slicing, Python's half-open interval, and comprehension; we came up with several ways to transpose a matrix, then transposed a transposed dataset to return it to its correct form. Finally, we learned about stacks, queues, and recursion. In the next chapter, we will work in several SciPy libraries that are commonly used when working on datasets.

SciPy 16

As soon as we started using Python as a calculator in Chapter 9, we've been making use of the SciPy software stack. IPython, NumPy, SciPy, Pandas, SymPy, and Jupyter notebooks—all of these make up a substantial part of the tools created, developed, and maintained by STEM researchers for use by STEM students and researchers. In this chapter and within the accompanying scripts and Jupyter notebooks, we will touch briefly upon some of the functionality within the SciPy software stack, especially as it pertains to working with datasets.

> How can it be that mathematics, being, after all, a product of human thought which is independent of experience, is so admirably appropriate to the objects of reality?
>
> —Albert Einstein, Sidelights on Relativity (1922)

> SciPy ("Scientific Python") is a collection of free and open source libraries designed for use by scientists and engineers.
> IPython, the interactive Python shell that we've been using and that was created by the physicist Fernando Pérez, is part of the SciPy collection.
> Using these libraries saves us from having to write our own objects and functions to work on and analyze our datasets. Much of the functionality they provide can also be used when we are using Python as a calculator.
> In this chapter, we'll review several of these libraries.

Because many of the code examples in this chapter are in Jupyter notebooks in the notebook directory of our repo, we will begin by copying the notebook directory into our home directory:

```
$ cp -a ~/repo/intro_to_programming/notebook ~
```

You may want to launch Jupyter notebook within the notebook directory:

```
$ cd ~/notebook && jupyter notebook
```

Many people prefer working within Jupyter notebooks to IPython. Jupyter notebooks are also favored by teachers for lessons, given that within the notebooks one can bundle not only code, images, and text, but also audio and video files, as well as code to run simulations.

16.1 matplotlib: Graphics with SciPy

Figure 16-1 Matplotlib. Scan or click the QR code to go to the homepage of the *matplotlib* site. https://matplotlib.org/

> The ability to visualize your data can be fundamental to understanding it.
> A relationship between two or more dimensions in your dataset made obvious at a glance can make all the difference in whether or not it makes an impact on your audience.
> To the furthest extent possible, show, don't tell, or show while telling.
> **matplotlib** is a comprehensive library for creating static, animated, and interactive visualizations in Python.
> Its functions, objects, and their methods are designed to be familiar to Matlab users.

For this lesson, we will be using two Jupyter notebooks in the repo similarly named:
G.1_intro_to_matplotlib.ipynb and **G.2_intro_to_matplotlib.ipynb**
We start by opening **G.1_intro_to_matplotlib.ipynb**.

```
%matplotlib inline
import matplotlib.pyplot as plt
```

Figure 16-2 Initializing *matplotlib.pyplot on Jupyter notebook*

We initialize matplotlib to render images within Jupyter notebook using the **%matplotlib inline** magic.
matplotlib.pyplot is used for rendering plots of curves.

```
# pyplot plots a list of numbers, when passed in as a single argument,
# as y values against their indices (x values).

plt.plot(list(range(10)))
```

The items of an ordered collection are index/value pairs.
When a single ordered collection of numbers (e.g., a list or ndarray) is passed into the **plt.plot()** function, a curve is rendered in which the indices are the values of the *x*-axis and their numbers are the values of the *y*-axis.
In a tabular dataset, the single ordered collection might be a single quantitative dimension (in other words, a column vector).

```
# if we give pyplot two lists, the first becomes the x values,
# and the second the y values.
# the lists must be of the same length.

plt.plot([2*x for x in range(10)], [x**2 for x in range(10)])
```

16.1 matplotlib: Graphics with SciPy

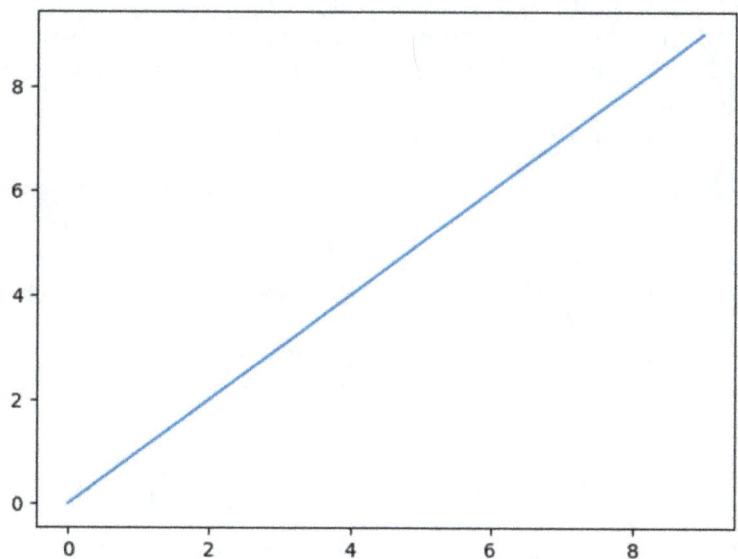

Figure 16-3 The least necessary to plot a curve is an ordered collection of numbers

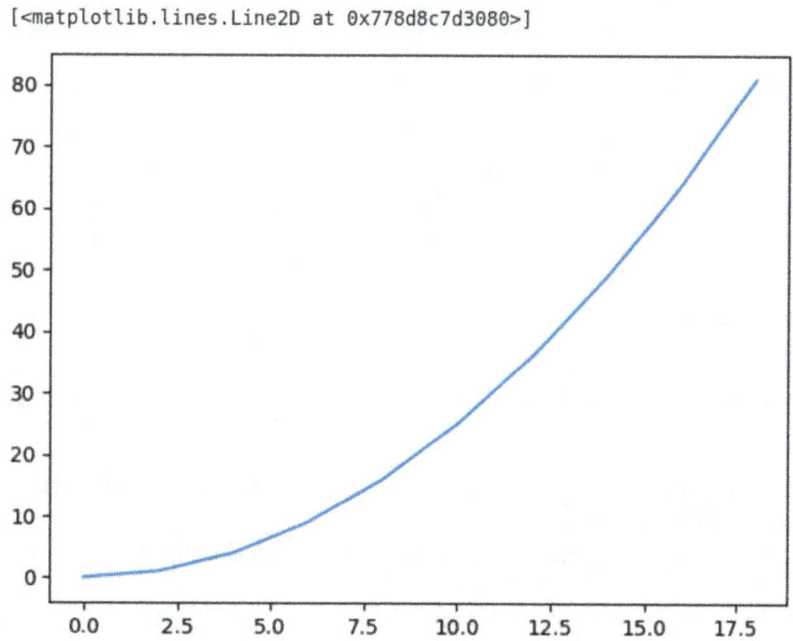

Figure 16-4 Passing two ordered collections into the *plt.plot()* function

As you may have already figured out, when we pass in two ordered collections, the first becomes the x values of the plot, while the second becomes the y values.

In this example, we pass in two list comprehensions to generate our x and y vectors. The first yields an ordered list of 2 * the natural numbers from 0 to 9, while the second yields an ordered list of the same numbers squared.

This may be useful to visualize a relationship between two column vectors in a tabular dataset.

```
# when the axes scales are unequal, the plot distorts the shape of the curve.
# to set the axes to the same scale, we use the plt.axis() method,
# passing in the string 'equal' as argument.
# note that matplotlib returns the tuple (xmin, xmax, ymin, ymax)

plt.plot([2*x for x in range(10)], [x**2 for x in range(10)])
plt.axis('equal')
```

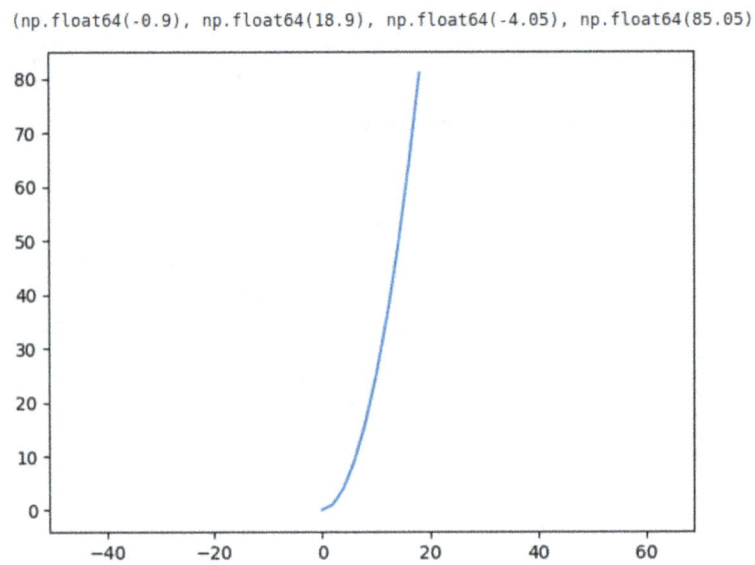

Figure 16-5 Setting the *x* and *y* axes equal

You may have noticed that the axes of the curve rendered in the earlier plots are not equal, creating a visual distortion of their curves.

That could result in your audience misinterpreting the relationship between the values in two vectors.

16.1 matplotlib: Graphics with SciPy

Here, we see what the curve in the last image looks like when we set the x and y axes equal.

```python
# the matplotlib inline magic allows
# for multiple curves to render on the same plot

plt.plot(list(range(10)))
plt.plot([2*x for x in range(10)])
```

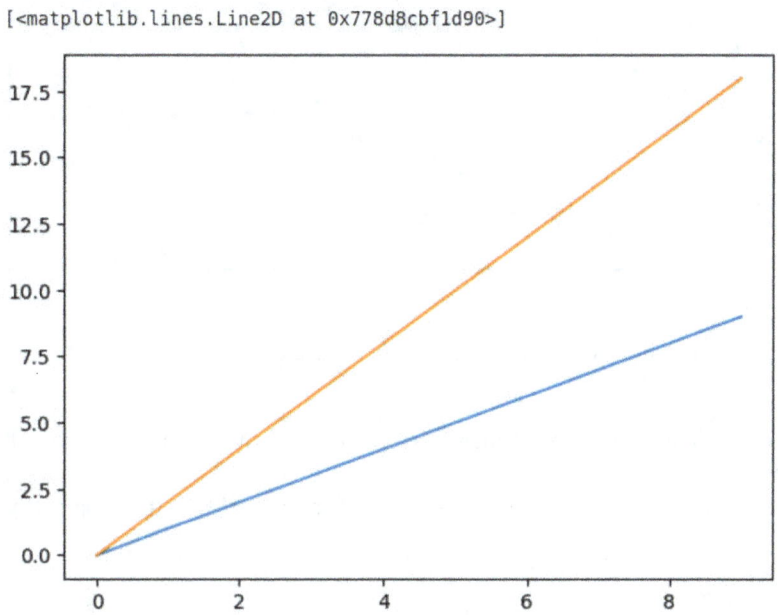

Figure 16-6 Rendering multiple curves in the same plot

Note that matplotlib sets attributes of curves (like color) to default values if none are passed in.

```python
# we can also make subplots
# first, we create an instance of the plt.figure() object
fig = plt.figure()
# then we add each plot to it as a subplot
# the add_subplot() method argument specifies:
# num_rows, num_cols, plot_number
ax1 = fig.add_subplot(211) # plot 1
ax1.plot(list(range(10)))
ax2 = fig.add_subplot(212)
ax2.plot([2*x for x in range(10)])
plt.show()
```

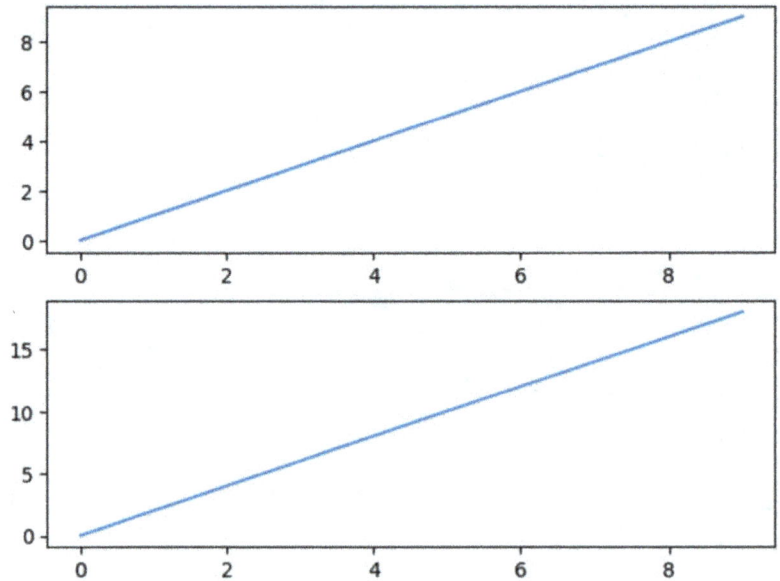

Figure 16-7 Subplots allow us to make side-by-side comparisons of curves

This can greatly aid audience comprehension of a point we may be making about the relationships between vectors.

The difference between these two curves is revealed in the scales of the subplots' y-axes.

```
# let's return to multiple curves on one plot.
# we can specify the colors of our curves
# we can add a grid; we can label our curves and axes,
# title our plot, and provide a legend

plt.plot(list(range(10)), label='x', color='magenta')
plt.plot([2**x for x in range(10)], label='x**2', color='cyan')
plt.grid(True)
plt.xlabel('indices')
plt.ylabel('values')
plt.title('linear v. quadratic growth')
plt.legend()
plt.show()
```

16.1 matplotlib: Graphics with SciPy

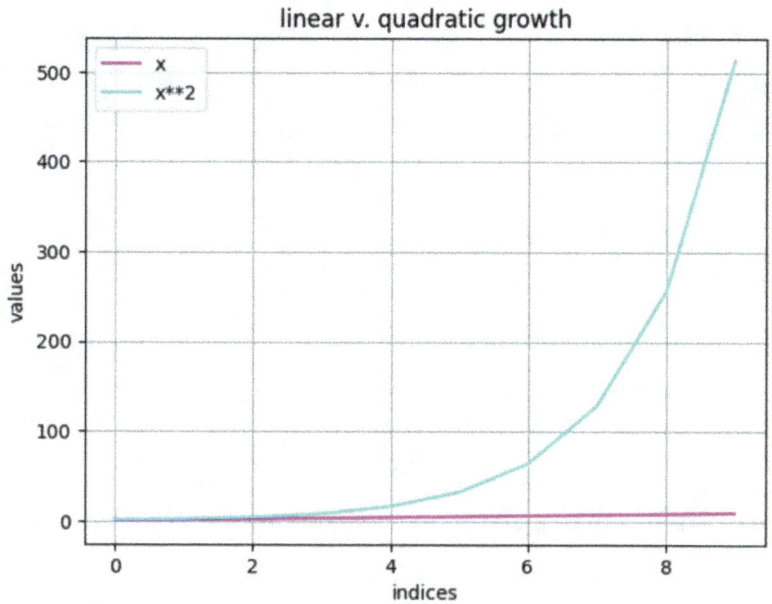

Figure 16-8 *matplotlib* gives us control over all the elements of a plot

Again, the point is to provide your audience a visual confirmation of whatever point about your data you're trying to make that is easily, quickly comprehended.

```python
from IPython.display import HTML
from scipy.stats import lingress
import numpy as np
import matplotlib.pyplot as plt
```

Figure 16-9 In the second Jupyter notebook, G.2_intro_to_matplotlib.ipynb, we consider different types of plots (scatterplots, image plots, and histograms), as well as colormaps

The YouTube video that is embedded in the notebook is a talk given at the SciPy conference in 2015 regarding colormaps. It lasts 20 minutes. Recommended.

```python
import matplotlib.pyplot as plt
import numpy as np
import os; home = os.path.expanduser('~')

with open(home + '/datafile/reformatted_Unigene.fa') as inFile:
    LoS = inFile.read().splitlines()
    LoL = []
    for record in LoS:
        ''' after splitting record string,
            get the length of nucleotide string
            (in index position 6)
            and append to LoL
        '''
```

```
        LoL.append(len(record.split()[6]))
    LoL = np.array(LoL)
binwidth = 1
plt.figure(figsize=(30, 5)) # set height and width of figure
plt.hist(LoL, bins=np.arange(LoL.min(), LoL.max() + binwidth, binwidth))
```

```
(array([1.08e+03, 9.54e+02, 9.21e+02, ..., 0.00e+00, 0.00e+00, 1.00e+00]),
 array([ 200.,   201.,   202., ..., 6614., 6615., 6616.]),
 <BarContainer object of 6416 artists>)
```

Figure 16-10 Histogram of the nucleotide string lengths in our reformatted fasta file

The histogram's width and height have been set by hand to get the axes of roughly equal length.

A histogram is defined by its shape—in this case, the shape of the curve that defines the top of the histogram.

Is there anything you can say about the lengths of the nucleotide strings in our dataset, given the shape of the histogram?

Can you describe the curve of the histogram with a mathematical expression?

16.2 NetworkX: Working with Graphs

Figure 16-11
NetworkX. Scan or click the QR code to go to the homepage of the *NetworkX* site. https://networkx.org

> NetworkX is a Python package for the creation, manipulation, and study of the structure, dynamics, and functions of complex networks.
>
> —From networkx.org site

As we saw in the lesson "Introduction to Graph Theory" in the last chapter, we can use Bash tools that we are already familiar with to extract simple, useful information about graphs.

However, if you need to do a deeper, more complex analysis of a graph, NetworkX is your friend.

```
# initialization
!cp ~/repo/intro_to_programming/datafile/hewitsoni_males.txt ~/datafile
```

16.2 NetworkX: Working with Graphs

```python
import os; home = os.path.expanduser('~')

# first, we read in the contents of the hewitsoni males file
with open(home + '/datafile/hewitsoni_males.txt') as inFile:
    LoS = inFile.read().splitlines()
    LoL = []
    for record in LoS:
        LoL.append(record.split('\t'))
# second, we create an edge_list_LoL
    edge_list_LoL = []
    for index in range(len(LoL)-1):
        if LoL[index][0] == LoL[index+1][0]:
            record = [LoL[index][1],\
                      LoL[index+1][1],\
                      LoL[index][0]]
            edge_list_LoL.append(record)
```

Figure 16-12 We will use an edge list that we make from the hewitsoni_males.txt dataset in our repo

```python
import networkx as nx
# each butterfly's recorded journey forms a separate graph.
# to capture all of them, we must us a multigraph object
G = nx.MultiGraph()
# we add each edge to the multigraph.
# a butterfly's number is the weight of each recorded edge
G.add_weighted_edges_from(edge_list_LoL, weight='specimen')
# we can find out how many times stations form the endpoints
# of edges using the .degree() method
# we can then sort on the value for each edge to determine
# which stations were most visited
sortedDegreeCnt =\
    sorted(dict(G.degree()).items(), key = lambda x:x[1])
sortDict = dict(sortedDegreeCnt)
# the nodes' degrees by node:degree pairs, in ascending order
print(sortDict)
# station 690 has highest degree, and is therefore the most visited
dict(G.degree())['690']
```

Figure 16-13 Using networkx to analyze the graph formed from our edge list

In this case, we wish to find out which nectar-feeding stations were the most visited by the butterflies.

Notice that we have created our graph as a **MultiGraph**. NetworkX has several graph types you can render your dataset of nodes and edges into. The MultiGraph is for networks with directed edges, in which there can be several edges between any two nodes.

16.3 NumPy: Foundational Library of SciPy

Figure 16-14 NumPy. Scan or click the QR code to go to the homepage of the *NumPy* site. https://numpy.org

> NumPy ("Numerical Python") was created by Travis Oliphant to provide the means to significantly speed up numerical computation in Python, especially quantitative datasets.
>
> The default collection of NumPy is the ndarray. "ndarray" means "n-dimensional array." To speed up computations, NumPy requires the elements of an ndarray to be of the same datatype or object. In other words, the elements must be homogenous.
>
> NumPy also uses vectorized operations to speed up computation. Vectorized operations make use of single-instruction multiple data (SIMD) registers in the CPU cores. AMD added them to their CPUs to speed up audio-visual processing. Intel followed, adding them to the Pentium II in 1997. At the time, Intel called them "MMX (multimedia) registers."
>
> The number and width of hardware-parallel SIMD registers in current Intel processors varies. The AVX-512 offers 32 512-bit registers, each of which holds 8 64-bit floats (or 16 32-bit floats) at a time, and performs the same operation on them simultaneously. The width and number of SIMD registers are expected to increase in future CPUs.
>
> Vectorized operations that make use of SIMD registers are known as ufuncs (or "universal functions").
>
> By design, the default datatype for the elements of an ndarray is the float (64-bit float for 64-bit operating systems and 32-bit float for 32-bit operating systems). Users can resize how many bits their data occupy based on the accuracy and precision they need. Using fewer bits for each datum frees up memory and speeds up calculations.
>
> NumPy and the ndarray provide a rich array of linear algebra functions and methods to use on datasets.

16.3.1 The ndarray

"NumPy" stands for "numeric Python." Travis Oliphant wrote NumPy to address one of the biggest complaints researchers using Python to process datasets have with the language—its runtime speed. Compared to compiled programming languages, Python runs slow. Although Python is written in C and makes use of functions in the glibc library, a script written in Python can run up to 100× slower than a functionally equivalent C program.

There are many reasons for this performance hit, but the ones that concern us now have to do with mutable Python collections—in particular, the Python list.

16.3 NumPy

The freedom to update mutable Python collections at runtime and to create lists with different types of items comes at a cost. The Python interpreter must check to determine if the type of item is conformable to an operation before that operation can be executed on the item. A compiler, on the other hand, must check only once, while compiling code.

By requiring that all items of an ndarray be of the same type, it is necessary for the Python interpreter to have to test only once to ensure that all the items in the ndarray are conformable for an operation.

16.3.2 Linear Algebra Has Three Objects: Scalar, Vector, and Matrix

> There are three objects in linear algebra: (1) the dimensionless number, or scalar; (2) a one-dimensional array of scalars, or vector; and (3) a collection of vectors, or matrix.

Linear Algebra: The study of linear sets of equations and their transformation properties
—Eric W. Weisstein, *CRC Concise Encyclopedia of Mathematics*, Second Edition.

$$\mathbf{v} = (1, -3, 2)$$

A vector.

The elements of a vector are scalars, or dimensionless numbers. In textbook format, vectors are rendered in boldface.

When we treat tabular datasets as matrices, we refer to vectors written out in a row like the one above as a **row vector**.

$$\begin{bmatrix} x_1 \\ x_2 \\ \vdots \\ x_m \end{bmatrix} \quad (16\text{-}1)$$

A column vector.

When we work with tabular datasets as matrices, records in the dataset become row vectors, and each dimension in the dataset becomes a column vector.

$$M = \begin{bmatrix} m_{11} & m_{12} & m_{13} & m_{14} & m_{15} \\ m_{21} & m_{22} & m_{23} & m_{24} & m_{25} \end{bmatrix}$$

A matrix.

In textbook format, matrices are rendered in capital letters, and the enclosure is square brackets. Their elements are rendered in the same letter, lowercase. The subscripts of the elements show their positions in the matrix by row and column indices.

The ndarray can represent vectors and matrices. The default ndarray vector is the row vector.

16.3.3 Single-Instruction Multiple Data Registers in CPUs

Figure 16-15 Scan or click the image to go to wikipedia article on SIMD registers. https://en.wikipedia.org/wiki/Single_instruction,_multiple_data

SIMD registers were widely introduced into desktop computers when Intel introduced MMX technology in its Pentium II CPUs in 1997. This was in the age of single-core CPUs, when CPUs still commonly processed audio and video signals.

SIMD registers are an example of hardware parallelization. They are very wide registers that can hold several instances of data of the same datatype, where all of these data are acted on simultaneously.

Audio and video signals are processed with linear algebra operations. SIMD registers greatly sped up the processing of these signals.

While these signals are not normally handled by the CPUs of personal machines today, the SIMD registers have remained, where they are available for other uses.

The core programmers of Python and R use them to process datasets using **vectorized operations**.

16.3.4 Universal Functions (ufuncs) and Vectorized Operations

Figure 16-16 Available universal functions (ufuncs) in NumPy. Scan or click the QR code to go to the documentation for *ufuncs* on the *NumPy* site. https://numpy.org/doc/stable/reference/ufuncs.html#available-ufuncs

16.3 NumPy

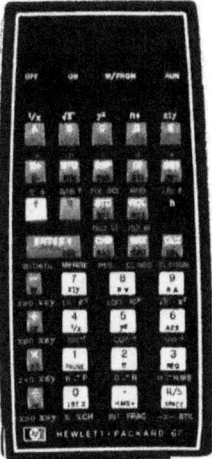

Figure 16-17 The set of NumPy ufuncs is reminiscent of functions available on a programmable calculator

There are more than 60 ufuncs, and they cover (1) math operations, (2) trig functions, (3) bit-twiddling functions, (4) comparison functions, and (5) float functions.

<blockquote style="text-align:center">"If you're using for-loops, you're doing it wrong."</blockquote>

NumPy gives us access to vectorized operations on arrays. Furthermore, implementing them is largely transparent to users. Always check first to see if you can process your array data using ufuncs.

16.3.5 Row and Column Vectors in Memory and Data Processing

The default vector in Python is the row vector. When a vector is moved into system memory, the memory manager tries to keep the elements in the vector contiguous in memory. This minimizes latencies as the elements are processed by the computer.

However, many STEM researchers work with recordsets not record by record, but by dimensions. When a dataset is read into system memory in row-major order, accessing just the data of one dimension introduces latencies, as the data of that dimension are not laid down in memory contiguously.

Because many STEM researchers work with recordsets dimension by dimension, languages specialized for research work like Fortran and R lay down a dataset into memory by column-major order.

NumPy offers this functionality, too, though the researcher must specify it when creating an ndarray.

16.4 Linear Algebra

16.4.1 Datasets As Matrices I

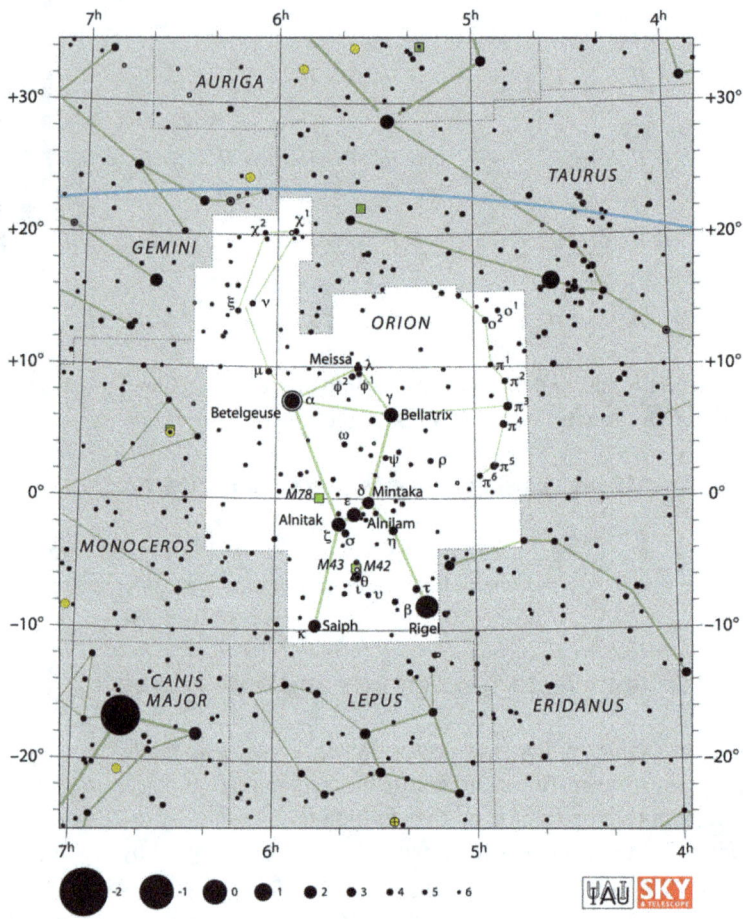

Figure 16-18 Astronomers use spherical coordinates analogous to the more familiar geographic longitude and latitude to locate objects in Earth's skies. Credit: IAU and Sky and Telescope, Creative Commons. Click the image to go to the image on the IAU site. https://www.iau.org/public/images/detail/ori/

These coordinates are called "right ascension," or RA, and "declination," or dec.

Right ascension lines, like lines of longitude, run from pole to pole; whereas longitude is measured in degrees, right ascension is commonly measured in hours, minutes, and seconds.

Likewise, declination lines, like lines of latitude, run as circles parallel to the equator, which in both is $0°$, with the declination of the north pole being $+90°$ and of the south pole being $-90°$.

16.4 Linear Algebra

The star map includes the constellations of Orion and Canis Major. In right ascension and declination, the brightest star in the sky, Sirius, is located at 06h 45m 09s RA, -16°40' dec; Betelguese is at 05h 55m 10s RA, + 07° 24' dec; and Rigel is at 05h 14m 32s RA, − 08° 12' dec.

By conceiving of our tabular datasets as matrices, we can make use of linear algebra operations to efficiently work with and analyze their contents. (In the last chapter, we saw how a linear algebra operator, **transpose**, lets us "flip" a dataset into its correct format from eight records of a half-million columns to a half-million records of eight columns.)

Our tabular datasets, when thought of as matrices, are made up of row vectors and column vectors. Let

$$M = \begin{bmatrix} m_{11} & m_{12} & m_{13} & m_{14} & m_{15} \\ m_{21} & m_{22} & m_{23} & m_{24} & m_{25} \end{bmatrix}$$

The row vectors of M are

$$\begin{bmatrix} m_{11} & m_{12} & m_{13} & m_{14} & m_{15} \end{bmatrix}$$

$$\begin{bmatrix} m_{21} & m_{22} & m_{23} & m_{24} & m_{25} \end{bmatrix}$$

and the column vectors are

$$\begin{bmatrix} m_{11} \\ m_{21} \end{bmatrix} \begin{bmatrix} m_{12} \\ m_{22} \end{bmatrix} \begin{bmatrix} m_{13} \\ m_{23} \end{bmatrix} \begin{bmatrix} m_{14} \\ m_{24} \end{bmatrix} \begin{bmatrix} m_{15} \\ m_{25} \end{bmatrix}$$

When we think of our dataset as a matrix of row vectors, we think of it as a collection of records—each row a record—and each record is a data point in a multidimensional space.

$$\begin{bmatrix} 5340 & GI541 & 16AlpBoo & Arcturus & 14.26103 & 19.18241 & K2IIIp \end{bmatrix}$$

A row vector in a tabular dataset is a data point in a multidimensional space.

When we think of our dataset as a matrix of column vectors—each column a dimension—we think alone of the values of the dimensions in that space and of how they might be related to each other.

In general, researchers think of their datasets in terms of column vectors. They may be interested in the statistics of certain dimensions, or in trying to determine if a relationship exists between two or more dimensions of their datasets; and if a relationship does exist, if it can be described mathematically.

In Figure 16-19, we see values in one dimension—in this case, time in datetime format.

Figure 16-19 A column vector in a dataset

V8
2018/9/24 16:10
2018/9/25 18:47
2018/9/26 20:35
2018/9/27 19:58
2018/9/28 16:26
2018/9/29 17:27
2018/9/30 19:37
2018/10/1 17:55
2018/10/2 18:12
2018/10/3 15:40
2018/10/4 22:13
2018/10/5 16:01
2018/10/6 18:43
2018/10/7 15:32
2018/10/22 15:53
2018/10/23 18:01
2018/10/24 17:00
2018/10/25 15:54
2018/10/26 18:28
2018/10/27 16:41
2018/10/28 18:27
2018/10/29 15:32
2018/10/30 15:26
2018/10/31 17:55
2018/11/1 18:49
2018/11/2 18:20
2018/11/3 20:00
2018/11/4 17:30
2018/9/10 15:34
2018/9/11 15:30
2018/9/12 15:29
2018/9/13 15:29
2018/9/14 15:43
2018/9/15 17:23
2018/9/16 15:30

Figure 16-20 Conversion of spherical to Cartesian coordinates

spherical -> cartesian coordinates

$$\bar{x} = cos(\bar{\theta}) * cos(\bar{\lambda}) * \bar{r}$$

$$\bar{y} = sin(\bar{\theta}) * \bar{r}$$

$$\bar{z} = cos(\bar{\theta}) * sin(\bar{\lambda}) * \bar{r}$$

16.4 Linear Algebra

Referring to Figure 16-20, one may find conversions listed like this in textbooks. The bar over each variable means that it represents a vector (in a tabular dataset like our star catalog, where each record represents the recorded dimensions of a star, these vectors are column vectors). Numpy's vectorized operations let us write out our conversion equations in a format that strongly resembles textbook format. Here we convert stars' spherical coordinates in the star catalog into rectangular coordinates.

```
!unzip ~/repo/intro_to_programming/datafile/hygdata_v41.zip -d ~/datafile/
import os; home = os.path.expanduser('~')
from numpy import loadtxt, savetxt, deg2rad, vstack, sin, cos

# because some of the dimensions contain string data,
# we'll read the entire dataset in as string data,
astroTable = loadtxt(home + '/datafile/hygdata_v41.csv',\
delimiter=',', skiprows=1, dtype=str)
# RA, dec, and dist are columns 7, 8, and 9
# here, we convert their values into floats:
sphCoor = astroTable[:, 7:9+1].astype(float) # a submatrix

# RA is in decimal hours, dec is in decimal degrees
# numpy's default angular measurement is radians
ra = deg2rad(15 * sphCoor[:, 0])
dec = deg2rad(sphCoor[:, 1])
r = sphCoor[:, 2]

# convert spherical coordinates -> rectangular coordinates
x = cos(ra) * cos(dec) * r
y = sin(ra) * r
z = cos(ra) * sin(dec) * r

# we vstack the row vectors, then transpose the vstack,
# which renders them as column vectors.
rectCoor = vstack((x, y, z)).T
savetxt(home + '/datafile/rectCoor.csv',\
rectCoor, fmt="%15.7f", delimiter=',')
```

Figure 16-21 Using vectorized operations to work with a dataset

Explaining the code NumPy has a **loadtxt()** function to read datasets in text files directly into NumPy ndarrays. Because this dataset has heterogeneous datatypes, we'll read everything in as strings, then convert the data in columns 7, 8, and 9 into floats when we slice them from **astroTable** into a submatrix that we call **sphericalCoor**. To enhance the readability of our code, we'll then create individual vectors for **ra**, **dec**, and **r**. Note that **ra**, **dec**, and **r** are column vectors, and transforming the spherical coordinates into Cartesian coordinates yields **x**, **y**, and **z** coordinates.

Finally, the specification calls for writing out the **x**, **y**, and **z** arrays as column vectors in a text file. To do this, we first bring **x, y, z** into a matrix using **vstack()**, passing into it a tuple of the vectors in the correct order, then transposing it. Finally, we use the NumPy function **savetxt()** to write out the matrix to a text file.

16.4.2 Making a Rotatable 3D Graph from Data in a Dataset

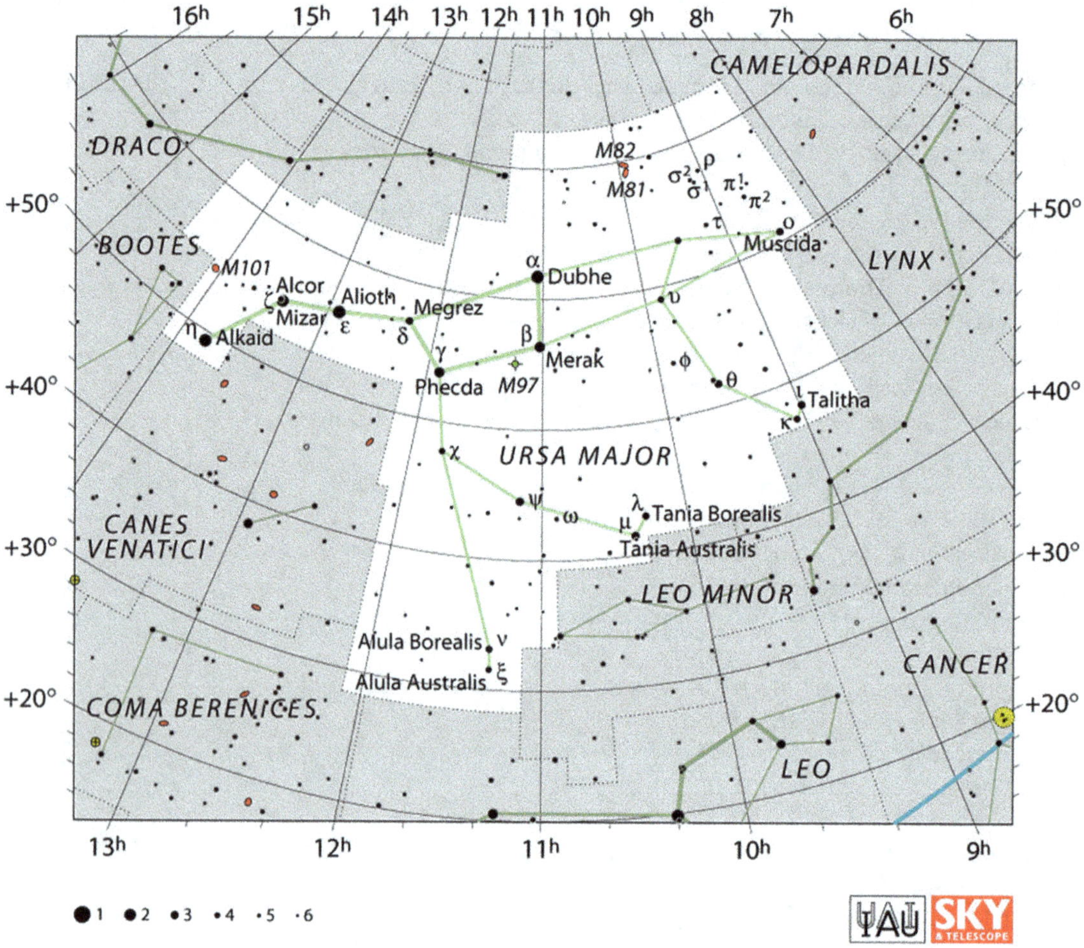

Figure 16-22 The Big Dipper is part of the constellation Ursa Major. Credit: IAU and Sky and Telescope, Creative Commons. Click the image to go to the image on the IAU site. https://www.iau.org/public/images/detail/uma/

The Big Dipper is made up of most of the brightest stars in Ursa Major

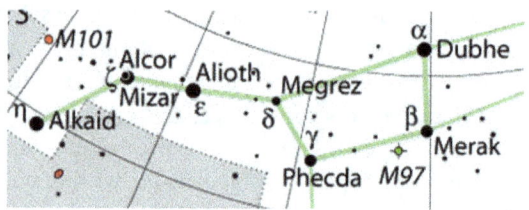

16.4 Linear Algebra

Table 16-1 The stars of the Big Dipper have names

Ursa Major	
α Ursae Majoris	Dubhe
β Ursae Majoris	Merak
γ Ursae Majoris	Phad
δ Ursae Majoris	Megrez
ϵ Ursae Majoris	Alioth
ζ Ursae Majoris	Mizar
η Ursae Majoris	Benetnasch
ι Ursae Majoris	Talita
λ Ursae Majoris	Tania Borealis
μ Ursae Majoris	Tania Australis
ν Ursae Majoris	Alula Borealis
ξ Ursae Majoris	Alula Australis
o Ursae Majoris	Muscida
ψ Ursae Majoris	Ta Tsun
80 Ursae Majoris	Alcor

```
zcat "$HOME"/repo/intro_to_programming/datafile/hygdata_v41.zip |#
tail -n +2 |# drop the label line
sed -e 's/""//g' |# replace empty strings with empty space
grep -E '(Alkaid|Alcor|Mizar|Alioth|Megrez|Phecda|Merak|Dubhe)'\
> "$HOME"/datafile/big_dipper.txt
```

Figure 16-23 We use the fact that the stars of the Big Dipper have names (see Table 16-1) to extract their records from our star catalog and write them into a text file

Given that there are only eight stars in the Big Dipper (two of them a double star), it is easier just to select their records by name.
$ cat ~/datafile/big_dipper.txt

```
53754,53910,95418,4295,Wo 9343,48Bet UMa,Merak,11.030677,56.382427,24.4499,81.66,33.74,-12.0,2.340,0.399,A1V,0.033,-13.103033,3.39835
8,20.360601,0.00000737,-0.00001191,-0.00000801,2.887824569114951,0.9840589862911813,0.000000395898851541666667,0.000000163576135,Bet,4
8,UMa,1,53754,,60.311481961781745,,,
53905,54061,95689,4301,,50Alp UMa,Dubhe,11.062155,61.751033,37.6790,-136.46,-35.25,-9.0,1.810,-1.070,F7V comp,1.061,-17.298705,4.3348
80,33.191332,0.00000478,0.00002450,-0.00001116,2.896065350203451,1.0777588446528075,-0.000000066157674848611111,-0.000000170896822,Alp,
50,UMa,1,53905,,233.3458062281002,,,
57828,58001,103287,4554,,64Gam UMa,Phad,11.897168,53.694760,25.5037,107.76,11.16,-13.0,2.410,0.377,A0V SB,0.044,-15.094867,0.406425,2
0.552678,0.00000862,-0.00001356,-0.00000990,3.1146712453081937,0.9371503534205525,0.000000522435222166667,0.000000054105206,Gam,64,U
Ma,1,57828,,61.54602373713163,,,
59592,59774,106591,4660,Gl 459,69Del UMa,Megrez,12.257086,57.032617,24.6853,103.56,7.81,-13.4,3.320,1.358,A3Vvar,0.077,-13.402309,-0.
903455,20.710384,0.00000906,-0.00001181,-0.00001099,3.2088975991391166,0.995406944309545,0.00000050207304758333334,0.000000037863948,De
l,69,UMa,1,59592,,24.9344618809783,,,
62757,62956,112185,4905,,77Eps UMa,Alioth,12.900472,55.959821,25.3100,111.74,-8.99,-9.0,1.760,-0.256,A0p,-0.022,-13.775959,-3.309169,
20.972944,0.00000732,-0.00001234,-0.00000824,3.377335590144558,0.9766831266334463,0.0000054173080665277778,-0.000000043584749,Eps,77,
UMa,1,62757,,110.25543321022239,Eps,1.776,1.746
65173,65378,116656,5054,NN 3783A,79Zet UMa,Mizar,13.398747,54.925362,26.3089,121.23,-22.01,-5.6,2.230,0.129,A2V,0.057,-14.115808,-5.4
13302,21.531272,0.00000646,-0.00001408,-0.00000630,3.507783854721718,0.9586284043094538,0.0000005877396249374999,-0.000000106707491,Z
et,79,UMa,1,65173,NN 3783,77.33925780489973,,2.336,2.196
67088,67301,120315,5191,,85Eta UMa,Alkaid,13.792354,49.313265,31.8674,-121.23,-15.56,-11.0,1.850,-0.667,B3V SB,-0.099,-18.529548,-9.3
94541,24.164506,-0.00000355,0.00001920,-0.00001010,3.6108299012782816,0.8606788389261799,-0.0000005877396249374999,-0.000000075437008
,Eta,85,UMa,1,67088,,160.99040762157054,,,
```

Figure 16-24 Resultset: records of the eight stars that make up the Big Dipper

```python
import pandas as pd
import matplotlib.pyplot as plt
import os; home = os.path.expanduser('~')

# we need the starTable's label line
starTable = pd.read_csv(home + '/datafile/hygdata_v41.zip',\
                       sep=',',\
                       compression='zip')
label_line = starTable.columns.tolist()

# now we label the columns in the big dipper dataframe
big_dipper = pd.read_csv(home + '/datafile/big_dipper.txt',\
                        index_col=0,\
                        names=label_line)

# make 3D rotatable plot of big dipper
fig = plt.figure()
ax = fig.add_subplot(projection='3d')
x, y, z = big_dipper['x'], big_dipper['y'], big_dipper['z']
ax.scatter(x, y, z)
plt.show()
```

Figure 16-25 We put these records into a Pandas dataframe, then use the rectangular coordinates of the Big Dipper stars to generate a scatterplot of those stars

Note that in Pandas, we can refer to column vectors by their labels.

Figure 16-26 A rotatable 3D scatterplot of the stars of the Big Dipper

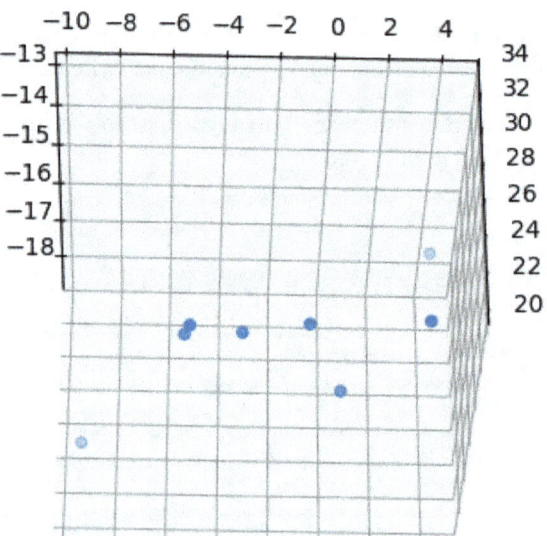

When I Heard the Learn'd Astronomer

When I heard the learn'd astronomer,
When the proofs, the figures, were ranged in columns before me,
When I was shown the charts and diagrams, to add, divide, and measure them,
When I sitting heard the astronomer where he lectured with much applause in the lecture-room,
How soon unaccountable I became tired and sick,
Till rising and gliding out I wander'd off by myself,
In the mystical moist night-air, and from time to time,
Look'd up in perfect silence at the stars.

—Walt Whitman
Drum-Taps, 1865

16.4.3 Datasets As Matrices II: Partitioning a Matrix

> We can break a matrix into pieces by dividing it up along its rows or columns. This is called partitioning a matrix.
> Each piece of a partitioned matrix is a submatrix of the original matrix.

id	hip	hd	hr	gl	bf	proper	ra	dec	dist	pmra	pmdec	rv	mag	absmag	spect	ci	x	y	z
0						Sol	0	0	0	0	0	0	-26.7	4.85	G2V	0.656	5E-06	0	0
1	1	224700					6E-05	1.089009	219.7802	-5.2	-1.88	0	9.1	2.39	F5	0.482	219.740502	0.003449	4.177065
2	2	224690					0.000283	-19.49884	47.9616	181.21	-0.93	0	9.27	5.866	K3V	0.999	45.210918	0.003365	-16.008996
3	3	224699					0.000335	38.859279	442.4779	5.24	-2.91	0	6.61	-1.619	B9	-0.019	344.552785	0.030213	277.614965
4	4	224707					0.000569	-51.893546	134.2282	62.85	0.16	0	8.06	2.421	F0V	0.37	82.835513	0.012476	-105.61954
5	5	224705					0.000665	-40.591202	257.732	2.53	9.07	0	8.55	1.494	G8III	0.902	195.714261	0.034068	-167.695291
6	6						0.001246	3.946458	55.0358	226.29	-12.84	0	12.31	8.607	MOV:	1.336	54.905296	0.017912	3.787796
7	7						0.00147	20.036114	57.8704	-208.12	-200.79	0	9.64	5.828	G0	0.74	54.367897	0.020886	19.827115
8	8	224709					0.001823	25.886461	200.8032	19.09	-5.66	-31	9.05	2.536	M6e-M8.5e Tc	1.102	180.654532	0.086213	87.668389
9	9	224708					0.002355	36.585958	420.1681	-6.3	8.42	0	8.59	0.473	G5	1.067	337.379614	0.207994	250.431996
10	10	224717					0.002424	-50.866976	92.3361	42.23	40.02	0	8.59	3.763	F6V	0.489	58.275424	0.037038	-71.623522
11	11	224720					0.002488	46.939997	239.2344	11.09	-2.02	-25.8	7.34	0.446	A2	0.081	163.34042	0.106439	174.793831
12	12	224715					0.002727	-35.960225	307.6923	-5.99	-0.1	0	8.43	0.989	K4III	1.484	249.053728	0.177782	-180.684145
13	13	224728					0.00278	-22.594705	100000	8.45	-10.07	0	8.8	-11.2	K0III	1.129	92324.548321	67.196978	-38421.000273
14	14	224726					0.003228	-0.36045	205.7613	61.75	-11.67	0	7.25	0.683	K0	1.2	205.757155	0.17389	-1.294442
15	15	236267					0.003356	50.791187	523.5602	13.88	5.47	0	8.6	0.005	K2	1.166	330.967664	0.290916	405.679189
16	17	224732					0.003401	-40.192392	136.4256	-34.46	-26.37	0	8.15	2.476	F3V	0.425	104.212982	0.092744	-88.043116
17	16						0.003469	-54.914363	751.8797	257.39	-96.63	0	11.71	2.329		0.421	432.180376	0.395981	-615.258522
18	18						0.003522	-4.05368	44.8229	-127.22	23.78	0	11.03	7.773	K5	1.567	44.710745	0.041225	-3.168578
19	19	224721					0.003554	38.30405	249.3766	-2.5	-15.07	16	6.53	-0.454	G5	0.955	195.693966	0.182078	154.572309
20	20	224723					0.004203	23.529228	96.6184	36	-22.98	0	8.51	3.585	G0	0.516	88.585158	0.097476	38.571692

Figure 16-27 The first columns and rows of the star catalog, including the label line

In tabular datasets that have them, the label line is generally the first row vector, and all of its elements are strings (each the name of the column vector it belongs to).

As you may recall, to work with the data in the star catalog, we skipped reading the first row—the label line—into the ndarray. When treating a dataset as a matrix, this is the same as partitioning the matrix, allowing us to work only with the data points in the dataset—creating a submatrix of the dataset.

id	hip	hd	hr	gl	bf	proper	ra	dec	dist	prox	prodec	rv	mag	absmag	spect	ci	x	y	z
0						Sol	0	0	0	0	0	0	-26.7	4.85	G2V	0.656	5E-06	0	0
1	1	224700					6E-05	1.089009	219.7802	-5.2	-1.88	0	9.1	2.39	F5	0.482	219.740502	0.003449	4.177065
2	2	224690					0.000283	-19.49884	47.9616	181.21	-0.93	0	9.27	5.866	K3V	0.999	45.210918	0.003365	-16.008996
3	3	224699					0.000335	38.859279	442.4779	5.24	-2.91	0	6.61	-1.619	B9	-0.019	344.552785	0.030213	277.614965
4	4	224707					0.000569	-51.893546	134.2282	62.85	0.16	0	8.06	2.421	F0V	0.37	82.835513	0.012476	-105.61954
5	5	224705					0.000665	-40.591202	257.732	2.53	9.07	0	8.55	1.494	G8III	0.902	195.714261	0.034068	-167.695291
6	6						0.001246	3.946458	55.0358	226.29	-12.84	0	12.31	8.607	M0V:	1.336	54.905296	0.017912	3.787796
7	7						0.00147	20.036114	57.8704	-208.12	-200.79	0	9.64	5.828	G0	0.74	54.367897	0.020886	19.827115
8	8	224709					0.001823	25.886461	200.8032	19.09	-5.66	-31	9.05	2.536	M6e-M8.5e Tc	1.102	180.654532	0.086213	87.668389
9	9	224708					0.002355	36.585958	420.1681	-6.3	8.42	0	8.59	0.473	G5	1.067	337.379614	0.207994	250.431996
10	10	224717					0.002424	-50.866976	92.3361	42.23	40.02	0	8.59	3.763	F6V	0.489	58.275424	0.037038	-71.623522
11	11	224720					0.002488	46.939997	239.2344	11.09	-2.02	-25.8	7.34	0.446	A2	0.081	163.34042	0.106439	174.793831
12	12	224715					0.002727	-35.960225	307.6923	-5.99	-0.1	0	8.43	0.989	K4III	1.484	249.053728	0.177782	-180.684145
13	13	224728					0.00278	-22.594705	100000	8.45	-10.07	0	8.8	-11.2	K0III	1.128	92324.548321	67.196978	-38421.000273
14	14	224726					0.003226	-0.36045	205.7613	61.75	-11.67	0	7.25	0.683	K0	1.2	205.757155	0.17389	-1.294442
15	15	236267					0.003356	50.791187	523.5602	13.88	5.47	0	8.6	0.005	K2	1.166	330.967664	0.290916	405.679189
16	17	224732					0.003401	-40.192392	136.4256	-34.46	-26.37	0	8.15	2.476	F3V	0.425	104.212982	0.092744	-88.043116
17	16						0.003469	-54.914363	751.8797	257.39	-96.63	0	11.71	2.329		0.421	432.180376	0.395981	-615.258522
18	18						0.003522	-4.05968	44.8229	-127.22	23.78	0	11.03	7.773	K5	1.567	44.710745	0.041225	-3.168578
19	19	224721					0.003554	38.30405	249.3766	-2.5	-15.07	16	6.53	-0.454	G5	0.955	195.693966	0.182078	154.572309
20	20	224723					0.004203	23.529228	96.6184	36	-22.98	0	8.51	3.585	G0	0.516	88.585158	0.097476	38.571692

Figure 16-28 Perhaps the most common partitioning of a dataset is blocking off the label line and reading in only the data

When we read in the star catalog dataset in NumPy, we passed an argument skiprows=1 into the function in order not to read the label line into the ndarray. We could just as well have sliced the ndarray to achieve the same result.

In the notebook named **DF.corals.ipynb**, the tabular dataset is processed in accordance with the specification using only out-of-the box Python.

sample	spp	island	site	Fam78_CA	Fam78_CA	Fam78_CA	Fam78_CA
19	A. hyacinthus	Pohnpei	south reef (Roj island)	170	172	174	0
23	A. hyacinthus	Pohnpei	south reef (Roj island)	172	174	0	0
24	A. hyacinthus	Pohnpei	south reef (Roj island)	170	176	0	0
26	A. hyacinthus	Pohnpei	south reef (Roj island)	172	174	0	0
27	A. hyacinthus	Pohnpei	south reef (Roj island)	156	176	0	0
30	A. hyacinthus	Pohnpei	south reef (Roj island)	170	176	0	0
31	A. hyacinthus	Pohnpei	south reef (Roj island)	172	174	0	0
34	A. hyacinthus	Pohnpei	south reef (Roj island)	170	176	0	0

Figure 16-29 Microsatellite data for coral symbionts

In order for this dataset to be read by the next program in the lab's workflow, each integer for a sample must be put into a column that holds only instances of that integer.

In other words, one column of the integer matrix could be labelled '170', and if a sample has the integer 170 in its row, we write '170' into the column.

sample	spp	island	site	Fam78_CA	Fam78_CA	Fam78_CA	Fam78_CA
19	A. hyacinthus	Pohnpei	south reef (Roj island)	170	172	174	0
23	A. hyacinthus	Pohnpei	south reef (Roj island)	172	174	0	0
24	A. hyacinthus	Pohnpei	south reef (Roj island)	170	176	0	0
26	A. hyacinthus	Pohnpei	south reef (Roj island)	172	174	0	0
27	A. hyacinthus	Pohnpei	south reef (Roj island)	156	176	0	0
30	A. hyacinthus	Pohnpei	south reef (Roj island)	170	176	0	0
31	A. hyacinthus	Pohnpei	south reef (Roj island)	172	174	0	0
34	A. hyacinthus	Pohnpei	south reef (Roj island)	170	176	0	0

Figure 16-30 Partitioning the matrix (red lines) into submatrices

16.4 Linear Algebra

Because the specification for this programming problem deals only with the data in the integer matrix, and the order of the samples will be preserved, we can think of the problem as requiring two partitions, one that cuts out the label line and one that cuts out sample descriptive text columns.

Figure 16-31 The coral dataset's submatrix that we've been calling its integer matrix

170	172	174	0
172	174	0	0
170	176	0	0
172	174	0	0
156	176	0	0
170	176	0	0
172	174	0	0
170	176	0	0

Note that you can use slicing to extract a copy of this submatrix from the dataset.

Note also that because the solution requires as many columns as there are unique instances of the integers, the integer matrix has to be resized (from four to five columns).

sample	spp	island	site	Fam78_CA 156	Fam78_CA 170	Fam78_CA 172	Fam78_CA 174	Fam78_CA 176	Fam78_CA 178
19	A. hyacinthus	Pohnpei	south reef	0	170	172	174	0	0
23	A. hyacinthus	Pohnpei	south reef	0	0	172	174	0	0
24	A. hyacinthus	Pohnpei	south reef	0	170	0	0	176	0
26	A. hyacinthus	Pohnpei	south reef	0	0	172	174	0	0
27	A. hyacinthus	Pohnpei	south reef	156	0	0	0	176	0
30	A. hyacinthus	Pohnpei	south reef	0	170	0	0	176	0
31	A. hyacinthus	Pohnpei	south reef	0	0	172	174	0	0
34	A. hyacinthus	Pohnpei	south reef	0	170	0	0	176	0

Figure 16-32 The coral dataset with its integer matrix fixed, in accordance with the specification

The code in **DF.corals.ipynb** that creates the submatrices is difficult to understand, making it difficult, if not impossible, to understand and maintain.

If we refactor our solution into one that works with submatrices that we'll call the **label_line**, **record_id_text**, and **integer_matrix**, we can set up solving the problem in a much more straightforward way using **NumPy**.

```
from numpy import array
dataInput = [['sample','spp','island','site','Fam78_CA','Fam78_CA','Fam78_CA','Fam78_CA'],
['19','A. hyacinthus','Pohnpei','south reef (Roj island)','170','172','174','0'],
['23','A. hyacinthus','Pohnpei','south reef (Roj island)','172','174','0','0'],
['24','A. hyacinthus','Pohnpei','south reef (Roj island)','170','176','0','0'],
['26','A. hyacinthus','Pohnpei','south reef (Roj island)','172','174','0','0'],
['27','A. hyacinthus','Pohnpei','south reef (Roj island)','156','176','0','0'],
['30','A. hyacinthus','Pohnpei','south reef (Roj island)','170','176','0','0'],
['31','A. hyacinthus','Pohnpei','south reef (Roj island)','172','174','0','0'],
['34','A. hyacinthus','Pohnpei','south reef (Roj island)','170','176','0','0']]
dataInput = array(dataInput)
label_line = dataInput[0, :]
label_line
```

```
array(['sample', 'spp', 'island', 'site', 'Fam78_CA', 'Fam78_CA',
       'Fam78_CA', 'Fam78_CA'], dtype='<U23')
```

```
record_id_text = dataInput[1:,:4]
record_id_text
```

```
array([['19', 'A. hyacinthus', 'Pohnpei', 'south reef (Roj island)'],
       ['23', 'A. hyacinthus', 'Pohnpei', 'south reef (Roj island)'],
       ['24', 'A. hyacinthus', 'Pohnpei', 'south reef (Roj island)'],
       ['26', 'A. hyacinthus', 'Pohnpei', 'south reef (Roj island)'],
       ['27', 'A. hyacinthus', 'Pohnpei', 'south reef (Roj island)'],
       ['30', 'A. hyacinthus', 'Pohnpei', 'south reef (Roj island)'],
       ['31', 'A. hyacinthus', 'Pohnpei', 'south reef (Roj island)'],
       ['34', 'A. hyacinthus', 'Pohnpei', 'south reef (Roj island)']],
      dtype='<U23')
```

```
integer_matrix = dataInput[1:, 4:]
integer_matrix
```

Figure 16-33 Using NumPy to partition the coral dataset into submatrices with slicing

```
array([['170', '172', '174', '0'],
       ['172', '174', '0', '0'],
       ['170', '176', '0', '0'],
       ['172', '174', '0', '0'],
       ['156', '176', '0', '0'],
       ['170', '176', '0', '0'],
       ['172', '174', '0', '0'],
       ['170', '176', '0', '0']], dtype='<U23')
```

Here we see the computation cells in **np_DF.corals.ipynb**.

Making use of **SciPy** libraries can greatly simplify our data processing tasks, but at the cost of disk space and memory—certainly a trade worth making!

We can now start putting the allele numbers into the correct columns.

16.5 Pandas: Working with Labeled Datasets in Pandas

Figure 16-34 Pandas. Scan or click the QR code to go to the homepage of the *pandas* site. https://pandas.pydata.org/

> Pandas builds on NumPy to provide Python users with the means to efficiently work with datasets.
> Wes McKinney wrote Pandas to work programmatically with datasets that others normally worked with in Excel.
> The main data structure of Pandas is the DataFrame.

As you may recall in an earlier lesson, when transforming spherical coordinates in our star catalog to rectangular ones, we used the index positions of column vectors to invoke and work with them.

Doing so works, but researchers don't normally refer to the column vectors in their datasets by indices, but rather by their labels.

16.5 Pandas: Working with Labeled Datasets in Pandas

Pandas allows us to work with columns by their names. This not only makes it easier for researchers to work with their datasets, it also makes it easier for their collaborators to read their code.

```python
from numpy import deg2rad, sin, cos
from pandas import read_csv, DataFrame
import os; home = os.path.expanduser('~')

starCatalog = read_csv(home\
                + '/repo/intro_to_programming/datafile/hygdata_v41.zip',\
                compression='zip')

ra = deg2rad(starCatalog['ra'] * 15)
dec = deg2rad(starCatalog['dec'])
r = starCatalog['dist']

rectCoor = DataFrame(columns=['x', 'y', 'z'])
rectCoor['x'] = cos(ra) * cos(dec) * r
rectCoor['y'] = sin(ra) * r
rectCoor['z'] = cos(ra) * sin(dec) * r

rectCoor.to_csv('rectCoor.csv', float_format='%.9f', index=False)
```

Figure 16-35 Converting spherical coordinates from the star catalog to rectangular coordinates using Pandas

The default data structure in Pandas is the DataFrame. Although NumPy underlies Pandas, we can import into a Pandas DataFrame a tabular dataset whose columns contain entries of different datatypes.

Note that we directly read a compressed datafile of different datatypes into a DataFrame called **StarCatalog**.

We create the one-dimensional DataFrames that we will invoke as we create the rectangular coordinates **x**, **y**, and **z** in a DataFrame we'll call "rectCoor." Next, we create the empty DataFrame with three empty column vectors labeled **x**, **y**, and **z**.

On the right-hand side of our next three assignment statements are conversion formulas that look very much like textbook format, making the code easy to read. The vector that each line generates is assigned to its proper column in **rectCoor**.

Finally, we read out the contents of the **rectCoor** DataFrame to a csv file.

Note that when the columns of a tabular dataset are labeled, after being read into a Pandas DataFrame, we can refer to the column vectors by their labels.

Likewise, we can write the contents of a column vector directly into a DataFrame (as we do the for the **rectCoor** DataFrame), using the column labels.

Using column labels to work with the dimensions of our records is more intuitive than working with indices.

16.6 Pandas: Using Masks to Query Recordsets

```python
from pandas import read_csv
import os; home = os.path.expanduser('~')
starCatalog = read_csv(home \
         + '/repo/intro_to_programming/datafile/hygdata_v41.zip',\
           index_col='id', compression='zip')
starCatalog.fillna({'con': ''}, inplace=True)
mask = (starCatalog['con'].str.contains('UMa'))\
    & (starCatalog['proper'].notna())
starCatalog[mask][['proper', 'con', 'x', 'y', 'z']]
```

Figure 16-36 Using a mask to select specific records from a recordset

id	proper	con	x	y	z
40572	Násti	UMa	-14.789600	21.444841	47.900183
41586	Muscida	UMa	-16.375480	21.290022	47.898272
44000	Talitha	UMa	-6.835882	6.883318	10.789878
44343	Alkaphrah	UMa	-53.667801	51.996165	80.572997
46339	Intercrus	UMa	-47.431774	36.836132	61.329924
50230	Tania Borealis	UMa	-27.815454	13.402145	28.706022
50655	Tania Australis	UMa	-48.161684	21.865099	46.794651
53565	Chalawan	UMa	-10.333319	2.794615	9.120037
53754	Merak	UMa	-13.103033	3.398358	20.360601
53879	Lalande 21185	UMa	-1.998000	0.504305	1.495504
53905	Dubhe	UMa	-17.298705	4.334880	33.191332
55055	Alula Borealis	UMa	-100.864256	18.476143	66.832099
57226	Taiyangshou	UMa	-37.766969	2.301619	41.698309
57647	Aniara	UMa	-67.531225	2.542591	106.655113
57767	Groombridge 1830	UMa	-7.187679	0.220247	5.561623
57828	Phecda	UMa	-15.094867	0.406425	20.552678
59592	Megrez	UMa	-13.402309	-0.903455	20.710384
62757	Alioth	UMa	-13.775959	-3.309169	20.972944
65173	Mizar	UMa	-14.115808	-5.413302	21.531272
65272	Alcor	UMa	-13.393436	-5.223608	20.521915
65983	Liesma	UMa	-48.051398	-20.903886	71.410393
67088	Alkaid	UMa	-18.529548	-9.394541	24.164506
118742	Alula Australis	UMa	-8.730890	1.610966	5.446747
118743	Alula Australis B	UMa	-8.730989	1.610983	5.446808

The mask is a one-dimensional array of bools the same length as the recordset. If bool is true, the corresponding record gets selected; else, it doesn't.

In this example, we use a mask to query our star catalog for all records of named stars in the constellation Ursa Major.

We get back the records of 24 stars.

Using masks, we can easily construct queries to extract matching records from our recordsets.

Note that in cell 3, we instruct the machine to replace all NaNs (missing values) in the 'con' column vector with empty strings. This allows the machine to then apply the **.str.contains**() method used to create the mask in the next cell.

In the last cell, we apply the mask on the starCatalog dataframe and extract from the records in the resultset just 5 columns: 'proper', 'con', 'x', 'y', and 'z'.

16.7 Pandas: Getting Statistics on Datasets

```
In [1]: !cp ~/repo/intro_to_programming/datafile/MLB.txt ~/datafile

In [2]: !wc ~/datafile/MLB.txt
1035    6208   45481 /home/user/datafile/MLB.txt

In [3]: !head ~/datafile/MLB.txt | cat -vet
Name^ITeam^IPosition^IHeight^IWeight^IAge$
Adam_Donachie^IBAL^ICatcher^I^I180^I22.99$
Paul_Bako^IBAL^ICatcher^I74^I215^I34.69$
Ramon_Hernandez^IBAL^ICatcher^I72^I210^I30.78$
Kevin_Millar^IBAL^IFirst_Baseman^I72^I210^I35.43$
Chris_Gomez^IBAL^IFirst_Baseman^I73^I188^I35.71$
Brian_Roberts^IBAL^ISecond_Baseman^I69^I176^I29.39$
Miguel_Tejada^IBAL^IShortstop^I69^I209^I30.77$
Melvin_Mora^IBAL^IThird_Baseman^I71^I200^I35.07$
Aubrey_Huff^IBAL^IThird_Baseman^I76^I231^I30.19$
```

Figure 16-37 We use our Bash tools within IPython and Jupyter notebook to get stats on our dataset in MLB.txt

The first number **wc** returns is the number of lines in a text file; the third number is the size of the file in bytes.

The pipeline gets the first ten lines of the file and pipes them into **cat -vet**, which represents some whitespace characters with "visible" characters. ^**I** represents a tab, and **$** represents a newline character. Note that in this dataset, the underscore (_) is used to represents a space and is used to separate first and last names.

The last command returns the number of lines, words, and bytes in the file. Because the first line is a label line, there are 1034 records in the dataset.

```
In [4]: !sed -i 's/_/ /g' ~/datafile/MLB.txt

In [5]: !head ~/datafile/MLB.txt | cat -vet
Name^ITeam^IPosition^IHeight^IWeight^IAge$
Adam Donachie^IBAL^ICatcher^I^I180^I22.99$
Paul Bako^IBAL^ICatcher^I74^I215^I34.69$
Ramon Hernandez^IBAL^ICatcher^I72^I210^I30.78$
Kevin Millar^IBAL^IFirst Baseman^I72^I210^I35.43$
Chris Gomez^IBAL^IFirst Baseman^I73^I188^I35.71$
Brian Roberts^IBAL^ISecond Baseman^I69^I176^I29.39$
Miguel Tejada^IBAL^IShortstop^I69^I209^I30.77$
Melvin Mora^IBAL^IThird Baseman^I71^I200^I35.07$
Aubrey Huff^IBAL^IThird Baseman^I76^I231^I30.19$
```

Figure 16-38 Using *sed* to clean up a dataset efficiently

sed means "stream editor." sed allows us to transform text. Here, we use it to substitute spaces for underscores throughout the MLB.txt datafile.

```python
import os; home = os.path.expanduser('~')
from pandas import read_csv
mlb = read_csv(home + '/datafile/MLB.txt', sep='\t')
mlb.iloc[0] # first record in dataframe
```

```
Name          Adam Donachie
Team                    BAL
Position            Catcher
Height                  NaN
Weight                180.0
Age                   22.99
Name: 0, dtype: object
```

```python
mlb.iloc[0]['Position']
```

```
'Catcher'
```

Figure 16-39 Extracting records and values using Pandas

```python
%matplotlib qt # use this in IPython session
# %matplotlib inline # OR use this in Jupyter notebook
import os; home = os.path.expanduser('~')
from pandas import read_csv
mlb = read_csv(home + '/datafile/MLB.txt', sep='\t')
mlb.describe() # descriptive stats
```

16.7 Pandas: Getting Statistics on Datasets

[3]:	Height	Weight	Age
count	1033.000000	1033.000000	1034.000000
mean	73.696999	201.689255	28.736712
std	2.306916	20.991491	4.320310
min	67.000000	150.000000	20.900000
25%	72.000000	187.000000	25.440000
50%	74.000000	200.000000	27.925000
75%	75.000000	215.000000	31.232500
max	83.000000	290.000000	48.520000

```
mlb.corr(numeric_only=True) # compute pairwise correlation of numeric columns
```

[4]:	Height	Weight	Age
Height	1.000000	0.532297	-0.073565
Weight	0.532297	1.000000	0.158282
Age	-0.073565	0.158282	1.000000

```
mlb.cov(numeric_only=True) # compute pairwise covariance of numeric columns
```

[5]:	Height	Weight	Age
Height	5.321861	25.781663	-0.732915
Weight	25.781663	440.642685	14.361168
Age	-0.732915	14.361168	18.665079

Figure 16-40 Working with the MLB dataset using Pandas in an IPython session or Jupyter notebook

Now that we've preprocessed our dataset, substituting underscores with spaces, we read it into a Pandas DataFrame in a Jupyter notebook. Jupyter notebooks make ideal containers to hold and process graphical info.

Pandas provides a record index by default (the far-left column). Pandas does let us set an index column, if one exists. Although Pandas can work with nonunique indices, this is in general not advised, as it can substantially slow down the execution of Pandas code. In other words, Pandas is optimized to work with recordsets whose record indices are unique. If the indices of your recordset are not unique, you should consider letting Pandas add its own index column.

Note also that Pandas set the column labels using the label line in the datafile.

Finally, Pandas fills empty values with NaNs. Pandas lets us decide how to handle NaNs.

```python
%matplotlib qt # use this in IPython session
# %matplotlib inline # OR use this in Jupyter notebook
import os; home = os.path.expanduser('~')
from pandas import read_csv
from pandas.plotting import scatter_matrix

mlb = read_csv(home + '/datafile/MLB.txt', sep='\t')
scatter_matrix(mlb, diagonal='kde')
```

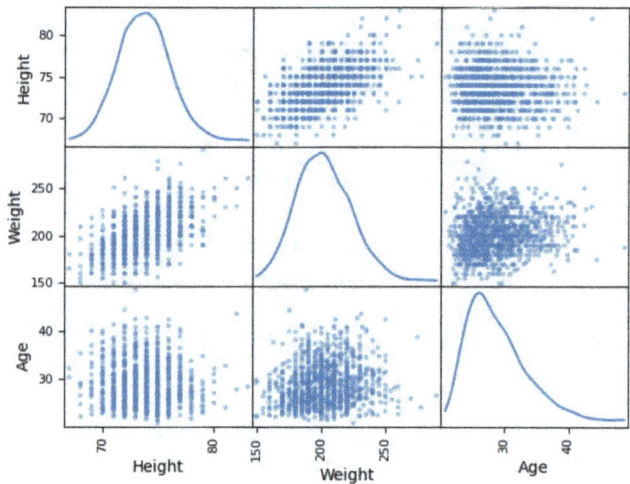

Figure 16-41 Statistical plots using Pandas: scatter_matrix()

16.7.1 Using Seaborn

Seaborn is a Python data visualization library based on matplotlib. It provides a high-level interface for drawing attractive and informative statistical graphics.

—From seaborn.pydata.org homepage

Figure 16-42 Seaborn. Scan or click the QR code to go to the homepage of the *seaborn* site. https://seaborn.pydata.org/

```
%matplotlib qt # use in ipython session
# %matplotlib inline # OR use in jupyter notebook
from pandas import read_csv
import os; home = os.path.expanduser('~')
mlb = read_csv(home + '/datafile/MLB.txt', sep='\t')
import seaborn as sns
sns.set_theme(style='darkgrid')
g = sns.jointplot(x='Height', y='Weight', data=mlb,\
                  kind='reg', truncate=False,\
                  xlim=(67, 83), ylim=(150, 290),\
                  color='m', height=7)
```

Figure 16-43 Statistical plots using seaborn

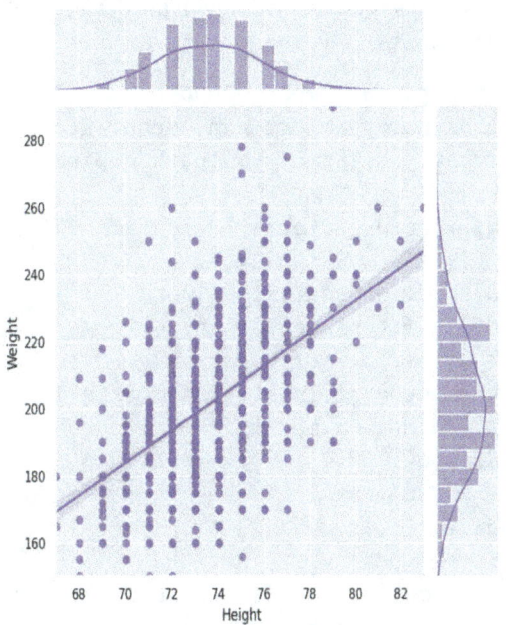

16.8 Pandas: Processing Datasets Programmatically

Mass spec datasets in the chemistry department are generated by Windows machines, which by design don't by default use the newline character to end lines, as Linux and Mac machines do (please refer to the ipython input/output below). Furthermore, each dataset comes out with an empty column (why is it there?).

In [1]: !cp ~/repo/intro_to_programming/datafile/mass_spec_data.csv ~/datafile

In [2]: !head ~/datafile/mass_spec_data.csv | cat -vet

```
Residue,Trial 1,Trial 2,Trial 3,^M$
1,0,0,0,^M$
2,0.000930221,0,0,^M$
3,0,0,0,^M$
4,0.000315431,0.000474183,0.000405405,^M$
5,0.000565901,0.000630124,0.000602657,^M$
6,0.000847624,0.000968444,0.000818597,^M$
7,0.000468794,0.000553492,0.000342596,^M$
8,0.000527281,0.000994546,0.000571512,^M$
9,0.000528844,0.000369776,0.000504031,^M$
```

Figure 16-44 The first ten rows of a mass spec dataset

The requirement is to write a script that, when run, cleans up the dataset, as well as calculating for each record the arithmetic mean and standard deviation of the trials if and only if two or three trials for a residue contain nonzero numbers.

Pandas is used to work with the datasets, while NumPy is used to calculate the means and standard deviations.

```python
from pandas import read_csv
from numpy import nan, mean, std
import os; home = os.path.expanduser('~')

df = read_csv(home + '/datafile/mass_spec_data.csv')

df = df.dropna(axis=1,how='all') # drop empty column
df = df.replace(0, nan) # replace zeros with NaN
# create a list, each value a sum of NaNs in a record
nanList = df.isnull().sum(axis=1).tolist()
# add column for arithmetic mean, fill with float zeros
df.loc[:,'average'] = 0.
# add column for standard deviation, fill with float zeros
df.loc[:,'std_dev'] = 0.

for row in range(len(nanList)): # this for-loop goes down the rows
    if nanList[row] < 2: # and if a residue's NaN count is less than 2, then...
        # write the mean of columns 1,2,3 in column 4
        df.iloc[row,4] = mean(df.iloc[row, 1:4])
        # write their standard deviation in column 5
        df.iloc[row,5] = std(df.iloc[row, 1:4])

# replace NaNs with zeros, restoring the numerical format of the data
df = df.replace(nan, 0)
# ...and write out the results
df.to_csv(home + '/datafile/mass_spec_fixed_csv',\
          float_format='%.9f',\
          index=False)
```

Figure 16-45 The script, still in development

Of the improvements we might want to make before putting it into production, we should consider making it invokable off the Bash command line, passing in the path to the mass spec datafile as an argument.

```
In [9]: !head ~/datafile/mass_spec_fixed_csv | cat -vet
Residue,Trial 1,Trial 2,Trial 3,average,std_dev$
1,0.000000000,0.000000000,0.000000000,0.000000000,0.000000000$
2,0.000930221,0.000000000,0.000000000,0.000000000,0.000000000$
3,0.000000000,0.000000000,0.000000000,0.000000000,0.000000000$
4,0.000315431,0.000474183,0.000405405,0.000398340,0.000065003$
5,0.000565901,0.000630124,0.000602657,0.000599561,0.000026310$
6,0.000847624,0.000968444,0.000818597,0.000878222,0.000064888$
7,0.000468794,0.000553492,0.000342596,0.000454961,0.000086652$
8,0.000527281,0.000994546,0.000571512,0.000697780,0.000210621$
9,0.000528844,0.000369776,0.000504031,0.000467550,0.000069875$
```

Figure 16-46 Resultset of the final script

16.9 SymPy: Symbolic Python

In accordance with the specification, the extra column has been removed from each record, and if two or three trials for a residue are nonzero, the average and standard deviation of the nonzero trials are computed.

Figure 16-47 *SymPy.* Scan or click the QR code to go to the homepage of the *SymPy* site. https://sympy.org

> SymPy is a Python library for symbolic mathematics. It aims to become a full-featured computer algebra system (CAS) while keeping the code as simple as possible in order to be comprehensible and easily extensible. SymPy is written entirely in Python.
>
> —The "about" blurb from the SymPy homepage.

```
$ mkdir -p ~/notebook && cd ~/notebook/
$ cp ~/repo/intro_to_programming/notebook/intro_to_sympy.ipynb ~/notebook
$ jupyter notebook
```

Figure 16-48 Because Jupyter notebooks use MathJax, SymPy output looks better in the notebooks than in IPython

Here, in Bash, we make a directory in our home directory to hold Jupyter notebooks, we copy the notebook we'll work in to this directory, then launch Jupyter notebook from within the directory.

This brief section is intended as a reminder that SciPy includes SymPy, a powerful and easy-to-use CAS (computer algebra system) for working with symbolic math expressions. Because of MathJax and other web technologies, I prefer working with SymPy in Jupyter notebooks.

```python
# initialize
# to initialize displaying webpages within the notebook
from IPython.display import IFrame
# to initialize sympy from ipython:
from sympy import init_session
init_session()
# to initialize sympy from the bash shell:
# isympy
```

IPython console for SymPy 1.13.3 (Python 3.13.2-64-bit) (ground types: python)

These commands were executed:
```
>>> from sympy import *
>>> x, y, z, t = symbols('x y z t')
>>> k, m, n = symbols('k m n', integer=True)
>>> f, g, h = symbols('f g h', cls=Function)
>>> init_printing()
```

Documentation can be found at https://docs.sympy.org/1.13.3/

Figure 16-49 SymPy is different from other SciPy libraries in that by default, initializing a session that uses it entirely loads the library into system memory

```
expr = x**3 + 3*x**2*y + 3*x*y**2 + y**3
factors = factor(expr)
pprint(factors) # show the factors of the expression
expand(factors) # now expand the factors expression
```

$$(x + y)^3$$
$$x^3 + 3x^2y + 3xy^2 + y^3$$

```
# we can substitute values into a sympy expression
expr.subs({x:1, y:2})
```

$$27$$

```
# we can substitute values for just some of the variables in the expression
expr.subs({x:1})
```

$$y^3 + 3y^2 + 3y + 1$$

```
# we can substitute expressions for variables in the expression, and solve
expr = x*x + x*y + x*y + y*y
simplify(expr.subs({x:1-y}))
```

$$1$$

Figure 16-50 Here, aside from showing how mathematical expressions are displayed, we see how easy it is to substitute values—including math expressions—for variables and solving

```
# the quadratic equation
a, b, c = symbols('a b c')
expr = a * x**2 + b * x + c
expr
```

$$ax^2 + bx + c$$

```
# solving the quadratic equation
ans = solve(expr, x)
ans
```

Figure 16-51 Solving the quadratic equation

$$\left[\frac{-b - \sqrt{-4ac + b^2}}{2a}, \frac{-b + \sqrt{-4ac + b^2}}{2a} \right]$$

SymPy includes powerful solvers.
Note that the 'ans' is a list that encloses the two parts of the algebraic answer.

To the furthest extent possible, writers of SciPy libraries must use existing datatypes and collections, instead of creating their own. Using existing datatypes and collections helps flatten the learning curve for using a new library.

```python
import matplotlib.pyplot as plt
from sympy.plotting import plot
x = symbols('x')

p1 = plot(x*x, (x, -10, 10))
```

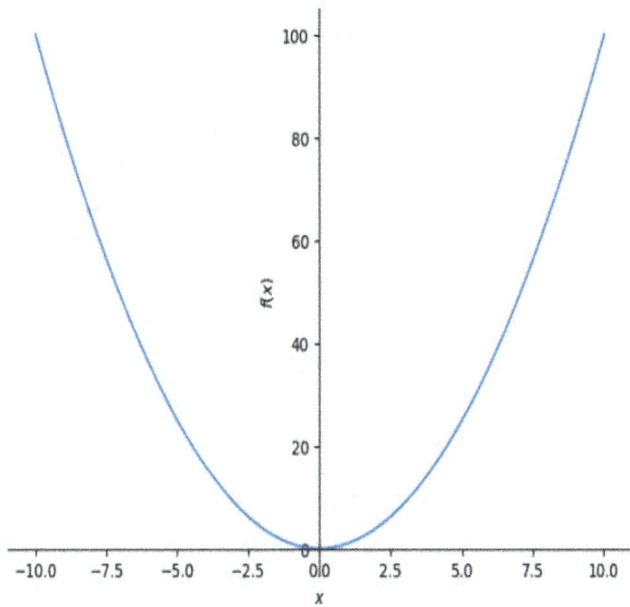

Figure 16-52 Plotting curves in *SymPy* is easy by design

Chapter Summary

In this chapter, we've revisited some SciPy libraries and we've been introduced to a couple more. These tools are meant to make your work easier as you process and analyze datasets. Before starting a project, you should spend some time figuring out which libraries may be useful, as well as how to use them efficiently.

Odds and Ends 17

In this next-to-last chapter, we consider a few topics that weren't covered in earlier chapter. Python sets can be made from records in a recordset to establish existence or determine membership of a record based on dimensions. In the section "Datetime in Datasets," we look at one way to fill in missing datetime entries in a recordset, allowing researchers to then further process their recordsets. Finally, we look at how we might use ipyparallel and a decorator function to somewhat easily render a function used to process records one-at-a-time "embarrassingly parallel" (yes, this is a term used in parallel programming). As always, the focus is on making the code as easy read and use as possible.

17.1 Writing Programs: Writing, Rewriting, and Matters of Style

> As with prose writing, strive to achieve a programming style that is simple, clear, and direct. Ideally, your code should be written and structured so that another programmer—including your future self—can understand it at a glance.
> Be generous with comments.
> Follow style guides. Python has one: PEP 8—
> https://www.python.org/dev/peps/pep-0008/
> **pylint** is a great tool for finding problems with your code and enforcing matters of style.
> Don't be afraid to break the rules of style—just make sure you have a damn good reason for doing so.

> The competent programmer is fully aware of the limited size of his own skull. He therefore approaches his task with full humility, and avoids clever tricks like the plague.
> —Edsger W. Dijkstra

> Don't comment bad code. Rewrite it.
> —Brian W. Kernighan

Do not put more into one Python statement than what you can explain in one simple sentence.
Just because Python allows you to nest functions 5 or 6 (or more!) deep doesn't mean that doing so is a good idea. The same goes for method chaining. Insofar as this guide was written for scientists at a research institution, and I imagine some scientists will leverage their newly acquired skillset to automate tasks in the lab, I ask you to consider that moment in your weekly lab or group meeting when you have to stand in front of your colleagues to explain your code.

By keeping your code simple to explain, you are helping not just yourself, but also your audience, whom (we hope) will find it easier to follow your explanations.

The same goes for coders, in general. As a sequence of instructions, the statements in a program detail how a computer transforms data line-by-line over time. We want those who read our code to be able to follow this transformation.

> I can tell the lion by his claw.
> —Johann Bernoulli, upon reading the solution to a calculus problem submitted anonymously and knowing that its author could be none other than Isaac Newton

As with writing, strive to write code that is simple, clear, and direct. Shun any affectation that draws attention to itself as "stylish." As you grow your skillset and develop as a programmer, you will certainly tend to favor algorithms you've used in the past and understand well. These tendencies will become part of your style. But there is another thing.

How programmers conceive of problems is reflected in their solutions. As your body of work grows, it will—for better or worse—reflect how you think about the problems you solve through your work. This, too, becomes part of your style; and fellow programmers familiar with your work may be able to identify the author of a piece you submit anonymously by no more than your tendencies and approach to thinking about and solving problems, all of which is reflected in your code.

Your goal is to be known by code that is as easy to understand and use as possible while being as efficient as possible. Good luck.

17.2 Python Sets

I admit that when I first read that Python includes in its fundamental collections the set, I was interested in learning more about it, but I couldn't think of a practical use for it.

How times have changed.

First, sets allow us to test for existence and membership of items. This means that you can create a set whose members share a trait, then iterate through your dataset to see if any records have that trait, and if they do, add their IDs to the set. Afterwards, coerce the set to a bool. **True** means your dataset contains at least one record with that trait, while **False** means not a single record in the dataset has that trait.

```
# SPECIFICATION: Update master record set with new record set. Some records in master
# record set will have their dimensions updated. When that happens, replace record in
# master record set with updated record.

# sample records have [recordID, dimension]
masterRecs = [['1', 3], ['2', 2], ['3', 4], ['4', 7], ['5', 6]]
newRecs = [['2', 3], ['4', 7], ['6', 3], ['7', 1]]

# to find updated records, we create sets of recordIDs
masterIDset, newIDset = set(), set()
for record in masterRecs:
```

```
            masterIDset.add(record[0])
    for record in newRecs:
        newIDset.add(record[0])

    # now we iterate through master record set finding shared records & removing them
    for record in masterRecs:
        for ID in masterIDset & newIDset:
            if record[0] == ID:
                masterRecs.remove(record)

    # finally, all new records are appended to the master record set
    for record in newRecs:
        masterRecs.append(record)
```

Figure 17-1 Using Python sets to find shared records (using intersection of record IDs)

According to the specification, shared records in the master record set are then replaced with their copies in the new record list.

We use a list for the master record set because lists are mutable, and the specification requires modifying the master record set.

BEST TO BACK IT UP BEFORE YOU DO!

It is important to keep in mind that the items of a Python set must be immutable. Tuples can be members of a set; lists cannot. However, lists can be coerced into tuples and added as tuples into sets. Likewise, a set cannot be a member of a set; however, Python provides a built-in function, **frozenset**(), to coerce a set into a **frozen set**, which can be a member of a set (the frozen set retains the property that its members are unordered, or behave as if they are).

You can find other examples of using sets and set operations in this book. We used frozensets so we could compare the sets of galactic coordinates captured using different algorithms in the section "Multiple Passes Through Dataset vs. Single Pass." We used the intersection operator when we created the mask in the section "Pandas: Using Masks to Query Recordsets." And we considered an approach using sets when finding range overlap in the section "Finding Intervals with Overlap."

When you go through the Python set notebook that accompanies this lesson, please think of the examples in terms of existence of items or attributes in your datasets, or of membership in multiple datasets.

17.3 Datetime in Datasets

17.3.1 Filling In Missing Datetime Entries

Time is an important dimension in many datasets. In these datasets, it is a leading dimension in the records, often the leading one.

In this case, a long-term research project requires volunteers to make one digital entry per day over two weeks. However, the volunteers being human, many forgot to make entries each day.

The researchers can use incomplete recordsets submitted to them; however, the software they use to process the entries requires 14 sequential entries per subject—they should be one per day—or it won't accept the dataset of volunteer entries.

As a result, lab members manually enter the requisite empty entries into their datasets by hand.

With Pandas and the built-in datetime module, we can automate the task.

Figure 17-2 Before Pandas and the datetime module fixes a dataset

43357	9/24/2012 15:57	MON	1
43357	9/25/2012 18:33	TUE	2
43357	9/27/2012 19:47	THU	4

This volunteer made only three entries. Fair enough. But the software that processes these datasets requires 14 sequential entries.

Figure 17-3 After researchers run the script against the dataset

43357	1	2012-09-24 15:57:00	MON	1
43357	2	2012-09-25 18:33:00	TUE	2
43357	3	2012-09-26 18:33:00		
43357	4	2012-09-27 19:47:00	THU	4
43357	5	2012-09-28 19:47:00		
43357	6	2012-09-29 19:47:00		
43357	7	2012-09-30 19:47:00		
43357	8	2012-10-01 19:47:00		
43357	9	2012-10-02 19:47:00		
43357	10	2012-10-03 19:47:00		
43357	11	2012-10-04 19:47:00		
43357	12	2012-10-05 19:47:00		
43357	13	2012-10-06 19:47:00		
43357	14	2012-10-07 19:47:00		

Note that aside from three columns, the filler records are blank. These three columns are the minimum the processing software requires to accept the dataset.

```python
import pandas as pd
import datetime as dt
import os; home = os.path.expanduser('~')

df = pd.read_csv(home + '/datafile/datetime_input.csv', sep=',', encoding='utf-8')

# convert datetime strings in datetime to datetime objects
# sort df: order first by subject, then by datetime
df['datetime'] = pd.to_datetime(df.datetime)
df.sort_values(by=['ID', 'datetime'], inplace=True)
df = df.reset_index(drop=True)
same_day_entries = 'same day entries for: '

newDF = pd.DataFrame(columns=df.columns)
newDF_row = 0

''' fill in gaps in dates with blank records
'''
# if (df.loc[1, 'datetime'].date() - df.loc[0, 'datetime'].date()).days == 1:
for row in range(len(df)-1):
    # if subject is the same
    if df.loc[row, 'ID'] == df.loc[row+1, 'ID']:
        #...and if the dates are the same
        if (df.loc[row+1, 'datetime'].date() - df.loc[row, 'datetime'].date()).days == 0:
            # update newDF, increment newDF_row
            newDF.loc[newDF_row] = df.loc[row]
            print(f"same_day_entries {df.loc[row, 'ID']}")
            newDF_row += 1
        # ...and if the dates are in sequence
        elif (df.loc[row+1, 'datetime'].date() - df.loc[row, 'datetime'].date()).days == 1:
            # update newDF, increment newDF_row
            newDF.loc[newDF_row] = df.loc[row]
            newDF_row += 1
```

17.3 Datetime in Datasets

```
            #...and if the dates have a gap
            elif (df.loc[row+1, 'datetime'].date() - df.loc[row, 'datetime'].date()).days > 1:
                newDF.loc[newDF_row] = df.loc[row]
                newDF_row += 1
                # iterate over the difference between the two dates
                for date_diff in range((df.loc[row+1, 'datetime'].date() -\
                                        df.loc[row, 'datetime'].date()).days-1):
                    # increment newDF_row, insert new record into newDF
                    newDF.loc[newDF_row, 'ID'] = df.loc[row, 'ID']
                    newDF.loc[newDF_row, 'datetime'] = newDF.loc[newDF_row-1, 'datetime'] +\
                                                       dt.timedelta(days=1)
                    newDF_row += 1
        else:
            # the subject is NOT the same
            newDF.loc[newDF_row] = df.loc[row]
            newDF_row += 1
newDF.loc[newDF_row] = df.loc[row+1]
```

Figure 17-4 The original plan

The original plan was to use a single for-loop to iterate through the dataset, find gaps in date entries for a volunteer, then fill the gap with the records and requisite column info—so fix the dataset in a single pass through it.

In other words, the planned time complexity of the script was to be **O(n)**.

Figure 17-5 The records of 3376 after passing through the first for-loop

```
113  3376  2012-11-27 00:04:00  TUE  2
114  3376  2012-11-27 18:10:00  TUE  2
115  3376  2012-11-28 18:35:00  WED  3
116  3376  2012-11-29 17:52:00  THU  4
117  3376  2012-11-30 20:27:00  FRI  5
118  3376  2012-12-01 17:40:00  SAT  6
119  3376  2012-12-02 20:06:00  SUN  7
120  3376  2012-12-03 20:06:00  NaN  NaN
121  3376  2012-12-04 15:27:00  TUE  2
122  3376  2012-12-05 20:45:00  WED  3
123  3376  2012-12-06 20:45:00  NaN  NaN
124  3376  2012-12-07 18:57:00  FRI  5
125  3376  2012-12-08 17:24:00  SAT  6
```

However, I couldn't get everything done in a single pass. Note that for 3376, there are only 13 records, which is true of many records, and that it contains two entries for the same date (but different times).

A pass of the modified dataset through a second for-loop is necessary to get the dataset into the state set by the specification.

```python
import pandas as pd
import datetime as dt
import os; home = os.path.expanduser('~')

# first, use powershell to change character encoding of file to utf8
# so that python can read it.
# PS C:\Users\cns-jderry> powershell -Command "Get-Content python\daily.txt
#    -Encoding Unicode | Set-Content -Encoding UTF8 python\daily_utf8.txt"

df = pd.read_csv(home + '/datafile/datetime_input.csv', sep=',', encoding='utf-8')

# convert datetime strings in datetime to datetime objects
# sort df: order first by subject, then by datetime
```

```python
df['datetime'] = pd.to_datetime(df.datetime)
df.sort_values(by=['ID', 'datetime'], inplace=True)
df = df.reset_index(drop=True)
same_day_entries = 'same day entries for: '

newDF = pd.DataFrame(columns=df.columns)
newDF_row = 0

# fill in gaps in dates with blank records
#   if (df.loc[1, 'datetime'].date() - df.loc[0, 'datetime'].date()).days == 1:
for row in range(len(df)-1):
    # if subject is the same
    if df.loc[row, 'ID'] == df.loc[row+1, 'ID']:
        #...and if the dates are the same
        if (df.loc[row+1, 'datetime'].date() \
            - df.loc[row, 'datetime'].date()).days == 0:
            # update newDF, increment newDF_row
            newDF.loc[newDF_row] = df.loc[row]
            print(f"same_day_entries {df.loc[row, 'ID']}")
            newDF_row += 1
        # ...and if the dates are in sequence
        elif (df.loc[row+1, 'datetime'].date() \
            - df.loc[row, 'datetime'].date()).days == 1:
            # update newDF, increment newDF_row
            newDF.loc[newDF_row] = df.loc[row]
            newDF_row += 1
        #...and if the dates have a gap
        elif (df.loc[row+1, 'datetime'].date() \
            - df.loc[row, 'datetime'].date()).days > 1:
            newDF.loc[newDF_row] = df.loc[row]
            newDF_row += 1
            # iterate over the difference between the two dates
            for date_diff in range((df.loc[row+1, 'datetime'].date() \
                                    - df.loc[row, 'datetime'].date()).days-1):
                # increment newDF_row, insert new record into newDF
                newDF.loc[newDF_row, 'ID'] = df.loc[row, 'ID']
                newDF.loc[newDF_row, 'datetime'] =\
                newDF.loc[newDF_row-1, 'datetime'] + dt.timedelta(days=1)
                newDF_row += 1
    else:
        # the subject is NOT the same
        newDF.loc[newDF_row] = df.loc[row]
        newDF_row += 1

newDF.loc[newDF_row] = df.loc[row+1]

'''update the df with the newDF, insert columns;
append entries for ID counts less than 14.
'''
print("\n")
df = newDF
df.insert(loc=1, column='entry_no', value=0)

newDF = pd.DataFrame(columns=df.columns)
newDF_row = 0
```

17.3 Datetime in Datasets

```python
entry_cnt = 1
for row in range(len(df)-1):
    # if subject is the same...
    if df.loc[row, 'ID'] == df.loc[row+1, 'ID']:
        df.loc[row, 'entry_no'] = entry_cnt
        entry_cnt += 1 # increment subject record counter
        newDF.loc[newDF_row] = df.loc[row]
        newDF_row += 1
    # if subject is not the same...
    elif df.loc[row, 'ID'] != df.loc[row+1, 'ID']:
        df.loc[row, 'entry_no'] = entry_cnt
        newDF.loc[newDF_row] = df.loc[row]
        newDF_row += 1
        if entry_cnt < 14:
            print(f"missing entries: {int(df.loc[row, 'ID'])} : {entry_cnt}")
            for date_diff in range(entry_cnt+1,15):
                # increment newDF_row, insert new record into newDF
                newDF.loc[newDF_row, 'entry_no'] = date_diff
                newDF.loc[newDF_row, 'ID'] = df.loc[row, 'ID']
                newDF.loc[newDF_row, 'datetime'] = newDF.loc[newDF_row-1, 'datetime'] \
                                                    + dt.timedelta(days=1)
                newDF_row += 1
        entry_cnt = 1 # reset to 1

newDF.to_csv(home + '/datafile/datetime_output.csv', sep='\t', index=False)
```

Figure 17-6 The final working script

The dataset in a Pandas dataframe is processed through a second for-loop.

In other words, the time complexity of the script is **O(2n)**.

Figure 17-7 The records of 3376 after passing through the second for-loop

```
128 3376   1    2012-11-27 00:04:00   TUE   2
129 3376   2    2012-11-27 18:10:00   TUE   2
130 3376   3    2012-11-28 18:35:00   WED   3
131 3376   4    2012-11-29 17:52:00   THU   4
132 3376   5    2012-11-30 20:27:00   FRI   5
133 3376   6    2012-12-01 17:40:00   SAT   6
134 3376   7    2012-12-02 20:06:00   SUN   7
135 3376   8    2012-12-03 20:06:00
136 3376   9    2012-12-04 15:27:00   TUE   2
137 3376   10   2012-12-05 20:45:00   WED   3
138 3376   11   2012-12-06 20:45:00
139 3376   12   2012-12-07 18:57:00   FRI   5
140 3376   13   2012-12-08 17:24:00   SAT   6
141 3376   14   2012-12-09 17:24:00
```

Although the researchers believe that this script is good enough to use, it should nevertheless be considered a working draft, one in need of further work.

This divergence of opinions brings up a new, practical issue with regard to the developing of code. How much time and effort should a programmer put into a script or function?

The real-world answer is: it depends.

If you are writing code that only you will use—and it's not many lines long and you will be using it only a few times—then leaving it as a working draft might be ok.

I say "might" because you might use it later, or you might want to provide it to a colleague later, in which case you'll want to ensure that it's easy to read and so easy to maintain and that it's easy for users to understand and run.

If you're sharing your code, and colleagues are reporting problems now and then using it, I believe it's time to refactor your code and try to resolve those issues.

This means you may have to make your code more robust, ensuring that only expected input is passed into your implementation of an algorithm by placing garbage filters between the user and the implementation. Or it may mean rewriting your code to accept more or broader conditions (a greater temperature range, for example) than you wrote your code originally to handle.

In this specific case, I believe that as long as users of the script are using it and aren't asking for changes, let it ride. Remember: Not only is their time valuable—so is yours.

17.4 Introduction to Parallel Programming

> In this class, we have seen examples of hardware parallelization in our computers: 64-bit buses, GPUs, multicore CPUs, and SIMD registers.
> In this lesson, we consider parallel programming by writing a parallelized function to process one of our datasets.
> Parallel programming takes advantage of "concurrency," which describes a computer's ability to execute more than one task at a time.
> In most of our lessons, we have made use of serial programming, meaning that a single core has processed the instructions in our program one at a time.
> Today, we can have multiple cores processing the same instructions through parallel programming in Python. The commonest parallel programming tasks written and run by STEM researchers are to process large datasets.

> The CPUs or cores that are used for a parallel programming job are all together referred to as a "cluster." The members of a cluster are referred to as "engines."
> In a cluster, one engine is designated the "supervisor"; the other engines are referred to as "workers."
> The supervisor is responsible for dividing up a dataset into roughly equal parts, broadcasting the subsets, along with the instructions to process the subsets, to the workers. The supervisor works on its own subset.
> As the workers finish processing their subsets, they send their resultsets to the supervisor, which is responsible for assembling them into a single resultset, preserving the order of the original dataset.

Perhaps the most common use of parallel programming by STEM researchers is to have a large dataset broken up into equally sized subsets, then have each subset processed by a computer or a core—all the computers or cores involved in this task using the same instructions to process their subsets—then have the resultsets put together into a single resultset, perhaps for further processing.

This is what we will do in this lesson.

We will be using the cores of our computer's CPU in an ipyparallel cluster that can backend either an IPython or Jupyter notebook session.

Before we begin, it bears noting that while the naïve programmer might believe that in parallel programming, if one core can complete a parallelizable task in one unit time, then surely two cores can complete it in 1/2 that time, three cores in 1/3 the time, and so on, the real situation is not so straightforward.

17.4 Introduction to Parallel Programming

Basically, only one part of the overall task has been parallelized. The other parts are still serialized—in other words, the other parts can be done by only one computer. This includes breaking up the dataset to be processed into subsets and later putting together all the resultsets into a single resultset while preserving the order of the original dataset.

Practically speaking, this can mean that eight cores working on a parallelized task complete that task in only half the time that a single core would by working on the serialized equivalent.

Fortunately, even laptops today come with many-core CPUs. If you have a sufficient quantity of cores, you too may find that allocating eight cores to a task in order to cut in half its time to completion worth it.

Other issues that touch upon running parallel programs that we should be aware of relate to the consumption of compute cycles and system memory. When running a parallel program, each core in the cluster needs its own fraction of system memory to run its subtask. You need to be aware of the fact that running too many subtasks for your system risks slowing your system to a crawl or even effectively freezing it, as well as exhausting the system memory.

Sizing a parallelized task for the system that will run it is a bit of an art; however, you should use only a fraction of the available cores and memory to run your task.

Now to run parallelized tasks.

Currently, one creates and starts a cluster in Bash. In your home directory, open a Bash terminal and type:

```
$ ipcluster start -n 4 --location=localhost
```

In the terminal window, you'll see messages regarding the state of the cluster. Most of them will come from the IPController. Once you see that all your engines are ready, you can start your session in the Jupyter notebook.

```python
from ipyparallel import Client
import os; home = os.path.expanduser('~')

with open(home + '/datafile/reformatted_Unigene.fa') as inFile:
    LoS = inFile.read().splitlines()
LoL = []
for record in LoS:
    LoL.append(record.split())
```

Figure 17-8 Initializing our parallel programming session

Aside from initializations we've seen throughout the book, we import **Client** from **ipyparallel**.

Now we're ready to rock.

```python
rc = Client()
dv = rc[:]

# the parallelized function,
# which renders the reverse complement
# from each record's data string,
# and appends it to the end of the record
@dv.parallel(block = True)
def process_LoL(LoL):
    def revCompl(nuclStr):
```

```
            outputStr, complDict =\
            '', {'A':'T', 'C':'G', 'G':'C', 'T':'A', 'N':'N'}
            for nucleotide in nuclStr:
                outputStr = complDict[nucleotide]\
                 + outputStr
            return outputStr

        for record in LoL:
            revc = revCompl(record[6])
            record.append(revc)
        return LoL

results = process_LoL(LoL)
```

Figure 17-9 The parallelized function

We start by creating an instance of a client, then specifying that our variable **dv** includes all the engines in the cluster.

The decorator function **dv.parallel()** parallelizes the function below. It has specific uses and limitations. Please refer to the online manual for ipyparallel.

Note that Python allows us to write functions within functions, and I have used this to get a copy of **revCompl()** to all of the cores in the cluster.

Finally, each core creates a reverse complement string of the nucleotide string in the records of its subset; then the reverse complement string is appended to the record.

Once the subset has been processed, the resultset is returned.

On the last line of the computation cell, we invoke the parallelized function, and the resultset becomes the value of a variable named "results" so we can either save the resultset or process it further.

```
# to see all the instances of python running in parallel
# first open a terminal window and run: top
# watch top after you start the profiling statement below:
%timeit process_LoL(LoL)

1.42 s ± 16.8 ms per loop (mean ± std. dev. of 7 runs, 1 loop each)
```

Figure 17-10 Profiling the running of our parallelized function with eight cores

We associate parallel programming with large improvements in the time it takes for a task to run to completion, and it's true that parallelizing tasks can greatly speed them up.

But it's worth noting that not all algorithms can be parallelized.

It's also worth noting that latencies, including the time it takes for the supervisor to send and receive instructions and data to and from the farthest worker, can slow down the overall performance of a cluster.

Finally, the performance increase, measured against core count, is not linear. In fact, at some point, adding cores to a cluster in no significant way improves time performance.

Chapter Summary

In this chapter, we've covered a few useful topics that we weren't able to fit into earlier chapters. We've looked at how we might use python sets when working with datasets, how to work with datetime stamps in datasets, and how to process large datasets using parallel programming.

Writing a Large Project   18

In our last chapter, we will take on a large project that will allow us to make use of many of the concepts we've learned. These include sketching out a top-down design, organizing our code into subroutines and a main routine using our top-down design as a guide, writing unit tests, then following the test-develop-test cycles of test-driven development.

18.1 Putting It All Together: Solving Triangles

> In this chapter, we will work on writing a function in which the user passes in the values of any three of six parts of a triangle—sides or angles—and the function returns a solution tuple with all the sides and angles for that triangle.[a]
>
> We will start with a specification, develop a top-down design, write the subroutines to solve the triangles, write the garbage filter to ensure that only expected input is passed into the function, and write unit tests for our code.
>
> As we go, will lint our code with pylint and implement its suggestions.
>
> Finally, we will refactor our code—that is, we will do major rewrites of it—with an eye on improving it. For this project, this means we will have three versions of our function as we go from a working rough draft of the function to a more polished product.
>
> I hope that working through a project together will give you the experience to start working through your own projects.
>
> ---
> [a]The astute reader who has studied plane geometry will immediately point out that there are exceptions. The angle-angle-angel triangle (the AAA triangle), in which the three knowns of a triangle are its angles, can be solved by an infinite number of congruent triangles. Additionally, the side-side-angle and angle-side-side triangles (the SSA and ASS triangles, respectively) are known as ambiguous cases because with the given information, two different triangles for each are possible. These cases will influence the choices we make while developing our function.

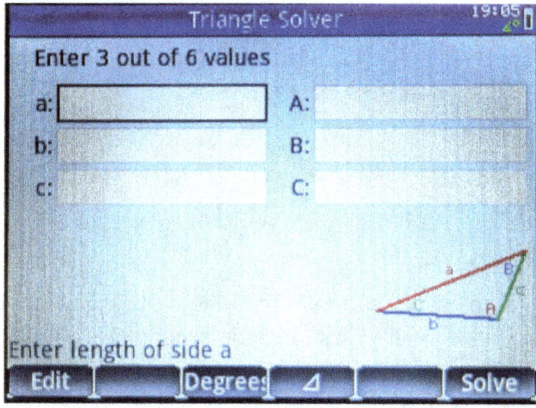

(a) HP Prime Calculator

(b) The Triangle Solver App

Figure 18-1 Programmable calculators since at least the 1970s (with the TI-58/59 calculators) have shipped with code that, given three of six values, computes the missing angles and sides of a triangle. Photos by author

These calculations make use of the Law of Sines and the Law of Cosines.

In this chapter, we will go develop our own **solve_triangle()** function, with a focus more on the development process than on the algorithms.

Note how clean and simple the user interface of HP Prime Triangle Solver App is.

Solving for the missing angles and sides of a triangle, given three of them, are standard geometry and trigonometry problems assigned to middle school and high school students.

In fact, these problems have been given their own names:

SSS triangle: In which the sides are known, solve for the angles
AAA triangle: In which the angles are known, solve for sides (setting one of unit length 1)
SAS triangle: In which two sides and the angle between them are known
ASA triangle: In which two angles and the side between them are known
AAS triangle, **SAA triangle**, **SSA triangle**, and the **ASS triangle**, preserving the order of sides and angles in the problem name.

These problems can be solved using The Law of Sines and The Law of Cosines.

Figure 18-2 Solving the triangles

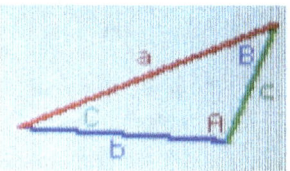

18.2 Design Considerations

Using the triangle drawn on the HP Prime Triangle Solver App as a reference, we see the ways in which the Law of Sines and Law of Cosines can be used to solve for the missing parts of different triangles.

Law of Sines.
$$\frac{sinA}{a} = \frac{sinB}{b} = \frac{sinC}{c}$$

Law of Cosines.

$$a^2 = b^2 + c^2 - 2 \cdot b \cdot c \cdot cosA$$
$$b^2 = a^2 + c^2 - 2 \cdot a \cdot c \cdot cosB$$
$$c^2 = a^2 + b^2 - 2 \cdot a \cdot b \cdot cosC$$

Figure 18-3 The Law of Sines and Law of Cosines

Figure 18-4 Law of Sines. Scan or click the QR code to go to the Wikipedia article. https://en.wikipedia.org/wiki/Law_of_sines

Figure 18-5 Law of Cosines. Scan or click the QR code to go to the Wikipedia article. https://en.wikipedia.org/wiki/Law_of_cosines

While developing our **solve_triangle**() function, we can use both our calculator and online tutoring sites to write our unit tests and to verify that our code returns correct answers.

18.2 Design Considerations

Modularize. Use subroutines.
> Kernighan and Plauger (Kernighan and Plauger. *The Elements of Programming Style*, 2d Edition. McGraw-Hill. 1978. p.61.)

Write and test a big program in small pieces.
> ibid(*ibid*, p77.)

Programming is an act of creativity, shaped—as are other acts of creativity—by knowledge and experience. We start by sketching the outlines of our program, what it should accept as input and what it should return as output, and build our code around that.

Given the specification—that our program should solve for the different triangles, named by the three given parts—we conceive that each triangle should be solved by its own subroutine.

And so the main routine should accept user input and return the output; and in between, it should pass user input to the correct subroutine.

This is the outline of our plan, to be filled in and refined as we go.

18.3 Input and Output

```
solve_triangle(side1=None, side2=None, side3=None,\
               angle1=None, angle2=None, angle3=None,\
               degrees=True, rnd=False, dec_digs=None)\
    -> tuple
```

Figure 18-6 We'll start by defining the name of the function, what it takes for input, and what it returns as output

Note that all of the arguments are named arguments. The first six are for inputting the three known parts of the triangle. Those that take no input from the user are set by default to **None**.

The next argument sets input/output of angle units in degrees or radians. And the last two let the user set rounding of output, as well as how many decimal digits to round to.

The function returns a tuple of all six parts of the triangle, in the same order as the parts in the function's argument list.

Note that this argument list of triangle parts is a knock-off of the Triangle Solver App, in that all six parts are uniquely labeled, allowing the user to exactly specify which parts are defined.

```
>>>solve_triangle(side1=7, side2=5, angle3=49, rnd=True, decDig=2)
(7, 5, 5.3, 85.59, 45.41, 49.0) # angles in degrees, rounding to 2 decimal digits
```

Figure 18-7 Input and output for an *SAS triangle*

The user specifies which parts of the triangle are given using **keyword=value** pairs. The user also specifies that output is to be rounded to 2 decimal digits. Because **degrees=True** by default, input and output angles are given in degrees.

What your program takes for input, and what it renders as output, makes up much, if not all, of the specification. Even now we should be asking ourselves if the function interface will be easy for our users to understand and work with. We may not really know until the function is working and we have a chance to play around with it ourselves (our even not until we've deployed it in our lab's production environment and our users start working with it); but it bears keeping in mind throughout development that the user interface (UI) should be as easy to use and as easy to work with as possible—intuitive, even.

And the more we get this right now, the less work we'll have to do to make it right later.

18.4 Organization of the Code

In Section 12.2, **"Writing Programs: Converting a Top-Down Design into a Program of Subroutines,"** we wrote our main routine and subroutines together, in the same file.

As programs get larger and more complex, we prefer to write their parts across several files. Again, this makes it easier to isolate units of code for troubleshooting and replacement.

In writing this function, we'll write our subroutines into a separate file, which we'll import into the file that holds the main routine. In other words, the **solve_triangle**() function takes two text files, one that we'll call **solve_triangle.py** and another that we'll call **solve_triangle_sbr.py** (**sbr** stands for **"subroutines"**).

And what code should we write as subroutines?

Answer: The segment of code that solves the **SSS triangle** should be its own subroutine, the segment of code that solves the **AAA triangle** should be its own, as well as the segment of code that solves the **SAS triangle**, and so on.

In other words, we are going to write a function for each of the eight different triangle problems, and each will return a tuple with all six parts solved.

The main routine will consist primarily of housekeeping chores:

1) ensure that user input is expected input (the garbage filter),
2) convert input angles to radians (the default angular unit of NumPy, as well as Python's built-in math module),
3) pass user input into the correct subroutine,
4) convert output angles to degrees if **degrees=True**; and
5) format output to user-specified number of decimal digits (or with full floating-point mantissa if **rnd=False**, which it is by default).

Please note that we have yet to write any code. We are still thinking about what we're going to write and, in outline, how we're going to write it.

18.5 Test-Driven Development (TDD) and Unit Testing

For years, I advised students to test, test, and test their code by hand and to ensure that the output of sample input is right or looks right. Of course, this assumes that students develop code knowing how it will transform or reformat input, that they already are in possession of test input/output, and that they don't forget to test their code with their test input.

Unit testing automates the testing of code with test input/output. We have to write unit tests for each unit of code we write (be it a function or a script); but once the unit tests are written, we simply invoke them on the Bash command line after we develop or revise our code to make sure that the code gives correct results once written and keeps doing so as we develop it further or refactor it.

There is a software development methodology called "extreme programming" that uses unit testing to do what is called "test-driven development," or TDD. In TDD, programmers write unit tests before they start programming. Basically, in TDD, you know what the output should be, given the input, and you write and revise until your code produces that output, given your test input.

Although I do not code this way habitually, I believe that it aligns with my own write-test-revise habits, and so although I did not write unit tests before developing the **solve_triangle**() function, in this chapter, we will do so. Our test cases will come from the Triangle Solver App on the HP Prime calculator, as well as online geometry/trigonometry tutoring sites that show how to solve these problems.

18.6 Linting Our Code

Finally, as we develop our code, we will run **pylint** against it to see how we might clean it up and improve our coding style.

18.7 Pencil to Paper: Our Top-Down Design

Specification: Write a function that takes three parts of a triangle (angles or sides) and solves for the other three parts. The input should allow a user to specify degrees or radians, as well as whether output values should be rounded. The output should be a tuple of the sides and angles, in that order.

Input	Transformation	Output
garbage filter	if...elif...else branch to choose correct subroutine for given parts	if degrees: convert angles from radians
		if rnd: round values to number of dec_digs
ensure number of parts == 3		
ensure given parts are positive reals		
ensure dec_digs is natural number		
ensure degrees and rnd are bools		

if degrees:
   convert angles to radians

solve_sss()	solve_aaa()	solve_asa()	solve_sas()	solve_saa()	solve_aas()	solve_ssa()	solve_ass()
Law of Cosines. $\cos(C) = a^2 + b^2 - c^2 / 2*a*b$	Law of Sines. infinite solutions! make 1 side unit length.	Law of Sines. ang3 = pi - (ang1 + ang2)	Law of Cosines. $a2 = b2 + c2 - 2bc \cos A$	Law of Sines to solve for the 2d angle		Law of Sines. 3 possibilities: 1) no solution 2) 1 solution 3) 2 solutions	sin A > a/c: no solution sin A = a/c: 1 solution sin A < a/c: 2 solutions

Figure 18-8 Top-down design for **solve_triangle()**, v1

Input includes the garbage filter and the conversion to radians.

The transformative functions are subroutines that we'll write into our second file.

Output ensures that angles are in the user-specified unit (degrees or radians) and that values are rounded if the user sets **rnd=True**.

The top-down design serves as our guide as we develop our code and, like everything else, can be changed as the need arises.

Now to Start Writing Code

> Say what you mean, simply and directly.
> Kernighan and Plauger (Kernighan and Plauger. *The Elements of Programming Style*, 2d Edition. McGraw-Hill. 1978. p9.)

When I develop code in a graphical desktop environment, I like to have two terminal windows open side by side. I use the left-hand terminal to develop in IPython, and I use the right-hand terminal as a scratchpad—I might use it to execute tasks in Bash, or try out some Python code to see if it works like I need it to before writing it into code in the left-hand terminal.

Make a directory in your home directory called "development"; and within it, another directory called "solve_triangle." Navigate into that directory and open two terminal windows.

```
$ mkdir -p ~/development/solve_triangle && cd ~/development/solve_triangle
```

In one, launch the IPython interactive shell. In the other, create three text files. Call the first "solve_triangle.py," call the second "solve_triangle_sbr.py," and call the third "test_solve_triangle.py." The first will hold our **solve_triangle()** function, the second will hold the subroutines, and the third, our unit tests.

Make sure that the working directory of both terminal sessions is:

```
~/development/solve_triangle
```

```
(left window)$ ipython
(right window)$ touch {solve_triangle.py,solve_triangle_sbr.py,test_solve_triangle.py}
```

Figure 18-9 Note that by enclosing our filenames in curly braces and separating them by commas, we can create all the files in a single statement

18.8 Our First Unit Test

Let's create our first unit tests before we start coding our function. Open **test_solve_triangle.py** in **vim**, and at the top of the file, write:

```
import unittest
from solve_triangle import *
from solve_triangle_sbr import *

class test_solve_triangle(unittest.TestCase):
```

We have to import the built-in module **unittest** to make use of Python's built-in unit tests. Then we have to import the modules whose functions we want to test. (We import **solve_triangle_sbr** in case we want to test individual functions within that file.)

Finally, the unit test module works by having us create an object that holds our unit tests as methods, so we write the class that, when run, creates an instance of the object. Hence the line:
class test_solve_triangle(unittest.TestCase):

At the bottom of the file, write:

```
if __name__== '__main__':
    unittest.main()
```

Save your changes but don't quit (just yet). In vim command mode, type:
   :w!
When we invoke **solve_triangle()** with these values:
(side1=7, side2=5, angle3=49, rnd=True, decDig=2)
we want it to return:
(7, 5, 5.3, 85.59, 45.41, 49.0)

The unit test for that is this method:

```python
def test_solve_triangle_sss1(self):
    result = solve_triangle(side1=3, side2=4, side3=5, rnd=True, dec_digs=2)
    self.assertEqual(result, (3, 4, 5, 36.87, 53.13, 90.0))
```

*

The start of your unit test should look like this:

```python
import unittest
from solve_triangle import *
from solve_triangle_sbr import *

class test_solve_triangle(unittest.TestCase):

    def test_solve_triangle_sss1(self):
        result = solve_triangle(side1=3, side2=4, side3=5, rnd=True, dec_digs=2)
        self.assertEqual(result, (3, 4, 5, 36.87, 53.13, 90.0))

if __name__ == '__main__':
    unittest.main()
```

Figure 18-10 test_solve_triangle.py, first draft

Now save your changes and quit:
:wq

18.9 Our First Draft of solve_triangle.py

```python
''' solve_triangle(). we put the function into this file.
'''

# initialization
from solve_triangle_sbr import \
    solve_sss, solve_aaa, solve_asa, solve_sas,\
    solve_ssa, solve_ass, solve_aas, solve_saa

def solve_triangle(side1=None, side2=None, side3=None,\
                   angle1=None, angle2=None, angle3=None,\
                   degrees=True, rnd=False, dec_digs=None) -> tuple:
    return ()
```

Figure 18-11 solve_triangle.py, first draft

Write your solve_triangle.py so it looks like this in **vim**.

We'll write a module comment at the top of the file, we'll write an initialization block in which we'll import the subroutines from the second file by name; and we'll create the function with its header, its tuple of named arguments, the type hint showing that the output is a tuple, and finally a return statement that returns an empty tuple.

---

* This test applies only to a **SSS triangle**.
In the finished unit test file, each of the types of triangle should be tested.

18.10 Running Our First Unit Test

```
$ python test_solve_triangle.py
Traceback (most recent call last):
File "/home/user/development/solve_triangle/test_solve_triangle.py", line 2, in <module>
from solve_triangle import *
File "/home/user/development/solve_triangle/solve_triangle.py", line 2, in <module>
from solve_triangle_sbr import \
ImportError: cannot import name 'solve_sss' from 'solve_triangle_sbr'
(/home/user/development/solve_triangle/solve_triangle_sbr.py)
```

Figure 18-12 Testing *solve_triangle.py*, first draft

In TDD (test-driven development), we test before we code, so we expect the first test(s) to fail, as indeed it does here.

However, it's not failing the unit test. Rather, the **Traceback** is reporting an **ImportError**.

It's telling us there is no function called "solve_sss" to import. In fact, all the subroutines we called to import in **solve_triangle.py** from **solve_triangle_sbr** are missing.

Let's fill them in.

```python
'''  subroutines of the solve_triangle() function.
'''


def solve_sss(side1, side2, side3, angle1, angle2, angle3) -> tuple:
    return side1, side2, side3, angle1, angle2, angle3

def solve_aaa(side1, side2, side3, angle1, angle2, angle3) -> tuple:
    return side1, side2, side3, angle1, angle2, angle3

def solve_sas(side1, side2, side3, angle1, angle2, angle3) -> tuple:
    return side1, side2, side3, angle1, angle2, angle3

def solve_asa(side1, side2, side3, angle1, angle2, angle3) -> tuple:
    return side1, side2, side3, angle1, angle2, angle3

def solve_saa(side1, side2, side3, angle1, angle2, angle3) -> tuple:
    return side1, side2, side3, angle1, angle2, angle3

def solve_aas(side1, side2, side3, angle1, angle2, angle3) -> tuple:
    return side1, side2, side3, angle1, angle2, angle3

def solve_ssa(side1, side2, side3, angle1, angle2, angle3) -> tuple:
    return side1, side2, side3, angle1, angle2, angle3

def solve_ass(side1, side2, side3, angle1, angle2, angle3) -> tuple:
    return side1, side2, side3, angle1, angle2, angle3
```

Figure 18-13 solve_triangle_sbr.py, first draft

Make sure to save changes to disk and quit vim.

And now let's rerun our unit test:

```
$ python test_solve_triangle.py
F
======================================================================
FAIL: test_solve_triangle_sss1 (__main__.test_solve_triangle.test_solve_triangle_sss1)
----------------------------------------------------------------------
Traceback (most recent call last):
File "/home/user/development/solve_triangle/test_solve_triangle.py", line 7, in test_solve_triangle_sss1
self.assertEqual(result, (3, 4, 5, 36.87, 53.13, 90.0))
AssertionError: Tuples differ: () != (3, 4, 5, 36.87, 53.13, 90.0)

Second tuple contains 6 additional elements.
First extra element 0:
3

- ()
+ (3, 4, 5, 36.87, 53.13, 90.0)

----------------------------------------------------------------------
Ran 1 test in 0.000s
```

Figure 18-14 Testing *solve_triangle.py*, first draft, second time

In test-driven development, we test before we code, expecting the test(s) to fail, as indeed it does here.

Now we see a failed unit test. **Traceback** is reporting an **AssertionError**, straight from our unit test.

The expected tuple and the returned tuple differ, which is what we expect.

Wonderful.

Insofar as we want failures and errors reported from the unit tests, this failure looks better than the first failure.

18.11 Running solve_triangle Function the First Time

```
In [1]: from solve_triangle import *

In [2]: solve_triangle(side1=3, side2=4, side3=5, rnd=True, dec_digs=2)
Out[2]: ()
```

Figure 18-15 Running our function the first time within IPython

First, we import the module that the file's in, then we invoke the function on the command line, passing in named arguments.

As expected, the function returns an empty tuple.

How things stand: We have a second file full of empty subroutines, a main function that returns an empty tuple, no matter what we pass into it, and a unit test that fails.

In the real world, our position looks pretty weak; but in the world of programming, we're off to a great start.

18.12 A Note on Structured Design

> **Stubs and Drivers**
> A **stub** is "[a] dummy procedure or function that helps in testing...A stub has the same name and interface as the procedure or function that actually would be called by the part of the program being tested, but it is actually much simpler."
> A **driver** is "[a] simple main program [or routine] that is used to call a procedure or function being tested." (Dale and Weems, *Introduction To Pascal and Structured Design*, 4th Edition. 1994. pg 339. *ibid*. pg 340.)

Our code starts as being just enough to run unit tests on. It is at its inception, in other words, no more than stubs and a driver.

But we're about to change that.

18.13 Adding Design Comments

At this point, we will add comments to our code regarding the design and implementation of our algorithm(s). These come largely from our top-down design and are meant to guide code development as we implement our proposed solution(s) into code.

Think of these as notes to ourselves. Even as we write them out, we may be thinking of how we will implement the steps they describe into Python.

```python
''' solve_triangle. we put the function into its own module.
'''
# initialization
from numpy import deg2rad, rad2deg
from solve_triangle_sbr import \
solve_sss, solve_aaa, solve_asa, solve_sas,\
solve_ssa, solve_ass, solve_aas, solve_saa

def solve_triangle(side1=None, side2=None, side3=None,\
                   angle1=None, angle2=None, angle3=None,\
                   degrees=True, rnd=False, dec_digs=None) -> tuple:
    '''(pos real, pos real, pos real, pos real, pos real, pos real, bool, bool, int)
        -> tuple,
        where "pos real" means positive real; i.e., positive int or float
    Requires NumPy.
    Given 3 parts of a triangle (sides or angles, as in 3 sides or 1 side and 2 angles),
    return values for all sides and angles.
    Angles can be either all in degrees or all in radians. The default is degrees.
    If rnd=True, results are rounded by the decimal degrees passed into the function.
    The default is no rounding.
    Output tuple follows the same ordering as the function's argument list:
    (side1, side2, side3, angle1, angle2, angle3)
    Examples:
    >>>solve_triangle(side1=7, side2=5, angle3=49, rnd=True, dec_digs=2)
        (7, 5, 5.3, 85.59, 45.41, 49.0) # angles in degrees, rounding to 2 decimal digits
    '''
    # begin garbage filter
```

```
    # ensure side and angle values are positive reals.
    # ensure degrees and rnd are bools.
    # ensure dec_digs is a natural number.
    # end garbage filter

    # convert degrees to radians for calculations.
    # numpy uses radians for angular measurements.

    ##### BEGIN MAIN #####
    # the conditional branching determines which subroutine applies
    # for the given input
    # each subroutine returns a return_tuple
    ##### END MAIN #####

    # convert radians to degrees if degrees==True

    # if rnd==True;
    #        value = round(value, dec_digs) # for each value in return tuple
    # return a tuple
    return () # return tuple
```

Figure 18-16 *solve_triangle.py* with comments

Writing out what your code should do is a great way to force you to think about how you're going to make the machine do what you want it to do.

Writing out the docstring makes it clear what users should enter for input, as you conceive it, as well as what your function should return to users.

```
''' subroutines of the solve_triangle() function.
'''

def solve_sss(side1, side2, side3, angle1, angle2, angle3) -> tuple:
    '''SSS: We solve using the Law of Cosines.
        cos(C) =  a^2 + b^2 - c^2 / 2 * a * b
    '''
    return side1, side2, side3, angle1, angle2, angle3

def solve_aaa(side1, side2, side3, angle1, angle2, angle3) -> tuple:
    '''AAA: We solve using the Law of Sines.
        Because there are an infinite number of SSS solutions,
        we normalize the result by setting the smallest side to 1.
    '''
    return side1, side2, side3, angle1, angle2, angle3

def solve_sas(side1, side2, side3, angle1, angle2, angle3) -> tuple:
    '''SAS: Given 2 sides, we can solve for the 3d using: a2 = b2 + c2 - 2bc cosA
        Given 3 sides, we can solve for the missing angles using the same formula,
        rearranged.
    '''
    return side1, side2, side3, angle1, angle2, angle3

def solve_asa(side1, side2, side3, angle1, angle2, angle3) -> tuple:
    '''ASA: We can solve for 3d angle with: 180 - (ang1 + ang2).
        We can solve for missing sides using Law of Sines.
```

18.13 Adding Design Comments

```python
        '''
        return side1, side2, side3, angle1, angle2, angle3

def solve_saa(side1, side2, side3, angle1, angle2, angle3) -> tuple:
        '''SAA: Given 2 angles, we use 180 - (angA + angB) to find the 3d.
           Then we use the Law of Sines to find the missing sides.
        '''
        return side1, side2, side3, angle1, angle2, angle3

def solve_aas(side1, side2, side3, angle1, angle2, angle3) -> tuple:
        '''AAS: Given 2 angles, we use 180 - (angA + angB) to find the 3d.
           Then we use the Law of Sines to find the missing sides.
        '''
        return side1, side2, side3, angle1, angle2, angle3

def solve_ssa(side1, side2, side3, angle1, angle2, angle3) -> tuple:
        '''SSA: We use the Law of Sines to solve for the 2d angle.
        '''
        return side1, side2, side3, angle1, angle2, angle3

def solve_ass(side1, side2, side3, angle1, angle2, angle3) -> tuple:
        '''ASS: We use the Law of Sines to solve for the 2d angle.
        '''
        return side1, side2, side3, angle1, angle2, angle3
```

Figure 18-17 solve_triangle_sbr.py with comments

We're now ready to fill in the spaces with code.

Let's review our two files.

solve_triangle.py holds the main function **solve_triangle**(). The function contains:

1) the garbage filter: allows to pass only expected input,
2) deg -> rad & rad -> deg conversions: when the user uses degrees,
3) if...elif branch: to invoke the correct subroutine to solve the triangle (the operational code lies in the subroutines); and
4) formatting output if user sets **rnd==True** by user-set **dec_digs**.

solve_triangle_sbr.py holds the subroutines, and they do the heavy lifting. Each takes a tuple of the three sides and three angles as input, with user input providing the given values, then calculates the missing values. The code in the subroutines is the reason users come to the **solve_triangle**() function; and that main function, basically, contains only the housekeeping chores—testing and formatting the input, then, as needed, formatting the output.

We could have broken the main function down even further. The garbage filter could be a subroutine, written into a separate function, as could the angular measurement conversions, and the rounding code.

Conceived this way, the **solve_triangle**() function would basically be nothing more than an if...elif branch deciding which subroutine to send the three triangle parts to, surrounded by functions testing and preparing input and output.

You could write your solution that way. In fact, there may be style guides in software companies that say you have to write it that way.

But for now, we'll leave our approach as is.

Please keep in mind that this is a rough draft. Recall from the Rules of UNIX Philosophy.

The Rule of Optimization: Prototype before polishing. Get it working before you optimize it.
(Eric S. Raymond. *The Art of UNIX Programming*. Addison-Wesley.2004. p.23)

An experienced programmer starts developing code at a point different than a beginner does, but even experienced programmers know that their rough draft is exactly that—a rough draft.

18.14 Writing Our First Draft

For now, we'll skip the garbage filter, we'll work on the parts of the main function that prepare the input and the output, and we'll write the first parts of the if...elif branch, along with the subroutines they invoke. Then we'll test.

```
# convert degrees to radians for calculations.
# numpy uses radians for angular measurements.
if degrees:
    if angle1:
        angle1 = deg2rad(angle1)
    if angle2:
        angle2 = deg2rad(angle2)
    if angle3:
        angle3 = deg2rad(angle3)

##### BEGIN MAIN #####
# the conditional branching determines which subroutine applies
# for the given input
if side1 and side2 and side3:
    solution_tuple = solve_sss(side1, side2, side3, angle1, angle2, angle3)

elif angle1 and angle2 and angle3:
    solution_tuple = solve_aaa(side1, side2, side3, angle1, angle2, angle3)

else:
    pass
# each subroutine returns a return_tuple
##### END MAIN #####

# convert radians to degrees
if degrees:
    # convert immutable tuple to mutable list
    solution_list = list(solution_tuple)
    # convert the angular values
    solution_list[3], solution_list[4], solution_list[5] =\
        rad2deg(solution_list[3]),\
```

18.14 Writing Our First Draft

```
            rad2deg(solution_list[4]),\
            rad2deg(solution_list[5])
        # coerce the list back into a tuple
        solution_tuple = tuple(solution_list)

    # return a tuple, with and without rounding
    if not rnd:
        return solution_tuple

    # in this return statement, we render a new tuple from converted values
    # in solution_tuple. note that we preserve the order of the values.
    return round(solution_tuple[0], dec_digs), round(solution_tuple[1], dec_digs),\
           round(solution_tuple[2], dec_digs), round(solution_tuple[3], dec_digs),\
           round(solution_tuple[4], dec_digs), round(solution_tuple[5], dec_digs)
```

Figure 18-18 Filling in the code in the main function

If the user uses/wants degrees, the machine has to convert her angular measurements to radians, as this is what NumPy—and even the built-in math module—uses. So if the bool **degrees** is true, convert the angular measurement inputs to radians using the NumPy function **deg2rad()**. The equivalent math module function is **radians(deg)**.

Likewise, if the user uses/wants degrees, the machine has to convert its angular measurement output to degrees. Again, we test if this is true using the bool **degrees**. Because tuples are immutable, we have to convert the **solution_tuple** to a list, modify the angular measurement values, then coerce the list back to a tuple.

Also, we have to tell the machine what to do if the user doesn't want rounded output, as well as what to do if she does. We have the machine test the value of the bool **rnd** to follow the correct option.

Please note that the solution has two **return** statements.

```
def solve_sss(side1, side2, side3, angle1, angle2, angle3) -> tuple:
    """SSS: we solve using the Law of Cosines.
        cos(C) =   a^2 + b^2 - c^2 / 2 * a * b
    """
    # calculate angles
    angle1 = arccos((side2**2 + side3**2 - side1**2)/(2 * side2 * side3))
    angle2 = arccos((side1**2 + side3**2 - side2**2)/(2 * side1 * side3))
    angle3 = arccos((side1**2 + side2**2 - side3**2)/(2 * side1 * side2))

    return side1, side2, side3, angle1, angle2, angle3

def solve_aaa(side1, side2, side3, angle1, angle2, angle3) -> tuple:
    """AAA: we solve using the Law of Sines.
        Because there are an infinite number of SSS solutions,
        we normalize the result by setting the smallest side to 1.
    """
    # calculate sines
    sin1, sin2, sin3 = sin(angle1), sin(angle2), sin(angle3)

    max_sin = max(sin1, sin2, sin3)
    if max_sin == sin1:
```

```
            side1 = 1 / max_sin
            side2 = side1 * sin2 / max_sin
            side3 = side1 * sin3 / max_sin
        elif max_sin == sin2:
            side2 = 1 / max_sin
            side1 = side2 * sin1 / max_sin
            side3 = side2 * sin3 / max_sin
        elif max_sin == sin3:
            side3 = 1 / max_sin
            side1 = side3 * sin1 / max_sin
            side2 = side3 * sin2 / max_sin
        else:
            pass

        # normalize values by setting smallest side to 1
        min_side = min(side1, side2, side3)
        side1, side2, side3 = side1/min_side, side2/min_side, side3/min_side

        return side1, side2, side3, angle1, angle2, angle3
```

Figure 18-19 The first two subroutines in the *solve_triangle_sbr.py* file

I recommend that if you are writing them out, you write and test them one at a time.

You can break down your development into even smaller pieces. For example, in the **solve_aaa()**, body of code is an if/elif branch. Write just the if-conditional first, test; then write the first elif conditional, test; and so on.

Don't forget that you can run the file against **pylint** to see if it can spot errors you're missing.

18.15 Testing Our Code

There is no royal road to geometry.
   Euclid to Ptolemy I Soter when the pharaoh asked if there was an easier way to learn geometry.

After you save your changes, test, and **EXPECT ERRORS**! This is normal. Everybody from beginners to experienced programmers has to deal with what are often just grammar, spelling, and punctuation errors.

Be easy on yourself when Python throws Tracebacks, revealing the errors it encounters one at a time.

Read the Traceback, go to the line number indicated, and see if you can find and fix the bug.

I think it helps to remind you that the results I post in this book are staged insofar as they're cleaned up and made "production-ready." You don't get to see all my mistakes simply because publishing all my mistakes would overwhelm those who've put this book together.

So if you're getting frustrated, it's time to take a break. Make yourself a snack, or go for a walk. Try not to think about the code that you can't seem to fix. Chances are, while you're not thinking about it, your mind might hit on something new to try that will fix that bug.

I don't know why, but that seems to be how our minds work. Just roll with it.

18.15 Testing Our Code

And remember, if you can't fix your bugs in this exercise, working scripts are in the repo that you can use, instead.

```
In [1]: from solve_triangle import *

In [2]: solve_triangle(side1=3, side2=4, side3=5, rnd=True, dec_digs=2)
Out[2]: (3, 4, 5, np.float64(36.87), np.float64(53.13), np.float64(90.0))
```

Figure 18-20 Running our code

Because we've written the subroutines to solve side-side-side and angle-angle-angle (SSS and AAA) triangles, we can now test them.

Figure 18-21 Verifying the output of our code

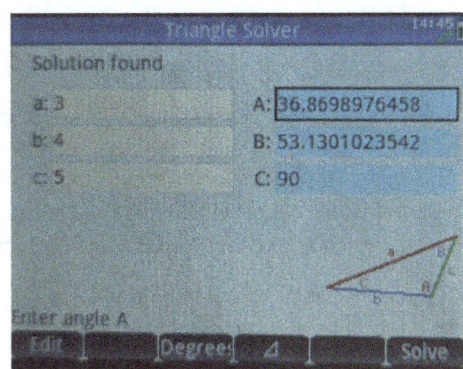

Looking good.

During code development, it's important to have input with either known output or output from at least one trusted source (which could be you, a pencil, and some paper).

A friendly reminder: the single unit test we've written so far into our **test_solve_triangle.py** file tests the subroutine for the side-side-side triangle. Let's run our unit test:

```
$ python test_solve_triangle.py
.
----------------------------------------------------------------------
Ran 1 test in 0.000s

OK
```

Figure 18-22 Running our unit test

The single dot above the dashed line signifies that one test has run. If the test had failed, Python would have printed an **F**, instead.

Now we can write unit tests for our other subroutines, as well as for the garbage filter that we're about to code.

18.16 The Garbage Filter: Writing Unit Tests and Coding

The garbage filter at the top of the main function catches bad input and lets the user know what's wrong with the input. For example, we're asserting that the six parts of a triangle must be positive reals. If any part isn't, our garbage filter should throw an **AssertionError** reminding our users that those parts must be positive reals.

```python
# this test must throw the assertion error
# of the garbage filter
def test_garbage_filter_1(self):
    ''' six parts of triangle
        must be positive reals
    '''
    with self.assertRaises(AssertionError):
        solve_triangle(side1=-3, side2=4, side3=5)
```

Figure 18-23 Our first garbage filter unit test

This unit test passes in one part provided by the user that is not a positive real number. The unit test asserts that an **AssertionError** must be raised.

This method goes in our unit test file, within the body of the class declaration.

```
$ python test_solve_triangle.py
F.
======================================================================
FAIL: test_garbage_filter_1 (__main__.test_solve_triangle.test_garbage_filter_1)
six parts of triangle
----------------------------------------------------------------------
Traceback (most recent call last):
File "/home/user/development/solve_triangle/test_solve_triangle.py", line 11,
in test_garbage_filter_1
with self.assertRaises(AssertionError):
^^^^^^^^^^^^^^^^^^^^^^^^^^^^^^^^^^^
AssertionError: AssertionError not raised

----------------------------------------------------------------------
Ran 2 tests in 0.000s

FAILED (failures=1)
```

Figure 18-24 Running our unit tests

We expect the garbage filter unit test to fail, and indeed, it does.

Please note the **F .** above the dashed line. This means the first unit test in the file—the garbage filter unit test—failed, while the second passed.

Reason for the fail: AssertionError not raised.

Of course not—we haven't yet written the code that will raise the AssertionError.

Let's do that now.

```python
# begin garbage filter
# ensure side and angle values are positive reals.
pos_reals = True
```

18.16 The Garbage Filter: Writing Unit Tests and Coding

```python
if side1 and not (isinstance(side1, (int, float)) and side1 > 0):
    pos_reals = False
if side2 and not (isinstance(side2, (int, float)) and side2 > 0):
    pos_reals = False
if side3 and not (isinstance(side3, (int, float)) and side3 > 0):
    pos_reals = False
if angle1 and not (isinstance(angle1, (int, float)) and angle1 > 0):
    pos_reals = False
if angle2 and not (isinstance(angle2, (int, float)) and angle2 > 0):
    pos_reals = False
if angle3 and not (isinstance(angle3, (int, float)) and angle3 > 0):
    pos_reals = False
assert pos_reals, "triangle sides and angles must be positive reals"
```

Figure 18-25 Our garbage filter ensuring that the three user-supplied parts of the triangle are positive reals

We start by setting a bool called **posReals** to True.

Let's analyze the first **if** statement (all the others that follow it are identical in structure and logic). All parts not given by the user are set to **None**, and **None**, coerced into a bool, evaluates as false. So **side1** can't be **None**, and it can't be zero. That's what "if side1" means.

The other side of the compound logic statement requires that **side1** must be an int or a float **and** the value of side1 must be greater than zero.

If these conditions are not met, **posReals** becomes false.

The same must be true of the other five parts of the triangle; hence, the **assert** statement: assert that posReals is true (it never gets flipped to False), or raise an AssertionError.

When I conceived of this garbage filter, I had an idea of what i needed to test for. Exactly how I was going to do it was still vague.

After a false start (trying to test for *everything* in a single assert statement), I reorganized into multiple conditionals in which each part is tested separately.

So: create and instantiate a bool to true before the conditional branches, and if any part of the triangle fails the test, flip the bool to false.

The next challenge was getting the compound logic statement for each branch correct. To do that, I developed the statement in the IPython interactive shell, starting by setting the bool to true and the value to **None**, and making sure the end state of the bool was correct, to setting the value to a positive real and testing; and finally setting it to bad values (negatives and imaginary numbers), all the while, making sure that the end state of the bool was correct.

The moral here is **getting even the parts of your project that may not be the most interesting parts correct can take effort and patience.**

```
$ python test_solve_triangle.py
..
----------------------------------------------------------------------
Ran 2 tests in 0.000s

OK
```

Figure 18-26 Running the unit tests with the garbage filter in place

Success.

At this point, I recommend that you add linting your code to the development cycles of this project.

pylint is an excellent linter, and the suggestions it makes regarding your code can influence the direction the development of your code takes, as well as help you learn good style.

18.17 Finishing solve_triangle(), v1

At this point, I will leave it as an exercise for you to finish coding the subroutines, the garbage filter, and the unit tests for the first version of our function.

Please keep in mind that your first working version of a program is a rough draft. It **is** a significant milestone so once you reach it, you should be proud of yourself for doing so. However, we are always on the lookout for improvements to our code, especially those that make it easier or more intuitive for users to use our code. We solicit feedback from our users, and we listen to their suggestions.

And we always think of how we can make our code simpler, cleaner, and faster.

Now for **solve_triangle**(), v2.

18.18 Improving solve_triangle(), v1

```
$ pylint solve_triangle.py
************* Module solve_triangle
solve_triangle.py:9:0: R0913: Too many arguments (9/5) (too-many-arguments)
solve_triangle.py:9:0: R0917: Too many positional arguments (9/5)
 (too-many-positional-arguments)
solve_triangle.py:66:9: R0916: Too many boolean expressions in if statement (9/5)
 (too-many-boolean-expressions)
solve_triangle.py:71:9: R0916: Too many boolean expressions in if statement (9/5)
 (too-many-boolean-expressions)
solve_triangle.py:76:9: R0916: Too many boolean expressions in if statement (9/5)
 (too-many-boolean-expressions)
solve_triangle.py:81:9: R0916: Too many boolean expressions in if statement (9/5)
 (too-many-boolean-expressions)
solve_triangle.py:86:9: R0916: Too many boolean expressions in if statement (9/5)
 (too-many-boolean-expressions)
solve_triangle.py:91:9: R0916: Too many boolean expressions in if statement (9/5)
 (too-many-boolean-expressions)
solve_triangle.py:9:0: R0912: Too many branches (21/12) (too-many-branches)

-----------------------------------
Your code has been rated at 8.12/10
```

Figure 18-27 Linting *solve_triangle()*, v1

pylint provides suggestions for improving the code in the file in our repo. These are in addition to, and separate from, fixing the problems with the **solve_ssa()** and **solve_ass()** subroutines.

First, can we reduce the number of arguments in the function's argument list?

And second, can we reduce the number of boolean expressions and simplify the if...elif...else conditional branching in the main part of the main function?

The answer to both questions is: **yes**.

The solution to one will influence the solution to the other.

And while we're considering reducing the number of arguments, we should revisit the need for the bool **rnd**. Turns out, it's redundant, given the possible values of **dec_digs**.

18.19 TI-59 Calculator: Triangle Solution, Master Library ROM Module—A Different Approach

Figure 18-28 The TI-59 programmable calculator

Introduced in 1977, its many features included swappable solid-state ROM modules that provided additional programs and functionality.

Please note the user-defined keys on the top row of the keyboard (labeled **A** through **E**); and above the keyboard, the card slot, which in this photo is holding nothing.

(I owned the less expensive and more modest TI-58C.)

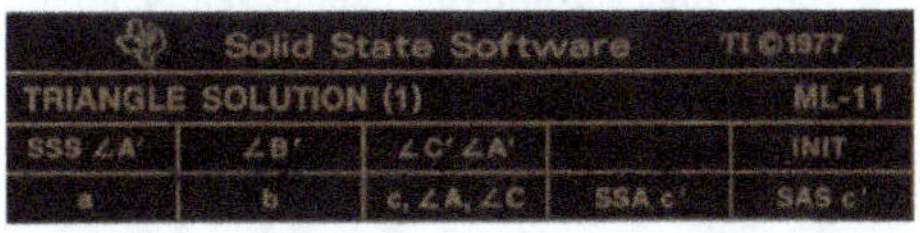

Figure 18-29 The TI-59: Triangle Solution I label card

ROM modules for the TI-59 came with manuals and packets of label cards. When using a program in a ROM module, the user would slide the program's label card in the card slot location below the display and above the keypad; and the label card showed how the keys **A** through **E** were defined by the program's writers.

In Table 18-1, we have the **TRIANGLE SOLUTION (1)** program from the Master Library ROM Module that shipped with each calculator. The two triangle solution programs in the library covered most of the possible triangles (SSS, ASA, etc., excluding AAA).

Table 18-1 Instructions on how to solve the SSS triangle using the *TRIANGLE SOLUTION* **program.**—table adapted from the *Programmable TI 58/59 Master Library*, "Triangle Solution (1)" (*Programmable TI 58/59 Master Library*, "Triangle Solution (1)". Texas Instruments. 1977. p.35.)

Step	Procedure	Enter	Press	Display
	Knowing SSS			
1	Enter a	a	A	a
2	Enter b	b	B	b
3	Enter c	c	C	c
4	Calculate ∠ A		2nd A	∠ A'
5	Calculate ∠ B		2nd B	∠ B'
6	Calculate ∠ C		2nd C	∠ C'

The user enters the known parts, referring to the labels on the label card to press the correct user-defined keys; then the user presses the key labeled **SSS** ∠A to get back the first angle (and the keys labeled ∠B and ∠C ∠A' to get angles B and C, respectively).

The approach taken by the programmers of the ROM module's TRIANGLE SOLUTIONs suggests the approach we'll take in redesigning the **triangle_solution()**'s interface.

Briefly, if we have our users start the argument list with a string defining *which* triangle they want to solve ('sss', 'aaa', etc.), they can then follow it with the three known parts in order, named *val1*, *val2*, and *val3*.

```
def solve_triangle(triangle: str, val1: (int, float),\
                   val2: (int, float), \
                   val3: (int, float)) -> tuple:
```

Figure 18-30 Partial redesign of our function header

The user must pass in which triangle the machine is to solve for, along with the known parts in ordered sequence.

This new approach takes four arguments, as opposed to the six of the old approach.

18.20 Losing the *rnd* Bool from the Argument List

It turns out that the value of **dec_digs**, which does not change throughout the main function's execution, can tell us everything that the **rnd** bool does:

> If dec_digs is **None** (the default value), no rounding.
> Else, round values to the number of dec_digs, a positive int.

This means that in our redesign, we lose one more argument from the function's argument list.

18.21 Rethinking the Main Section of solve_triangle()

> Quality code is the result of experience, effort, and patience.
> Code rewriting in programming is so standard that, when the rewrite improves the performance of the code without altering the code's external behavior, it has its own name: **refactoring**.
> In this section, we will consider different ways of writing the main section of solve_triangle(). These ways are summarized in Figures 18-33, 18-34, and 18-35.
> As we seek to improve the code in our projects, it is normal to come up with different approaches to solve the same problem.
> **pylint** may offer you refactoring suggestions that are at least worth considering.

Figure 18-31 *refactoring* **is part of the code development cycle.** Please scan or click the image to go to the Wikipedia article. https://en.wikipedia.org/wiki/Code_refactoring

Note that we did not start with the first approach listed in Figure 18-32, in which the code that solves particular triangles make up the blocks of the if...elif branches. This is indeed one approach, and you may see it used in production code.

Instead, we decided to move the code that solves each particular triangle into its own subroutine in a separate file.

If that code is in Python or another high-level modern programming language, you should consider refactoring it into an easier-to-read, easier-to-maintain format. This is especially true if those blocks of code are long.

```
# ASA Triangle
# main routine
    elif (angle1 and side3 and angle2) or \
         (angle2 and side1 and angle3) or \
         (angle3 and side2 and angle1):
        # from sbr
        # get missing angle
        if angle1 and angle2:
            angle3 = pi - (angle1 + angle2)
        elif angle2 and angle3:
            angle1 = pi - (angle2 + angle3)
        elif angle3 and angle1:
            angle2 = pi - (angle3 + angle1)
        else:
            pass

        # calculate sines
```

```
            sin1, sin2, sin3 = sin(angle1), sin(angle2),\
            sin(angle3)

            # calculate missing sides
            if side1:
                side2, side3 = sin2 * side1 / sin1, sin3 * side1 / sin1
            elif side2:
                side1, side3 = sin1 * side2 / sin2, sin3 * side2 / sin2
            elif side3:
                side1, side2 = sin1 * side3 / sin3, sin2 * side3 / sin3

            solution_tuple = side1, side2, side3, angle1, angle2, angle3
```

Figure 18-32 Here, we've synthesized the selection clause in the main routine and the associated code in the subroutine that solves the *ASA triangle*

This gives you an idea of how large and unwieldy the solve_triangle() function would be if all its parts had been written as a single function.

```
if side1 and side2 and side3:
    solution_tuple = solve_sss(side1, side2, side3, angle1, angle2, angle3)

elif angle1 and angle2 and angle3:
    solution_tuple = solve_aaa(side1, side2, side3, angle1, angle2, angle3)

elif (angle1 and side3 and angle2) or \
     (angle2 and side1 and angle3) or \
     (angle3 and side2 and angle1):
    solution_tuple = solve_asa(side1, side2, side3, angle1, angle2, angle3)

elif (side1 and side2 and angle3) or \
     (side2 and side3 and angle1) or \
     (side3 and side1 and angle2):
    solution_tuple = solve_sas(side1, side2, side3, angle1, angle2, angle3)
```

Figure 18-33 The if..elif clauses in the main routine invoking the subroutines to solve the SSS, AAA, ASA, and SAS triangles

Note the structure of the compound logic statement in the second elif clause to invoke the *solve_asa()* function.

```
three_parts = bool(side1), bool(side2), bool(side3),\
              bool(angle1), bool(angle2), bool(angle3)

func_dict =\
 {(1, 1, 1, 0, 0, 0): solve_sss,\
  (0, 0, 0, 1, 1, 1): solve_aaa,\
  (0, 0, 1, 1, 1, 0): solve_asa,\
  (1, 0, 0, 1, 1, 0): solve_aas,\
  (1, 0, 0, 1, 0, 1): solve_saa,\
```

```
    (1, 0, 1, 0, 0, 1): solve_sas,\
    (1, 1, 0, 1, 0, 0): solve_ssa,\
    (1, 0, 1, 1, 0, 0): solve_ass}
```

Figure 18-34 Replacing the if..elif clause with a dictionary

The Boolean values making up the tuples that serve as keys are determined by which parts of the triangle the user provides.

The keys in turn determine which subroutine gets invoked.

```
func_dict =\
   {'sss': solve_sss, 'aaa': solve_aaa, 'asa': solve_asa,\
    'sas': solve_sas, 'ssa': solve_ssa, 'ass': solve_ass,\
    'aas': solve_aas, 'saa': solve_saa}
```

Figure 18-35 Using strings as keys

Each key corresponds to a triangle.
The evolution of developing different ways to do the same thing:

In Figure 18-32, we have an if..elif clause in which all the code to solve a triangle (in this case, the ASA triangle) is in the clause's block of code.
In Figure 18-33, we put the functional code that solves each triangle into a function, then invoke the function within the clause's body of code. This is the approach we took in **Version 1**.
In Figure 18-34, we replace the if..elif branches with a dictionary. First, we create a tuple of bools (or ToB) that shows which parts of the triangle the user has provided, then matches the ToB with the ToB keys in the dictionary. When a key matches, its value—the name of the corresponding subroutine—is returned, a tuple of the provided values is concatenated to the subroutine name, and the subroutine is invoked.
In Figure 18-35, we rewrite the subroutines so they take only three parts of a triangle specified by the user.

In my opinion, the major split in these four different approaches occurs between approaches 2 and 3, when we move from using logical statements in if..elif clauses to using keys in dictionaries. A logical comparison requires more CPU cycles than doing a lookup in a dictionary in memory. The first is a computation, then second isn't. Using a lookup table should be faster than making computations.

Generally speaking, sometimes computation is necessary, as when the amount of data, or the variance of the data, makes it difficult, even impossible, to create a dictionary that covers all options. (Note, too, that to come up with a dictionary's keys, it may be necessary to do computations that are not part of your code so even coming up with a fast, useful dictionary—and implementing it—may require doing some preprocessing.)

18.22 solve_triangle(), v2

```
def solve_triangle(tri_type: str,\
                   val1: (int, float),\
                   val2: (int, float),\
                   val3: (int, float),\
                   degrees=True,\
                   dec_digs=None) -> tuple:
```

Figure 18-36 solve_triangle(), v2

In this version, users pass in a string that is the triangle they want to solve for and the three known parts of the triangle, in order. The first value entered is always either **side1** or **angle1**. The function returns a six-element tuple with values for all parts of the triangle.

Users also do not have to set a bool declaring if they want rounded results or not.

```
if degrees:
    deg_dict =\
        {'sss': (val1, val2, val3),\
         'aaa': (deg2rad(val1), deg2rad(val2), deg2rad(val3)),\
         'asa': (deg2rad(val1), val2, deg2rad(val3)),\
         'sas': (val1, deg2rad(val2), val3),\
         'ssa': (val1, val2, deg2rad(val3)),\
         'ass': (deg2rad(val1), val2, val3),\
         'aas': (deg2rad(val1), deg2rad(val2), val3),\
         'saa': (val1, deg2rad(val2), deg2rad(val3))
        }
    val1, val2, val3 = deg_dict[tri_type]
```

Figure 18-37 deg_dict

We use a dictionary to convert angular measurements from degrees to radians before passing the values into **main**.

```
func_dict =\
    {'sss': solve_sss, 'aaa': solve_aaa, 'asa': solve_asa,\
     'sas': solve_sas, 'ssa': solve_ssa, 'ass': solve_ass,\
     'aas': solve_aas, 'saa': solve_saa}

solution_tuple = func_dict[tri_type](val1, val2, val3)
```

Figure 18-38 funct_dict

We use a dictionary in **main** to choose the correct subroutine, given the triangle type (denoted by a string).

The subroutines are functions that take only three arguments and return a six-value tuple.

```
# return a tuple, with and without rounding
if dec_digs is None:
    return solution_tuple

# in this return statement, we render a new tuple from converted values
# in solution_tuple. note that we preserve the order of the values.
return round(solution_tuple[0], dec_digs), round(solution_tuple[1], dec_digs),\
       round(solution_tuple[2], dec_digs), round(solution_tuple[3], dec_digs),\
       round(solution_tuple[4], dec_digs), round(solution_tuple[5], dec_digs)
```

Figure 18-39 *dec_digs* functioning as a bool

If **dec_digs** is **None**, return values without rounding. Else, round values by the int value of dec_digs.

Running pylint against our Version1 of the solve_triangle main routine motivated the refactoring that resulted in Version2. Because of pylint comments, we reduced the number of arguments passed into the function, and we replaced conditional branches with dictionaries. How does pylint assess the result of all our effort?

```
$ pylint solve_triangle.py
************* Module solve_triangle
solve_triangle.py:12:0: R0913: Too many arguments (6/5) (too-many-arguments)
solve_triangle.py:12:0: R0917: Too many positional arguments (6/5) (too-many-positional-arguments)

-----------------------------------
Your code has been rated at 9.00/10
```

Everyone's a critic.

18.23 What's Left to Do?

Figure 18-40 The SSA and ASS triangles and their multiple calculation outcomes. Scan or click the QR code to go to the online article at **mathworld**. https://mathworld.wolfram.com/ASSTheorem.html

Given the values for a side-side-angle or angle-side-side triangle, there are four possible outcomes, as made clear in this article.

The first one is, if $sin A > a/c$, there is no solution.

The second one is, if $sin A = a/c$, there is one possible triangle.

The third and fourth occur if $sin A < a/c$, in which case side b has two possible lengths.

To reflect these different cases in our code, we will **assert** that $sin A$ cannot be greater than a/c.

If $sin A = a/c$, in the six-value tuple returning all the values of the triangle, side b will show a single number.

But if $sin A < a/c$, the angles and side with two possible answers in the six-value return tuple will themselves be two-value tuples.

Finally, in **solve_triangle(), v3**, we will replace **numpy** with Python's built-in **math** module.

This allows our function to run with only a Python3 interpreter and its built-ins.

The trig functions in **math** module, like the trig functions in **numpy**, take and return angular measurements in radians. Also, like **numpy**, the **math** module includes functions that convert degrees to radians and radians to degrees.

```python
# test if ASS or SSA triangle has no solution
if (tri_type == 'ass') and sin(val1) > val3/val2:
    raise AssertionError('there is no solution for this angle-side-side')
if (tri_type == 'ssa') and sin(val3) > val2/val1:
    raise AssertionError('there is no solution for this side-side-angle')
```

Figure 18-41 In the garbage filter code at the top of our function's body of code, we assert that the condition for SSA and ASS triangles that result in *no solution* raises an error

```python
def solve_ssa(side1, side2, angle1) -> tuple:
    '''SSA: We use the Law of Sines to solve for the 2d angle.
    sin A < a/c : b = c cos A +/- (a**2 - c**2 sin**2 A)**(1/2) [two solutions]
    sin A == a/c : [one solution]
    https://mathworld.wolfram.com/ASSTheorem.html
```

```
    if sin(angle1) < (side1 / side2):
        # side3 = side2 cos(angle1) +/- (side1**2 - side2**2 sin**2(angle1))**(1/2)
        side3a = side2 * cos(angle1) + (side1**2 - side2**2 * sin(angle1)**2)**(1/2)
        side3b = side2 * cos(angle1) - (side1**2 - side2**2 * sin(angle1)**2)**(1/2)
        side3 = (side3a, side3b)

        angle2a = acos((side1**2 + side3a**2 - side2**2)/(2 * side1 * side3a))
        angle2b = acos((side1**2 + side3b**2 - side2**2)/(2 * side1 * side3b))

        angle3a = pi - (angle1 + angle2a)
        angle3b = pi - (angle1 + angle2b)

        angle2 = (angle2a, angle2b)
        angle3 = (angle3a, angle3b)

    else:
        # Law of Sines
        # a2 = b2 + c2 - 2bc cosA
        angle2 = asin(side2 * sin(angle1) / side1)
        angle3 = pi - (angle1 + angle2)
        side3 = (side1**2 + side2**2 - (2 * side1 * side2 * cos(angle3)))**(1/2)

    return side1, side2, side3, angle1, angle2, angle3
```

Figure 18-42 solve_ssa(), v3

In the body of the code, we handle the other possible outcomes.

The **else** clause handles the single outcome while the body of code for the **if** clause handles the ambiguous case.

Recall that Eric Weisstein's article shows us how to solve for each side b in the ambiguous case.

```
# has embedded tuple. round values in embedded tuples,
# and other values in solution_tuple
solution_list = list(solution_tuple)
for index, value in enumerate(solution_list):
    if isinstance(value, tuple):
        temp_list = list(value)
        for list_idx, list_value in enumerate(temp_list):
            temp_list[list_idx] = round(list_value, dec_digs)
        solution_list[index] = tuple(temp_list)
    else:
        solution_list[index] = round(solution_list[index], dec_digs)
solution_tuple = tuple(solution_list)
return solution_tuple
```

Figure 18-43 And now, solution_tuple may or may not itself have tuples for values

The challenge comes when the user wants results rounded.

In this solution, we have the machine test if the solution_tuple's values are tuples, one by one. If one is, the machine then rounds each of the inner tuple's values.

Chapter Summary

Programming is a creative process. Even if we are handed a specification and told to write a program that meets the specs, for all but the most trivial programs, we still rely on imagination, experience, and insight to assemble collections, algorithms, and program features into a solution that is robust and easy to use. It takes time and effort to become good, if not decent, at programming; but if you find yourself not noticing the time passing and loving the effort while writing programs, you might have what it takes to become not just a decent, and not just a good, but a great programmer. Good luck.

Suggested Reading

Chapter 1

The Harvard Computers. https://en.wikipedia.org/wiki/Harvard_Computers

Colossus. https://en.wikipedia.org/wiki/Colossus_computer

ENIAC. https://en.wikipedia.org/wiki/ENIAC

The Altair 8800. https://en.wikipedia.org/wiki/Altair_8800

© James R. Derry 2026
J. R. Derry, *Introduction to Programming for Researchers*,
https://doi.org/10.1007/979-8-8688-1615-4

The Xerox Alto. https://en.wikipedia.org/wiki/Xerox_Alto

The Turing Machine. https://en.wikipedia.org/wiki/Turing_machine

Chapter 2

Transistor

Integrated Circuit

Fairchild Semiconductor

Logic Gate

Suggested Reading

NAND Gate

Arithmetic Logic Unit

Moore's Law

Moore's Law

The Bit.

George Boole.

Boole, George. An Investigation of the Laws of Thought

Boole, George. The Mathematical Analysis of Logic

Claude Shannon, *A symbolic analysis of relay and switching circuits*. Master's Thesis, 1940.

MIT Technology Review Editors."Claude Shannon: Reluctant Father of the Digital Age", *MIT Technology Review*. 2001.

Siobhan Roberts. "Claude Shannon, Father of the Digital Age, Turns 1100100". 2016.

Central Processing Unit.

The Instruction Cycle.

Chapter 3

Operating System

CTSS

MULTICS

UNIX

Linux

Dennis Ritchie, M. 1984. *The Evolution of the Unix Time-sharing System.* **AT&T Bell Laboratories Technical Journal 63 No. 6 Part 2**. October 1984.

Chapter 6
Wikipedia
Richard Hamming

Hamming Code

Chapter 7

Wikipedia
Numerical Analysis

IEEE 754

References

Chapter 1

Section 1.1.2

Turing, A.M. 1937. On Computable Numbers, with an Application to the Entscheidungsproblem. *Proceedings of London Math Society* s2-42, pg 250, 251, 252, 253, and 254.

Ghiselin, Brewster. 1985. *The Creative Process: A Symposium.* CALIFORNIA PAPERBACK EDITION. pg 23. Oakland: University of California Press.

Quote in Figure 1.9 caption. https://www.columbia.edu/cu/computinghistory/704.html

Section 1.2

Turing, A.M. 1937. On Computable Numbers, with an Application to the Entscheidungsproblem. *Proceedings of the London Mathematical Society* s2-42 (1): 230–65.

Penrose, Roger. 1989. *The Emperor's New Mind, With A New Preface By The Author*, 54. Oxford: Oxford University Press.

Chapter 2

Section 2.1.4

Figure 4.3. Max Roser, Hannah Ritchie and Edouard Mathieu. "What is Moore's Law?" Published online at OurWorldinData.org. 2023.

Retrieved from: 'https://ourworldindata.org/moores-law'

Section 2.1.5

Upton, Eben, et. al. 2016. *Learning Computer Architecture with Raspberry Pi*, 95. Hoboken: Wiley.

Section 2.2.1

Soni, Jimmy, and Rob Goodman. 2017. *A Mind At Play: How Claude Shannon Invented the Information Age*, 38. New York: Simon and Schuster.

Shannon, Claude, and Warren Weaver. 1949. *The Mathematical Theory of Communication*, 60. The Urbana: University of Illinois Press.

op. cit. pg 44

J. R. Derry, *Introduction to Programming for Researchers*,
https://doi.org/10.1007/979-8-8688-1615-4

Section 2.2.2
Kahn, David. 1996. *The Codebreakers: The Story of Secret Writing*, 744. New York: Scribner.

Roberts, Siobhan. 2016. Claude Shannon, Father of the Digital Age, Turns 1100100. Online article.

Section 2.4
Irvine, Kip. 2015. *Assembly Language For x86 Processors*, 7th ed., 33–35. London: Pearson.

Chapter 3

Section 3.1.1
Kernighan, Brian. 2020. *UNIX: A History And A Memoir*. Seattle: Kindle Direct Publishing.
Ritchie, Dennis. 1984. The Evolution of the Unix Time-sharing System. https://www.read.seas.harvard.edu/~kohler/class/aosref/ritchie84evolution.pdf

Section 3.2
Kernighan, Brian. 2020. *UNIX: A History and a Memoir*, 32. Seattle: Kindle Direct Publishing.

Chapter 4

Section 4.6
Raymond, Eric S. 2004. *The Art of UNIX Programming*, 11–25. Boston: Addison-Wesley.

Section 4.7.4
Aho, Alfred et al. 2018. *Compilers: Principles, Techniques, and Tools*, 2nd ed., 11 & 85. London: Pearson.

Section 4.10
Kernighan, Brian. 2020. *UNIX: A History And A Memoir*, 67. Seattle: Kindle Direct Publishing

Section 4.11
Raymond, Eric S. 2004. *The Art of UNIX Programming*, 24. Boston: Addison-Wesley.

Chapter 5

Section 5.2.1
Kernighan, and Plauger. 1978. *The Elements of Style*, 2nd ed., 54. Columbus: McGraw Hill.

Section 5.4
IAU and Sky & Telescope, Creative Commons. https://www.iau.org/public/images/detail/ori/

Section 5.5
IAU and Sky & Telescope, Creative Commons. https://www.iau.org/public/images/detail/ori/

Section 5.8
Kernighan, Brian. 2020. *UNIX: A History and a Memoir*, 73. Seattle: Kindle Direct Publishing.

Section 5.8.1
ibid. p72.

Section 5.9
Frédéric Mahé, Creative Commons. https://www.biostars.org/p/17680/

Chapter 6

Section 6.1.1
The American Heritage Dictionary of the English Language, 5th ed. Version 15.1.722. Boston: Houghton Mifflin Harcourt Publishing. 2025.

Section 6.1.2
Knuth, Donald E. 1968. *The Art of Computer Programming, Vol. I: Fundamental Algorithms*, 4–6. Boston: Addison-Wesley.

Section 6.2
Kernighan, and Plauger. 1978. *The Elements of Style*, 2nd ed., 2. Columbus: McGraw Hill.
    Martin, Robert C. 2009. *Clean Code: A Handbook of Agile Software Craftsmanship*, 7–8, 10. Upper Saddle River: Prentice Hall.
    Kernighan, Brian. 2020. *UNIX: A History and a Memoir*, 12–13. Seattle: Kindle Direct Publishing.

Chapter 7

Section 7.2
Kneusel, Ronald T. 2017. *Numbers and Computers*, 2nd ed., 130–131. Berlin: Springer.

Section 7.3
mpmath.org https://mpmath.org/

Chapter 9

Section 9.3
Packard, Hewlett. 1979. *The HP-41C Alphanumeric Programmable Scientific Calculator: Owner's Handbook and Programming Guide*, 8–11. Hewlett Packard.

Section 9.5
Andersen, P. K., and G. Bjedov. 1997. "Chemical stoichiometry using MATLAB". Purdue University.

Section 9.7
Fermi, Enrico. 1956. *Thermodynamics*, 10. Garden City: Dover Publications.

Chapter 10

Section 10.2
Masterminds of Programming: Conversations With the Creators of Major Programming Languages, ed. Federico Biancuzzi, and Shane Warden, 26–27. Santa Rosa: O'Reilly Media.

Section 10.5
Kernighan, Brian, and P.J. Plauger. 1978. *The Elements of Programming Style*, 2nd ed., 2. Columbus: McGraw-Hill.

Section 10.7
National Human Genome Research Institute, NIH, DNA fact sheet, 24th August 2020. https://www.genome.gov/about-genomics/fact-sheets/Deoxyribonucleic-Acid-Fact-Sheet.
   Image : https://www.genome.gov/sites/default/files/media/images/2024-05/DNA_2024a.jpg

Chapter 11

Section 11.9
Strogatz, Steven. 2016. *Infinite Powers*, 42–57. Houghton, Miflin, Harcourt.

Chapter 12

Section 12.4
Raymond, Eric. 2003. *The Art of UNIX Programming*, 23. Boston: Addison-Wesley.

Chapter 14

Section 14.1
Biancuzzi, Federico, and Shane Warden, eds. 2009. *Masterminds of Programming: Conversations with the Creators of Major Programming Languages*, 109. Santa Rosa: O'Reilly.

Section 14.7.2
Raymond, Eric S. 2004. *The Art of UNIX Programming*, 22. Boston: Addison-Wesley.

Chapter 15

Section 15.2
Raymond, Eric S. 2004. *The Art of UNIX Programming*, 22. Boston: Addison-Wesley.

Section 15.4.1
Donovan, Alan, and Brian Kernighan. 2015. *The Go Programming Language*, 22. Boston: Addison-Wesley.

Dijkstra, Edsger. Why Numbering Should Start at Zero. https://www.cs.utexas.edu/users/EWD/ewd08xx/EWD831.PDF

Section 15.8
Watson, James D. 1976. *Molecular Biology of the Gene*, 3rd ed., 281–282. New York: W.A. Benjamin.

Section 15.13.1
Sigler, L.E. Translator. 2003. *Fibonacci's Liber Abaci*, 3. Berlin: Springer Verlag.

Chapter 16

Section 16.4.1
IAU and Sky & Telescope, Creative Commons.
https://www.iau.org/public/images/detail/ori/

Section 16.4.2
IAU and Sky & Telescope, Creative Commons.
https://www.iau.org/public/images/detail/uma/

Chapter 18

Section 18.2
Kernighan, Brian, and P.J. Plauger. *The Elements of Programming Style*, 2nd ed., 61. Columbus: McGraw-Hill.

ibid, p77.

Section 18.9
ibid, p9.

Section 18.12
Dale, N. B., and C. Weems. 1994. *Introduction To Pascal and Structured Design*, 4th ed., 339. Lexington, Mass. : D.C. Heath.

ibid. pg 340.

Section 18.13
Raymond, Eric S. 2004. *The Art of UNIX Programming*, 23. Boston: Addison-Wesley.

Section 18.19
Programmable TI 58/59 Master Library, "Triangle Solution (1)". Texas Instruments. 1977. p. 35.

Index

A

agrep (approximate grep), 108–109
Algorithm
    The Art of Computer Programming, 118–119
    bubblesort, 125–128
    computer algorithms, 115
    control flow
        conditional branching, 119–121
        for/while loop, 121–122
        loop structures, 121–122
        sequential flow, 119
        while loop, 122
    definition, 115
    Euclid GCD algorithm, 123–124
    halting problem, 129, 130
    libraries, 116–117
    little hummer card trick, 124–125
    methods, 115
    mystical history, 129–130
    programming (*see* Programming style)
    programming style, 206–211
    pseudocode, 115
    recipes, 118
American Standard Code for Information Interchange (ASCII), 46–47
Antonelli, Kay, 247–248
Arithmetic and logic units (ALUs), 17, 24
Automate testing, 200–203
awk programming language, 88–92

B

Bash
    agrep (approximate grep), 108–109
    awk programming language, 88–92
    calculator, 104
    character encodings/text file formats, 45–48
    command-line prompt, 36–37
    datafiles
        bit/byte/nibble/word, 52–53
        character-encoding standards, 53
        data/instructions, 52
        pointers, 52
        process datafiles, 53–54
    datetime integer, 96–98
    files (LINUX)
        base-8 numbers (Octals), 44–45
        chmod command, 43–44
        clobbering, 42–43
        file creation, 41
        newFile, 42
        noclobber option, 43
        path, 40–41
        programs and executable scripts, 40–41
        read-write-execute permissions, 43
        session noclobber option, 45
        set/clear flag commands, 44
        text file, 43
        working directory, 41
    format print function printf(), 94
    history, 37
    interpreter
        assignment statements, 50
        environment variables, 50–51
        installation scripts, 51
        interpreter, 51
        symbol tables, 49
        symbol tables/variables, 51–52
        variables, 49–50
    LINUX filesystem
        absolute path, 37–38
        cd (change directory) command, 38
        command line, 37
        grep command, 40
        hidden text file, 37
        history file, 39
        list directory contents, 38
        return type, 39–40
        working directory, 37
    pipelines (*see* Pipelines/scripts (bash))
    profilers, 55
    queries, 92–94
    recordsets, 105–108
    regular expressions (grep-E), 98–104
    scripts (*see* Script languages (bash))
    shell, 35–36
    Thompson, Ken, 56
    time/watch commands, 54–55
    UNIX philosophy, 48
    user input, 95–96

© James R. Derry 2026
J. R. Derry, *Introduction to Programming for Researchers*,
https://doi.org/10.1007/979-8-8688-1615-4

Bhakat, Priyanka, 219–224
Boole, George, 20–22
Bubblesort algorithm
  array index, 126–127
  data structure, 126
  for loop, 127–128
  pseudocode, 127
  sorting algorithms, 125–126
  value comparison, 128

C

Calculators
  annotations and comments, 153
  assignment statements, 155–156
  climate datasets, 173–179
  COVID-19 pandemic, 151–153
  datetime module, 152
  digital signal processing, 179–181
  dimensional analysis, 161
  falling bodies
    Ernesto's home directory, 168–169
    jupyter notebook, 169
    nsimplify(), 171
    quadratic equation, 168
    SymPy initialization, 170–171
    webpage, 169
  format printing, 157
  GC content percentage, 155–157
  gravitational acceleration, 163–164
  Harris, Danny, 153–154
  heat loss problem, 154–155
  ideal gas law problem, 161–162
  image-driven data analysis, 182–187
  ipython interactive shell, 155
  Jupyter notebooks, 165–168
  nucleotide string, 155–157
  print directive, 157
  solving date problems, 153–154
  sound pressure, 164–165
  spherical trigonometry, 171–173
  str.lower() method, 156
  symbolic Python (SymPy), 157–161
  thermodynamic systems, 163
Central processor unit (CPU)
  arithmetic and logical operations, 18
  calculations/logical operations, 24
  clock cycle, 25
  fetch-decode-execute cycle, 25
  hypothetical microcomputer, 24
  logic gates, 17–18
  machine cycle, 25
  program execution/data processing, 31–32
  transistor, 18–20
  wait states, 25
Climate datasets
  Camp Mabry dataframe, 176–177
  dataframe, 178–179
  dataframe.agg() method, 177
  home directory, 174–175
  Jupyter notebook, 175
  NOAA datasets, 173–174
  pandas dataframe, 175–176
  site homepage, 174
  TMAX and TMIN, 178
Computer Age
  Alan Turing's bombes, 3–4
  bombe, 3
  Colossus, 3, 5
  digirule counting program, 9–11
  digital computers, 7
  EDVAC, 4–6
  ENIAC, 3–5
  Harvard Observatory computers, 2–3
  history, 2–3
  instruction set and reserved registers, 10
  Mauchly, John, 4
  Moore's Law, 7, 10
  tremendous progress, 7
  war information, 6–7
  Xerox Alto, 8–9
Computer algebra system (CAS), 391
COVID-19 pandemic, 151–153

D

Datasets
  Bash commands, 277
  list of lists (LoL), 277–280
  list of strings (LoS), 278–279
  method chaining, 278
  minimum and maximum values, 281
  nesting collections, 280–281
  parsing
    definition, 282
    fasta recordset, 282–287
    if clause, 283–284
    metadata/data sequence lines, 283
    tabular recordset, 284
  preprocessing data, 287–288
  splitlines() method, 278
  text file
    home directory, 288
    ipython session, 291
    line count, 289
    listdir() function, 289
    pickle directory, 291
    resultsDict file, 292
    working function and testing, 290
  unsorted collection, 281
Datetime format
  datasets, 397–398
  for-loop, 399–401
  long-term research project, 397
  planned time complexity, 399
  reporting problems, 401–402
  sequential entries, 398
  source code, 398–399
  working script, 401
Decimal fractions/binary conversion

Bhakat, Priyanka, 219–224
binary fraction, 219–220
Brahmagupta (598–668CE), 225
calculation, 220
garbage filter, 222–224
interval number, 219
positional values, 221
range() function, 218–219
Digital computation
  addresses, 22
  Boole, George, 20–22
  data/instructions/pointers, 22–23
  fetch/decode/execute, 24–25
  fundamental physical unit, 15–17
  real-world application, 23
  Shannon, Claude, 20–22
  transistors
    CPU design, 18, 19
    electronic circuits, 16, 17
    financial budgets, 19
    integrated circuits (ICs), 17
    logic gates, 17–18
    Moore's Law, 15–19
    physical miniaturization, 17
    Shockley, William, 16
    vacuum tube, 16
  xcircuit, 23–24
Digital signal processing
  code cell and blinking, 180
  Jupyter notebook, 179–180
  notebook page, 180
  plotting signal, 181
  signal wave, 179
  SymPy symbol, 180–181

E

Electronic Discrete Variable Automatic Computer (EDVAC), 4–6
Electronic Numerical Integrator and Computer (ENIAC), 3–5
Error-trapping code, 132
Euclid GCD algorithm, 123–124
Euler, Leonard, 248

F

Floating-point numbers
  arithmetic issues, 136
  definition, 133
  herbie, 138–140
  integers, 135
  internal representation, 135
  module's objects/functions, 135
  mpmath, 137–138
  Python interpreter, 134
  representative number, 134
  working process, 136–137
Floating-point unit (FPU), 19
Function design recipe (FDR), 250

Functions
  calculus textbooks
    anonymous functions, 265
    Archimedes' method, 258–259
    area and multiplication, 257
    derivative() function, 265
    differentiation, 264–266
    Gates-Dell Complex (GDC), 259
    integral values, 259–262
    numeric integration, 256–258
    NumPy/Python, 262–264
    quad() function, 263
    rectangular method, 260–261
    SymPy, 266–267
    time-velocity graph, 257
  concise functions, 256
  Euler, Leonard, 248
  function design recipe (FDR), 250
  import keyword, 249
  lambda, 247
  lambdas, 255–256
  modules, 249
  namedtuple() function, 254
  positional *vs.* named argument
    argument list, 251
    array() function, 252–253
    keyword=value pairs, 251
    tuple collection, 251–252
  return statement, 253–255
  self-documenting code, 250
  subroutine, 247–248
  symbol, 248

G

Gates-Dell Complex (GDC), 259
Gökkr, Ilayda, 157–161, 244–246
Graph theory
  datafile directory, 318
  edges, 317
  Euler, Leonhard, 317–318
  hewitsoni_males.txt file, 318–321
  lexicon of, 317
  pickling, 322–323
Graphical user interface (GUI), 8

H

Hamming, Richard, 131–132
Harris, Danny, 153–154
Hilbert, David, 12

I

Ideal gas law, 161–162
Image-driven data analysis
  calculation results, 186
  default tiff file, 186
  download page, 183
  flood mitigation project, 182

higher-resolution images, 186–187
image files, 184
management and urban planning, 182–183
online documentation, 184
statistics and displaying results, 184–185
Integrated circuits (ICs), 17
International Astronomical Union (IAU), 88

J
Josephus problem, 350–353
Jupyter notebooks
   command line, 166–167
   NumPy (Numeric Python), 166
   Pérez, Fernando, 167–168
   SciPy (Scientific Python), 359
   SymPy (Symbolic Python), 165–166
   working directory, 167

K
Kernighan, Brian, 131–132

L
Large language model (LLM), 242
Linux operating system
   application writer, 27, 28
   bash history, 37–45
   graphical user interfaces (GUIs), 33
   hardware manufacturers, 27
   mass-storage devices, 31
   memory manager, 31–32
   Process ID (PID), 33
   process scheduler, 31–33
   standardization, 28
   UNIX (*See* UNIX)
List of lists (LoL), 277–280

M
Modern computers
   communication devices, 1–2
   computational devices, 11–14
   computer age (*see* Computer Age)
   personal computers, 1–2
Moore's Law, 15, 17–19

N
National Oceanic and Atmospheric Administration (NOAA), 173
Nucleotide string
   approach, 237–238
   clockwise (CW), 230
   Deoxyribonucleic-Acid-DNA, 230–231
   empty string, 232
   for-loop, 232
   input string, 233
   Python collections, 231–234

rev_compl() function, 235
test-driven development, 234–238
NumPy (Numerical Python)
   foundational library, 368
   linear algebra, 369–370
   MMX (multimedia) registers, 368
   ndarray, 368–369
   Oliphant, Travis, 368
   row and column vectors, 371
   SIMD registers, 368, 370
   universal functions (ufuncs), 370–371
   vectorized operations, 371

O
Odds/ends
   datetime, 397–402
   ipyparallel/decorator function, 391
   parallel programming, 402–405
   Python sets, 396–397
   shared records, 397
   writing program, 395–396
Operating system, 27–33

P
Pandas
   labeled datasets, 382–383
   processing datasets program
      mass spec dataset, 389
      resultset, 390–391
      script development, 390
   query recordsets, 384–385
   rectCoor DataFrame, 383–384
   spherical coordinates, 383
   StarCatalog, 383
   statistics
      datasets, 385–386
      extracting records and values, 386
      IPython session, 387
      seaborn, 388–389
      statistical plots, 387–388
      stream editor, 386
Parallel programming
   cluster, 402
   concurrency, 402
   decorator function, 404
   hardware parallelization, 402
   home directory, 403
   initializations, 403
   ipyparallel cluster, 402–403
   parallelized function, 403–404
   resultset, 404
Pérez, Fernando, 167–168
Pickering, Charles, 2
Pipelines/scripts (bash)
   definition, 55–56
   documentation, 56–57
   Eric Raymond, 57
   executable scripts

Index

foundational code, 109
interact_mk_proj_fs, 112
makeProjectFS, 110–111
nucleotide strings, 109–110
recurring code, 110
tree project, 111, 113
extraction/analysis
    datafiles, 82
    directory/copying files, 83
    gawk/awk interpreter, 84–85
    GET statement, 83
    getMaxHitCount method, 87
    Google Stack Overflow, 84
    scripting process, 86–87
    specification, 82–83
    uniq command, 85
programming style, 57
script, 59–60
shellcheck, 58–59
Thompson, Ken, 56
Unix philosophy, 56
Poincaré, Henri, 3
Programming efficiency
    algorithms
        index/value pairs, 295–297
        linear time, 293
        time complexities, 293–295
    binary tree $O(\ln_2 n)$, 304–307
    dataset *vs.* single pass
        algorithm, 312
        decimal points, 311
        equivalent code, 312–313
        extending solution, 314–315
        galaxy_coordinates.txt, 310
        linear-runtime algorithm, 313
        list of lists (LoL), 310–311
        problem/solution, 310–314
    functional equivalence/profiling code
        algorithms, 308
        lookup table *vs.* conditional testing, 308–309
        minimum and maximum values, 309–310
    nested loop $O(n^m)$/time complexity
        cubic time complexity, 303–304
        inner/outer loop, 297–302
        output, 303
Programming style
    algorithms
        built-in collections, 209
        coding, 209–211
        data structures, 243–244
        for-loop clause, 210
        high-level language, 206–207
        interpreter, 206
        IPython interactive shell, 208
        nested math functions, 208
        Python, 206–207
        Rossum, Guido van, 207
        while loop, 210–211
    counting symbols/strings
        assignment statement, 239
        constraint-free function, 238
        error-trapping, 238–240
        exception handling, 239
        KeyError, 239
        symbol-counting function, 240
    decimal fractions/binary conversion, 219–225
    enumerate() function, 212–214
    error-trapping code, 132
    Euclid GCD algorithm
        assignment statements, 214–215
        bool function, 214
        compound logic statement, 215–216
        euclid_gcd() function, 216
        remainders, 215
        unit testing, 217–218
    f-strings, 211
    garbage filter, 212
    Hamming, Richard, 131–132
    IPython magics, 240–241
    Kernighan, Brian, 131–132
    nucleotide string, 230–238
    pipelines/scripts, 57
    program (*see* Simple programming)
    programmer, 241–242
    stoichiometry code, 244–246
    test-driven development, 132
    trapping errors, 130
    unit testing, 225–230
    writing code, 130–131
Public Health Emergency (PHE), 151
Python
    amino acid strings/nucleotides
        bioinformatics collection, 341
        codon sequence, 340
        function, 341–342
        genetic information, 339–340
        reading frames, 340
    attributes/methods, 147–148
    built-in types, 141–142
    calculator (*see* Calculators)
    collections, 142–143
    comprehension, 342–344
    comprehension/slicing, 343
    enumerate function, 211–214
    eratosthenes, 344
    error-reporting module, 143–144
    Euclid GCD algorithm, 214–218
    find intervals/overlap
        genomic sequences, 332–337
        max() and min() functions, 331
        natural number intervals, 330–331
        range() function, 331–332
        sequences, 329–330
    function (*see* Functions)
    genomic sequences
        basic structure, 336
        BED files, 334–335
        comparison, 334–335

datafile directory, 332–333
numbering system, 333
session memory, 335–336
working code, 336–337
half-open interval, 328–329
interactive scripts, 327–328
IPython interactive shell, 144–147
Josephus problem, 350–353
method chaining, 148
nucleotide string, 231–234
objects, 147–148
operations, 143
overload operators, 148
queues, 349–350
range()/slicing operations, 328–329
recursion, 354–358
Rossum, Guido van, 141
scripts
    dictionaries, 326
    initialization, 325–326
    matches, 327
    netsh command, 324–325
    ports/protocols/attributes, 325
    standard interface, 323–324
    windows defender firewall, 324
sets, 396–397
slicing lists/strings, 338–339
stacks, 348–349
Traceback, 143–144
transpose matrix
    empty matrix, 346
    linear algebra, 345
    list comprehension, 346
    nested loops, 345
    operational statement, 345–346
    tabular dataset, 347–348

R

Recursion function
    command line, 354–356
    conditional branch, 355
    definition, 354
    Fibonacci sequence, 357–358
    functions, 356–358
    memoization, 357–358
    nested dolls, 354
    pythontutor visualizer, 356
    recursFibonacci, 357
    sorting algorithms, 358
Regular expressions (grep -E)
    anchor modification, 100
    character class, 101
    contiguous characters, 102
    dictionary file match, 102
    fasta format, 105
    find command, 98–99
    literal strings, 98
    matches, 99–100
    metacharacters, 99–101

parentheses metacharacters, 103
parsers, 106
recordset, 108
sed command, 105–106
sequential deletions/replacements, 107
sprung OR spring, 104
string literal, 98–99
zcat, 105
Rossum, Guido van, 141

S

SciPy (Scientific Python)
    definition, 359
    home directory, 359
    linear algebra
        Big Dipper, 377–378
        conversion equations, 375
        datasets, 372
        geographic longitude and latitude, 372
        integer matrix, 381
        loadtxt() function, 375
        matrices, 379–382
        multidimensional space, 373–374
        rotatable 3D graph, 376–379
        spherical/cartesian coordinates, 374
        tabular datasets, 373–374
        vectorized operations, 375
    matplotlib
        differences, 364–365
        fundamentals, 360
        histograms, 365–366
        ordered collections, 361
        plt.plot() function, 361
        rendering multiple curves, 363
        side-by-side comparisons, 363–364
        tabular dataset, 360–361
        vectors, 362
    NetworkX, 366–367
    notebook directory, 359
    NumPy (*see* NumPy (Numerical Python))
    pandas (*see* Pandas)
    SymPy, 391–393
Script languages (bash)
    assignment statement, 69
    bit execution, 67
    command/edit mode, 62–64
    control flow, 62
    executable files, 61
    graphical desktop environment, 68
    hash-bang (shebang) line, 63
    home directory, 62
    initialization, 64
    line numbering, 64–65
    linters, 70–72
    makeProjectFS, 69–70
    mkdir lines, 66
    PATH string, 68–69
    review, 72
    syntax highlighting, 65

tr (*see* Translate/delete characters (tr command))
    tree structure, 66–67
    Ubuntu system, 68
Self-documenting code, 132
Shannon, Claude, 20–22
Simple programming
    assert statement, 198–200
    error-trapping, 198
    functions
        autoreloading edited module, 196–198
        coders and users, 193–195
        comments, 194
        docstring, 190–205
        garbage filters, 190, 191, 193
        header, 192
        IPython session, 196–198
        modules, 190, 195–196
        nucleotide string, 189–192, 193
        Rossum, Guido van, 191
        self-documenting code, 194
        testFunc() method, 192–193
        type hints, 194–195
        users/programmers, 195
        working process, 191–192
    GC content, 189
    garbage filters, 198–200
    linters (pylint), 203–205
    unit tests, 200–203
Single-instruction multiple data (SIMD), 155, 368, 370
Software design. *see* Top-down design (TDD)
Spherical trigonometry, 171–173
SymPy (Symbolic Python)
    assignment statement, 160
    calculus textbooks, 266–267
    chemical equation, 157–158
    chemical stoichiometry, 244–246
    computer algebra system, 157
    Gökkr, Ilayda, 157–161, 244–246
    homogenous equations, 158
    Jupyter (*see* Jupyter notebooks)
    linear algebra equation, 244–246
    pydroid, 158–159
    rational number, 245
    reshape() method, 160
    SciPy (Scientific Python)
        CAS (computer algebra system), 391
        datatypes/collections, 393
        mathematical expressions, 392
        plotting curves, 393
        quadratic equation, 392
        system memory, 391–392
    symbols() function, 159–160

T

Test-driven development (TDD)
    code development, 203
    nucleotide string, 234–238
    programming, 225
    triangle, 411

    unit testing, 132
Top-down design (TDD)
    definition, 269
    development, 413
    files, 273–274
    garbage filters, 272
    graphical desktop environment, 412
    methodology, 270
    prescriptive, 274–275
    routine/subroutines, 271–273
    specification, 271
    triangle, 412–413
Traceback, 143–144
Translate/delete characters (tr command)
    bit bucket, 75
    command line, 81
    command mode, 79–80
    dict file, 80
    dictionary file, 78, 81
    egrep command, 75
    grep statement, 80
    grep tool, 75
    input string, 76–77
    Linux files converter, 81–82
    lowercase equivalents, 77–78
    punctuation, 76
    remove punctuation, 76
    spellchecker pipeline, 72–74, 78–80
    stackoverflow, 75
    string literal, 79
    substitute uppercase chars, 77
    timesharing, 80
    wc command, 73
Triangle
    angle-angle-angel (AAA), 407, 433–434
    code organization, 410–411
    design comments, 417–420
    design considerations, 409–410
    input/output, 410
    Law of Sines/Law of Cosines, 409
    lint/coding style, 411
    programmable calculators, 408
    refactoring, 429–431
    return statements, 421
    rnd bool (argument list), 428
    ROM module, 428
    rough draft, 420–422
    side-side-angle (SSA), 407–408, 433–434
    solve_triangle.py, 414–416, 426–427
    solve_triangle() function, 408–409
    stubs and drivers, 417
    TDD/unit testing, 411, 413–414
    testing process, 422–423
    TI-59 programmable calculator, 427–428
    top-down design, 412–413
    TRIANGLE SOLUTION program, 428
    v2 solve_triangle(), 431–433
    Turing machines (TMs). *See* Universal Turing machine (UTM)

U

Unit testing
  advantages, 230
  AssertionError, 424
  automate testing, 200–203
  bash script, 229–230
  garbage filter, 424–426
  running process, 415–416
  solve_triangle function, 416, 426–427
  test_solve_triangle.py, 413–416
  testing process, 422–423
  triangle, 411
  unittest_template.py file, 225–229
Universal Turing machine (UTM). *See* virtual universal Turing machines (vUTMs)
UNIX
  advantages, 28
  bash, 48
  batch processing, 28
  hardware resources, 28
  history, 28–29
  Linux filesystem, 30–31
  MULTICS, 28–30
  Paterson, Tim, 29
  tree structure, 30

V

virtual universal Turing machines (vUTMs), 11, 13, 15

W

World Health Organization (WHO), 151

GPSR Compliance

The European Union's (EU) General Product Safety Regulation (GPSR) is a set of rules that requires consumer products to be safe and our obligations to ensure this.

If you have any concerns about our products, you can contact us on

ProductSafety@springernature.com

In case Publisher is established outside the EU, the EU authorized representative is:

Springer Nature Customer Service Center GmbH
Europaplatz 3
69115 Heidelberg, Germany